Debates in Religious Edu

Wha ~~to tay?~~

BAR

Deba explores the major issues all RE teachers encounter in their early professional lives. It encourages critical reflection and aims to stimulate both novice and experienced teachers to think more deeply about their practice, and link research and evidence to what they have observed in schools.

This accessible book tackles established and contemporary issues enabling you to reach informed judgements and argue your point of view with deeper theoretical knowledge and understanding. Taking account of recent controversy, and challenging assumptions about the place of religion in education, expert contributors cover key topics such as:

- effective pedagogy in RE teaching
- exploring thinking skills and truth claims
- the relationship of science and religion in the classroom
- the place of school worship in contemporary society
- the role of RE in spiritual and moral development
- diversity in the RE classroom.

With its combination of expert opinion and fresh insight, *Debates in Religious Education* is the ideal companion for any student or practising teacher engaged in initial training, continuing professional development or Masters level study.

L. Philip Barnes is Reader in Religious and Theological Education at King's College London, where he is currently Director of the MA in Religious Education and the MA in Jewish Education.

Debates in Subject Teaching Series

Series edited by: Susan Capel, Jon Davison, James Arthur and John Moss

The **Debates in Subject Teaching Series** is a sequel to the popular **Issues in Subject Teaching Series**, originally published by Routledge between 1999 and 2003. Each title presents high-quality material, specially commissioned to stimulate teachers engaged in initial training, continuing professional development and Masters level study to think more deeply about their practice, and link research and evidence to what they have observed in schools. By providing up-to-date, comprehensive coverage the titles in the **Debates in Subject Teaching Series** support teachers in reaching their own informed judgements, enabling them to discuss and argue their point of view with deeper theoretical knowledge and understanding.

Other titles in the series:

Debates in History Teaching
Edited by Ian Davies

Debates in English Teaching
Edited by Jon Davison, Caroline Daly and John Moss

Debates in Citizenship Education
Edited by James Arthur and Hilary Cremin

Debates in Art and Design Education
Edited by Lesley Burgess and Nicholas Addison

Debates in Music Teaching
Edited by Chris Philpott and Gary Spruce

Debates in Physical Education
Edited by Susan Capel and Margaret Whitehead

Debates in Religious Education

Edited by L. Philip Barnes

Routledge
Taylor & Francis Group

LONDON AND NEW YORK

First edition published 2012
by Routledge
2 Park Square, Milton Park, Abingdon, Oxon, OX14 4RN

Simultaneously published in the USA and Canada
by Routledge
711 Third Avenue, New York, NY 10017

Routledge is an imprint of the Taylor & Francis Group, an informa business

British Library Cataloguing in Publication Data
A catalogue record for this book is available from the British Library

Library of Congress Cataloging-in-Publication Data
A catalog record has been requested for this book

ISBN13: 978-0-415-58392-3 (hbk)
ISBN13: 978-0-415-58391-6 (pbk)
ISBN13: 978-0-203-81380-5 (ebk)

Typeset in Galliard
by Saxon Graphics Ltd, Derby

MIX
Paper from
responsible sources
FSC
www.fsc.org FSC® C004839

Printed and bound in Great Britain by
CPI Antony Rowe, Chippenham, Wiltshire

Contents

Illustrations

Tables

Figures

Introduction to the series

This book, *Debates in Religious Education*, is one of a series of books entitled *Debates in Subject Teaching*. The series has been designed to engage with a wide range of debates related to subject teaching. Unquestionably, debates vary among the subjects, but may include, for example, issues that:

- impact on Initial Teacher Education in the subject;
- are addressed in the classroom through the teaching of the subject;
- are related to the content of the subject and its definition;
- are related to subject pedagogy;
- are connected with the relationship between the subject and broader educational aims and objectives in society, and the philosophy and sociology of education;
- are related to the development of the subject and its future in the twenty-first century.

Consequently, each book presents key debates that subject teachers should understand, reflect on and engage in as part of their professional development. Chapters have been designed to highlight major questions, and to consider the evidence from research and practice in order to find possible answers. Some subject books or chapters offer at least one solution or a view of the ways forward, whereas others provide alternative views and leave readers to identify their own solution or view of the ways forward. The editors expect readers will want to pursue the issues raised, and so chapters include questions for further debate and suggestions for further reading. Debates covered in the series will provide the basis for discussion in university subject seminars or as topics for assignments or classroom research. The books have been written for all those with a professional interest in their subject and, in particular, student teachers learning to teach the subject in secondary or primary school; newly qualified teachers; teachers undertaking study at Masters level; teachers with a subject coordination or leadership role, and those preparing for such responsibility; as well as mentors, university tutors, CPD organisers and advisers of the aforementioned groups.

Books in the series have a cross-phase dimension, because the editors believe that it is important for teachers in the primary, secondary and post-16 phases to look at subject teaching holistically, particularly in order to provide for continuity and progression, but also to increase their understanding of how children and young people learn. The balance of chapters that have a cross-phase relevance varies according to the issues relevant to different subjects. However, no matter where the emphasis is, the authors have drawn out the relevance of their topic to the whole of each book's intended audience.

Because of the range of the series, both in terms of the issues covered and its cross-phase concern, each book is an edited collection. Editors have commissioned new writing from experts on particular issues, who, collectively, represent many different perspectives on subject teaching. Readers should not expect a book in this series to cover the entire range of debates relevant to the subject, or to offer a completely unified view of subject teaching, or that every debate will be dealt with discretely, or that all aspects of a debate will be covered. Part of what each book in this series offers to readers is the opportunity to explore the interrelationships between positions in debates and, indeed, among the debates themselves, by identifying the overlapping concerns and competing arguments that are woven through the text.

The editors are aware that many initiatives in subject teaching continue to originate from the centre, and that teachers have decreasing control of subject content, pedagogy and assessment strategies. The editors strongly believe that for teaching to remain properly a vocation and a profession, teachers must be invited to be part of a creative and critical dialogue about subject teaching, and should be encouraged to reflect, criticise, problem-solve and innovate. This series is intended to provide teachers with a stimulus for democratic involvement in the development of the discourse of subject teaching.

Susan Capel, Jon Davison, James Arthur and John Moss December 2010.

Contributors

David Aldridge is Senior Lecturer in Religious Education at Oxford Brookes University.

David Armstrong is Senior Lecturer in Religious Studies at Stranmillis University College, Belfast.

L. Philip Barnes is Reader in Religious and Theological Education at King's College London.

Vivienne Baumfield is Professor of Pedagogy, Policy and Practice in the School of Education, University of Glasgow.

Lat Blaylock is editor of *RE Today* magazine, and an RE adviser with *RE Today*.

Trevor Cooling is Professor of Christian Education and Director of the National Institute for Christian Education Research at Canterbury Christ Church University.

Tony Eaude works as an independent consultant and is a Research Fellow, Department of Education, University of Oxford.

Nigel Fancourt is a PGCE tutor in religious education at the University of Oxford.

Marius Felderhof is Senior Lecturer in Systematic and Philosophical Theology at the University of Birmingham.

Leslie J. Francis is Professor of Religions and Education in the Institute of Education, University of Warwick.

J. Mark Halstead was formerly Head of Department and is currently Research Professor in the School of Education and Professional Development at the University of Huddersfield.

Roger Homan is Professor Emeritus of Religious Studies at the University of Brighton.

Paul Hopkins is the leader of the PGCE religious education course at the University of Hull and a consultant on the use of ICT across the UK and internationally.

Robert Jackson is Professor of Religions and Education in the Institute of Education at the University of Warwick, UK; he is also Professor of Religious Diversity and Education at the Council of Europe-related European Wergeland Centre in Oslo, Norway.

William K. Kay is Professor of Theology at Glyndŵr University, Wales.

Stephen McKinney is Senior Lecturer in the School of Education, University of Glasgow.

David Lundie is a researcher on a major project, sponsored by the AHRC Religion and Society Programme, investigating the aims and practices in religious education in secondary schools, at the University of Glasgow.

Gemma O'Dell is Head of the Humanities Faculty at Barton Court Grammar School, Canterbury, Kent.

Mark A. Pike is Reader in Educational Values and Pedagogy, in the School of Education, University of Leeds.

Michael Poole is Visiting Research Fellow in Science and Religion at King's College London.

Brenda Watson is a former Director of the Farmington Institute, Oxford.

Kevin Williams is Senior Lecturer in Education at Mater Dei Institute of Education, Dublin City University.

Rosemary Woodward is Schools' Adviser for the Diocese of Lichfield.

Andrew Wright is Professor of Religious and Theological Education at King's College London.

Elina Wright is a postdoctoral researcher at the University of Helsinki.

Acknowledgements

'See-saw diagram showing relationship between predictability and impact' from *Christianity in Culture: A Study in Dynamic Biblical Theologizing in Cross-Cultural Perspective* by Charles H. Kraft (2005: 125). Reprinted with permission of Orbis Books.

'Community Cohesion through Primary RE' © *RE Today, course materials on respect for all in primary RE, http://www.retoday.org.uk*. Reprinted with permission.

Entering the debate

L. Philip Barnes

In all probability religious education (RE) is the most divisive subject in the school curriculum. No other subject generates so much discussion or elicits responses from so wide an audience. Even those uninterested in curricular developments in education generally often have definite views on RE; typically expressed on the issues of whether it should or should not be taught in schools and whether the subject, if taught, should be compulsory. Popular interest in the fortunes of RE is matched by professional interest, and again much of this interest focuses on the legitimacy and compulsory nature of the subject. What distinguishes scholarly debate from popular philosophising is often, as one would expect, the more nuanced nature of the conclusions reached. For example, in 1994, David Hargreaves, at that time Professor of Education at the University of Cambridge and subsequently Chief Executive of the Qualifications and Curriculum Authority (then one of the chief official policy-making and implementation agencies in the United Kingdom), while advocating an expansion of religious schools within the state system (a conclusion enthusiastically taken up by New Labour under Tony Blair; see Walford 2008), argued that RE in non-religious schools should be abolished and replaced by citizenship education, on the grounds that RE can underwrite moral education only in schools that are religiously uniform (as in faith schools) and not in religiously diverse 'secular schools'. Interestingly, Hargreaves went on characterise modern multi-faith RE in Britain as a 'pick 'n' mix tour of religions' that 'trivialises each faith's claims to truth' (Hargreaves 1994: 34), a viewpoint not uncommon among educators generally but not religious educators. More recently, Professor John White (2004) has similarly questioned the contribution of RE to moral education and by implication its contribution to the social aims of education; he also concluded that it should become an optional rather than a compulsory subject for pupils.

Debates in RE, however, are not confined to its current compulsory status in schools, as this volume amply illustrates. Like all other subjects, RE in schools embraces aims, objectives, methodologies, content, assessment techniques and learning outcomes, and relates to whole school issues such as gender and diversity; and like any other school subject it is regulated by legislation, conditioned by a range of formal and informal policy initiatives emanating from a host of official and semi-official organisations, and so on. At each point of influence the potential is created for debate and discussion. Take the issue of aims, for example. What are appropriate aims for RE? Should RE focus on the challenge of providing pupils with knowledge and understanding of religion or should it incorporate the challenge of enabling pupils to evaluate religion? Should the thrust of RE be on 'responsible citizenship' and social cohesion or are such concerns distractions from the real concerns of the subject? Basically should the aims of RE be instrumental to the shifting social agenda of the nation state or should religious educators look askance upon such influences and allow the nature of religion and the interests of pupils to determine what is taught? This last question takes us back to the positions of Hargreaves and White, who both assume that the main purpose of RE is to further the moral development of pupils and to inculcate positive social values in the young. A variation on this theme is the idea that RE should be focused on challenging religious extremism (secular political extremism, of the sort that occasioned two world wars in the twentieth century, presumably will be challenged elsewhere in the curriculum!). The terrorist attacks of 7 July 2005 (7/7) on London by Islamists, all of whom were born in England and attended 'community' schools, have provided support for the view that RE could conceivably help dissipate religious extremism: in his only formal parliamentary reference to RE, former Prime Minister Gordon Brown commended the *National Framework for Religious Education* (QCA 2004) within the context of a 'Statement on National Security' (Brown 2007). Here is an instrumentalist view of RE that takes social reality and the context of religion seriously, but fails to ask the critical question whether the form of RE recommended by the *National Framework* actually contributes to social cohesion or exacerbates the alienation felt by some pupils from minority communities. The subject of instrumentalist verses non-instrumentalist aims does not exhaust the debates that surround RE; there are many other issues in RE to consider. Every issue opens up new questions and controversies, and provides insights that in turn illuminate other issues and debates.

The purpose of this collection of essays is to introduce readers to the breadth and depth of current debates in RE, and hopefully to provide a positive introduction to the contested field of theory and practice that is RE. An attempt is made to represent the rich variety of opinions and ideas that characterise contemporary discussions in RE and to take account of the diversity of issues that constitute and impact upon RE. No single ideological agenda is common to the contributors and individual essays deliberately aim to be inclusive of different positions and to take account of different arguments; this does not exclude the endorsement sometimes of controversial positions, but it does ensure that the reader has the essential content to reach informed conclusions on the basis of the evidence. The essays aim to initiate dialogue and reflection on important issues in RE and they are written in that spirit. Some essays are more provocative than others, some more restrained, some more widely focused, and some more narrowly. All aim to educate and collectively to convey a sophisticated understanding of the nature and practice of RE in the United Kingdom and Ireland.

The structure of the book

While there is no overall unifying *grande narrative* and each chapter is self-contained, there is, nevertheless, a discernible structure to the book.

Section 1: History, policy and purpose

Section 1 provides the essential context for an appreciation of the nature and role of RE in British and Irish society. In Chapter 1, Brenda Watson considers the aims of RE and their relevance to contemporary education and to society, under the title 'Why religious education matters'. Chapter 2 is devoted to a critical review of the recent history of RE in the four nations of England, Northern Ireland, Scotland and Wales. An account is provided of recent developments in legislation, policy and classroom practice, along with an introduction to the different types of schools and the implications of this for the practice of RE. What emerges is a complex picture of commonalities and differences between the different countries reviewed. In some cases, under examination, oft-quoted distinctions between national forms of RE reveal themselves to be unsustainable, such as that RE throughout Ireland is necessarily confessional but non-confessional elsewhere. In other cases, commonly used descriptions disguise different meanings. In England, for example, 'multi-faith' RE typically denotes a study of at least six different religions (and if the guidance of the *National Framework* is followed a study of significantly more), in other countries RE is still 'multi-faith', but the number of religions to be studied may be considerably fewer. Religious educators in different countries have much to learn from each other and much to reflect upon: for example, the English model of multi-faith RE is not the only model and perhaps not the best model for challenging religious intolerance and developing positive relationships between different communities (see Barnes 2009a). There are strengths and weakness both in the theory and the practice of RE across the five countries.

In Chapter 3 William K. Kay provides an historical account of the way in which local influence over RE has been enshrined in legislation and practised in the form of locally agreed syllabuses. Many view such syllabuses as expressions of local democracy, which serve to relate RE to local history and to empower local communities to work together on a common educational project. The reality of course can often be different, with local communities following national 'advice' and simply replicating what is deemed to be 'politically expedient'; since 2004 this has meant following the controversial 'guidance' of the *National Framework*, which was produced with the expressed intention of bringing about a greater degree of uniformity in RE. The result of course has been to lessen local influence and to further strengthen national influence over RE: the 'long march' towards the centralisation of RE in the hands of a few influential organisations and individuals continues.

Section 2: Educational issues and religious education

This section introduces a range of educational issues that impact upon RE. Chapter 4 considers the issue of moral and religious diversity and the challenges posed to society and to education by such diversity. Attention chiefly focuses on developments and responses to diversity in England and Wales; and account is taken of current concerns about how successful RE has been in challenging discrimination and fostering respect for others. It is particularly difficult to discuss this issue dispassionately, as any suggestion that RE has not been particularly successful in promoting mutual respectfulness between individuals and between communities is met with resistance by those who enjoy influence in directing policy, on the grounds that criticism at this point threatens to undermine the status and compulsory position of RE in the curriculum; hence the rhetoric of success that often accompanies 'official' discussion of this and related matters.

Chapter 5 begins by discussing the issues of gender in education from the 1970s until the present day. It notes how explanations for the difference in educational achievement between boys and girls have emphasised the role of gender identity as a central factor for consideration in schools. The implications and significance of findings from educational research into gender are considered in relation to RE, in particular concerns about RE being viewed as a 'feminine' subject. Constructivist and interpretive approaches are advocated as ways forward for RE practitioners to help pupils develop a more fluid understanding of gender identities. Finally, it is suggested that the understanding of one's own plural identity, including gendered identity, can in turn lead students to appreciate the heterogeneous character of religious traditions.

Part of the professional role of the RE teacher is to be an advocate for the subject. The challenge of course is how to be an advocate for the subject without requiring religious commitment of pupils. On what basis is religion to be taught in schools and in what ways? Furthermore, what is the relevance of religion to the wider curriculum, given that not every teacher or pupil endorses or practises religion? Trevor Cooling address these questions and other related questions in Chapter 6, chiefly by exploring the relevance of religion to a small sample of whole school issues. His aim is to show the educational potential of religion across the curriculum.

The issue of 'faith schools' is one of the most controversial subjects in education. There are two main concerns: first, the very existence of schools 'with a religious character'; and second, the issue of whether such schools should be funded by the state. In Chapter 7 J. Mark Halstead considers some of the deeper issues that emerge in discussions and arguments about faith schools. The chapter begins with a clarification of the concept of 'faith school' and then summarises the history of faith schooling in Britain: reference is made to current policies and recent legislation, and attention is given to international comparisons. The nature of the academic and political arguments about faith schools is then explored, and four different but intertwined debates are identified. Finally, the arguments and counter-arguments are examined directly: seven main arguments in support of faith schools are outlined and evaluated, and seven main arguments against.

In Chapter 8 Mark Pike challenges popular assumptions about citizenship and human rights by demonstrating how important beliefs and practices are often interpreted, and responded to, in quite different ways. He shows how educational values such as 'freedom', 'equality', 'rights', 'reason', 'autonomy' and 'tolerance' can be interpreted differently by religious believers and by secular citizens. The problem in education is that secular interpretations of these values, under the guise of neutrality, are typically accorded normative force; consequently religious interpretations and contributions to citizenship and human rights are marginalised. Pike argues that in societies characterised by diversity, the freedom of citizens of faith to bring legitimate religious convictions to readings of secular state-sponsored values should be encouraged and respected. In conclusion he explains why Christianity should be a vital part of citizenship education in the diverse, plural, liberal democracies of the West.

Although spiritual development is not a new theme in British education (reference is made to spiritual development, for example, in the 1944 Education Act, see Barnes and Kay 2002: 27) the conjunction of moral development alongside spiritual development dates from the 1988 Education Reform Act. This innovation is susceptible to different readings. On one reading the specification of the requirement of schools to further moral development merely makes explicit what was always the case, that is, that education is concerned with morality and moral values; on another reading it indicates that politicians were aware of declining standards in public and private life and that the moral component of education needed new emphasis and direction. This in turn relates to a wider debate about the effects of secularisation on society and on schools, and the perception that the decline in religious commitment and observance in society is correlated to a decline in moral standards and behaviour. A link between spiritual development and moral development is entirely natural, in that there is accumulating empirical evidence of the positive effects of spirituality both for individuals and for society in general. Education can endorse such links, albeit not uncritically. Secularists could object to the need for schools to promote spiritual development, if the meaning of spirituality is tied too closely to religion. This presumably explains both why the term 'spiritual' development is preferred in the legislation over *religious* development (for the former is capable of a secular, non-religious interpretation) and why the notion of spiritual development in education is defined in terms of a process rather than in terms of substantive outcomes: through spiritual development pupils should be enabled to 'reflect', 'consider' and 'appreciate,' but not to espouse particular religious beliefs or values. This debate is addressed and reflected in Tony Eaude's discussion of spiritual and moral development in Chapter 9. The nature of spiritual and moral development and its place in education in the light of social and cultural change are considered, as well as being related to fundamental questions of identity, meaning and character.

Chapter 10 by Rosemary Woodward considers the issue of community cohesion in education, an issue that has come to the fore in the last decade, prompted by increasing evidence both of segregation between different communities and of a growing sense of alienation among members of ethnic communities from mainstream (secular) society. She explains how community cohesion in education aims to demolish barriers of division and mistrust within British society, by offering equal opportunities for all, celebrating diversity and challenging stereotypes. This chapter explores the contribution of RE to developing pupils' self-awareness by encouraging an open-minded exploration of the shared concepts that provide common ground between faiths. As pupils develop confidence in their own cultural roots, they can begin to develop the skills needed to bridge the divisions within society, including those between faith communities, at local, national and global levels. Promoting community cohesion, however, raises controversial issues of relevance, intolerance and conflicting truth claims.

Chapter 11, by Marius Felderhof, addresses the controversial issue of whether humanism and humanist perspectives should be incorporated into RE. While few educators question the need to include critical perspectives on religion in RE (though historically, for ideological reasons, this has been largely absent from RE in England and Wales; see Barnes 2006), there are strong legal, educational and philosophical objections to extending the scope of the subject to incorporate humanism. For example, it is not at all obvious that the category of religion is appropriately extended to include humanism as a species of the wider genus; and given that legally RE is concerned with religion, this would seem to exclude humanism as a subject for study in RE. There is also the objection that because the number of professed humanists in the United Kingdom and Ireland is so small, it would be controversial to privilege it for study over that of religions that attract many more adherents but are not included in the RE curriculum. In any case, historically humanists have been much more preoccupied with denying religious truth and criticising religion than with developing the positive dimensions of humanism; consequently much of the critique of religion that is so central to humanism is appropriately and currently integrated into good RE.

In Chapter 12 Leslie Francis provides an overview of empirical research in RE in the UK during the fifty-year period from 1960 until 2010. His focus is on qualitative and quantitative studies concerned with the religiosity of young people and the relevance of their findings to school-related RE. Four phases of research are identified during this period: the pioneering researchers of the 1960s; the quantitative studies developed in the 1970s; the qualitative traditions shaped in the 1980s and 1990s; and the collaboration and consolidation emerging during the 2000s. The review of research by Francis illustrates that there is an important vein of rich empirical data on the attitudes, beliefs and values of young people, classroom pedagogy and a host of other topics relevant to RE in the curriculum and in the classroom that is sometimes overlooked by teachers and educators.

Robert Jackson's discussion of European developments in RE in Chapter 13 provides a useful complement to Francis's review of empirical research. At the very least, as Jackson notes, acquaintance with the European discussion provides examples of different educational systems, traditions and approaches and serves to challenge insular attitudes and preoccupations. Some British religious educators neglect a comparative European perspective and simply assume that RE in Europe should follow the British model without seriously considering what can be learnt from the theory and practice of RE elsewhere. Jackson alerts us to the potential of developments and innovations in European RE to stimulate new thinking and challenge 'sacred' assumptions in RE in the UK and Ireland.

Section 3: Issues in teaching and learning in religious education

In this section we turn to a series of issues that are of immediate concern to teaching and learning in RE. In Chapter 14 Roger Homan raises the provocative issue of how religion is represented in the classroom, an issue that find its stimulus in recent discussions of methodology in religious studies and in theology. He illustrates and explores the ways religion is constructed for educational purposes. This construction is attributed to a number of influences or agencies: the Piagetian paradigm of cognitive stages, promulgated by Goldman as the principle of 'readiness'; the element of PR or spin when representatives of faith communities are invited to contribute their own accounts; the sanction of examination boards whose candidates are coached to recite particular distortions; and the discontinuity between research and teaching. The essential point for teachers to note is that 'religion' is a contested and variously interpreted category of meaning and explanation.

Chapter 15 addresses what Ofsted describes as 'the way to structure and define a clear process of learning in RE' (Ofsted 2010: 41), that is, the issue of developing coherent schemes of work and lesson plans that facilitate pupil learning. David Aldridge argues that the theoretical literature of RE has not sufficiently engaged with the challenge of planning and delivering effective RE lessons. He considers the disconnection between academic discussions of pedagogy in RE and the fragmentary, tool-kit teaching approaches adopted in practice in many classrooms. Finally, he compares two recent attempts to develop an integrated approach to structuring learning in RE, before encouraging teachers to reflect more critically on the different factors that influence what is taught and how it is taught in the RE classroom.

The focus on learning and how teachers can initiate and further pupil learning in RE is continued in Chapter 16 by Vivienne Baumfield. Pedagogy is defined as intentional and systematic intervention in order to influence the development of the learner; moreover, pedagogy is a cultural activity that is not disinterested or neutral. Attention is given to recent discussion of 'learning about' and 'learning from' religion and the ways in which these two emphases may usefully complement each other. The aim of effective pedagogy is to create experiences from which pupils can learn something that is meaningful to them in the here and now, while cultivating an interest in continuing to learn in the future.

Chapter 17, by Nigel Fancourt, explores how differentiation in RE is affected both by general educational issues, as well as by subject-specific teaching and learning. The nature of pupil difference is considered, as are the ways in which differences between pupils condition learning and achievement. The chapter concludes by reviewing arguments about strategies for dealing with these differences, such as setting, mixed-ability teaching and thinking skills.

In many educational circles, the notion of 'thinking skills' remains popular and classroom activities are often constructed to reflect and test such skills: in 2001 the last Labour government renamed the (then) Department for Education and Employment, the Department for Education and Skills. In recent years, however, the topic of thinking-skills in education in general, and in RE in particular, has been the subject of debate and controversy. In Chapter 18 Elina Wright and Andrew Wright provide an overview both of current theory about the nature of thinking skills and of the application of this theory to the RE classroom. They then go on to develop a critique of skills-centred approaches to teaching and learning in RE, focusing in turn on issues raised by philosophy, theology and pedagogy. They conclude more positively by proposing that the cultivation of a set of pedagogic virtues – attentiveness, intelligence, reasonableness and responsibility – ought to take priority over the cultivation of specific thinking skills.

Chapter 19 by Lat Blaylock outlines the positive possibilities of applying methods from Assessment for Learning and from 'Assessing Pupils' Progress' to RE in ways that challenge RE professionals to be clear about their aims and learning intentions and about the kinds of evidence that demonstrate achievement in RE. The argument is that the wide range of interdisciplinary learning methods in RE, including the conceptual, the creative, the spiritual and the phenomenological, all offer routes through which evidence of achievement can be collected and assessed. When this process is informed by the insights of assessment for learning, it not only measures achievement but it can also enable enhanced achievement. Blaylock argues for alertness to the range of inter-disciplinary learning opportunities offered by RE (e.g. philosophical, creative, moral, spiritual, historical, personal) and for subjecting any assessment requirements to a rigorous questioning: is it fit for purpose in RE, fair, valid and manageable?

Information and communication technologies are an essential aspect of the lives of all those who teach and an essential and core part of all teaching and learning in schools. Chapter 20 by Paul Hopkins considers some of the underlying principles about the use of technology in relation to teaching and learning in RE and some of the ways religious groups use technology. He then offers six practical strategies for using technology to enhance teaching and learning; and concludes by looking at the process of becoming 'e-mature.'

The relationship between science and religion and the challenges posed by science to religion are perennial topics of debate and controversy. Adherents of what is often referred to as 'the new atheism' characterise science as objective and rational, and contrast this with religion, which is characterised as subjective and irrational. The majority of scientists, however, do not think in such terms; and while most contend that there is no necessary conflict between the conclusions of science and those of religion, culturally the metaphor of conflict endures in the public imagination. Given the prominence and status of science and scientists in society, it is important that RE addresses some of the points at which scientific research impacts on religion and on religious faith. Indeed there is a strong case for concluding that issues to do with the relationship of science and religion are much more relevant to the interests and experience of pupils than some of the expressly religious content (drawn from an ever widening category of different religions) that is often studied in RE. In our final chapter, Michael Poole discusses a range of scientific topics that are relevant to religion and to RE. The topics considered are: worldviews and the nature and scope of science and scientific explanations; laws and the concept of miracles; creation and origins – evolution/chance/design and 'ID'; and finally the character of scientific and of religious language.

More could be said by the contributors about all of the topics considered in this book, and chapters on other topics could be added, but enough is said to provide a fairly comprehensive overview both of RE as it is theorised and practised in the UK and in Ireland and of the influences that shape it as a curriculum subject. Controversy and debate may abound, which perhaps should not surprise, given that RE as a field of study draws upon and relates to a diverse array of subjects and topics that meet at the intersection between education and religion, but the hope is that after reading this book, the reader will be better equipped to make an informed decision about his or her own position across the range of issues most relevant to the theory and practice of RE. Read on!

History, policy and purpose

Chapter 1

Why religious education matters

Brenda Watson

Despite the continued official presence of religion in Britain, most people today will concede that we live in a profoundly secular society. That RE survives in state schools and is indeed in many respects flourishing is a remarkable tribute to its practitioners (see Copley 2008).

Christine Gilbert, chief inspector of schools, linked the importance of RE to 'good teaching based on strong subject knowledge and clarity about the purposes of RE' (reported, *Sunday Telegraph*, 6 June 2010). Nevertheless there is widespread uncertainty in our society both about what religion constitutes and about why it is on the school curriculum. A recent *Handbook for RE Teachers* notes: 'Your English or Maths colleagues seldom get the question, "What's the point of doing this subject?" You will' (Wood 2009: vii).

Overview of aims

Traditional approaches

From the 1944 Education Act and into the 1960s in Britain, two major inter-related reasons were given for RE: (i) that of passing on the truth of the religion which had sustained society in the past – the 'confessional' approach; and (ii) that of ensuring the moral stability of society, thus appealing to non-religious people who subscribed to Christian values in general.

The second of these aims has metamorphosed into concern for the 'spiritual, moral, cultural, mental and physical development of pupils' (1988 Education Reform Act). But it risks rendering RE redundant. Thus Hargreaves (1994) argued for the replacement of RE by citizenship education in the common school on the grounds that RE's moral purpose cannot be achieved when there is no consensus on religion. Emphasis on human rights and its accompanying 'political correctness' shorn of any essential links with religion has now effectively taken its place as a driver towards social justice. Various initiatives such as *Whole Education* (see http://www.wholeeducation.org) take this aspect of education seriously without any mention of a need for RE. A simple equation of moral stability and

RE is no longer possible, even though links with religion are still important (see Jackson 2002; Gearon 2004; and Stern 2006: 80–94).

Confessionalism has been ousted from the curriculum on similar grounds. In the pluralist society which Britain has become, teaching any faith as true to a non-voluntary, immature and therefore vulnerable audience from diverse backgrounds can attract censure as attempted proselytising. Guarding against insensitive pressurising of pupils was not sufficiently widely appreciated or practised. The notion of the school being simply an extension of nurture is well illustrated in the allied issue of compulsory worship assemblies. Terms such as 'Let us pray' were regularly used instead of issuing a properly educational invitation such as 'Listen to this prayer and pray if you wish' (see Watson and Thompson 2007: 186–188). Consequently the confessional approach was open to some justified criticism which brought about its downfall.

The phenomenological approach

A world religions approach focused on an empathetic study of the phenomena of religions has taken its place in justifying the retention of RE on the curriculum (Schools Council 1971; SCAA 1994b). It was, and is, advocated as helping to create a harmonious society. Whether this is so is not however so clear. Panjwani (2005: 375), for example, is worried by what is taught about Islam, and considers 'that RE has yet to fulfil its potential in this regard'.

The phenomenological approach has been heavily criticised on several grounds including:

(i)   providing an indigestible diet for pupils of miscellaneous facts, referred to as 'mish-mash' (Hulmes 1979: 44; Hull 1991);
(ii) failing to relate to pupils' real needs and personal development (e.g. Grimmitt 1987; Hammond *et al.* 1990; Jackson 1997);
(iii) teaching a false impression of religion through generalisations which deny the diversity within religions (e.g. Jackson 1997; Geaves 1998);
(iv) creating a divide between how religion is seen by religious believers and how it is presented in the classroom (e.g. Grimmitt 1987; Barnes 2007c);
(v)   promoting relativism through failure to engage pupils critically with religious truth-claims (e.g. Wright 1996; Thompson 2004);
(vi) ignoring the central importance of Christianity in British society (e.g. Thompson 2004).

Beyond the phenomenological approach

This is quite a formidable critique and recent decades have seen many different approaches designed to meet at least some of these criticisms. (*Pedagogies of RE,* edited by Michael Grimmitt (2000b) gives a good overview of these different approaches to RE.) Whilst objections (i)–(iv) have been well addressed by most more recent approaches, (v) has proved to be more difficult. Grimmitt (1991: 78), for example, acknowledged the problem of relativism but his postmodernist constructivist pedagogy reinforces the view that truth-claims only reflect their advocates' opinions (see Kalve's critique, 1996). To avoid relativism discussion of the possible truth of truth-claims must form part of RE. Copley (2008: 206) gives the example of irreconcilable Christian and Muslim views on the crucifixion of Jesus: 'Is RE supposed to sweep this under the proverbial carpet in the interests of multicultural harmony?'

Regarding objection (vi), attempts to reinstate a form of confessionalism ran up against the multicultural trend of the times, and were not helped by political manoeuvring (see Thompson 2004: 111–123). Appeal to the legal arrangements, which in Britain have helped RE to survive the advance of secularisation, does not offer sound educational reasons against an educational objection – even if the latter is politically used. Thus the argument for teaching Christianity as true because our society is built on principles derived from Christianity has not been taken seriously enough, for it offends dominant political progressivism. Frank Furedi (2009) provides a devastating exposure of such progressivism in education in general.

For the purposes of this chapter, purely educational reasons for RE, whether in common or faith schools, will be discussed. Only slowly have consciously educational approaches emerged which may seriously be regarded as effectively dealing with the two criticisms of promoting relativism and down-playing religious insight. These include: Copley (2005), Cooling (1994) and Watson and Thompson (2007). They all are concerned about pupil integrity in opening up, not foreclosing, questions of the truth of religious beliefs (see e.g. Wright's 1997 discussion of Cooling).

These educational approaches are nevertheless contested. Erricker (2010: 180), for example, whilst sympathetic to many of the approaches associated with Wright and Copley, is critical of what he sees as their implying that religious traditions are true instead of leaving that to pupils to decide for themselves. 'They are making claims as to the religious or spiritual truth in what religions say and this translates into their advocacy of pedagogies that call for the recognition of that truth.' In order to answer this criticism various inter-related issues need to be considered.

Issues relevant to avoiding relativism and playing fair with religious truth-claims

Unavoidability of contentious commitment

Advocacy in the classroom of a contentious point of view cannot be avoided, for beliefs and values govern everyone's behaviour, reactions and intentions. There is no neutrality possible in the teaching of any subject (Hulmes 1979; Ashton and Watson 1998: 187–189). The worldview that governs what we select to teach and how, and what we omit, cannot be excluded, for it is the model from which we work.

Wright notes (1996: 173):

> Every framework within which human beings choose to live, including the doctrinal systems of the world's religions, and the systems of scientific naturalism, liberal experiential-expressivism and postmodernism, entails, whether implicitly or explicitly, a fundamental ontology, an account of what is fundamentally true about reality.

Erricker (2010: 144) gives an interesting example of how his postmodernist commitment influences his assessment of the impact on pupils of a lesson on the resurrection of Jesus. 'Remarkably most of them came to the conclusion that Jesus was resurrected ... This, of course, is nonsense.' Is it? (See Watson 2004: 153–172.)

Pernicious indoctrination was summarised in a compelling phrase by Basil Mitchell (1970: 358) as producing 'closed minds and restricted sympathies'. What guards against this is openness in the way that the 'confessional' content, of whatever nature, is taught. The educator must have a commitment *also* to the integrity of the pupil from the youngest child upwards. This is what defines education as opposed to indoctrination, giving those who are taught space to reflect and freedom to disagree if they wish. Elmer Thiessen (1993: 232–242) has argued that that there is no more essential link between Christian nurture and indoctrination than in any other form of nurture (see also Lloyd 2007).

Fears of latent neo-confessionalism are still so strong that this key difference from the traditional confessional model for RE must be insisted upon, namely, sharing truth-claims in a way that acknowledges their controversial nature. Instead of simply assuming the truth of the content imparted, the teacher should promote open, critical and investigative learning in RE. It is important also to acknowledge that openness needs to transcend the commonly held cognitive/affective divide. Real understanding involves hearts as well as minds (see Astley 2007).

If educational concern for the integrity of the pupil is in place the teacher can then safely open up questions concerning truth without indoctrinating. A recent research project found significantly that 'Christians believe that sharing their faith would be unprofessional whereas atheists believed that sharing their beliefs could be a positive contribution to an RE lesson' (Revell 2010). This finding reflects the actual pressures of society as a whole on professions of individual religious commitment. Pernicious indoctrination in the West is much more likely to be against religion than for it, except for those pupils from homes where religion is practised in exclusivist ways.

The need to challenge secularist indoctrination

Copley (2005: vi) asks:

> Why is it that we are on constant alert against religious indoctrination while at the same time almost completely unprepared for secularist indoctrination? Religious discourse and options in favour of belief have been effectively closed down or edited out for many people.

It is important to realise that much of this may not be the result of deliberate pressurising but, as Copley (2005: 5) suggests, it may be by omission. McLaughlin (2002: 84) noted that common schools can be complicit in producing indoctrinated people. For indoctrination happens most effectively through failure to present alternatives – what has been termed the null curriculum – which alongside the explicit and implicit curricula govern what pupils actually receive as a result of their schooling (Eisner 1985: 87–108; Watson and Thompson 2007: 24–28).

This null curriculum especially affects religion because, unless God is talked about, effective atheism tends to become the norm. Education, as it has developed in the West since the Enlightenment, tends to imply atheism. As Marsden (1997) recognises, education routinely starts from the assumption that God does not exist. The positivist agenda which assumes that only scientific or empirical methods of investigation lead to knowledge has been powerfully at work in schools governing the priorities of the curriculum, the way in which their content is taught and the inexorable stress on assessment (see Watson 2009). This has affected everyone who has been through the educational system. The positivist outlook provides the single most important reason why people question why RE matters. Bausor and Poole (2002: 18) note that 'in many people's eyes ... science displaces religion and therefore challenges the very appropriateness of the activity of religious education.'

The seriousness of indoctrination by omission is made far greater by the strong anti-religious undercurrent present in the West. Mention of religion in the media, ordinary conversation and academic discourse tends to be unfavourable. The fulminations of Dawkins are widely publicised. Influential philosophers like A. C. Grayling (2007b: 89) liken belief in God to believing there are fairies at the bottom of the garden. A popular book on *Bad Thinking* cites as an example those who believe in the doctrine of the Trinity, on the grounds that it is bad mathematics (Whyte 2003: 23). Well may Copley ask (2005: viii):

> What if young people are never in a real position to choose between a religious way of life and a non-religious way of life? What if they irresistibly acquire a non-religious worldview in the same way they acquire a taste for jeans, logo trainers and pop music?

RE needs to challenge this kind of secularism (Watson 2000). It is very far from being values and beliefs free. It incorporates a variety of atheistic and agnostic ideologies that give the lie to its presumed neutrality. Moreover, such secularism falls foul of its own proclaimed principles of openness and non-dogmatic critical enquiry. As Laborde (2010: 13) argues, the secular state should not be hostile to religion because 'neither the view that religion is true, nor the view that religion is false ... can be proven according to widely accepted epistemological standards'. Instead there should be mutual respect and open debate, both of which the positivist worldview closes down regarding religion.

Postmodernism has helped many to see that the secularist worldview, developed so markedly in the West since the Enlightenment, is not the only possible one: nurturing the young into it can be just as indoctrinatory as nurturing them into any other worldview. Jackson (2004b: 14) argues that RE needs to be more critical of its Western assumptions; and Ipgrave (1999: 156) calls for 'much more than Westernised liberals talking to each other'. An RE which fails to challenge secularism has already effectively committed suicide.

Dealing with diversity

Similarly, an RE which fails to challenge the pre-eminence in the West of values such as tolerance is short-changing pupils. Tolerance cannot stand the weight placed upon it: tolerance of intolerance, for example, is logically and existentially incoherent. Constant appeal to it therefore has tended to disable the use of critical faculties regarding diversity. In the light of recent international happenings, RE has a responsibility to move beyond such values 'rather than merely papering over the cracks of society through a vacuous blanket appeal to tolerance when so much around us is unambiguously unworthy of acceptance' (Barnes, Wright and Brandom 2008: 1).

The shared language of the secular state should centre on what is truly universal and ethically required whether people are religious or not: such as concern for truth and honesty, respect for all people as persons, empathy and concern for justice for all (Sacks 1995; Parekh 2000). Values such as tolerance are secondary values, dependent on deeper values being in place (see Wright 2007: 38).

Because religious convictions can be so strong and well defined, RE has a special role to play in enabling society to accommodate diversity fairly. It should provide an atmosphere of welcoming openness and permitting a safe space for expressing disagreement. It can therefore help pupils learn that disagreement should be based on understanding, not on ignorance, bias or misinterpretation. The principle elsewhere termed 'critical affirmation' is relevant (Ashton and Watson 1998: 190–192). If initially we look for insights in positions different from our own, and are generous-minded in trying to understand them, then we are in a strong position to be able to critique them appropriately, again in a spirit of respect.

Dogmatism, or imagining one can have absolute unchallengeable certainty, is the real enemy. References to the need for 'epistemological humility' (Cush and Francis 2001: 54) are crucial but should not be interpreted as betraying reasonable trust in one's own commitment. Rather, they should signify perceiving the provisionality and partiality of all our presumed knowledge. Wright notes (1996: 172) 'The absolute certainties of positivistic science and religious fundamentalism' need to be transcended, for our explorations 'will always be provisional, being grounded in a contingent rationality'. Laura (1983: 46) speaks of the need for 'fallibilistic realism'.

Such awareness ought to come naturally to religious people 'given the limitations of the human mind and the transcendent nature of the final truth' (Mitchell 1994: 95). Discussing faith and rational choice, Mitchell (1994: 108) further notes that in our on-going task 'progress consists in the achievement at any given time of as full an approximation to the truth as the circumstances of that time allow'. The pronounced difficulty which many have with this is because the intensity of their convictions leads them to overstate their understanding. Through dialogue with others, which RE can open up, pupils may be enabled to extend the boundaries of their understanding and sympathies.

Confronting the dark side of religion

Failing to take the dark side of religion seriously gives a utopian view of religion to the exclusion of what Gearon (2002: 148) calls 'dystopian realities.' Concern for this in RE is long overdue. RE needs openly to discuss the reality of the abuse of religion and what can be done to guard against such abuse. But to speak of the violence and injustice associated with religion as abuse is already to enter controversial waters. Erricker (2010: 175), for example, accuses some religious educators of favouring an approach that 'argues for the good in religion and rejects the bad as not the real thing', but this, he believes, fails to meet the required 'level of objectivity in relation to the phenomenon of religion'. Appeals to objectivity in religion, however, are notoriously controversial. Just how abusive is religion? Is all abuse accredited to religion truly religious? If Christians say they follow Jesus who taught a message of God as love, for which he lived and died, then anti-Semitism cannot be an *authentic* part of their religion. RE should open up a positive way of dealing with this misinterpretation. It should share, for example, properly critical analysis of biblical texts used to support anti-Semitism (see e.g. Watson 2004: 133–135).

Similarly, Muslims who claim to follow Allah are denying Allah when they succumb to violence (see Sardar 2004 for a sensitive study of this). It is cautionary to note the poor quality of the RE which the four 7/7 bombers had received (see REC 2005, with the Ofsted Reports on the schools attended by them). An RE which promotes real debate on the meaning of Islam might seriously help to prevent dangerous extremism. It could cite, for example, the 600-page *fatwa* of ul-Qadri Muhammad Tahir which notes that violence separates people from Allah and from the destiny of paradise: 'Violence is violence. It has no place in Islamic teaching' (see http://www.quilliamfoundation.org).

Presenting religion in a positive light should not mask its propensity for evil. Rather it provides grounds for evaluating how religious ideals are or are not lived up to (see Watson and Thompson 2007: 92–110). Such a focus is an essential aspect of spiritual and religious literacy.

Conclusion

The following resumé is a talking-point for readers of why RE matters today within a modern Western educational system.

1   RE matters because it opens up for pupils a perspective on knowledge that is concerned with belief in Transcendence – what most religions called God. This aim goes beyond imparting mere information to helping pupils have the wherewithal to begin to consider intelligently and sensitively for themselves the truth or otherwise of religious truth-claims.
2   RE matters because it offers an opportunity for pupils to challenge prevailing anti-religious assumptions which are common in the West. As such it is a powerful anti-indoctrinatory subject promoting thinking in depth.
3   RE matters because it can demonstrate a generous-minded but critical openness to others who think differently – an openness that goes beyond problematic tolerance. This is particularly important for a flourishing pluralist society because of the diversity of religious beliefs and the intensity of conviction in which they are held.
4   RE matters because it can help politically to render the world a safer place. The potential for violence found within religions can be discouraged through exposure to the search for truth and goodness within the major world religions.
5   RE matters because it can aid pupils' personal and spiritual development. It encourages the capacity for mature judgement-making on matters of ultimate significance which give meaning to life.

Questions

How far do you agree with this summary of why RE matters?

Compare this account of the aims of RE with that in the *National Framework* (QCA 2004: 8–9). Which is more realistic, and why?

How should the five aims outlined above be advanced in the classroom?

Further reading

Copley, T. (2005) *Indoctrination, Education and God*, London: SPCK. Incisive and powerfully argued.

Erricker, C. (2010) *Religious Education: A Conceptual and Interdisciplinary Approach for Secondary Level*, London: Routledge. Controversial and challenging.

Felderhof, M., Thompson, P. and Torevell, D. (eds) (2007) *Inspiring Faith in Schools: Studies in Religious Education*, Aldershot: Ashgate. Valuable collection of thought-provoking essays.

Watson, B. and Thompson, P. (2007) *The Effective Teaching of Religious Education* (2nd edn), Harlow: PearsonLongman. Embraces concerns for both education and religion – of practical as well as academic interest.

Chapter 2

Religious education in the United Kingdom and Ireland

INTRODUCTION, BY L. PHILIP BARNES

The tendency in some circles is to equate religious education (RE) in the United Kingdom with British RE, and then equate British RE with RE in England. There is some logic to these reductions, but it is not compelling. Such a strategy fails to capture the diversity of arrangements, policies and accommodations that characterise RE in the four nations that comprise the United Kingdom: England, Northern Ireland, Scotland and Wales. Certainly there is a case for considering England and Wales together, for both are subject to the same legislation, and this is the strategy adopted below, yet attention to the fact that there are two different sets of national guidelines to interpret the legislation (QCA 2004; DCELLS 2008) should caution against overhasty reductions or generalisations. Scotland and Northern Ireland are considered separately. This account of RE in the United Kingdom is then complemented by an account of RE in the Republic of Ireland; this adds a comparative dimension that is often overlooked by religious educators.

ENGLAND AND WALES, BY DAVID LUNDIE

> In my RE lessons I have learnt to become more broadminded, to accept other people's beliefs and faiths and to not let race or religion come in the way of what you see in an individual.
>
> (QCA 2004: 6)

> RE is one of my favourite subjects and the reason for that is that most of the time in lessons we discuss issues that make me look inside myself and think very deeply about the world, behaviour, my personality and my beliefs.
>
> (DCSF 2010: 32)

The above statements set out, in carefully selected examples of student feedback reported in policy documents, the two attainment targets which have come to dominate curriculum development at the national level: learning about religions and learning from religions. RE's unique policy context in English education is characterised by tensions between local and national policy determination and tensions between attainment-driven academic goals and claims made for its significance for students' spiritual, moral and interpersonal development. Understanding the historical and legislative origins of these tensions is essential to help any RE teacher to navigate within the subject.

Legislative developments

The history of RE in the curriculum

Up until the introduction of the National Curriculum in 1988, RE remained the only subject mandated by law to be taught in all schools in England and Wales. As early as the 1870 Elementary Education Act, a clause provided for compulsory Religious Instruction, though from its inception, RE in the 'county school' was to be non-denominational, not following the catechism or formulary of any one church. From its beginnings, therefore, the unique character of English RE was established – unlike the French or American education systems, religion is seen as an essential component of public education, but unlike the Irish, Spanish or Norwegian education systems, RE was not to be a nurturing in the state religion. The compulsory nature of Religious Instruction, and its non-denominational character, was retained in the 1944 Education Act.

The 1988 Education Reform Act

The contemporary legal context for RE in England and Wales is provided by the Education (Reform) Act 1988. In a few brief paragraphs in Sections 8 and 84–88, the subject is addressed. The basic requirements, and much of the language, of the 1944 Act are, for the most part, retained and reiterated, although the subject is tellingly re-named from 'Religious Instruction' to 'Religious Education'. Among these enduring requirements – the compulsory nature of RE, the right of parents to withdraw their children from RE (along with sex education, this remains the only subject in the curriculum with this right of withdrawal), to which is added the right of teachers to refuse to teach RE. A number of additional demands are made by the 1988 Act:

(i)   That any new syllabus for RE 'shall reflect the fact that the religious traditions in Great Britain are in the main Christian whilst taking account of the teaching and practices of the other principal religions represented in Great Britain' (Section 8.3).

(ii) Standing Advisory Councils for RE (SACREs) *must* be established, and are granted extended functions, including the power to make determinations (exceptionally) to remove the requirement for Collective Worship to be of a broadly Christian character.

(iii) Further, SACREs are required to convene a statutory Agreed Syllabus
Conference to review the locally agreed syllabus, at least every 5 years – the
committee of the Agreed Syllabus Conference to be composed of:

- Committee A – religious groups other than the Church of England, to
  include the principal non-Christian religions represented in the area.
- Committee B – representatives of the Church of England
- Committee C – representatives of the teaching unions (note that the
  representatives are drawn from teaching *unions* and do not necessarily
  include RE teachers)
- Committee D – representatives of the local authority.

All of these provisions were retained by the 1996 Education Act.

Interpreting the legislation – department circulars

In the period immediately following the 1988 Act, debate continued in the
professional community around what it meant for a syllabus to acknowledge that
Great Britain's religious traditions are 'in the main Christian', and in what way to
determine the other 'principal' religions and 'take account' of them. In response,
the Department for Education and Science issued Circular 3/89, which broadly
reiterated the language of the legislation, doing little to interpret or answer the
kinds of questions teachers and SACREs were asking – how many religions were
to be studied? How much time was to be devoted to Christianity and how much
to other religions? Should students learn about the traditions and customs of
other religions, or are they expected to gain personal insight from the teachings
of each of the religions? The position expressed in the circular was that it was for
the local education authority to determine whether or not a syllabus produced by
its syllabus conference conformed to the new legal requirements. To date, there
have been no challenges or determinations on the legal requirements in a court
of law, and it remains for Department Circulars and local authorities to interpret
the legislation.

It must be borne in mind that this legislation did not impose requirements 'out
of the blue'; as early as 1971, Schools Council Working Paper 36 had drawn
attention to the increasingly secular nature of British society, and suggested the
need for a phenomenological, multi-faith approach to RE which rejected the
implicit Christian faith formation of previous approaches. Many locally agreed
syllabuses, following the example set by the 1975 Birmingham Agreed Syllabus
Living Together, had included teaching about non-Christian religious traditions
for some years. There was still a great deal of variation in practice, however, and
John Hull, at the time one of the most respected theorists among British RE
professionals, writing in an influential piece as editor of the British Journal of RE,
remarked on the 'assumed Christian monopoly' which persisted in some syllabuses
(Hull 1989: 60). Hull's interpretation of the new requirements was that they
gave legislative force to the kind of multi-faith RE already widely practised in

Britain 'for the past fifteen years or so ... There is absolutely no suggestion [in the 1988 Act] that RE should be "Christian based", "Christian centred" or should offer an undue emphasis on Christianity' (Hull 1989: 60). With hindsight, some commentators (e.g. Thompson 2007) have seen this as an undue departure from what is, on the face of it, legislation requiring RE to be in the main Christian. In Hull's view, no syllabus meets the requirements to take account of the other principal religious traditions represented in the UK unless it includes the teachings and practices of 'Judaism, Islam, Hinduism, the Sikh faith, and Buddhism' (Hull 1989: 61).

The view that RE ought to comprise the study of these five religions plus Christianity quickly established itself in classroom practice. In 1994, this view received government approval with the publication of Circular 1/94, and of two 'Model' syllabuses by the School Curriculum and Assessment Authority (SCAA), intended to exemplify good practice. Model 1, entitled Living Faiths Today followed in the phenomenological tradition, and can be seen as the fore-runner of Attainment Target 1: learning about religions. Model 2, Questions and Teachings, focused on religious belief and practice, and has more of a focus on the skills which would later form Attainment Target 2: learning from religions. These model syllabuses, promulgated by the same body with responsibility for National Curriculum subjects, represented a significant shift in the meaning of 'local' determination of the agreed syllabus for RE. In many ways, the processes leading to the drafting of these syllabuses, involving national representatives of the major faith communities, teachers and education professionals, and policy makers, mirrors the composition of Agreed Syllabus Conferences on the local level.

The SCAA model syllabuses have subsequently been superseded by a single *Non Statutory National Framework* (QCA 2004) which, while retaining the emphasis on the study of six major faiths, with the study of Christianity at each key stage, also 'recommends' the study of a range of further traditions 'such as the Baha'i faith, Jainism and Zoroastrianism' and 'secular philosophies such as humanism' (QCA 2004: 12). Recent guidance from the Department for Children, Schools and Families (DCSF 2009) intended as a successor to Circular 1/94, explicitly stated that 'the Framework and its implementation are the basis of Government policy' (DCSF 2009: 18). This advice, however, has been promptly superseded by further DCSF guidance (DCSF 2010), which makes no mention of the *Framework*, but recommends that Agreed Syllabus Conferences should 'reflect curriculum developments nationally ... as set out in the RE programmes of study and learning' (DCSF 2010: 23). The 2009 and 2010 guidance makes two notable departures from previous circulars: first, it de-couples RE from Collective Worship, treating only of the former; and second, in acknowledging, in line with moves in the wider curriculum, that a cross-curricular approach to RE, particularly in the primary school, may be appropriate.

From policy into practice

The Non-Statutory National Framework and the programmes of study

While local determination remains a legal reality, on a number of practical levels, the influence of the Non-Statutory National Framework, published in 2004, mirrors that of the National Curriculum in other compulsory subjects: the framework includes level descriptors using the National Curriculum 8-level scale to standardise the assessment of student attainment in RE, and while Ofsted inspectors will look to see that the LEA Agreed Syllabus is taught in schools, they will measure student attainment relative to the level descriptors in the National Framework. The Qualifications and Curriculum Agency (QCA) has recently published exemplification materials to demonstrate to teachers how to assess student work using these level descriptors – the exemplification materials cover content drawn from the National Framework. The most recent version of the Framework (QCA 2007b and 2007c) has also been included in the National Curriculum handbook for teachers, albeit with a footnote explaining the non-statutory status of the guidance on RE.

Perhaps the greatest challenge of the National Framework has been bringing together the two competing conceptions of RE represented by the two previous model syllabuses, and this has resulted in the two attainment targets mentioned above. The distinction was first made by Michael Grimmitt in his 1987 book Religious Education and Human Development – Grimmitt distinguishes between 'learning religion', understood as a catechetical or faith formation approach, 'learning about religions', as a phenomenological or sociological process of learning about a particular faith's beliefs and practices, and 'learning from religion', as a personal reflective approach, encouraging a personal encounter with the key moral and metaphysical questions which religions seek to address. Writing in 2006, Mary Hayward notes that phenomenological approaches to learning about religions rooted in the model developed in the 1970s still dominated many agreed syllabuses in English RE (Hayward 2006: 157). The balance achieved by the Non-Statutory Framework represented a tension between the continuing strength of followers of a phenomenological pedagogy and an emerging personal reflective approach, drawing on sources including the ethnographic work of Jackson (2004b). In practice, however, this compromise had led to some confused and unhelpful pedagogical approaches, with some schemes of work separating entire lessons, or even entire topics into a 'learning about' unit and an unrelated 'learning from' unit. In Grimmitt's model, and in the model proposed by the Framework, learning from religions is intended to require a background in learning about religions, and the depth of understanding gained by learning from religions is intended to aid pupils in learning about the same. The idea that these three dimensions, the cognitive, reflective and affective approaches to religious learning, can be separated has been criticised by, among others, Marius Felderhof, on the grounds that any attempt to communicate the '"truths" of religious life' must make a claim on the emotions and commitments of the learner (Felderhof 2007: 91). Emerson-Moering (2007: 11) describes the Framework as 'an "English compromise", pragmatic, written by QCA officials ... clear but flexible and inclusive with a set of values whose origins are unclear', and is critical of the amorphous nature of the Framework's conceptual underpinnings, while acknowledging the enormous breadth of consensus between religious groups and teaching professionals in the agreeing of such a document.

With these difficulties in mind, the QCA published a series of programmes of study in 2007–2008, intended as a supplement to the *Non-Statutory Framework*. For the first time, programmes of study recommend a particular pedagogy, 'key concepts', as a means of integrating the two attainment targets without artificial separation. Aside from this, the main changes introduced by the programmes of study are the integration of RE with the language and aims of the National Curriculum and other cross-curricular policy developments such as *Every Child Matters* and the recognition, at Key Stage 4, of the possibility of studying philosophy and ethics as the central focus of RE, reflecting existing practice in many schools and the popularity of the Philosophy and Ethics paper in GCSE RE.

The locally agreed syllabus

The Standing Advisory Council on RE (SACRE)

In a strict sense, educational policy is determined by the relevant legislation and the application of this legislation by government bodies and the courts. As we have noted, in the case of RE, legislation makes provision, in the form of locally agreed syllabuses, for the local determination of content, the local authority having discretion over whether the agreed syllabus complies with legislation. The SACRE, as noted above, is required by law to reflect the principal religious traditions in the area. An examination of the composition of English SACREs in 2008 confirms that there is broad variation based on the make-up of the local community: the St Helen's SACRE, for example, representing the local authority with the highest population of Christians in the UK (86.9%, information from the 2001 census (see ONS 2006)) was composed entirely of representatives of the Christian Churches – 5 from the Church of England, 4 Roman Catholics and one representative of the Free churches; by contrast, the composition of the Tower Hamlets SACRE, representing the local authority with the largest number of non-Christian religious adherents (ONS 2006), was much more diverse – 7 Muslim representatives, 4 from the Church of England, 3 Roman Catholics, 1 representative of a black-majority Christian church, 1 Free churches representative, 1 Jewish, 1 Buddhist, 1 Hindu and 1 Sikh representative, a total of 20 members on Committees A and B. While these changes to composition have provided some impetus for the changes in RE, those who frame and produce locally agreed syllabuses do not work in a vacuum, as we have seen. A contentious issue exists at present around the representation of non-religious beliefs. While the *Non-Statutory Framework* recommends the study of non-religious life stances, Humanist representatives are not permitted to sit as full members of Committee A, though they may be co-opted. Recent government advice (DCSF 2010: 19–20) has recommended an expanded role for SACREs in the wider educational life of the local authority, suggesting activities such as consultation on community equality strategies, operating inter-faith study centres and organising themed education weeks. The increasing centrality of RE to the community cohesion strategies of government is evident in such suggestions.

The Agreed Syllabus Conference

The Agreed Syllabus Conference is a separate body, convened by the SACRE, with a legal mandate to review the locally agreed syllabus every five years. In recent years, syllabus conferences have tended to adopt the National Framework, or to incorporate it in some form, although there are exceptions, most notably the 2007 Birmingham Agreed Syllabus. It is at this level that the trajectories of local policy, with continuities of practice and interest over many years, intersect with the trajectory of national policy, with its increasingly precise pedagogical and social intentions. The ways in which these policy trajectories collide do result in variation, although an analysis of a sample of 24 agreed syllabuses, drawn from a range of areas, urban and rural, more and less diverse, from local authorities under different political control, demonstrated mostly differences in quality and prescriptivity. Agreed syllabuses in the sample varied from 15 to 192 pages in length, some accompanied by web-based teaching materials.

Some of the problems an agreed syllabus conference can encounter may include the influence of a single vocal member who insists on a radical departure, either in pedagogical terms, or in terms of their personal understanding of a particular religious tradition, from the nationally or locally agreed norms. Nonetheless, the history of the development of RE in policy and practice in England and Wales has shown the effectiveness of some locally agreed approaches in influencing the national situation. The 1975 Birmingham Agreed Syllabus has already been addressed as perhaps the most prominent example. More recently, the idea of 'key concepts', adopted in the non-statutory programmes as a pedagogical device to bridge the gap between the two attainment targets, was borrowed directly from a similar pedagogy, 'conceptual enquiry' which was pioneered in the Hampshire Agreed Syllabus, subsequently adopted by Portsmouth, Southampton, Westminster and others, representing a meso-level through which local determination serves to disseminate best practice, as was also the case with the changes which filtered outward from Birmingham in the 1970s.

The National Exemplar Framework for Wales

The common legislative character which English and Welsh RE had previously shared was ended with the publication in 2008 of the Welsh Assembly government's *National Exemplar Framework for Religious Education* (DCELLS 2008). The Welsh *Framework* enumerates three core skills for RE: engaging with fundamental questions, exploring religious beliefs, teachings and practice(s) and expressing personal responses. This approach represents a similar move to the introduction of key concepts in England, seeking as far as possible to bring out the 'learning from' dimension of RE. While the Welsh *Framework* refers to 'Christianity and the other principal religions', no other religions are named. It must be borne in mind, however, that this *Framework* comes in the wake of 20 years of common policies and syllabuses with England, as discussed above.

Inspecting RE

Although Section 5 of the Education Act 2005 requires Ofsted inspectors to inspect whether RE is being provided in accordance with the locally agreed syllabus, their responsibility to inspect pupil progress also means that they will usually have recourse to the level descriptors in the *Non-Statutory National Framework*. This places a constraint on local syllabuses to be compatible, in terms of general standards, with these level descriptors, and it is precisely the lack of pupil understanding of their progress in RE that has been highlighted for criticism in recent inspectorate reports (Ofsted 2010). Exemplar materials are available through the QCA on how to assess in accordance with these descriptors across a range of syllabus aims. RE is not always singled out as a priority for inspectors. The arrangements for inspecting RE in schools with a religious character (Section 48 inspection) fall within the bounds of the religious organisation sponsoring the school, and are discussed below.

Assessment in RE

Besides the statutory bodies addressed above, the most significant influence on RE curriculum practice in the secondary school is the increasing importance of examinations. An increasing number of schools, often following the advice of their local agreed syllabus, or responding to resource-linked pressures to raise attainment, seek to provide their compulsory RE at Key Stage 4 through the medium of a GCSE. The recent Ofsted report, Transforming Religious Education, notes the rise in examination entry as a positive development (Ofsted 2010: 5) but does not address the apparent tension experienced by many teachers between the academic aims of RE as an examined subject and the expectations of the subject in 'promoting pupils' spiritual development', except to note that the demands of assessment could at times lead to a lack of continuity between Key Stages 3 and 4, '[i]n the worst cases, this lack of continuity distorted pupils' understanding of religion and belief' (Ofsted 2010: 6). RE is the only subject, besides Citizenship education, to be offered as a 'short course' qualification, comprising half of a standard GCSE. Examination boards are required to meet Ofqual standards, which mandate two assessment outcomes: AO1, focusing on knowledge and understanding, mapping neatly to Attainment Target 1, and AO2, measuring personal response, similar to Attainment Target 2 (QCA 2007a: 5). Examination boards are also, it must be borne in mind, subject to commercial pressures in a market environment in England and Wales. The market in exam-board approved textbooks further reinforces the effect of the market, generating a critical mass of candidates for examinations in Christianity alone, Christianity and Islam and philosophy and ethics, but creating difficulties for teachers or students wishing to specialise in Sikhism or Buddhism at Key Stage 4.

In the 15 years since the publication of Circular 1/94, the prevalent trend in RE in England and Wales has been for a greater centralisation of 'strong' advice and guidance for the subject – guidance backed up by inspection and examination regimes, moving ever closer to a position of equivalence with the subjects in the National Curriculum. The government's recent decision to scale back 'initiatives on PSHE, Citizenship and RE' (Gove 2010) may see the increasing importance, for RE, of relying on its credentials as an examined, academic subject, located firmly in the Humanities, and separated from its former 'soft skills curriculum' bedfellows of PSHE and Citizenship.

Schools with a religious character

A further significant influence on RE in England is the increasing diversity of school provision, with the promotion of 'schools with a religious character', voluntary aided schools and academies (e.g. DCSF 2007a), which are exempt from the provisions of their local authority agreed syllabus, but for whom the 2009 DCSF guidance still recommends the Non-Statutory National Framework. In a joint statement in 2006, leaders of the main faith communities endorsed the values of the National Framework and the importance of RE for community cohesion and students' spiritual development (Ekklesia 2006). The 2010 guidance clarifies a number of issues around this complex area – voluntary controlled and foundation schools are still required to follow the agreed syllabus, as are academies of a non-religious character; voluntary aided schools must operate a double opt-out – parents may request their children be withdrawn from denominational RE and offered the locally agreed syllabus instead, as well as having a right of withdrawal as in community schools. The contribution of Church schools in particular to the teaching of Christianity may come to the fore in the coming years, as state schools seek to respond to inspectors' concerns around 'specific weaknesses in the teaching about Christianity', including a lack of depth and systematic study (Ofsted 2010: 6) a concern also raised by a recent review of classroom resources (Jackson *et al.* 2010).

The School Census from 2005 showed that there were 1,710,400 pupils in maintained Christian schools, 1,770 pupils in maintained Muslim schools, 14,670 pupils in maintained Jewish schools and 640 pupils in maintained Sikh schools in England. Religious organisations sponsoring schools of a religious character are responsible for inspecting RE in those schools (Section 48 inspections) – the Church of England, Roman Catholic Church and Board of Deputies of British Jews have formal education bodies established to carry out such inspections.

The Church of England

The Church of England, one of the largest providers of denominational schooling, established the principal of 'additionality' in the provision of its syllabus for RE, accepting the *National Framework* in its entirety, but also making provision for additional aims:

> In a Church of England school RE also helps students:
> (a) engage with the living faith
> (b) understand how religious faith can provide a vision to sustain and develop their spiritual life
> (c) develop a sense of themselves as significant, unique and valued
> (d) become active citizens, understanding and serving their neighbour.
>
> (National Society n/d: 12)

Interestingly, in enumerating the key concepts set out in the QCA programmes of study, the Church of England advice and guidance suggests that the first three key concepts are 'predominantly learning *about* religion', with the latter three 'predominantly learning *from* religion' (National Society n/d: 12–13), aptly illustrating the ability of mediating bodies to entirely misinterpret the aims of a new pedagogy in the interests of continuity.

The Roman Catholic Church

While the Roman Catholic Church's advice and guidance on RE shares the principle of additionality discussed above, the form taken by Catholic guidance is somewhat different. While the Church of England's additionality is evident from the outside, the Catholic approach has been to present the key aims of the national guidelines, but from entirely within a Catholic faith framework. While acknowledging the changes that have taken place, and officially endorsing the new *Framework*, the Church has retained its *Icons* scheme of work, published with the support of the Bishops' Conference, and first published in 2001, though many schools supplement this work with other activities. The Catholic Church has also made explicit the desire for all pupils in Catholic schools to take accredited examinations (GCSEs and A levels) in RE at Key Stages 4 and 5, and several examination boards offer a syllabus tailored to the Catholic tradition. In recent years, there has been some debate about the effectiveness of Catholic RE, in part prompted by the work of Bishop O'Donoghue (2007), whose advice recommended a return to the catechism, prayer and the sacraments, and avoiding an overly simplified phenomenological approach based on personal experience.

Academies and independent schools

A number of religious organisations have established networks of academies in recent years. These have the freedom to establish a syllabus in keeping with their principles. However, following controversy in some schools (e.g. Walker 2006), the DCSF guidance of 2007 states an obligation on all schools, including those in the independent sector, to promote community cohesion, while the 2010 guidance also grants ministers a right of determination in agreeing a syllabus for RE in academies. The increasing diversity of school provision which may be afforded by the new Conservative government's plans to fund small independent 'free schools' may bring new dimensions to these debates and controversies.

Questions

What are the pressures teachers face in balancing the pressures of national, local and faith community demands on their teaching?

What are the threats posed by a National Curriculum in RE? Who are they a threat to?

What are the challenges facing policy makers when proposing models of good practice for RE?

Further reading

City of Birmingham Agreed Syllabus Conference (2007) *The Birmingham Agreed Syllabus for Religious Education*, see http://www.birmingham-asc.org.uk. One of the few agreed syllabuses to openly challenge the non-statutory guidance, the Birmingham syllabus is notable for its distinctive focus.

Grimmitt, M. (1987) *Religious Education and Human Development*, Essex: McCrimmons Publishing Company. Grimmitt's work established the distinction between 'learning about' and 'learning from' religions – although many subsequent developments are a departure from the pedagogy he proposes, this distinction has been used in subsequent policy debates.

Erricker, C. (2010) *Religious Education: A Conceptual and Interdisciplinary Approach for Secondary Level*, Oxford: Routledge. Moving beyond Grimmitt's work, Clive Erricker's ideas, which had a significant impact on the Hampshire Agreed Syllabus, and subsequently on the non-statutory Programmes of Study, seek to integrate the aims of learning about and learning from religions.

Qualifications and Curriculum Authority (QCA) (2004) *Religious Education: Non-Statutory National Framework*, London: QCA. The key curriculum document proposed by government, it forms the backbone of the majority of locally agreed syllabuses, and is fundamental to understanding the current stated aims of RE in England.

NORTHERN IRELAND, BY DAVID ARMSTRONG

Northern Ireland's 'Troubles' frequently drew attention to the place of religion in the Province's schools and for some popular commentators (Dawkins 2006; Grayling 2006) Northern Ireland is the paradigm example of all that is wrong with linking education and religion. Religious education (RE) is one of the most heavily legislated subjects in the curriculum, a feature Northern Ireland shares with many other European countries (see Kuyk *et al.* 2007). Friesen's (1999: 235) remark that 'Combining religion and education in discussion is rarely a boring activity' is certainly true of RE's history in Northern Ireland. While the provision of RE in schools has been compulsory for some time, it is only recently (1996) that a statutory RE syllabus was specified. The Church of Ireland along with the Catholic, Presbyterian and Methodist Churches were invited by the Department of Education to draw up a 'core' syllabus for use in the Province's grant-aided schools. Of course, the Churches' interest in the control of schooling since the establishment of Northern Ireland (1921) has been well documented (Akenson 1973; McGrath 2000) and is reflected in the 'dual' system of Catholic and Protestant schools which, despite a small integrated sector, remains the default position today. The power to fashion and transmit religious belief has been a priority for the Churches who have been 'arguably the single biggest influence on the development of Northern Ireland educational law' (Lundy 2000: 10). RE has been, and remains, a key concern for the Churches. Given this history and the continuing 'separateness' of schooling, the provision of an agreed Churches' RE syllabus was a considerable ecumenical achievement and welcomed by government. While the syllabus has come in for some criticism from professional educators (Barnes 1997; Nelson 2004; Richardson 2007), the Churches' control of the syllabus has provoked little controversy from parents or teachers.

Northern Ireland 1921 – organising education

In 1921, when the 'new' jurisdiction of Northern Ireland was established, schooling was organised on denominational lines. In the 1830s Lord Stanley proposed national schooling to 'unite in one system children of different creeds' (Williams 2005: 38). Religious instruction and secular education were to be differentiated with teachers required to display a classroom sign indicating whether what was taking place was religious or secular. Clergy could teach their own 'flock' in the schools but outside the school day. The reality of Church influence, however, meant that the National Schools established under the

'Stanley' Education Act were 'gradually amended from a non-denominational scheme into a network of denominational schools' (McGrath 2000: 16).

After partition, the Northern Ireland government established the Lynn Committee to bring forward proposals for the reorganisation of the Province's schools' estate. Lord Londonderry, the first Education Minister, sought to end denominational schooling and bring education under public control. He ignored the recommendations of the Lynn Committee which proposed a common Scripture programme for schools. Londonderry's 1923 Education Act was clear, 'the education authority shall not provide religious instruction'. Londonderry's schools were labelled 'godless' schools which banned the Bible.

In the 'new' jurisdiction, the Catholic authorities, 'opposed to any dilution of clerical power and wary of alienating a militant nationalist electorate, refused to cooperate with the devolved government's education scheme' (McGrath 2000: 15) and refused to transfer Catholic schools to state control. The Protestant Churches transferred their schools to 'state' control and welcomed the removal of the financial responsibility. This 'transfer of control' gave rise to what are now called 'controlled' schools with certain governance rights in these schools given to the Church 'transferors'. The Protestant Churches secured important changes to Londonderry's Education Act with respect to religious instruction. In 1925 a further Act provided for 'simple Bible instruction' in schools with a 1930 Act securing non-denominational religious instruction in 'transferred' schools. Teachers in these schools were required to give this instruction although pupils could be exempted under a 'conscience' clause.

Thus from its inception the Northern Ireland schools' estate reflected the religious status quo and subsequently developed along these religious 'fault' lines. These early debates and arrangements precipitated the 'dual' system that has been maintained through most of the twentieth century.

The Education Act (Northern Ireland) 1947

This important post-war Act made a number of important amendments to the provision of religious instruction. It introduced a conscience clause allowing teacher exemption from religious instruction and excluded religious instruction from inspection by Education Department officials. It stipulated that religious instruction in 'county' (state) schools should be based upon the Holy Scriptures but must exclude 'instruction as to any tenet which is distinctive of any particular religious denomination'.

Northern Ireland 2010 – the schools' estate

Almost all the Province's schools are state financed. Catholic education is funded via the Council for Catholic Maintained Schools; the Northern Ireland Council for Integrated Schools operates the small integrated (Christian) sector; Irish language education is funded under the Comhairle na Gaelscolaíochta. According to the Department of Education, controlled schools (mainly Protestant) 'are not a recognised sector as such. They are the schools that do not fit into any other category and are owned and managed by government. They lack the sense of shared identity and ownership that is evident in other sectors' (see DENI 2007). Controlled schools are state schools in which the Protestant Churches have certain historic governance rights. In recent years the Protestant Churches have expressed serious concerns about future educational proposals 'directed towards providing a school sector which has had the Protestant church ethos removed as of right' (Transferor Representatives' Council 2007).

Barnes (2007a: 232) refers to controlled schools as state schools whose largely Protestant populations give them a 'Protestant character' but notes that these schools 'lack both the overtly confessional orientation of Catholic schools and the measure of control enjoyed by the Roman Catholic Church over its schools'. While Nelson (2004: 251) acknowledges that controlled schools lack the overt confessionalism of Catholic schools, he maintains 'there is no doubt that within the majority of controlled schools a Christian and Protestant ethos is promoted.' Richardson (2008a: 2) correctly notes that these schools 'are not in any sense official Protestant church schools'. Arthur (2006: 136) argues that the secularisation of previously Christian educational institutions is hastened when they are no longer connected with a particular Christian Church. He maintains that a general religious identification 'erodes the religious uniqueness of the particular denomination's contribution'. On this analysis, the Protestant Churches' fears that their 'contribution and rights ... far from being respected and protected, are in fact being undervalued and ... systematically eroded' (General Assembly of the Presbyterian Church in Ireland: 2008) are well founded.

The school category or type influences the delivery of RE. While RE is compulsory in all grant-aided schools, only in controlled schools must RE be 'undenominational'. Acknowledging the risk of oversimplification, Schreiner (2007: 11) writes, 'In general it is possible to differentiate between two main models of RE in Europe: the Religious Studies and Denominational or Confessional approach.' The 'undenominational' nature of RE in controlled schools, certainly in controlled secondary schools, has tended towards the subject's development in a religious studies direction. In this sector teachers are more likely to regard themselves as impartial educators whose task is to promote the value of a religious studies approach, perhaps sympathetic to Christianity, but eschewing the nurture of a specific religious tradition. This contrasts with the Catholic sector where primary school teachers require a recognised certificate of RE to deliver a confessionally Catholic programme.

Contemporary legislation

The Education Reform (Northern Ireland) Order 1989 states that every grant-aided school must 'include provision for RE for all registered pupils at the school'.

Earlier provision that RE in 'state' schools must be undenominational and based upon the Holy Scriptures is retained. The Order invited 'persons having an interest in the teaching of RE' to draft a syllabus. The resulting Churches' produced syllabus was specified in 1996 and revised in 2006 and drafted into legislation.

The 1996 syllabus was entirely Christian in its content. Each key stage is organised around the same three learning objectives: the Revelation of God, the Christian Church and morality. The syllabus required students to study 'two traditions' of the Christian Church at Key Stage 4, whereas the 2006 syllabus was more specific in stipulating that the Christian Church should be studied from 'the Roman Catholic tradition and at least one Protestant tradition'. Significantly, the revised syllabus incorporated the study of two world faiths (in addition to Christianity) at Key Stage 3. While Richardson (2007) objects to the Churches' 'ownership' of the syllabus and the insufficient attention given to world religions, Barnes (2002b: 19) argues that the English model of multi-faith RE is 'inappropriate to the Northern Irish educational and cultural context'. However, Copley (1997: 186) claims that the syllabus 'would not have been culturally, politically or socially acceptable in more openly plural and secular England and Wales'. The 2009/10 Department of Education school census statistics reveal that only half of 1 per cent (0.55%) of students in Northern Ireland's schools are from non-Christian backgrounds and lend force to Barnes's (2002b) claim.

While the content of the syllabus is mandatory, it does not 'prevent or restrict the inclusion of any other matter, skill or process'. In other words, schools may expand the core syllabus to suit their needs. However, it is unlikely that schools will commit extra time and resources to teach material over and above what is prescribed. Similarly, the statutory requirement to deliver the syllabus at Key Stage 4 serves to restrict schools from choosing GCSE Religious Studies specifications which do not cover the prescribed core content. The prescription that controlled schools deliver 'undenominational' RE conflicts with the core's requirement to study the Christian Church from the Roman Catholic and at least one Protestant tradition (see Armstrong 2009).

Developments in religious education

Controlled schools

Since 1925 various committees and councils have designed RE programmes supporting the legislative requirement to provide 'simple Bible instruction'. The courses reflect an orthodox Protestant understanding of Scripture and focus on the teachings of Christ and the New Testament message of redemption. The 'RE Council, Northern Ireland' (established in 1966) recognised the need for specialist RE teachers. The developing cadre of professional religious educators valued the Durham Report's (1970) emphasis on the study of religion in its universal rather than exclusively Christian experience. The Council's 1978 consultative report *Design for Religious Education* recommended the study of Christianity in an 'open exploratory spirit, as the most appropriate way of promoting understanding of and insight into the religion that is nearest to most children and also of providing a basis for the wider study of religion' (1978: 23). The report called for discussion of the subject's aims and objectives. It recommended 'strict objectivity' in the study of the Bible and distinguished this from the Bible's use in evangelism and Christian nurture. None of the courses produced throughout this period was statutory and it is difficult to gauge their uptake or impact. Richardson (2008b) writes, 'Despite various attempts to provide uniform teaching materials, the controlled schools in Northern Ireland during this period reflected a very unsystematic – some might say *chaotic* – approach to schemes and programmes of work.' Today's statutory core may have removed this chaos but the question of RE's aims is left (deliberately?) vague by the syllabus.

Catholic schools

RE in Catholic schools has been centrally organised with catechetical materials and programmes of study made available through a national publisher. The primary programme *Children of God* was in use from the 1970s until the early 2000s when it was replaced by *Alive O*. These are confessional programmes aimed at preparing children for First Confession, Communion and Confirmation. The *Christian Way* and *Fully Alive* secondary courses complemented the primary curriculum and overall these programmes present a coherent Catholic RE throughout the school years. These brief comments on Catholic RE fail to do justice to the subject's curriculum development, especially the more recent efforts to present the subject as one which both forms and informs students. The attempt to combine personal formation with critical reflection from within a Christian tradition distinguishes Catholic RE from RE in the controlled sector. The Catholic sector cannot, however, be complacent about its future. While 'Catholic schools seek to reflect a distinctive vision of life and a corresponding philosophy of education' (Irish Catholic Bishops Conference 2008) it is not axiomatic that the religious ethos of Catholic schools necessarily secures 'the full and uncritical support of all school members' (Donnelly 2000: 144). Catholic schooling faces unprecedented challenges: the disappearance of religious orders which served to staff RE; a Catholic laity which increasingly questions its allegiance to the Church in the aftermath of clerical child-abuse revelations and allegations of cover-up. The Church's commitment to RE in Catholic schools is unquestioned. The question, however, of the continuing role of RE in schools to sustain Catholic faith formation is moot.

Conclusion

For some, particularly in the controlled sector, a Churches' syllabus compromised the subject's independence and precipitated a debate about the 'ownership' of the subject (Nelson 2004). Others, however, regarded the Churches' co-operation in establishing a statutory agreed syllabus as a positive development which guaranteed the subject's status in the curriculum. This is especially true in the controlled sector where RE was rarely afforded the time, resources or status enjoyed by the subject in Catholic schools.

Historically, the approaches to RE in controlled and maintained schools might be described as respectively neo-confessional and confessional. Today, the situation in controlled schools is rather more complex. A largely Christian core syllabus 'sits less comfortably in "state" schools where the connection between RE and Christian nurture is either rejected or is at least ambiguous' (Armstrong 2009: 310). The character of RE has evolved differently in the two main sectors. RE in Catholic schools remains confessional whereas in controlled schools the movement towards *educational* RE is clearly discernible. However, the distinction between confessional and educational RE is not that helpful. Christian 'identity formation' (Schreiner 2007: 12) need not exclude an educational religious studies approach. Indeed, Schreiner (2007: 12) thinks that in different European classrooms 'there is a tendency for practice to converge in spite of the different "theories"'. In Northern Ireland, the joint Churches' syllabus has assisted that convergence. RE cannot be divorced from its cultural context. This is especially relevant in Northern Ireland where broadly Christian RE continues to reflect a societal consensus. Present legislation may require some minor amendment but it need not be discarded as the 'cultural hangover' (Copley 1997: 127) of a Christian past.

Questions

Is it acceptable that a statutory RE syllabus for use in grant-aided schools should be under the control of the Christian Churches?

To what extent are the aims of *confessional* RE compatible with *educational* RE?

Legislation may make RE compulsory but to what extent should it specify the subject's aims?

Further reading

Akenson, D. H. (1973) *Education and Enmity: The Control of Schooling in Northern Ireland 1920–50*, Newton Abbot: David & Charles. A history of the schools' estate in Northern Ireland.

Armstrong, D. (2009) 'RE and the law in Northern Ireland's controlled schools', *Irish Educational Studies*, 28: 297–313. Examines the legislation in some detail pointing out anomalies and possible solutions.

Barnes, L. P. (2002b) 'World religions and the Northern Ireland curriculum', *Journal of Beliefs & Values*, 23: 19–32. Barnes assesses the arguments for and against including world religions in the RE curriculum.

McGrath, M. (2000) *The Catholic Church and Catholic Schools in Northern Ireland: The Price of Faith*, Dublin: Irish Academic Press. A detailed history of Catholic schooling in Northern Ireland.

SCOTLAND, BY STEPHEN MCKINNEY

This is an appropriate point to assess the development and contemporary position of religious education (RE) in Scottish schools. The implementation of *Curriculum for Excellence*, the new Scottish Government curricular guidelines for ages 3 to 18, in autumn 2010 confirms religious and moral education as one of the curriculum organisers for all Scottish schools. This is remarkable progress from the pre-1972 era when the practice in RE, in the non-denominational sector, was reported to be anachronistic and ill suited to late twentieth-century Scotland. This section will begin with a concise overview of the history of Scottish state-funded schools before discussing two main stages of the history of RE in the late twentieth to early twenty-first centuries. First, the 1970s and 1980s that includes the impact of the 1972 Millar report, the Education (Scotland) Act 1980 (and Circular 6/91) and the Scottish Catholic church response to the post-Vatican II era. Second, the 1990s to 2010 that highlight the 5–14 curricular guidelines, the introduction of Higher Still, the establishment of the Scottish Catholic Education Service, and *Curriculum for Excellence*. Finally, the section will conclude by discussing some recent debates in RE. It is important to note that nomenclature in the Scottish context can be confusing and the terminology will be explained as it emerges in this short historical account.

Scottish state-funded schools

Scotland, like other Western English-speaking countries, attempted to introduce some form of standardised state-funded schooling in the late nineteenth century, to ensure quality of education and equity for all children (Miller 2000: 156–157; Paterson 2003). The Roman Catholic schools, founded as a result of waves of Irish Catholic immigration, were anxious that they would lose their denominational status in the state-funded sector and declined the offer to become state-funded under the 1872 Education (Scotland) Act (Fitzpatrick 1986). In a possibly unique accommodation between a state and organised religion, the 1918 Education (Scotland) Act awarded Roman Catholic schools (and other denominational schools if they wished) full state funding, but allowed these schools to retain their denominational status, follow their own RE programmes and approve their own teachers (Anderson 2008: 210). The state school system was composed, then, of two main sectors: the denominational and the oddly titled non-denominational. The state-funded denominational schools in Scotland have become practically synonymous with Roman Catholic schools – apart from one Jewish primary school that has been state funded since 1982 and a handful of schools that claim to be Episcopalian (Caldwell 1998). Currently there are 2,708 schools in Scotland: 2,151 primary, 375 secondary and 182 special (Scottish Government School Estate Statistics 2009). Within these overall figures, the Roman Catholic schools account for 384 schools: 325 primary, 53 secondary and 6 special. The Roman Catholic schools have been disputed in the political, academic and public arenas and sometimes mistakenly presumed to be a root cause of (ill-defined) sectarianism, but have been viewed more favourably by the Labour–Liberal Coalition Scottish Executive (1999–2007) and by the leader of the Scottish Nationalist Party Scottish Government (2007–) (see McKinney 2008a: 54–55; Davis 2008: 66; Scottish Government online (n.d.), *About the Scottish Government*).

The 1970s and 1980s

The Millar Report of 1972 is the catalyst for change in late twentieth-century non-denominational RE, but also had significant impact on the organisation of RE in Roman Catholic schools (Scottish Education Department 1972). The Millar Report was an audit of RE in non-denominational schools and of stakeholders' views on the present and future vision of RE. The audit revealed that RE was poorly resourced, very limited in scope and overly focused on Christianity and bible study. There was often insufficient time, no examinations and no inspections. There was no teaching qualification for RE and, therefore, no specialist teachers and no departments. As a result the teaching frequently lacked imagination and motivation. This was compounded by the decreasing religious literacy of the teachers (reflecting the decline of mainstream Protestant Christianity in Scotland) who felt ill-trained and lacked confidence in this subject (McKinney 2010: 136–137). Moreover, the cultural, ethnic and, importantly, religious landscape in Scotland was changing, and cities such as Glasgow were experiencing the growth of Muslim, Hindu and Sikh communities (Maan 1992: 165–168; Maan 2008: 201–204).

The Millar Report and the subsequent SCCORE documents (Bulletin 1 and Bulletin 2) proposed some radical changes in terms of rationale, aims and scope of RE in school education (Scottish Central Committee on RE, 1978, 1981). The title of the subject was amended to Religious and Moral Education (RME) to reflect moral viewpoints that were not based on a religious perspective. The subject aimed to explore the search for meaning as articulated in religion by studying this under three main themes: Christianity (preserving the historical importance of Christianity for Scotland); world religions; and pupil search for meaning – ultimately reflecting changes in Scottish educational thinking, demography and religious diversity (McKinney 2010: 137–138). Teachers were to be trained in RE at all levels and training courses were introduced, as were public examinations. The qualified specialist teacher of RE began to be recognised as an important addition to the non-denominational secondary school.

The Approach to RE in the Catholic Secondary School (1974) was the Scottish Catholic Church response to the General Catechetical Directory (1971) and, unsurprisingly, outlined a Christocentic and confessional vision to RE (Sacred Congregation of the Clergy 1971; National RE Committee 1974). The Roman Catholic schools in the early 1970s used a national syllabus for RE in the primary schools approved by the hierarchy. The provision of RE in the secondary schools was less co-ordinated and the resources varied from diocese to diocese. Interestingly, many Catholic teachers in secondary schools, similar to their counterparts in non-denominational schools, felt ill-equipped and lacked confidence in teaching RE. This was caused by post-Vatican II changes, overpopulated classes (at a time of teacher shortage), increasing professional demands of the subject and the lack of resources. In a striking parallel to the Millar Report, the recommendations were that each secondary school should establish an RE department, headed by a qualified specialist teacher, supported by a chaplain and, where possible, a diocesan RE advisor (usually a priest). The specialist teacher would direct and support the non-specialist teachers (later to be known as generalists). The Roman Catholic schools moved quickly to appoint specialist teachers and establish departments by the end of the 1970s and by the early 1990s there were very few Catholic secondary schools that did not have a principal teacher (head of department). While many non-denominational schools also began to appoint principal teachers for new departments of RE, there could be a tendency, in smaller schools, to appoint at assistant principal teacher level.

The rapid increase in the professional status of RME, prompted by the Millar Report and the SCCORE *Bulletins*, was to be consolidated by the Education (Scotland) Act 1980 which provided a legal guarantee of the right of children to receive 'instruction in religion' (and religious observance), though there is a parental right to withdraw children (Office of Public Sector Information 1980; see Hartshorn 2008: 375). This was re-emphasised in the 1991 Scottish Office Education Department Circular 6/91 which stated that RE had a 'fundamental place in the curriculum' (Scottish Office Education Department 1991; see McKinney and Conroy 2007: 225). Further consolidation occurred in the introduction of public examinations in Religious Studies (RS) at Ordinary Grade (1982) and Higher Grade (1985) (see Nixon 2008: 558–559). The subject began to be inspected by Her Majesty's Inspectorate in 1983 (see McKinney and Conroy 2007: 224). The inspections are in relation to the quality of teaching and learning and take place in both non-denominational and denominational schools. Religious Studies would be included in the major changes in public examinations from Ordinary Grade to Standard Grade.

The 1990s to the present

In the late 1980s, there were growing concerns in Scotland about the educational efficacy of the transitions from primary school to secondary school (and between stages within the secondary school) and the co-related impact on continuity and progression in learning. The 5–14 national curricular guidelines in the early 1990s introduced a common structure, organising language and concepts for all subject areas, including Religious and Moral Education (Scottish Office Education Department 1992). The three main areas of focus were Christianity, other world religions and personal search. There was some disquiet about the continued privileged position of Christianity and the reference to 'other' world religions. Personal search was conceived as being contained within the study of Christianity and other world religions, but was perceived by some teachers to be a separate focus of study. Originally, it was envisaged that the same guidelines, with an appendix, would be used by the Roman Catholic sector. The Roman Catholic sector rejected this proposal as the guidelines failed to recognise the distinctive nature of Roman Catholic schooling and RE. After a period of consultation with Roman Catholic schools, educationalists and other stakeholders, a document entitled '5–14 Religious Education (Roman Catholic Schools)' was published in 1994 (Scottish Office Education Department/Catholic Education Commission 1994). These guidelines, though adapted from the non-denominational guidelines, were contextualised within the vision of Christian faith formation of Catholic education. Religious and Moral Education was deemed to be an inappropriate title, as morality was perceived to stem from religion. There was greater emphasis on Christianity, though other world religions would be taught. The Roman Catholic guidelines included a greater focus on sacraments and liturgy and personal search was understood to be within the context of Catholic Christianity for Catholic pupils.

There were further changes in public examinations as the Higher examination became the more encompassing 'Higher Still'. These changes, like the move to Standard Grades, were designed to create a more inclusive examination system for a wider range of ability, a consequence of the raising of the school leaving age to sixteen (Pickard 2008: 214, 220). Within the move to Higher Still, Religious Studies was changed to Religious, Moral and Philosophical Studies (RMPS) (see Nixon 2008: 558–559). The change in nomenclature reflected the importance of moral philosophy and an increasing, but contested, diversification within the subject. The Roman Catholic sector was considerably strengthened with the appointment of Michael McGrath in 2003 as the first director of the Scottish Catholic Education Service (SCES), the operational arm of the Scottish Catholic Education Commission.

A national debate in education was conducted in 2002 and the consequent recommendation for a Curriculum for Excellence (CfE) was accepted by the Scottish Executive in 2004 (Scottish Government 2004). The underlying purpose is to enable all children to develop their capacities as successful learners, confident individuals, responsible citizens and effective contributors to society. The aim is to produce a curriculum that is less crowded, more flexible and better connected but retain the breadth and depth associated with the Scottish tradition in education. The expectations for learning and progression are expressed within a series of experiences and outcomes, contained within curriculum organisers, which are intended to be inter-connected and will contribute to developing the four capacities. There will also be a revision of the national qualifications. The eight curriculum organisers include Religious and Moral Education, which is sub-divided into RME and RERC (RE in Roman Catholic schools). This is the only curriculum area which has two different sets of experiences and outcomes (Learning and Teaching Scotland 2004).

The rationales for Religious and Moral Education and RE for Roman Catholic Schools are outlined in the two *Principles and Practice* documents (Scottish Government online n.d.). The *Curriculum for Excellence: Religious and Moral Education* remains within the vision of the post-Millar Report tradition, with some modification. Christianity continues to be emphasised because of its historical and contemporary importance in Scotland. Other world religions are now studied under the less pejorative title of world religions. Personal search has been replaced by development of beliefs and values. *Religious Education for Roman Catholic Schools* has been organised under eight strands of faith, which, in the spirit of CfE, are not mutually exclusive. These are: Mystery of God; In the Image of God; Revealed Truth of God; Son of God; Signs of God; Word of God; Hours of God and Reign of God. The Curriculum for Excellence initiative appears to have consolidated the position of Religious and Moral Education in the curriculum for non-denominational schools and created an opportunity for the Roman Catholic sector to articulate a clearer theological vision.

Recent developments and contemporary debates

As the Higher Education sector faces severe cuts in funding and as teacher education in Scotland faces review and rationalisation, the serious anxiety about the commitment of University Faculties or Schools of Education to the subject of RE becomes intensified (see McKinney and Conroy 2007: 228). The staffing at Strathclyde and Edinburgh universities, for example, has been reduced. The responsibility for RE in the majority of universities resides with one or possibly two persons, apart from the University of Glasgow. Similarly, there are anxieties about the position of the teacher of RE in the non-denominational school. As schools have moved from subject departments to faculties that embrace a cluster of subjects, RE has often been subsumed into a Faculty of Social Subjects. This has resulted in the loss of many posts of principal teacher of RE, though a few have become Head of Faculty. There are concerns about the long-term effects on the status of the teacher of religious and moral education in the non-denominational schools. There are further concerns about the time allotted to RME because schools are encouraged to be more creative with curriculum architecture. Encouragingly, the Scottish government remains committed to the subject as an essential part of the curriculum for all young people. Roman Catholic schools, on the whole, have maintained the position of principal teacher of RE. During the consultation period for Curriculum for Excellence: Religious and Moral Education, it emerged that there remains a lobby for inclusion of Christianity within world religions. Christianity, however, was reconfirmed as an important and relevant area for special emphasis. There also emerged a small but vociferous lobby for a greater focus on philosophy, but the majority of practitioners consulted remained adamant that religion was the principal focus of RME. These debates do not appear to be completely resolved and the relationship and balance between Christianity and world religions and also between religion and philosophy in RME will continue to be subjects for on-going debate.

The Catholic documentation, while remaining part of the national initiative, has adopted a more catechetical approach than was evident in the 5–14 curriculum. Depending on the position one adopts, this can be viewed as an unwelcome and unhelpful discordance between the approaches to RE in the two sectors, or as a much stronger affirmation of the uniqueness of the approach in the Roman Catholic sector. It remains to be seen how this catechetical approach will be congruent with the diverse pupil population of Scottish Catholic schools, especially the secondary schools, which include children of other denominations, other faiths and of no faith. This approach will require considerable expertise and sensitivity in the classroom and the development of the teachers has been identified as a major priority.

The development of *Curriculum for Excellence* has highlighted new modes of support for RE in both sectors. The once strong and influential complement of advisors for the non-denominational sector and the number of full-time advisors in the Roman Catholic sector has been depleted. Patricia Watson, HMIE National Specialist for RME, however, has established a strong and close working relationship with schools and universities, consistent with the current climate of closer communication and links between the inspectorate and practitioners (http://www.hmie.gov.uk). Learning and Teaching Scotland, a government agency, have been engaged in developing resources and support materials for *Curriculum for Excellence* for both Roman Catholic and non-denominational sectors. The Scottish Catholic Education Service has worked in close partnership with Roman Catholic schools, university colleagues, diocesan advisors, HMIE and the Scottish government. It has produced supplementary materials for *Curriculum for Excellence: Religious Education* such as *This is Our Faith* and offers support and opportunities for in-service training (SCES online n.d.).

Questions

If *Curriculum for Excellence* has consolidated the policy position of RME, how strong is it its position, in practical terms, in non-denominational schools?

What are the long-term implications of the reduction of staff devoted to RME in teacher education?

How will the shift towards a more catechetical paradigm in Roman Catholic RE cohere with the mixed school population of Roman Catholic schools?

Further reading

Bryce, T. G. K. and Humes, W. (eds) (2008) *Scottish Education* (3rd edn) *Beyond Devolution*, Edinburgh: Edinburgh University Press). This is a comprehensive collection of historical and contemporary accounts of the different aspects of Scottish education.

Learning and Teaching Scotland (LTS) *Understanding the Curriculum*. Available online: http://www.ltscotland.org.uk/understandingthecurriculum/ (accessed 16 August 2010). This is an essential website as it provides access, and updates, to all of the *Curriculum for Excellence* documentation including the RE documentation.

McKinney, S. J. (2010) 'Communicating faith through Religious education', in J. Sullivan (ed.) *Communicating Faith*, Washington DC: The Catholic University of America Press. This provides a more detailed account and analysis of recent documents that relate to RE.

Scottish Catholic Education Service (SCES). Available online: http://www.sces.uk.com/ (accessed 16 August 2010). Contains all supplementary materials and resources produced by SCES for Roman Catholic RE.

Scottish Qualifications Authority (SQA). Available online: http://www.sqa.org.uk/sqa/5656.html (accessed 16 August 2010). Provides all relevant information and updates on Scottish national examinations.

REPUBLIC OF IRELAND, BY KEVIN WILLIAMS

Following some very brief comments on the historical context, this section considers the arrangements for religious education (RE) in the Republic of Ireland and then examines the legal framework. It concludes with an account of the continuing controversy regarding the pervasiveness of religion in most primary schools.

The Reformation marks the moment at which native Irish identity assumed an explicitly Catholic character. Gaelic Ireland resisted the attempts made by the English crown to promote the Protestant faith. This resistance led to an identification of Catholicism with freedom from foreign interference and this in turn prompted the development of a version of national consciousness that saw a fusing of religious, political and cultural elements. The closing years of the sixteenth century heralded the emergence of the tradition of Catholic nationalism that has endured to the present. Conversely, the later Plantation of Ulster was to lead to the development of a version of Irishness which was eventually (particularly in the nineteenth and twentieth centuries) to associate its political identity with Britain and with Protestantism. To this day many people associate their political and cultural sense of who they are with religion.

Awareness of the potential for social disharmony deriving from the conflicting identities formed part of the impulse behind the attempt to introduce a multi-denominational school system in the nineteenth century. The aim of the architects of the system of national education that was eventually established in Ireland in 1831 was to promote a shared identity on the part of the inhabitants. The multi-denominational system that was introduced limited the remit of the state to secular learning and assigned responsibility for RE to the respective churches. The multi-denominational project was strenuously resisted by all the churches with the result that education in practice assumed a denominational character. This character was reinforced by the Irish state from its foundation in 1922 to the 1990s.

Arrangements for religious education in Irish schools

At primary level schools are largely state aided, with the state providing the major proportion of capital and current expenditure in order to supplement the educational initiatives of denominational and other bodies. Excluding some 125 schools for children with special educational needs, according to the most recent figures, there are 3,175 primary schools. Of those, 92 per cent are under Catholic management, 1.45 per cent are Educate Together schools, about 5 per cent are run by other faiths and about 1.55 per cent are Irish medium. Single religion faith schools are not likely to be the main model of the primary schools of the future and already five multi-denominational schools under the local authority Vocational Education Committee have been established.

At primary level one half-hour per day is devoted to what is called 'religious instruction' (see below). This is provided under the guidance of the relevant religious authorities and the state's only role is to ensure that no child is obliged to attend religion class against the wishes of his/her parents. Normally the regular class teacher also takes the daily lesson in RE and teachers in denominational primary schools are indeed expected to do so. Where, however, a teacher objects on grounds of conscience, then in practice arrangements may be made for that teacher to undertake other duties while someone else takes the class in religion.

The arrangements for RE in Educate Together schools are very different. Autumn 2004 saw the publication of the sector's common programme in moral, civic, spiritual and religious education. Entitled *Learn Together: An Ethical Education Curriculum for Educate Together Schools*, it is compulsory for all pupils. In this programme, pupils are taught about worldviews with the aim of fostering tolerance and respect for different traditions in the context of promoting an agreed set of moral principles. Provision for denominationally specific religious instruction for those parents who seek it is made outside of schools hours.

Within the schools under the Vocational Education Committee, RE of a catechetical character is made available within the school. The religious programme is made up of common and denominationally specific elements. Another inter-denominational model has been developed within the context of some *Scoileanna Lán Ghaeilge* (Irish medium) schools. This involves a joint Catholic and Protestant inter-denominational religious programme. The teaching of religion is conducted on an ecumenical basis to all pupils in the same classroom during school hours. Protestant children may either be offered special instruction during the time allocated for preparation for the Catholic sacraments or may remain as part of the class. As with the schools within the Vocational Education Committee framework, much of the fine detail regarding the provision of RE is still being worked out on the ground.

The situation at second level

At second level the state provides much of the finance to support schools (i.e. 391 schools) owned largely by religious bodies. Almost one-third of second level schools (248) (known as vocational schools and more recently community colleges) are, however, directly state owned and funded through local authorities. From the late 1960s, a new model of second-level school, known originally as comprehensive schools and subsequently as community schools, has emerged. There are some 91 of these schools and they combine, through a deed of trust, a management partnership of state/local authority and denominational interests. They also provide a model for school amalgamations and the community school or community college model of second-level schooling is likely to be favoured in the future.

Teachers of religion are paid the normal incremental salary by the state to provide two hours teaching of religion to each class per week. In state schools their appointment must be approved by the 'catechetical inspectorate' and provision can be made to transfer teachers of religion to other duties if they cease to be acceptable to the relevant religious authorities (see Department of Education 1979 and Association of Community Schools 1992). Until the introduction of RE as an examination subject, made possible by the Education Act in 1998 (discussed below), the curriculum in RE was solely within the control of the relevant denominational authorities. In the current situation, schools offer RE on a catechetical basis or for examination purposes or as a combination of both.

The rationale for the syllabus in RE curriculum is inclusive and consistent with liberal democratic principles. Underpinning the approach is the conviction that membership of a complex liberal democracy requires an understanding of a variety of religious and of secular worldviews (Department for Education and Science 2000: 3–4). The syllabus gives ample scope for searching and detailed study of Christianity as expressed in its different traditions. It also 'seeks to promote an understanding and appreciation of why people believe, as well as tolerance and respect for the values and beliefs of all' (ibid.: 4). One of the aims of RE is to prepare students for citizenship by exploring the 'unique role' of the Christian tradition 'and its denominational expressions in Irish life' (ibid.). As RE has become established as an examination subject fears that examinations in religion may be incompatible with formative learning appear to have abated.

The legal framework

There are two important documents governing the status of religion in Irish schools. The first is the Irish Constitution and the second is the Education Act of 1998.

The Constitution

The association of the nation with Christianity is very explicitly made in the Constitution of 1937 and its general tone is theocentric, as the French philosopher Régis Debray (2002: 44–45) has noted in some apparent surprise. Yet the document is also informed by liberal principles. This is clear from the following clauses that appear in Article 44 and which are still in force.

> 2.1 Freedom of conscience and the free profession and practice of religion are, subject to public order and morality, guaranteed to every citizen.
> 2.2 The State guarantees not to endow any religion.
> 2.3 The State shall not impose any disabilities or make any discrimination on the ground of religious profession, belief or status.
>
> (Constitution of Ireland 2004)

Moreover, in the provisions relevant to education, the Constitution confers upon the state no direct role in the religious formation of citizens. In Article 42, which deals with education, an undertaking is given that the 'State shall ... as guardian of the common good, require in view of actual conditions that the children receive a certain minimum education, moral, intellectual and social' (Constitution of Ireland 2004, Art. 42. 3. 2) but the article offers no undertaking in respect of a minimum education in religion. Responsibility is assigned to parents 'to provide, according to their means, for the religious and moral, intellectual, physical and social education of their children' (ibid., Art. 42. 1). To this end, the 'State shall not oblige parents in violation of their conscience and lawful preference to send their children to schools established by the State, or to any particular type of school designated by the State' (ibid., Art. 42. 3. 1). Those who drafted this guarantee could hardly have envisaged how this guarantee would be invoked against denominational schooling. This neatly illustrates one of the lessons of history in church–state relations, namely, that laws can have unpredictable consequences.

In its support of education, the state must show 'due regard ... for the rights of parents, especially in the matter of religious and moral formation' (Constitution of Ireland 2004, Art. 42. 4). This regard is reinforced by the provision in Article 44 (which deals with religion). It states that:

> Legislation providing State aid for schools shall not discriminate between schools under the management of different religious denominations, nor be such as to affect prejudicially the right of any child to attend a school receiving public money without attending religious instruction at that school.
>
> (Constitution of Ireland 2004, Art. 44. 2. 4)

The guarantees in the Constitution regarding the right to withdraw from RE reflect the historical provisions made in respect of primary schools that were to be repeated later in respect of vocational schools/community colleges and community schools. In these schools parents have the right 'to request in writing that their children be withdrawn from classes in religious instruction' (Department of Education 1979). In community schools, religious instruction and religious worship are provided 'except for such pupils whose parents make a request in writing to the Principal that those pupils should be withdrawn from religious worship or religious instruction or both religious worship and religious instruction' (Association of Community Schools 1992: 23).

The Education Act

The attempt to reconcile the claims of religious and secular versions of human self-understanding in modern Ireland was an important feature of educational policy in the late 1990s. Educational policy was one aspect of a general attempt to determine the relationship between church and state in contemporary Ireland. The two pillars of state policy were to remove from the State any role in prescribing the character of the ethos of schools on a national basis and to confer on individual schools discretion with regard to the ethos that they wished to embrace. The repeal in the Act of a rule in the Intermediate Education Act of 1878 prohibiting examinations in religion allowed for the provision of RE as a examination subject. The choices within the syllabus accommodate an approach tailored to the requirements of individual schools.

Yet there is a tension at the heart of provisions of the Education Act 1998 between the right of patrons to maintain a particular ethos (Government of Ireland 1998, Section 15 [b]) and the principle of 'respect for the diversity of values, beliefs, traditions, languages and ways of life in society' (ibid. [e]) with regard to accommodating the children of parents who dissent from this ethos. This ethos pervades the curriculum and the whole life of the school so the right to withdraw from lessons in religion would not prevent children being exposed to religion. The pervasive presence of religion as part of the school's ethos at primary level remains a very contentious issue concerning the role of religion in Irish schools.

The right to withdraw from RE

The teaching of religion in the overwhelming majority of primary schools is catechetical in character. This means that it has as its purpose the continued initiation of young people into the faith and the consolidation of their commitment to it. Although parents have the right to withdraw their children from religion class, it is not always possible for schools for practical reasons regarding space and personnel to make alternative arrangements to accommodate children withdrawn from RE. Even where parents ask to have their children withdrawn, this withdrawal could be said to have a stigmatising effect leaving the children vulnerable to teasing and bullying (see Williams 2005: 63; 110–114). Withdrawal is even more complicated in the years when children are being prepared for Communion and Confirmation, as activities related to this preparation often require a more extensive time allocation than the normal half hour per day.

But the law does not oblige schools to change their ethos to accommodate the wishes of parents who have no option but to send their children to faith schools. This was made clear in the Supreme Court judgment in response to the challenge to the payment from public funds of chaplains in community schools. The essence of this challenge was that individuals were in receipt of state salaries in order to exercise denominational ministries directed at co-religionists in public institutions. Payment of such salaries, however, was judged to be consistent with the Constitution. The court also found that the right not to attend religious instruction could not protect a child 'from being influenced to some degree, by the religious "ethos" of the school' (see Bredin 1998: 101; 81–101). Accordingly, school management is 'not obliged to change the general atmosphere of its school merely to accommodate a child of a different religious persuasion who wishes to attend that school' (ibid.). But this does not affect the right to withdraw from RE and, moreover, any attempt at proselytism is explicitly ruled out (ibid.). This means that parents who send their children to a school animated by different beliefs and values from theirs, whether these be religious or secular, cannot expect that school to change its ethos to affirm the beliefs that they wish to have fostered in their children.

Though, as already noted, single religion faith schools are not likely to be the main model of the primary schools of the future, the status of religion within schools remains in the forefront of educational discourse in this decade. This debate retains a high profile in the media and at times prompts the same antagonistic feelings that have historically informed the debate concerning secularism in France.

Questions

In the Republic of Ireland, the Catholic school at primary level often serves as a common school for all irrespective of the religious affiliation of parents. Can a programme of RE in Catholic schools be open enough to accommodate the children of non-Catholic parents?

In the common school serving a pluralist constituency, can a progamme of RE be designed that will meet the requirements of formative initiation into faith as well as more general education in worldviews?

Is the solution to the growing pluralism in Ireland the exclusion of formative RE from schools following the Educate Together model?

Further reading

Byrne G. and Topley, R. (eds) (2004) *Nurturing Children's Religious Imagination: The Challenge of Primary Religious Education Today*, Dublin: Veritas. This volumes offers contributions on the teaching of religion from academics and practising teachers.

Hogan, P. and Williams, K. (eds) (1997) *The Future of Religion in Irish Education*, Dublin: Veritas. The volume contains different perspectives on the place of RE in Ireland and the topics explored remain relevant today.

Williams, K. (2005) *Faith and the Nation: Religion Culture and Schooling in Ireland*, Dublin: Dominican Publications. The issues raised in this part of the chapter are explored in detail in this book.

Chapter 3

Agreed syllabuses

William K. Kay

In England and Wales religious education (RE) is provided in the vast majority of schools according to a syllabus that has been agreed at local level. This arrangement, which places the teaching of religion within the tax-supported educational system, often amazes visitors to the UK. The reasons for the existence of the relevant legal and administrative machinery are historical. By this is meant that the current situation has arisen over a long period of time. It has been tested over many generations, in times of peace and war, and passed through differently constituted parliaments, many of which included educational amendments or reforms within their programmes. In this way the current situation has been reached through a succession of modifications and adjustments while, surprisingly, holding consistent to a series of principles (set out below) that have helped to define the nature of British society.

How we reached the present position

It is traditional to seek the explanation of the desire to read to the post-Reformation social and religious changes that wrested the Bible from clerical control, turned it from inaccessible Latin and placed it, freshly translated, in the hands of ordinary men and women. Luther wrote a 30-page tract entitled *To the Councilmen of All Cities in Germany that they Establish Christian Schools* (1524) in which he argued that the public purse should fund new schools. Subsequent revivalistic movements across Europe generated further educational drives. In Britain from the eighteenth century onwards the education of the working class was stimulated by Methodism, a process that eventually ebbed into the life of trade unionism (Thompson 2002).

The same process also inspired enormous philanthropic efforts that began with the establishment of Sunday schools in the 1790s. By 1795 there were over 250,000 children enrolled in this way, and the figure rose to over 900,000 by 1835 (Cruickshank 1963: 2). Religious philanthropy continued from 1808 onwards with the establishment of the British and Foreign Schools Society, founded by the Quaker Joseph Lancaster, and followed in 1811 by Andrew Bell's foundation of the National Society, an Anglican organisation. Both these new societies were concerned to educate the children of the poor in weekday schools and, although the mid-century industrial revolution may have benefited from a greater dissemination of elementary education, these early initiatives were religiously motivated. Boys and girls could learn the Ten Commandments and the Lord's Prayer, and read the Bible. The government of the day was content to leave matters entirely in the hands of religious charities, partly on the grounds that the burden of taxation was thereby minimised and partly out of a laissez-faire political philosophy.

For the next 60 years the churches were almost entirely responsible for the education of the vast bulk of British children. It is true that political moves to support the schools began early and that, by 1833, £20,000 was voted for 'the erection of schoolhouses for the education of the poorer classes in Great Britain' (Smith 1931: 139). Money continued to be granted annually and by 1850 Methodists and Roman Catholics 'were drawn into co-operation with the government' and opened their own schools so that a 'vast denominational system' that included all religious groups apart from 'Congregational Dissenters' had come into being (Murphy 1971: 37). Some of this money was granted by central government and some came out of local taxation or rates but it is estimated that in 1861 government only paid about a third of the cost of educating each child at church schools. The remainder was more or less equally divided between school fees and church contributions.

Although this system put an enormous financial burden upon the churches, and although provision expanded considerably so that in the late 1860s there were over 18,000 church schools in existence, the rate of growth of the population in the new industrial cities was overwhelming. By 1870 there were 4.3 million children of school age in England and Wales but the church only catered for 1.3 million. As many as 2 million children were completely outside any educational provision and the remainder were in low-grade 'dame schools' of the kind excoriated in the novels of Dickens (Jenkins 1995: 322). The general election of 1870 was a turning point. When Gladstone's Liberal party was swept to power, he addressed the problem of creating a national system. He decided to the 'fill the gaps' left by the church system so that new schools might be built where church schools were missing. In this way the new 'board schools' complemented the church schools rather than competing with them, and the two kinds of school were brought together into what became a unified dual system.

The question of religion immediately arose. Within all types of church schools prayers had been said and the Bible had been taught. What should happen in the new schools? The parliamentary debate was passionate and prolonged but reached consensus when Cowper-Temple's famous amendment was adopted. It stated that in every grant-aided school 'no religious catechism or religious formulary, which is distinctive of any particular denomination shall be taught in the school'. By this means religious teaching derived from the Bible was moved to the centre ground, and statutory expression was given to the assumption was that there were matters of common agreement that all religious groups and none could assent to. In addition, a 'conscience clause' was passed and this allowed parents to withdraw their children from any religious instruction in either type of school. These two principles – of seeking common ground within religion (so as to gain the widest acceptance) and permission to withdraw on the inner basis of conscience alone – have continued to be operative until today. Together they constitute a vital form of religious freedom.

Although the board schools were allowed to dispense with RE, a report in 1888 showed only 7 out of 2,225 in England did so (Murphy 1971: 69). In other words, the vast majority of school boards were happy to use public money to teach the historic religion of the country. And church schools, despite failing to keep pace with the population, were still numerous: by the end of the century the Church of England was still able to offer 60 per cent of available school places (Curtis 1961: 282). The differences between church schools and board schools lay in their levels of funding, with the church schools having less to spend per child. In 1902, a new Education Act consolidated the entire system and equalised funding by drawing both kinds of school together through the creation of local education authorities. Over 2,500 boards were absorbed into the 300 new local education authorities (Curtis 1961: 315).

The dual system was now well established in the sense that church schools and what came to be called 'county schools' were indistinguishable at several important points: facilities were almost the same, teachers could transfer between one kind of school and another, and the RE in both was recognisably Christian.

Such wholesale structural reforms to the education system as might have been made in the years after 1902 were blighted by the economic impact of the 1914–1918 war and the financial uncertainties of the 1920s. However, in 1923 one of the local education authorities in Yorkshire produced its own syllabus for RE and this was followed in 1924 by the widely influential Cambridgeshire syllabus. Both these syllabuses were produced by committees seeking consensus between religious groups within their geographical areas and for this reason can be seen as the forerunners of legally established agreed syllabuses.

The Education Act 1944

Normal British politics were suspended during the 1939–1945 war. A wartime coalition government made up of Conservative and Labour members was formed, and this gave its legislation a peculiar authority. R. A. Butler was made president of the Board of Education by Churchill, the prime minister (Butler 1973). Butler produced a White Paper entitled *Educational Reconstruction* in July 1943 in which he outlined many of the ideas that later informed his Bill. The White Paper (paragraph 36) stated:

> There has been a very general wish, not confined to representatives of the churches, that RE should be given a more defined place in the life and work of the schools, springing from the desire to revive the spiritual and personal

values in our society and in our national tradition ... [paragraph 37] in order to emphasise the importance of the subject provision will be made for the school day in all primary and secondary schools to begin with a corporate act of worship[1]

By publishing his proposals in advance Butler gave the opportunity for interested parties like the teaching unions or parents' groups to respond. There was a similar opportunity provided by press reports. Into this mix we should also add the formidable figure of William Temple, then Archbishop of Canterbury, whose published thinking on the role of religion within democratic society and within education had reached the point where he was able to argue that only Christianity provides the resources for fulfilling the important double functions of fostering individual development and of creating bonds of union with all fellow citizens (Temple 1942).

Butler inherited a dual system that was in need of renovation. Many of the church schools required repair; the school leaving age was still stuck at 14 and needed to be raised (implying many expensive new buildings); free secondary education for everyone was not yet available; there was rivalry and suspicion between the churches. The Roman Catholics were worried about state control of their schools; and Nonconformists were worried about having to send their children to Anglican or Roman Catholic schools where they might receive religious teaching contrary to their consciences. Butler's genius lay in his ability to reconcile all these competing religious demands while creating a vision of post-war education that could appeal to moderate Conservative and diehard Labour supporters.

Despite its non-adversarial nature, legislation in the wartime parliament was scrutinised according to proper procedure. The 111 sections of the Bill were met with over 1,000 amendments, although only 340 of these were actually debated. The entire document passed through the House of Commons and then went to the House of Lords in the normal way before returning for a final reading in the Commons. The whole process took 17 days to complete and the record in Hansard demonstrates that MPs took their work seriously. Despite a few dissenting voices the great majority of parliamentarians saw Christianity as providing a moral bulwark against the ravages of fascism and dictatorship.

When the Act is examined, its structure shows that it conceived of RE as being made up of two components, collective worship and classroom instruction. Collective worship might be understood to be the practical or experiential aspect of the teaching that was given in the classroom. The conscience clause applied to each component and in all maintained schools (Chapter 31, section 25.4; see also *The Fourth R* 1970: para. 86f.).

The discussion of agreed syllabuses demonstrated that the vast majority of members of parliament had no objection to the principle of Christian teaching in school. What concerned them was whether denominational teaching according to an agreed syllabus was adequate. The discussion was complex because of the different categories of church school that were established to run alongside the county schools (as they were then called). Two different kinds of church schools were aided (which were aided by the state and gave a majority on the governing body to church appointees but which required a larger financial contributions from the church) and controlled (which were controlled by the state, gave a majority on the governing body to local authority appointees and which lessened the financial contributions of the church). Agreed syllabuses were taught in the county and controlled schools. They also applied where the only school in an area was aided; there they might be taught at the request of parents who did not want their children to receive denominational education (Chapter 31, section 28.1).

Although the discussion was complicated and the separate categories of school might have been unwieldy, the principle of equity behind the arrangements was simple: where the church contributed more finance to the running of the school, the RE it provided might be more precisely focused on its own theological tradition and doctrine; where the church contributed less, religious teaching was more general and reached out to Christian common ground. And, even when the church made no financial contribution as was the case in county schools, agreed syllabuses ensured that religious teaching could go ahead.

But how were the agreed syllabuses to be constructed? Here the legislation enabled all local education authorities to set up a special conference with four committees, each of which had one vote (see Chapter 31, schedule 5, section 29). Syllabuses could only be adopted after receiving all four votes. This structure allowed disagreement within the committees but not overall. The four committees represented interested parties: one included representatives of religious denominations which the local authority considered should be present; the second include representatives of the Church of England (except in Wales where the Church of England was disestablished – and in this case Anglicans found seats on the first committee); the third included representatives of teachers; and the fourth included representatives of the local authority itself. In this way the Church of England had a clear voice in England and the other religious denominations together also had a clear voice of their own. Teachers' representatives might or might not be religious but they were the people who had to deliver the syllabus in the classroom and for this reason they were included. And the local authority as the political and administrative hub of local education was also heard. The system was designed to allow local religious variation to be reflected in local syllabuses. Methodist Cornwall was qualitatively different from Roman Catholic Lancashire, and the syllabus-producing machinery was sensitive to such religious demographics. Moreover, either before or after the agreed syllabus had been written, the local authority had the power to set up a Standing Advisory Council 'to advise the authority on matters connected with religious instruction' (Chapter 31, section 29.2).

From 1944–1988

In the 1950s socially conservative attitudes predominated (Lewis 1978). Leisure time was limited, money was short and a rebellious counter-culture had no opportunity to develop. Agreed syllabuses were Bible-based, the indigenous population was almost entirely Christian, or nominally so, and teaching methods retained vestiges of the unimaginative Victorian era. Corporal punishment in schools was still practised and, although the churches did not manage to attract even half the population to worship, Sunday schools boomed.

Roughly 20 per cent of the pupils were selected to attend grammar school and about half of them stayed on beyond the age of 16. The majority of pupils attended secondary modern schools and left at 15. Bible stories were taught in primary schools and in the lower forms of secondary schools and, if world religions were addressed, they only appeared to those who stayed on after 16. Agreed syllabuses appear to have been geared in the main towards academic pupils. Only occasionally, as in the West Riding syllabus in 1966, were biblical themes linked with the notion of the personal or intellectual development of pupils.

By the 1960s a plethora of changes began to be felt within English and Welsh schools. Theology itself was reeling from the effects of academic reinterpretations of Christianity as exemplified in Bishop John Robinson's book *Honest to God* (1963) which popularised the liberal Protestantism of Tillich, Bultmann and Bonhoeffer. *The Fourth R* (1970: paras 113, 114), in reviewing the period since 1935, showed how theology itself was flowing away from biblical studies to a more open-ended and exploratory style of discourse. These currents began to filter into agreed syllabuses. Socially, Britain was becoming more plural as Commonwealth citizens from Pakistan, India, Ceylon and the West Indies arrived: it was no longer possible to think of Indian religions as being distant and exotic (ONS 1971: no. 108, table 19). Educationally, unforeseen changes were being unleashed by the dismantling of the selective system of education that had been in place since 1944. Grammar schools and secondary modern schools were combined into comprehensive schools in a process that can usually be dated to circular 10/65 (i.e. the 10th circular in 1965 sent by the Department of Education and Science, as the Board of Education had now become). These new schools were much bigger than any previously seen, and this had an immediate negative effect upon the holding of school assemblies and enforcement of collective worship. It became almost impossible to gather the whole school in one place at the start of the day. In addition, as a spin-off from the comprehensive ideal, mixed ability classes were introduced and these made it almost impossible for the syllabuses of traditional RE to be delivered, however skilful the teacher.

At this critical point Ronald Goldman published his research findings (Goldman 1964, 1965). They were based upon interviews with 200 pupils and said to demonstrate that pre-pubescent pupils were unable to understand the Bible; the symbolic nature of many events was beyond them. Educationalists heralded

Goldman's findings enthusiastically and the Bible was all set to disappear from primary schools and from agreed syllabuses. Roughly contemporaneously it became clear that the Hindu, Muslim or Sikh children now in British primary schools could best understand the religions of their homes through stories. A period of flux followed and it may not be too cynical to say that, when the dust settled, the Bible, which had seemed too difficult for young children to understand, was welcomed back and Goldman was forgotten.

By the 1970s the transformation of Britain from a selective to a comprehensive system was more or less complete. New examinations were being trialled and the Schools Council, a body that included government and trade union appointees, was driving forward curriculum innovation. RE can be said to have veered between a child-centred style of teaching and a style that was determined by the subject matter of religion itself. The 1971 Schools Council Working Paper 36 entitled *RE in Secondary Schools* was definitely in the latter category. A new generation of agreed syllabuses began to emerge, some of them claiming to use the phenomenological methods outlined in the Working Paper. Because the entire educational system was yet to be centralised, local variation across the whole curriculum was still at a premium.

The agreed syllabus conferences began to include members of other world faiths in the first committee; they sat alongside representatives of the Nonconformist churches. This was to stretch the meaning of the word 'denomination' in the 1944 Act but was a legitimate extension. Once Sikhs, Muslims, Jews, Hindus and others were included on the committee, they naturally pressed hard for the inclusion of their religions within the syllabuses (*pace* Jackson 2004b: 178). The consequence of this was that the syllabuses grew fatter and fatter by the addition of more and more religions. Classroom teachers tried to make sense of these increased demands by thematising religious material and, in a parallel development, school assemblies began to include reference to, or celebration of, non-Christian festivals.

The Education Reform Act 1988

This Act revolutionised education in England and Wales by establishing a new centrally controlled and inspected curriculum and by bringing into existence a new type of school, free from local authority control. Only RE, having been established by statute within the 1944 Act, was handled separately from other curriculum subjects. The national curriculum comprised 10 subjects (11 in Wales where Welsh was included) and these were divided up into four key stages, two at primary and two at secondary level. When RE was added, the whole was referred to as the 'basic curriculum' (section 2.1 of the Act).

The agreed syllabus conferences which had functioned since 1944 continued almost unchanged apart from one significant alteration. Non-Christian groups were specifically included as participants; the matter was not left at the discretion of local education authorities. Additionally, arrangements for RE were made more flexible to make the subject more attractive to non-Christian groups and collective worship was to be 'wholly or mainly of a broadly Christian character' without making it syncretistic and while retaining the conscience clause (1, 9, 3c) and the right for parents to withdraw their children. As a further strengthening of the subject, Standing Advisory Councils for RE (SACREs for short) became obligatory, and they had the power to authorise non-Christian worship where this was a reasonable request. The new syllabuses, according to section 8 of the Act, were required to '[r]eflect the fact that religious traditions in Great Britain are in the main Christian whilst taking account of the teaching and practices of the other principal religions represented in Great Britain'.

To illustrate what the new agreed syllabuses might look like, one of the statutory bodies set up by the Act to advise on non-religious subjects, the Schools Curriculum and Assessment Authority (SCAA), published two model RE syllabuses. Neither model was thematic. By now a consensus had been reached that the six principal religions in Great Britain were Christianity, Judaism, Islam, Hinduism, Sikhism and Buddhism. The educational pattern of the new syllabuses often required children to study Christianity and one or two other religions per key stage and, in this way, cover all six. The notion that at each key stage all six religions should be covered was, in the classroom time available, impractical and too demanding for pupils (Kay and Smith 2000; Smith and Kay 2000); Kay and Smith (2002) showed that just over a third had indeed studied six religions by the time they had reached 13–14 years of age.

Once the national curriculum was in place, it was monitored by the inspectorate (Ofsted in England, Estyn in Wales) and enormous emphasis was based upon raising standards as defined by the attainment targets reached by pupils.[2] The 'delivery' of the curriculum became subordinate to the directives of government agencies in a way that had been unknown before. The effect upon RE was threefold: first, a new generation of agreed syllabuses reflected the key stages of education; second, a distinction was made between 'learning about' and 'learning from' religion, and this had the effect of neatly combining the demands of the subject matter and the development of the individual; third it was argued that, because RE was omitted from the national curriculum and subjected to slightly different inspectorial provisions, it tended to slip down the curricular pecking order and thereby lose classroom time or funding.

The current situation

Agreed syllabuses continued to vary in quality and style and so unofficial moves were made to prepare for the inclusion of RE within the national curriculum. This would, of course, have been complicated given that the conscience clause would have been anomalous in applying to what was otherwise compulsory. In any case Kenneth Baker, then Education Secretary, argued that by joining RE with all national curriculum subjects and calling this the 'basic curriculum', RE would be 'definitely *primus inter pares*' (Baker 1993: 207). This proved to be incorrect. By 2003 several knowledgeable educationalists privately expressed the view that unless RE was inspected on the same basis as all other subjects, it would continue to be eroded. As a first step towards placing RE within the national curriculum, a *Non-Statutory Framework for RE* published by the QCA was composed with the probable intention of bringing agreed syllabuses into line with each other and with the salient features of other curriculum subjects. The *Framework* was launched in October 2004 by the then Secretary of State for Education and Skills, Charles Clarke. Senior members of the Anglican National Society publicly supported the move.

The *Framework* was put together by a large working group, including Humanists, members of the ISCKON educational services and Baha'is. The document set out what pupils 'should study in RE' and to 'establish an entitlement' for pupils (QCA 2004: 9). It also stated, 'the national framework sets out a structure for ASCs [Agreed Syllabus Conferences] and faith communities to use to determine what pupils should be taught in RE' (p. 10). Marius Felderhof (2004) criticised the *Framework* for 'subtly and illicitly' seeking to subordinate SACREs and ASCs to its own prescriptions. Precisely because the *Framework* was non-statutory it could only offer guidance, and no more.

By 2007 Birmingham, the second-largest city in England, launched its new RE syllabus, and it did so without letting itself be shaped by the *Non-Statutory Framework*. It accepted that pupils would need to learn about religious traditions as well as to learn from faith but it also took note of the role of RE in relation to the overarching aims of the Education Reform Act 1988. Pupils were to be challenged to develop as spiritual, moral, social and cultural beings and the RE curriculum was to be required to work in partnership with parents, faith committees and wider society (see Barnes 2008). The Birmingham syllabus argued that 'pupils should be offered a holistic view of religious traditions, their beliefs, their expressions, and their practical actions' and in this way sought to allow pupils to grasp the religions they studied as coherent entities rather than as disjointed contributors to conveniently pre-selected themes. In addition, unlike the *Framework*, the syllabus takes a flexible approach to the selection of content (in fact illustrative material is available from nine religions) and makes it clear that not all religious traditions should be studied at every stage or in every school. Indeed it says, 'the study of three religions (one of which will be Christianity) may well be more appropriate than the study of six' (Preface). Furthermore, the 'learning from' aim is prioritised over the 'learning about' aim. In this way, the Birmingham syllabus answers many of the questions identified by those who posited the *National Framework* as an answer. The support of the faith communities for their children, the proper funding of the Birmingham ASC and the quality and range of the pedagogical materials it offers (and which are rooted in local relevance) prevents the erosion of RE and its loss of classroom time.

Questions

To what extent should the teaching on religion be informed by studies on the psychological capacity of pupils?

Do you think there is a danger that pupils can become muddled up if they learn about several religions at once? If there is a danger, what should be done about it?

How can we make sure that pupils learn about and learn from religion? Do pupils need to learn about religion before they can learn from religion?

Notes

1 The Act itself later spoke of 'collective worship'. The distinction between collective and corporate appears to have been that, whereas the latter implied uniformity, the former implied the possibility of an individual response even within the group setting of a school assembly.

2 The position of RE in Wales is broadly similar to that in England, especially as there was no Welsh Assembly Government until 1999. Further details about RE and collective worship is found at: http://wales.gov.uk/docrepos/40382/4038232/4038211/4038298/religious-education-circula2.pdf?lang=en.

Further reading

The Fourth R: The Durham Report on RE (1970) London: SPCK. Good historical guide with interpretive comments.

Kay, W. K. and Smith, D. L. (2002) 'Classroom factors and attitude toward six world religions', *British Journal of RE*, 24: 111–122. Critical empirical comparison of thematic and systematic approaches.

Priestley, J. (2006) 'Agreed syllabuses: their history and development in England and Wales, 1944–2004', in M. de Souza, G. Durka, K. Engebretson and R. Jackson (eds), *International Handbook of the Religious, Moral and Spiritual Dimensions in Education* (Part 2), Dordrecht, The Netherlands: Springer Publishing. Detailed historical account of the development of agreed syllabuses.

Section II

Educational issues and religious education

Chapter 4

Diversity

L. Philip Barnes

RE in this country has never had it so good; no wonder that we are viewed by our continental European colleagues as in an enviable position.

(Gates 2007: 5)

RE in much of the UK is in a good position to help other parts of Europe ... RE of the kind needed across Europe is being articulated and provided in the UK.

(Keast 2006: 15)

Expressions of confidence in British religious education (RE), such as these two quotations above, could easily be multiplied. When read in context it is clear that both Brian Gates and John Keast do not chiefly mean by their comments that pupils in Britain know more about religion than pupils elsewhere (though this may be believed to be true by them as well), rather they mean that pupils in Britain possess and show, as a result of their RE, a more respectful attitude towards those who are perceived as 'different'.

The view that a form of RE has evolved in British education (chiefly English and Welsh education) that is uniquely equipped to contribute to harmonious relations between the diverse multi-ethnic, multi-faith communities that make up the population is a common refrain among contemporary religious educators, as is the view that other national educational systems have much to learn from our example. Increasingly, however, there are also critical voices raised within RE that challenge its 'official' self-congratulatory tone and contend that alongside undoubtedly positive achievements, the numbers of pupils who take formal, external examinations in the subject, for example, there are negative features that should caution educators from elsewhere uncritically adopting the British model of RE. Indeed there are complaints that current policies and methodologies are not particularly well suited to cultivating dialogue and respect between different ethnic and religious communities. In other words, British RE is defective at precisely that point at which its success is most vocally sounded by its official representatives. According to its critics, the distinctively British model of multi-faith RE is championed by those who have been instrumental in its creation and who enjoy the prestige of its success (Brian Gates is chairperson of the Religious Education Council of England and Wales; John Keast oversaw the production of the *National Framework for Religious Education*, QCA 2004), even though such claims are largely unsupported by evidence (see Barnes 2009a: 22–25).

The aim of this chapter is both to review and to assess the contribution of RE to the social aims of education in the pluralist democracy of the United Kingdom, where 'social aims' are chiefly understood in terms of developing respectful and responsible relationships between the different communities in contemporary society. Just how successful is RE in challenging religious intolerance and effecting positive relationships between communities? What are the strengths and weaknesses of different educational strategies and policies in relation to religious pluralism? Attending to these questions will provide insights and evidence that bear on the evaluation of the positive social influence of RE. The content relevant to our concerns is structured in the following way: an overview is provided of religious diversity in the United Kingdom; this is followed by a short critical analysis of the nature of contemporary religious pluralism and its relevance to RE; and finally there is a review of a range of responses within RE to the challenges of an increasingly diverse moral and religious population and to the discussion and debate these responses have stimulated.

Religious diversity in the United Kingdom

Table 4.1 provides the most recent and reliable data on the religious composition of the United Kingdom, expressed in terms of religious affiliation. Of course interpreting the census statistics is not without its challenges, both internal and external. Internal challenges relate to the fact that the question on religious identity was answered by respondents on a voluntary basis and that the data from the four different nations do not represent responses to the same identically worded question or include the same pre-set options for response (there were three separate censuses: England and Wales, Northern Ireland and Scotland). External challenges relate to the consistency of results with those of empirical measures of religiosity. Other datasets present a different picture, indicating much lower levels of commitment to religion, than might be inferred from census results. For example, in the European Values Survey, to a question on how important religion is in your life, 12.6 per cent of respondents in Britain said 'very important' and 24.8 per cent said 'quite important', while 33.0 per cent said 'not important' and 29.7 per cent said 'not at all' (Halman 2001: 33). Clearly affiliation to religion does not necessarily correlate to a strong appreciation of the importance of religion in one's life. Equally there is evidence that formal religious affiliation does not always translate into either religious practice or commitment to religious beliefs consistent with one's religious affiliation: only 15 per cent of adults in the United Kingdom attend church at least once a month (Ashworth and Farthing 2007: 6) and while more than 2 in 3 (67 per cent) of people in Britain believe in God (similar, earlier evidence prompted Grace Davie in 1994 to

Table 4.1 Religious responses in the 2001 census by country of the UK

Religion	England	Scotland	Wales	Northern Ireland	UK Total	UK %
Buddhist	139,046	6,830	5,407	533	151,816	0.3%
Christian	35,251,244	3,294,545	2,087,242	1,446,386	42,079,417	71.6%
Hindu	546,982	5,564	5,439	825	558,810	1.0%
Jewish	257,671	6,448	2,256	365	266,740	0.5%
Muslim	1,524,887	42,557	21,739	1,943	1,591,126	2.7%
Sikh	327,343	6,572	2,015	219	336,149	0.6%
Other Religion	143,811	26,974	6,909	1,143	178,837	0.3%
Total	38,190,984	3,389,490	2,131,007	1,451,414	45,162,895	76.8%
No religion	7,171,332	1,394,460	537,935	*	9,103,727	15.5%
Not stated	3,776,515	278,061	234,143	*	4,288,719	7.3%

* In Northern Ireland separate statistics for those of 'No religion' and 'Not stated' are not available.

Table reproduced from Inter-Faith Update 21. 3, the newsletter of the Inter-faith Network for the United Kingdom. Due to rounding, percentages may not total 100%.

speak of 'believing without belonging'), only 1 in 4 (26 per cent) believe in a *personal* God (Barley 2007: 1). This is not the context, however, to resolve such issues or to pursue a sociologically nuanced account of contemporary religious diversity in the United Kingdom. It is enough for our purposes to be familiar with the broad contours of diversity, as revealed in Table 4.1 above; comment will be confined to a number of statistics that are most relevant to curriculum planning and provision in RE.

Clearly Christianity commands the greatest number of adherents throughout the different nations that collectively make up the United Kingdom, and by a sizeable margin. The statistical significance of Christianity is of course complemented by its cultural, historical, legal, political and social significance as well. Table 4.1 also shows that Islam is the largest minority religion throughout the United Kingdom, though its strength varies from over one and a half million Muslims in England to under 2,000 in Northern Ireland. Alongside Muslims there are adherents of all the major 'world' religions and the diverse and numerous religious traditions and movements that one would expect to find in a modern European, liberal democratic state with a colonial history. Altogether, however, as Table 4.1 shows, fewer than 6 per cent of the population in the United Kingdom belong to a religion other than Christianity. The table also shows that the distribution of this 6 per cent is not uniform across the four different nations; other data from the censuses show the equally variable distribution levels of religious adherents in different areas and regions within the different countries. One of the effects of differentiated patterns of religious distribution is that outside the main, industrial cities and the main areas of 'new' religious settlement, which followed immigration to Britain in the 1950s and 1960s, many schools are much less diverse religiously than one might have imagined from acquaintance with overall statistics. Yet a note of qualification needs to be sounded immediately, for the term religious diversity need not apply only to diversity between religions, diversity is also a feature within religions. One naturally thinks of the denominational variety within Christianity, the Sufi/Sunni division within Islam, the schools and sects of Hinduism, and so on. These conventional distinctions within religions, however, often fail to capture the diversity of practice and belief at the level of lived experience in diverse social and community settings; and of course some religions are more diverse than others: though if recent research is to be believed, British Muslims are one of the most homogenous religious groups in all of Europe with regard to beliefs and to moral valuations, particularly with regard to sexuality issues (Gallup 2009: 30–33). Recognition of this, however, does not detract from the central point about the existence of diversity within religions.

The acknowledgement of diversity within religions and religious traditions raises another issue for educational provision that takes us back to the disparity we noted between the number of adherents to Christianity in Britain and empirical measures of their commitment to traditional Christian beliefs, practices and values. Research reveals a wide diversity of beliefs and values among Christian 'adherents', with many expressing scepticism not only towards distinctively Christian beliefs but also towards basic theistic beliefs, such as belief in a personal God or in the after-life, for example. Moreover, this scepticism is most marked among the young and those of secondary school age. When this evidence is complemented by empirical measures of religious agnosticism and atheism (in the census for England and Wales 15.5 per cent of the population in England and Wales described themselves as having 'no religion') it becomes clear that the concept of religious diversity, if it is to be both meaningful as a descriptive term and relevant to curriculum planning and pedagogy, needs to include some reference to the different varieties and degrees of religious scepticism that exist within the United Kingdom.

Conceptualising diversity and its implications for education

Religious diversity in the United Kingdom has increased in the last 50 to 60 years in three distinguishable ways: an increase in the variety of religions that are practised; an increase in the diversity within religions and religious traditions; and finally growth in the number of people who are either entirely sceptical about religion or sceptical about some of the central claims of religion (see Weller 2008: 47–52). Moreover, it is not just that religious diversity *per se* has increased; it is also that perceptions of the importance and social relevance of diversity have undergone profound changes. The nature of these changes justifies distinguishing three different (historically successive) forms of religious diversity in the United Kingdom, which for convenience we shall call traditional, modern and postmodern diversity.

Traditional diversity

Up until the late 1960s Britain was perceived as a Christian society (the perception of Northern Ireland as such still remains), where particular forms of 'established' Christianity enjoyed cultural hegemony in the different countries and, pertinent to our concerns, educational hegemony. By teaching in schools a broad non-denominational version of Christianity in a nurturing environment, it was hoped to inculcate Christian beliefs and values in the young and thus lay down a firm moral foundation for subsequent employment and life.

Modern diversity

In the 1970s traditional diversity gave way gradually to modern diversity. At one level modern diversity differs from traditional diversity in straightforward quantitative terms: society became more diverse morally and religiously, largely as a result of increasing secularisation and of post-war immigration. Unfortunately alongside increasing religious diversity in society went increasing evidence of religious discrimination and intolerance. This created an obvious challenge to schools and to RE in particular, and from the 1970s on RE began to perceive its chief contribution to the curriculum as that of challenging negative attitudes to adherents of other religions.

Postmodern diversity

By the 1990s modern diversity in Britain was giving way to what can be termed *postmodern* diversity. In the last 10 to 15 years there has been both a significant rise in net immigration, alongside a diversification of countries of origin (Vertovec 2006: 4), and a new awareness of cultural and sub-cultural forms of diversity. Ironically new forms of diversity have resulted not just from the process of (what sociologists call) individualisation, whereby meaning and identity in a culture shift from institutions and structures to the self who chooses from a range of identities, but also as a consequence of globalisation, either as a critical reaction to it or as the cultivation of minority identities that are facilitated by digital forms of communication. The challenge for education and schools in this context is to provide pupils with the knowledge and skills to construct their own identities from the diverse and often contradictory materials of culture.

Policy and practice in relation to diversity

Much of the recent history of RE and its innovations in policy in the United Kingdom has been in response to increasing religious diversity in society and to the desire for RE to be in the forefront of challenging intolerance and in contributing to respectful relationships between the different ethnic and religious communities. Mindful that other chapters in this volume review and refer to pedagogy, legislation and policy developments, and the need to avoid exact duplication of content, our focus will fall on the policy decisions and strategies that have a direct bearing only on responding to the educational challenge of moral and religious diversity.

Non-confessional religious education

The publication of *Working Paper 36* in 1971, written under the direction of Ninian Smart, by the Schools Council, represented a watershed in British RE and brought about a transition from confessional to non-confessional RE, which in the document was equated with a phenomenological approach to RE. *Working Paper 36*'s case against confessionalism was effectively two-fold (see Barnes 2002a): the accusation that confessional RE entails indoctrination and the contention that confessionalism is inappropriate in a secular and pluralist society. The argument that confessionalism entails indoctrination, with hindsight, now looks much less convincing for both philosophical and educational reasons (see Thiessen 1993). The second argument is much more persuasive. The essential point is that the particular constituency of modern Britain, that is, its multi-faith and value pluralist nature, entails that it would be inappropriate in state maintained (now termed 'community') schools, which are intended to cater for pupils from diverse social and religious backgrounds, to pursue confessional RE, which by its nature is partisan and exclusionary. In a society where many individuals and parents do not subscribe to or practise Christianity and where there is no widespread support for Christian nurture in state schools, then it is inappropriate.

It may be acknowledged that there are still religious educators who write in support of confessional RE in community schools. Penny Thompson (2003) is a sophisticated and able example, who is able to take advantage of the weaknesses of current provision and the incoherence of some forms of non-confessional RE to strengthen her case. But it is a case that is difficult to sustain. The debate about confessional RE is now typically (and in my view rightly) considered within the context of arguments for and against faith schools (see Chapter 7).

The phenomenological approach to religious education

Working Paper 36's equation of non-confessional religious with the 'undogmatic approach' of phenomenology (alongside the equation of confessional RE with 'a dogmatic approach') was influential in this country and elsewhere in convincing educationalists of the former's methodological appropriateness to secular and pluralist societies where pupils of different religious and non-religious persuasions are educated in common schools. In the late 1970s and early 1980s, however, when criticisms were beginning to be raised against phenomenology, some professional educators reacted defensively on the assumption that a rejection of the phenomenological approach heralded a return to some form of Christian confessionalism in education. Criticism of phenomenological RE was interpreted as criticism of educational neutrality, religious tolerance and personal autonomy, and hence liberal education *per se*. The alternatives were clear: either confessional RE or non-confessional, phenomenological RE. Such a set of oppositions, while faithful to the distinctions of *Working Paper 36* and still influential among some religious educators, is unwarranted and has served only to frustrate genuine concerns about the educational appropriateness of a phenomenological approach.

Criticisms were raised against phenomenological RE as early as the late 1970s. The most telling was that exposing pupils to a range of religions seemed to do little to challenge religious intolerance and discrimination or to develop respect for those who were perceived as different. *Working Paper 36* optimistically concluded that as pupils become acquainted with the beliefs and values of the various religions, so they will simultaneously become appreciative of religious difference and respectful of those who belong to different religions. The phenomenological approach encouraged pupils to suspend judgement and bracket out their own commitments in considering other religions; this it was believed would enable them to enter into the experience of others and so gain a 'sympathetic understanding of the[ir] inner life' (Schools Council 1971: 23). Such a position soon came to be regarded as hopelessly naive and limiting. For a start many pupils in schools proved incapable (conceptually and psychologically) of adopting a viewpoint contrary to their own: they lacked the psychological maturity necessary for 'entering into' the experience of others (see Kay 1997). Furthermore, the mere act of setting aside one's own prejudices and attempting to place oneself in someone else's situation may not contribute to any sense of appreciation of the other person's beliefs or worth. What is needed is a much more critical approach where one's prejudices and values are brought out into the open and interrogated; subjected to the scrutiny of reason and argument. The complaint is that by 'bracketing out' critical questions and one's initial assumptions in order to gain an understanding of religion and religious phenomena the issue of religious truth is ignored. This failure to address the conflicting nature of religious truth claims is regarded by critics as trivialising religion and endorsing religious relativism. The problem, some suggest, is compounded by the fact that the phenomenological approach tends to represent the truth of religion as something interior and intensely private, a position that is in keeping with its Liberal Protestant lineage, where the essence of religion is located in non-conceptual or pre-conceptual religious experience (Barnes and Wright 2006). In this way religion is effectively divorced from the public world of economics, morality, politics and social policy, and of course shielded from rational scrutiny and criticism. Lest we digress too far from educational representations of phenomenology, it may be useful to point out that the kind of Liberal Protestant interpretation of religion outlined above is precisely the interpretation of religion advanced by Michael Grimmitt in his endorsement of phenomenological RE in *What Can I Do in Religious Education?* (1973): this book was widely influential and remained a standard text among students of RE up until the late 1980s (for discussion and criticism, see Barnes 2001). Other criticisms of the phenomenological approach include accusations that it provides a superficial account of religion, chiefly because too many religions are studied; that the juxtaposition of material on common themes from different religions leads to confusion among pupils (Kay and Smith 2000; Smith and Kay 2000); that it misrepresents the varying significances that particular themes hold within different religions; and that the over-preoccupation with explicitly religious material fails to engage the interests and concerns of school children.

The attitude of many professional educators is that criticisms of the phenomenological approach are surmountable (see Jackson 1997: 12). This has led to a vigorous and at times heated debate that focuses on a number of issues: the proper interpretation of Ninian Smart's contribution to the emergence and adoption of the phenomenological approach; the extent to which familiar criticisms of the phenomenological approach can be answered; and the extent to which the later practice of phenomenology faithfully represented the position of *Working Paper 36,* alongside the contention that early versions are not vulnerable to criticism in the same way as later versions (contrasting views on these issues are debated in O'Grady 2005; Barnes 2007b; O'Grady 2009; Barnes 2009b). What makes this debate so controversial and topical is that supporters and critics alike recognise both that the phenomenological approach is foundational to the history of modern British RE and that its assumptions and commitments are implicit in much contemporary policy and practice.

Religionism

As we have noted above, phenomenological RE endorsed Liberal Protestant assumptions about the nature and character of religion, one of which is the view that the different religions embody different yet complementary revelations and experiences of the divine. Even critics, however, acknowledge that in the phenomenological approach to RE this assumption is implicit rather than explicit. Yet it is precisely this assumption that Professor John Hull, then of the University of Birmingham and editor of the *British Journal of Religious Education,* made the cornerstone of his positive social agenda for RE. In a series of writings in the 1990s he introduced and used the word 'religionism' to refer both to the view that one religion is true to a degree denied to other religions and to the attitude of superiority that expresses itself as intolerance towards adherents of other religions (Hull 1992: 70; cf. Hull 2000b: 76). Religionism, he affirmed, is rather like racism – there is the racist belief that one's own race is better than others and there are racist attitudes that show themselves in acts of discrimination against individuals from other races. It is the denial of the truth of other religious traditions than one's own that is the cause of religious bigotry and intolerance. That Hull believed his liberal reading of religion to be *superior* to other readings, and therefore in his own terms to 'justify' intolerance of those who disagree with him, somehow escaped his notice (see Barnes 2002c for an extended discussion and critique of Hull).

There is a range of problems with this strategy for challenging intolerance and prejudice in society, which are by now well developed in the literature and familiar to religious educators. In a sense Hull's solution to the problem of diversity is to deny the ultimate nature of diversity, for if the different religions are complementary then diversity is secondary to essential agreement: every religion initiates a saving encounter with the divine. This is hardly a position that endears itself to orthodox religious believers who look to their own religion as uniquely true. Indeed, some will feel that their religion is being misrepresented in the name and cause of social harmony. The assumption that all religions are true also encourages educators both to overlook the doctrinal aspect of religion (where disagreement is most obvious) and to bypass the controversial issue of religious truth claims and their assessment.

One of the most serious and damaging criticisms that has recently been voiced to the thesis of the essential unity of religions and to the kind of liberal theology that is implicit in much British RE is that strategies that assume these commitments are not well equipped to develop respect from pupils for religious difference. Consider the underlying logic of the strategies. You are encouraged to accept adherents of other religions and to relinquish intolerance of them on the ground that their ultimate convictions are in agreement with your own. You adopt a positive attitude to others because they share a similar and complementary commitment to the divine. Acceptance of the religious 'Other' is predicated on religious agreement (in essential experience). But this carries the implication that no such respect for difference may be forthcoming in those cases where there is genuine disagreement – no respect for those who resist the liberal temptation to view all religions as true. Yet if there were true respect for religious difference there would be no need to assume essential agreement between the religions (either by explicit or implicit teaching and methodologies). Furthermore, this liberal strategy has the capacity to 'demonise' others just as effectively as those who believe in the exclusive nature of the truth of their particular religious commitment and community. The line between insiders and outsiders is drawn in a different place, this time between inclusivists and exclusivists rather than say between Muslims and others, or Christians and others, but the same binary distinction is employed. Respect for religious difference is compromised when those who are to be accepted and affirmed must first relinquish any claim to uniqueness or religious distinctiveness.

The number of religions to be studied

Almost a century and a half ago the distinguished German philologist and Orientalist Friedrich Max Müller remarked that '[h]e who knows one [religion], knows none' (Müller 1873: 16). Few would dispute the fact that in order to gain an educationally responsible understanding of religious beliefs and practices it is necessary to study a range of different religions. This is surely part of the strength of a multi-faith RE, whether a phenomenological approach is employed or not.

Accurate and reliable descriptions of the beliefs and practices of different religions challenge crude caricatures and distorted accounts of religious phenomena, which are used by some to encourage intolerance of the beliefs and values of minority communities.

In England and Wales the 1988 Education Reform Act required that any new Agreed Syllabus 'shall reflect the fact that the religious traditions in Great Britain are in the main Christian whilst taking account of the teaching and practices of the other principal religions represented in Great Britain' (Section 8.3). For the most part this flexibility of legal provision that allows Agreed Syllabuses Committees to decide for themselves which religions to study has not resulted in flexibility of practice. Most Syllabus Committees follow John Hull's counsel that six religions should be studied. In his view '*taking account of* the teaching and practices of the other principal religions' means that no Agreed Syllabus meets the requirements of the Act unless it includes the teachings and practices of 'Judaism, Islam, Hinduism, the Sikh faith, and Buddhism,' alongside Christianity (Hull 1989: 61). The view that these six religions should be studied in schools was reinforced in 1994 with the publication of two 'Model' Syllabuses that were intended to exemplify good practice by the School Curriculum and Assessment Authority (SCAA). These Model Syllabuses have subsequently been superseded by a single *Non-Statutory National Framework* (QCA 2004) which, while retaining an emphasis on the study of six major religions, also 'recommends' the study of a range of further traditions 'such as the Bahá'í faith, Jainism and Zoroastrianism', and 'secular philosophies such as humanism' for all pupils (QCA 2004: 12). There is no doubt that the recommendation by the *National Framework* for pupils to study over ten different religious traditions has occasioned debate among educators and for some detracted from the overall credibility of the document (see Felderhof 2004 and 2005). It is difficult to know (for no justification is given) on what basis the Bahá'í faith, Jainism and Zoroastrianism are included as 'principal religions', and even more difficult to know why humanism is recommended for study by all pupils when it is not a religion, never mind a *principal* religion. The problem with this expanding project of requiring pupils to study so many religions is that it fails to identify what is significant to religion and how best to gain an understanding of the nature of religion. In addition there is the educational challenge of what can reasonably be studied given the limitations on curriculum time, the specificities of our culture, the knowledge and capabilities of the teacher and the intellectual capacities of pupils. A study of over 10 religions to many educators suggests itself to be a recipe for superficial knowledge and truncated understanding.

A much better approach to the issue of how many religions should be studied is provided by the most recent Birmingham Agreed Syllabus (2007). The Syllabus does not stipulate which religions should be studied alongside Christianity. Instead it provides a set of criteria on the basis of which teachers decide which religions it is appropriate to study in their particular context. The Syllabus looks to the professional judgement of teachers and prescribes certain basic principles for the exercise of that judgement. One selects the religious material to be used *for a reason*: e.g. does it reflect the family background of the children in the class, does it reflect the historic and cultural roots of the city and country, will it deepen or broaden the spiritual or moral dimension, will it lead to social cohesion and solidarity, does it meet the learning requirements set by the age, aptitude and daily experience of pupils, and so on. This seems a much more educationally sound way of determining how many religions should be studied by pupils, even if it results in far fewer religions being studied than the number recommended by the *National Framework*.

Conclusion

This review of some of the debates in relation to diversity and to representations of diversity in RE has of necessity been limited in scope and sophistication. Clearly many of the other chapters in this volume bear on the issue of diversity and therefore complement, qualify or possibly challenge what is said here. There is no straightforward or uncontroversial answer to the question of how successful RE in the United Kingdom has been and is in furthering respectful relations both between different communities and between individuals with different religious outlooks. Recent policies and strategies, as recommended by the *National Framework*, for example, provide some grounds for optimism: in the *Framework* curriculum planners are encouraged to give more attention to the issue of religious truth, to the diversity within religions and to the concerns and interests of pupils. Progress is being made, though our review of earlier debates suggests that overall RE has as yet not fully realised its potential in relation to the creation of a more humane, tolerant and inclusive society. The realisation of that potential remains a challenge both to curriculum planners and to contemporary religious educators.

Questions

What challenges to RE in schools are posed by increasing religious diversity in society and what do you judge to be educationally appropriate responses?

What are the strengths and weaknesses of the different policies and strategies in relation to diversity described in this chapter?

How successful do you think RE in the United Kingdom has been in challenging religious intolerance and furthering respect for those who belong to minority communities?

Further reading

Barnes, L. P. (2009a) *Religious Education: Taking Religious Difference Seriously*, London: Philosophy of Education Society of Great Britain. Short, provocative critique of current policy and practice in relation to diversity in RE.

Barnes, L. P. (2010) 'Enlightenment's wake: religion and education at the close of the modern age', in G. Durka, E. Engebretson and L. Gearon (eds) *International Handbook of Inter-religious Education*, Philadelphia: Springer. An attempt to initiate a critical dialogue between religious educators and political philosophers on the issue of education in a pluralist society.

Jackson, R. (2004b) *Rethinking Religious Education and Plurality*, London: RoutledgeFalmer. Excellent resource that discusses diversity in relation to a range of different methodologies in RE.

Weller, P. (2008) *Religious Diversity in the UK*, London: Continuum. Good up-to-date account of the nature of religious diversity in the United Kingdom.

Chapter 5

Gender

Gemma O'Dell

Educationalists are finding that the growth in plurality and pluralism in society is reflected in classrooms and schools, which are increasingly multi-cultural, multi-faith, multi-ethnic amongst other markers, which denote the multiplicity of the identities of learners. Education must equip pupils for the challenge of questioning and developing an understanding of their own and others' identities in environments that are changing and evolving.

This chapter charts the change in focus on issues of gender in education from the 1970s until the present day. It addresses how explanations for the difference in educational achievement between boys and girls have emphasised the role of gender identity as a central factor for consideration in schools. The implications and significance of findings from educational research into gender are looked at in relation to religious education (RE) and it is suggested that the understanding of one's own plural identity, including gendered identity, can in turn lead students to appreciate the heterogeneous character of religious traditions.

Overview of perspectives on gender in education

Gender in education (and gender as an analytical category and variable within educational research) has had a prominent place within discussions of educational achievement since the 1970s and was largely prompted by feminist works addressing the role and status of women within society at large. In feminist research 'gender' was viewed as a more appropriate category of analysis than 'sex' as it focused on social constructions of gendered beings rather than fixed biological factors (Oakley 1972).

In the 1970s and 1980s the focus was initially upon the marginalisation and sexual discrimination of females within schools. Attention was given to how school curriculum and structures helped to perpetuate stereotypical sex roles; the monopolisation of the teacher's time and the domination of the classroom by boys at the expense of girls. Difference in attainment between boys and girls was an issue in terms of the type of subject boys and girls opted to take for O level and their relative performance in these subjects. During the 1970s greater numbers of girls were in fact obtaining 5 or more A–C grades at O level than boys. However boys were performing better in subjects such as mathematics and science, which had more prestige than so called 'feminine' subjects such as home economics, and which ultimately could lead to employment with the prospect of relatively higher earning power (Francis and Skelton 2001: 1).

The introduction of the National Curriculum in England and Wales in 1988 made it compulsory for boys and girls to study the same core subjects and with this came a significant shift in the perception of the achievement of female students. Female students began to close the gap in achievement in traditionally 'masculine' subjects such as mathematics and science. It became more noticeable that male students were behind female students in their attainment in traditionally more 'feminine' subjects such as English, modern foreign languages and humanities. This was followed by a change of focus in discussions on educational equity. Despite the fact that since the 1980s the performance of both males and females has been improving (Younger and Warrington 1996), from the 1990s onwards attention has turned to the position of boys within education – particularly the perceived 'underachievement of boys'. This kept gender as a central issue in discussions about educational performance, although quite often without making explicit the fact that it is not boys *per se* who are underachieving, for there is less of a gap between boys and girls from higher socio-economic backgrounds. Indeed care must be taken when using gender as a separate variable in educational research and the multi-variable complexity of for instance gender, class and ethnicity must remain in the forefront of a researcher's mind (see Hammersley 2001).

The trend for girls to outperform boys in education is not specific to the UK but concerns of this sort are found across the Western world (in many European countries, Canada, North America and also South American countries such as Chile and Brazil (Francis and Skelton 2005: 36–38)). Attempts to understand and explain the difference in educational attainment between, broadly speaking, boys and girls have ranged from discourses on gender stereotypes, subject choice and various masculine identities to studies of behaviour and the contribution of boys in lessons, boys' overall work ethic and the 'feminisation of schools'. Explanations given for the current differentiation in educational achievement between boys and girls largely depend on the theoretical positioning of the researcher and influence not only the way in which this issue is seen but also how this issue should be addressed.

Key debates on gender in education

Gender differences: the nature/nurture debate

The nature/nurture debate is one that plays out strongly in education, especially as differences in educational attainment naturally lead to questions as to why such differences emerge. The positioning on either side of this debate cannot be seen to be entirely a-political. Various forms of feminism have usually positioned themselves on the nurture side of the debate, maintaining that gender is a social construct, which allows for the domination of 'femininity' by 'masculinity'. It is important to note that one does not need to be male to access the privilege endorsed by 'masculinity' (females may embody hegemonic masculinity). Butler (1990) drew attention to the understanding of the 'performativity' of gender identities and unhinged the differences between sex and gender and the way in which these terms had been used by feminists and social constructivists. Instead gender was not seen as something someone has/is but rather performances that create a mirage of 'gender identity'. In education such concepts put a spotlight on gender discrimination, which we saw during the 1970s and 1980s as a focus on the inequalities faced by girls.

Those on the side of the nature debate may claim that boys and girls are essentially different, whether this is due to intrinsic natural biological/genetic differences such as brain difference or the influence of hormones. Arguments which allude to brain differences (Gurian 2002) for instance position themselves with arguments suggesting that boys and girls learn differently, develop at different stages and develop different skills; hence explanation is given for the variation in subject preference amongst boys and girls, different behaviour seen in male and female students and a disparity in the achievements of boys and girls. The danger of overemphasis on these findings is that it can lead to a resigned acceptance that boys and girls learn in particular ways and so will excel in different subjects or a resigned acceptance that behaviour expectations *should* differ for boys and girls. Further it could direct educationalists to resort to essentialist teaching strategies that accommodate different learning styles for boys and girls, which may perpetuate gender differences and discrimination and isolate students who do not fall into archetypal 'boy/girl' categories. This is not to say that there are not gendered tendencies to prefer certain learning styles; however social constructivists would argue that as is the case with gender, these are socially engineered and should not be endorsed uncritically. Critiques of brain difference perspectives have drawn attention to the fact that the brain responds to external stimuli and as such develops in line with experience. This presents a further way of responding to this debate with the proposal that cognitive abilities are shaped as a result of both nature and nurture, accounting for gendered difference in educational achievement (see Francis and Skelton 2005: 76–79). Other critiques of this approach reject 'brain difference explanations' in accounting for gendered difference in achievement on the basis of the lack of evidence in comparison to the large body of evidence that shows achievement to be affected by social factors (see Francis and Skelton 2005: 79–82).

The impact of gender constructs on achievement

Educational feminist research during the 1980s found that stereotypical gender expectations of woman as home-maker and man as bread-winner led to very different career aspirations for girls and boys (Spender 1982). By the 1990s however the aspirations of girls appeared to be changing. New pressures on girls became evident as girls (in the main, middle-class girls) aspired to the image of a successful woman in contemporary society as being attractive as well as high academic achievers (see Francis and Skelton 2005: 108). During the 1990s focus largely turned away from the experience of girls in education to the study of boys, rotating on concerns of underachievement. Discussions have focused on the impact of 'hegemonic masculinities' (dominant forms of masculinity which exercise the most authority; see Connell 1995) amongst male students (and indeed some male teachers). Emphasis was placed on constructed and embodied 'masculinities'; principally those that place themselves in opposition to what is perceived as 'feminine' (which for some included a work ethic and displaying behaviours which jeopardise educational achievement) and how these impact on the lives and schooling of all.

Such discourse treats the concept of gender as an on-going, social/discursive construct, which is historically and spatially situated and evolving. The idea that there exists one unified form of masculinity is now dated. 'Masculinity' is to be viewed as fluid rather than fixed. The work on 'masculinities' in schools referred to imposed regimes whereby boys establish and construct their masculinities in relation to regulated 'gender boundaries', which are policed by conformity to heterosexual norms (Martino 1999: 260). Thus sexuality becomes a category for defining acceptable masculinity and homophobic comments become a tool for doing so (ibid.: 256). Significantly it was apparent that there was a trend for boys to establish their masculinity in opposition to femininity, which involves a rejection and denigration of what they consider to be feminine attributes or behaviours (ibid.: 244). In rejecting feminine attributes or behaviours boys may be rejecting what they consider to be markers of homosexuality (Butler 1990).

The construct of masculinity in opposition to femininity has implications for the activities boys choose to get involved in. Askew and Ross (1988: 23) found that boys had a greater need than girls to identify certain activities as 'male' or 'female' and then avoid activities which are seen to be female. This may have implications for subject preference amongst boys and religious educationalists must consider where their subject stands in relation to dualistic allocations of subjects along the spectrum of feminine/masculine.

The work into femininities/masculinities went some way to challenging notions of homogenous gender identities and paved the way for more individualised learning needs to be addressed, such as a 'Which boys? Which girls?' approach to looking at where resources and support should be targeted to address underachievement. It also placed emphasis on the diverse nature of identity, which opened a gap in the popularised field of gender in education and allowed for the suggestion that other factors of identity such as class, race or sexuality should also come into an analysis of the impact of a student's identity on their achievement. However some scholars deliberately choose not to draw on such discourse. Francis (2000: 14–15) gives two reasons for not drawing on the notion of masculinities/

femininities: first, she suggests that drawing on the idea of different versions of masculinity, some more dominant than others, suggests something more fixed about gender identity than is the case. Second, she argues that such categorisations raise problems with the very concepts of masculinity and femininity, which are purely notional concepts. Francis draws on work that suggests that underlying writings on masculinity/femininity is the conflation of sex/gender. Without drawing on what holds notions of masculinity or femininity together (which many theories of masculinity/femininity don't do) then these terms become reduced to essential sex difference. Weaver-Hightower (2003) points out a number of further criticisms of theory based and practice based works on masculinities. First, practice based policy approaches to masculinities with a focus on test scores make themselves vulnerable to political influence. Second, practice based approaches have sometimes led to 'tips for teachers' style suggestions, which provide simplistic answer to complex questions and which fail to take on board a 'which boys?' analysis. In terms of theoretical approaches Weaver-Hightower is critical of the focus on the most obvious boys, those at the top or bottom of the achievement scale, whilst 'ordinary boys' receive little attention.

Are boys really underachieving?

A number of scholars have questioned whether there is such a need to focus on boys' achievement to the extent it has been looked at in recent years. Not only are there fears that the attention given to the prominence of boys in educational research and education policy has been prompted by media hype, emerging in the 1990s surrounding the alleged 'crisis of masculinity' but also some question whether boys are actually 'underachieving' at all. Weaver-Hightower (2003) discusses a number of points made by researchers that suggest that concerns over boys' achievement in education have been inflated. These concerns vary and include the inadequacy of using only test scores as a measure of boys' underachievement. Multiple variables such as race and class may make boys versus girls analysis insufficient. Further points suggest that measures of academic equality should be based on factors other than test score; for instance despite boys' 'underachievement' in test scores males go on to surpass females in the work place (Weaver-Hightower 2003: 485–486). Although these are certainly valid sentiments two points are worth considering. First, it is problematic to look at simple boy-versus-girl statistics without considering other variables such as race or socio-economic status. However even when two variables are used such as gender and social class then it is clear that girls are outperforming boys in some subjects. At the most emotive level, any parent of a son would have genuine reason to question why this might be the case and what should be done about it and deserve to have these questions taken seriously. Second, the case that males in many societies have a privileged position does not justify recuperative and almost punishing neglect of boys in schools, when ethically educationalists have a responsibility to do their best for all students in their care.

Does the focus on boys' experience of education further marginalise girls?

The shift in focus from girls' achievements in education during the 1970s and 1980s to boys' achievements during the 1990s has been coined the 'boy turn'. Concerns that were raised by the 'crisis of masculinity' put much blame on feminist movements in education for prioritising the needs of females over males and as a result boys are underperforming in relation to girls. However the extent to which girls are outperforming boys is debatable and the tendency to present the success of middle-class girls as representative of girls *per se* hides the reality that some girls, like boys, are still disadvantaged in the education system (Lucey 2001).

Significance for religious education

Research into gender and education highlights a particular concern for RE. An unease centres round the relationship between gender stereotypes or expectations and subject choice: 'the notion of a gendered curriculum'. RE is a subject described specifically by an Ofsted review as preferred by girls:

> Science, mathematics, technology, IT and PE are rated as 'masculine' by pupils and preferred by boys; English, humanities, music, PSE and RE are rated as 'feminine' and preferred by girls.

> (Ofsted 1998: 31)

Dualistic allocations of school subjects along the spectrum of masculine/feminine may well feed into a student's essentialist understanding of themselves and have detrimental effects for the potential of RE to be an inclusive subject, open and accessible to all students. An Australian study by Engebretson (2007: 206) researched teenage boys' spirituality, revealing that teenage boys did not find it easy to talk without embarrassment about issues that related to belief in or experience of God. Francis (2000) reports on RE being preferred less by boys than girls in comparison to other subjects. RE was marked as the fourth least favourite subject for boys, whilst it was the sixth least favourite subject for girls. This was despite a 'blurring of the traditional preferences between girls and boys, supported by a lack of clear gender delineation between "science" and "arts" subjects' (Francis 2000: 46). Genuine discourse between pupils about religious matters and truth, religious identity and diversity and the role of religion in life and society (all of which feature as central questions in RE) can take place only when all pupils are comfortable, confident, engaged and perceive such discourse as important to their own lives and identities.

Gender representations in the content of religious education

Other concerns of a 'gendered curriculum' raise questions as to how curriculum material may promote gender stereotypes, which disadvantage both boys and girls. This is an issue for RE given feminist criticism of the patriarchal nature of religions. Teachers of RE have been said to have 'an ethical, as well as professional responsibility to reveal the patriarchal bases in the world's religions which continue to constrain women's visibility' (Hanlon 2002: 132–133). Hanlon writes that teachers should challenge 'religious sexism by omission' and exploit the flexibility within local agreed syllabuses and write women back into RE (ibid.: 133). Michael Grimmitt's social constructivist pedagogy for RE (to which I shall return) further suggests RE pedagogy should encourage students to 'be sensitive to the positive and negative effects of religion upon human life, including its intrinsic sexism and racism' (ibid.: 224). Grimmitt goes further still and opens up the possibility for RE to 'challenge concepts and practices which have become *reified* by tradition and which may no longer be worthy of support or toleration' (ibid.: 225). Such challenges to RE are not unproblematic and certainly the development of pedagogies that push a teacher's personal agenda and personal worldviews are not to be encouraged. Asking questions such as 'who judges which practices are to be upheld for scrutiny as being worthy of toleration and support?' would be justified. Presenting different representations of the roles of men and women within religious traditions and different responses from within faith communities to the role and status of men and women would certainly give students a more balanced account for their own consideration.

Report on the findings of a small-scale action research study into gender and religious education

As part of Warwick University's Community of Practice research for the EC funded REDCo Project a small-scale action research project set within one school was carried out looking into the influence of gender on students' engagement in RE (O'Dell 2009). The study investigated the hypothesis that perceptions of gender acted as a barrier to dialogue in RE for boys. The project reported that there was a significant perception among boys that RE was a girls' subject and religion was something that 'women talk about'. Explanations for this finding were due to a combination of boys' perceptions that RE involved talking about personal opinions and feelings. Boys were not necessarily averse to talking about either; however there was the belief that this was something which girls were better at doing and therefore they were consequently better at and more likely to succeed in RE. One of the advantages boys perceived girls as having over them in this subject was 'open-mindedness' in comparison to boys' cynicism. There were further concerns expressed by boys that the pressure to conform to a 'macho' image was not in keeping with expressing an interest in

RE. Avoiding being seen as 'weak' was also important to boys and for some boys appearing to have changed your mind on an issue may expose you to this criticism. This certainly reduced the scope and potential of dialogue in the classroom. There were aspects of RE which boys found difficult including the fear of embarrassment by unintentionally causing offence or receiving unwanted and patronising attention from girls, for simply expressing maturity and a sense of responsibility.

Questions then arise about what actually can be done to address such concerns and whether or not the findings from such small-scale research can have anything to offer to other educational settings. Certainly the enactment of gender in this study is particular to its setting and the issues of concern identified may not be matters of concern in other settings. When one takes an anti-homogenous view of gender and does not refer to male or female 'gender identity', but instead recognises differences amongst boys and girls and asks 'which boys? which girls?' then one must recognise that no two educational settings (or indeed students) will be the same and matters of gender in education will differ from establishment to establishment. This makes it almost impossible to offer pragmatic and pedagogic solutions and suggestions for best practice; however the fact that the project is related to teaching goals in order to develop self-awareness and help students appreciate religious diversity and community understanding may then produce some points to consider for teachers who share the same goals (Ipgrave and O'Grady 2009: 171).

A pedagogical framework: deconstructing gender through the interpretive approach

During the REDCo Project a pedagogical framework was developed to encourage deep reflection on self-identity and critical assessment of gendered identity. It might well offer suggestions for how a teacher can unpack gender issues in their classroom (both in terms of offering a critique of RE as 'a gendered subject' and also in terms of raising a critical awareness amongst students as to how RE may present gender). The framework was informed by and employed alongside the interpretive approach to exploring religious diversity. It was also influenced by Grimmitt's (2000a) social constructivist approach. This framework was used in on-going questioning of students' ideas about classroom material they encountered. It aimed to encourage student reflexivity and proposed that it should directly include the following dimensions:

1　*Ontology*: students must question their being in the world – what do they think is important in making them who they are? Students should question whether their identities are fixed or evolving. Are certain aspects of their identity fixed – how might this impact on their lives? Concerning gender, questions should arise about *what does it mean to them to be male/female?*

2   *Construction*: how are our identities constructed by and in relation to others? Particularly, *are there certain ways a boy/girl should act?* Who decides upon these ways? How do we learn about these ways? Do we agree with these ways? Do we have any control over 'construction'? This should be linked back to considerations about representation and interpretation found in the interpretive approach.

3   *Evaluation:* does our identity influence our own responses to material we are presented with? Does our identity influence the way people respond to us? *Does being male/female influence my response to the material I am presented with?* Does it make any issues particularly important to me? Would I like to look at this material in a different way, or look in detail at a different aspect of this tradition? 'How does this religious text, belief, practice or value present the possibilities of being female and male?' (Grimmitt 2000a: 225)

4   *Reflection on ontology:* does this process add to my understanding of self-identity? What is it to be male/female (for me)? Does it change/confirm my initial idea? What else is important in making me 'me' – is *my* idea of 'me' fixed or can it change? What might influence the way I respond to others? Do I recognise influences on the identity of others? Are the identities of others fixed or evolving? (O'Dell 2009: 61)

In combining self-analysis (in this case in terms of gender identity) with the analysis of religious groups studied impetus is placed on how, in order to fully appreciate the complexity of another's identity, one must first be conscious of the complexities of one's own identity. The approach taken here towards gender construction is complementary to the way in which an interpretive approach to RE approaches culture and religious traditions. An interpretive approach to RE employs a hermeneutic of learning about religious diversity through looking at the relationship between an individual, group and tradition. The interpretive approach (Jackson 1997) is applied to foster a sense of the understanding of plural identities and an understanding of diversity not only between but also within religious traditions. It leads students into a reflexive process as part of their learning, with special consideration given to the nature of the representation of traditions and the interpretation of them in the light of their own experience.

Students are further encouraged to see their own identity as complex, diverse and evolving. As a pedagogical framework the interpretive approach encourages the type of self-study which is needed in order to address fixed ideas of gender, and in turn by fostering an understanding of one's own identity as diverse one is brought closer to understanding religious identities and diversity.

Conclusions

The findings of such a small-scale study should not be taken as generalisations for practice; however they do have overlaps with other theories in education pertaining to the achievement of boys and girls and find resonance with popular discourses such as those on masculinity/femininity and the dualistic allocation of subjects along such lines, the pressure amongst students to conform to gender stereotypes and the warnings of a 'gendered curriculum'. It is for each educator in his or her own context to be aware of discourses on gender and critically assess their pertinence to the individual situation. Owing to the particularity of each educational setting and the various forms of gender construction it is not appropriate, realistic or desirable to offer 'tips for teachers' on best practice in RE. However drawing on research in education a number of important insights seem worthy of note and consideration.

It is important to engage students in processes that help them to realise the plurality of their own identities. Attention should be brought to the negative effects of homogenous concepts of gender and how these can restrict personal development and stand in the way of students' learning. Particular attention should be drawn to discourse on gender as a cultural construct and the impact this has on students' lives: 'it is important for those working in schools to help boys to develop specific capacities for understanding the effects of certain currencies of masculinity in their lives' (Martino 1999: 260). Bearing in mind discussions that are critical of the emphasis on boys' achievements for further marginalising girls, it is important when considering strategies to address gender concerns that these benefit all students in meaningful ways. It simply cannot do to hold the view that when the perceived needs of one sex are addressed then either all within that sex benefit or the opposite sex automatically benefits. Proactive steps to improve education should benefit all students directly. Further, students should be discouraged from making comparisons between boys and girls as if they were homogenous groups, instead encouraging a 'which boys? which girls?' approach. Careful thought should be given to the theoretical underpinnings of explanations for difference in achievement between boys and girls and the 'solutions' offered. Caution should be taken with pedagogies that are based on essentialist views of the difference between boys and girls as these may help perpetuate gender stereotypes. The classroom environment must support students' freedom to hold fast to their own beliefs and opinions. Understanding one's self as having a plural identity does not mean that there is a lack of continuity of self! It must however also be established that it is acceptable to change and develop an outlook and even change the way we view ourselves. Educationalists should critically assess how they portray sex and gender in their teaching but also teachers must engage in a whole school approach to assessing gender policy. It is important to question critically the ways in which school structures open up ways of being 'male'/'female' to students, whether this be through dialogue in the school and the language used to discuss gender, curriculum materials, teaching strategies or expectations of student behaviour based on stereotypical gender expectations.

Questions

Have recent concerns over boys' achievement further marginalised the needs of female students?

Do the curriculum and teaching adequately tackle gender stereotypes, which can impede the development of students and should be challenged within a RE framework?

How can pupils best be encouraged to deconstruct their own identities, including their gender identity?

Further reading

Arnot, M. and an Ghaill, M. M. (eds) (2006) *The RoutledgeFalmer Reader in Gender and Education,* London: Routledge. This book consist of contributions from leading international gender researchers and addresses current debates about gender, power, identity and culture relating to concerns about boys' and girls' schooling.

Francis, B. and Skelton, C. (eds) (2001) *Investigating Gender: Contemporary Perspectives in Education,* Milton Keynes: Open University Press. This book provides an overview of contemporary and theoretical debates in the field of gender and education.

Francis, B. and Skelton, C. (2005) *Reassessing Gender and Achievement: Questioning Contemporary Key Debates,* London: Routledge. Looks at the debate around boys' 'underachievement'. It reviews the work on gender and performance and critically assesses evidence supporting explanations for gender differences and strategies used to tackle them.

Martino, M., Kehler, M. and Weaver-Hightower, B. (eds) (2009) *The Problem with Boys' Education: Beyond the Backlash,* London: Routledge. Collected essays on analysis of theories and policies on boys' education around the world; special attention is given to how masculinities intersect with race, class and sexuality.

Chapter 6

Faith, religious education and whole school issues

Trevor Cooling

My grandmother's front room always intrigued me because of the curiosity cupboard. You don't see them much nowadays, but this was where her memorabilia were stored. It was a great place for a wet afternoon and the stories she told about the contents captivated me. However a fascinating half hour around the curiosity cupboard was enough. Then it was downstairs to the powerhouse of their home; the kitchen. This was where the conversations and decisions that determined everyday life in the family happened.

I began my teaching career as a science specialist in Banbury where I generally found that pupils trusted my scholarly authority. They certainly didn't question the validity of the subject matter that I taught. I also taught a little religious education (RE) and became captivated by the subject. So, after two years of teaching science, I returned to student life, theology this time, and subsequently switched to being an RE specialist in Aylesbury, teaching a little science as my second subject. However, I had a rude shock when, in RE lessons, I came up against the repeated refrain, 'Oh, that's just an opinion'. I had little scholarly authority. Indeed I even found some pupils questioning my ability to teach them science because I was an RE specialist. It was then that I realised that being identified with the 'God slot' on the curriculum posed a unique epistemological challenge. RE wasn't respected because many of the pupils did not see religion as credible knowledge. Religion was 'just an opinion' and not very relevant to the business of life at that. Being the RE teacher felt like being in charge of the school's curiosity cupboard. Science was the kitchen of the school curriculum.

My experience illustrates one of the major challenges facing RE teachers in Britain. We work in a culture where religion is not really seen as relevant or credible. Young people are increasingly sceptical about it. Society at large doesn't really take it seriously or even understand it. This attitude extends to the highest levels of academia. Revd Michael Reiss, Professor of Science Education at the Institute of Education in London University, experienced this in 2008 when he found himself at the centre of a controversy about creationism (Bickley 2010). Reiss is no creationist, but just suggesting that science teachers ought to accord the respect of hearing out pupils who had creationist views arising from religious convictions led to his resigning his position as Education Officer for the Royal

Society. His views were deemed 'open to misinterpretation'. Indeed some influential Royal Society members even felt it was inappropriate that such a position should be occupied by a clergyman. It appears that religious commitment was somehow thought to taint this Reverend's scientific credentials. The problem appears to have been that Reiss's comments might have implied that religion is of some relevance to a scientific education.

In such a climate many RE teachers find their subject is the Cinderella of the curriculum. Head teachers seem quite willing to overlook its significance in comparison with supposedly more serious subjects. Educational bureaucrats seem not to know or care about its legal status. The RE Council of England and Wales has to expend considerable energy on persuading politicians not to marginalise the subject in the inevitable next curriculum review. It is not then surprising that RE teachers feel that a significant part of their professional role is to defend the place of their subject in their schools' curriculum. The British approach to RE is highly prized by those who teach the subject and attracts interest and respect from all over the world. It is a treasure worth defending. The proud RE teacher therefore battles to maintain the position and integrity of the RE slot on the curriculum. Religion is unique, distinctive and important in its own right, we argue; it therefore needs its own specialist attention.

But could this passion for defending RE itself be exacerbating the 'God slot' problem that I experienced at Aylesbury and which countless RE teachers face on a daily basis?

Religion: irrelevant clutter or serious knowledge?

One of the important choices that RE teachers have to make is an epistemological choice. Basically we have to decide how we will represent the place of religion in human knowledge to our pupils and their parents and to our colleagues through the way we approach the promotion of our subject. Put rather crudely, the choice is between an Enlightenment view which highlights the concept of objective rationality and regards education as a neutral activity, or a constructivist view which acknowledges the role of belief and interpretation in human knowing (Cooling 2010 and Grimmitt 2000a).

The pursuit of objective rationality: religion as clutter

In the mid-1970s, Paul Hirst, then Professor of Education at the University of Cambridge, published what were to prove to be highly influential ideas (Hirst 1972 and 1974). His assertion was that 'there has emerged in our society a concept of education which makes the whole idea of Christian education a kind of nonsense' (Hirst 1974: 77).

The significance of Hirst's assertion for RE lies in his adherence to the theory of the secularisation of knowledge and his rejection of reliance on religious beliefs for generating a philosophy of education. A key element in Hirst's notion of secular knowledge was the concept of objectivity, which defined what it meant to be rational. Rationality is a *universal and shared* human characteristic, which transcends the particularity of religious differences. On this basis Hirst later distinguished between primitive approaches to education, which consist of passing on the contentious beliefs and ideas of particular religions, and sophisticated approaches, which are concerned only with transmitting objective knowledge and promoting rational thought (Hirst 1981). He was therefore uneasy with church schools and would have been appalled by their growing influence and popularity over the last ten years and particularly horrified by the idea that they offered a distinctively Christian approach to the curriculum. Although his particular focus was Christianity, his conclusions applied to all religions.

For RE, Hirst's views lead to one important conclusion. It is fine, in sophisticated education, to teach *about* religion because pupils need to know and understand people's religious beliefs and practices. RE is therefore a worthy subject, providing pupils with knowledge about religions and helping them to make their own autonomous choices. However the practice of religion is a private matter that should not impinge on the objective, educational task of promoting rationality. RE should not therefore take a confessional approach which is designed to nurture the pupil in a particular religious faith, but should rather focus on the objective study of religion.

Even though he wrote over 40 years ago, Hirst's ideas are still highly influential. For example, amongst RE professionals in Britain it is hard to find anyone who will argue for a confessional approach, with the marked exception of Penny Thompson (Thompson 2003). In wider educational circles, this ideal of objectivity pervades the thinking of most people. Religion is, if you are lucky, regarded as a fascinating topic for objective study in RE, but it is not thought of as an integral component of the concept of an educated person. Rather that person is objective and rational.

Professor Richard Norman is a humanist philosopher who has an active interest in RE. In his book *On Humanism*, Norman explains humanist belief about what it means to be human (Norman 2004). Humans are, he claims, characterised by their capacity for rational thought and flourish when that rationality is promoted. In the case of morality, this rational nature is evidenced by the shared moral values which are clearly identifiable in the midst of cultural and religious diversity. According to Norman, these shared values 'are entirely independent of religious belief' (2004: 114). They are, in contrast to faith-based values, objective and are therefore universal. In a telling metaphor, Norman states that religious beliefs are 'clutter' and 'humanists will want to remove the clutter' (2004: 118). Furthermore, in another book that he edited for the Humanist Philosophers Group, Norman asserts that: 'There has long been a free-thinking tradition in this country which has questioned religious belief' (2007: 6). Not only, therefore, are religious beliefs 'clutter' but to question them apparently characterises 'free-thinking'. Humanists are deeply sceptical about the concept of faith and are at pains to point out the difference between irrational faith in religious beliefs and warranted confidence in the rational, evidence-based beliefs of their secular philosophy (Law 2002). Like Hirst, most humanists are in favour of the study of the curious phenomenon of religious faith in RE lessons, but they do not want to accord it the credibility of rationality by allowing it to have a wider impact on the mainstream of school life. That is the preserve of things rational.

Herein lies the dilemma for the RE teacher. By campaigning to protect our subject from the forces that seek to eliminate it are we thereby reinforcing the message that religion is in fact irrelevant clutter, a private hobby that doesn't have that much significance in the greater picture of human endeavour and that can be appropriately parked in this peculiar slot called RE? Are we somehow conveying a secular view of religion which regards it as tolerated clutter to be studied in RE but not to be allowed into the mainstream of the curriculum? Is the problem exacerbated if we seek, for example, to protect RE from infiltration by seemingly irrelevant content by resisting the introduction of secular beliefs into the syllabus because they are 'not religions'? Are we then reinforcing the view that religious faith is somehow different from secular worldviews and thereby hastening the demise of our subject? One day will those with political influence ask the question: 'Why are we giving so much time to this clutter? What other private hobby gets this amount of attention in the curriculum?'

Two brief examples

Such has been the controversy surrounding creationism that the government produced guidelines for schools on dealing with the issue (DCSF 2007c). There is much helpful advice in this document. However the pertinent point is the recommendation that creationism should not be discussed in science lessons because it is not a scientific theory, but should rather be considered in RE. The danger is, to put it bluntly, that this advice reinforces the notion that science deals with that part of the curriculum that teaches rational, credible knowledge, whereas RE is where you study all the crazy things that religious people believe. That message will not help to improve the status of religion as a credible component in human thought.

The second example is a piece of recent research on the attitudes of Christian and atheist students training to teach RE in secondary schools to their own beliefs (Revell and Walters 2010). The researchers found that Christian students were generally hesitant about talking about their faith in their lessons, believing it was unprofessional to do so. The atheist students, in stark contrast, were happy to talk about their beliefs thinking that made a positive contribution to the lesson. When it came to their professionalism, the Christians apparently saw their beliefs as unhelpful clutter whereas the atheists saw theirs as objective and neutral.

How then can we avoid creating the impression that RE is the curiosity cupboard of the curriculum?

The role of interpretation: religion as serious knowledge

In contrast to the objectivist view, the constructivist approach to knowledge offers insights that will help to rehabilitate the credibility of religion. This can be illustrated by considering the writings of Richard Dawkins and Francis Collins, both leading geneticists with prestigious reputations and vocal exponents of opposing views in matters of religious belief. Dawkins is an atheist who believes passionately that evolution alone explains the origins of life on earth. For Dawkins, God is a delusion (Dawkins 2006). Francis Collins, in contrast, is a Christian convert who was the Director of the Human Genome Project. For him the natural world does not make sense unless one sees it as the result of God's design (Collins 2007).

Dawkins and Collins are scientific colleagues. They share the same knowledge base and work with complete integrity within the same discipline. Their different religious beliefs make no difference to their professional capacity to practise as geneticists. There is a shared scientific activity which is based on rational principles. In that sense their respective atheist and religious beliefs could be described as clutter.

However they differ fundamentally when it comes to the *meaning and significance* that they attribute to their shared enterprise of genetics. For Collins, genetics only makes sense in a world where there is a Creator, but for Dawkins it convinces him that God does not exist. Dawkins and Collins have both written books designed to persuade others of the truth of their beliefs. For both of them the shared activity of science is important; but the interpretation of the meaning and significance of science is even more so. *In this highly important sense their respective beliefs are not clutter but are, in fact, integral to their understanding of the world. Without a framework of beliefs, or worldview, neither of them could begin to make significant sense of the world of science.* True they would still have their scientific facts, but being educated is not about accumulating facts; it is about making meaning and judging significance.

Both Dawkins and Collins construct an understanding of the meaning of reality in response to their encounter with science. To do this they are dependent on their respective worldviews which enable them to make sense of the information they encounter. They are therefore constructing knowledge as they seek to give meaning to what they learn. Our beliefs enable us to do this. It is this hermeneutical behaviour which characterises human learning. The results are not 'just opinions'. The key difference between an objectivist approach and this constructivist approach is that the former takes individual scepticism about faith as its starting point whereas the latter honours faith as the starting point of interpretation (Thiselton 2009). What then are the implications of these observations for RE teachers?

First, we should proclaim the importance of our subject as the place in the curriculum where pupils attend to this highly significant process of meaning making. We are not just providing the curiosity cupboard of the curriculum. Rather we are the kitchen of learning where the truly important art of making meaning is the focus.

Second, we should not make the mistake of confining ourselves to studying religions and ignoring other worldviews. Every person is involved in this rational process of constructing meaning, be their worldview religious or non-religious. RE should treat all influential beliefs as worthy objects of study and reflection. If we are to answer the 'I don't want to be a vicar' objection to studying RE, then we must demonstrate its relevance to all pupils by embracing both religious and non-religious worldviews.

Finally, and most importantly from the perspective of this chapter, we should not adopt a bunker mentality. Meaning making happens throughout the school. As RE teachers it is our duty to take a lead in showing how religious and non-religious worldviews play a part in this process.

Religious education and whole school issues

As well as advocating the importance of RE as a distinct subject, we will not, therefore, succeed fully as RE teachers unless we are committed to showing how the subject is relevant to whole school issues. Two examples follow.

Hermeneutical pedagogy

Fundamentally to see RE as a hermeneutical subject (meaning that it engages pupils with the process of constructing meaning from the knowledge they acquire) is to be an advocate for an approach to pedagogy that puts interpretation at the heart of learning. Perhaps one of the greatest gifts that RE teachers can make to a school is to model and promote the insight that *the importance of pupils learning about worldviews is to learn something about themselves from them* so as to promote their development as people (Grimmitt 1987). It is true that there is some debate about the helpfulness of distinguishing these two attainment targets of learning about and learning from religion because the temptation is to treat them as two distinct, unrelated processes, which they are not. As with a coin, they are simply the two indispensable sides of the one hermeneutical process of learning. Some commentators therefore argue for combining them into one (Erricker 2010). It is also true that many teachers find the learning from attainment target difficult both to understand and to implement (Teece 2010). But the jewel in the crown of modern RE is undoubtedly the insight that teaching should actively support pupils in the business of rational thought, which is to construct meaning by interpreting the world through the lens of worldview. It should never be reduced to the accumulation of curious information about the bizarre world of religion.

One priority for every RE teacher should, therefore, be to develop a pedagogy that helps pupils to articulate their own worldview and to draw on its resources in interpreting the knowledge that they encounter in the wider school curriculum. Another priority should be to help pupils to understand worldviews other than their own and to encourage them to hear other voices that may challenge their own interpretations. Fortunately in RE we are blessed with a number of innovative approaches which offer a variety of ways with which to approach this task (Grimmitt 2000b).

But this vision should not be restricted to RE; it should characterise every subject on the curriculum. Allow me to illustrate from science, partly because it throws light on my personal experience of my early years of teaching, but mainly because a lot of the problems that RE teachers experience with being condemned to occupy the 'God-slot' lie in the perceptions that people have of the relationship between science and religion.

Many science teachers may regard worldviews as irrelevant to their work. Science is after all, they say, objective, concerned with established facts and theories and with the promotion of scientific method. However this is a very narrow view of science because it ignores the place of worldviews as providing the context from within which people make decisions about the meaning and significance of science and about how the knowledge gained will be applied. Returning to the debate between Richard Dawkins and Francis Collins, this narrow view of science education is saying 'we don't think their debate about meaning and significance is of much importance compared to knowledge of the scientific information that they share'. But this is to imply that science teachers are not employed to contribute to the personal development of their pupils through their subject teaching, only to increase their head knowledge. Do schools not care whether, for example, their science teaching produces concentration camp or refugee camp doctors? Teaching without a concern for personal development is not education.

If science teachers are silent about the role of worldviews, then they implicitly promote Dawkins' secular interpretation of science over a religious view like that of Collins. The message from silence is that religion has nothing to do with science; in other words it is clutter. It does not take long in a web search to find reviews of Francis Collins' book that deride and mock his Christian faith and express incomprehension that a scientist could succumb to such nonsense. Silence in science teaching about the role of worldview will, unfortunately, reinforce this widespread negative perception of religious faith. That's bad news for RE.

Clearly the RE teacher should not lecture the science department on such matters. But I suggest there are at least three ways in which gentle influence can be exercised, all of which can of course apply to colleagues in other subject areas:

1   Seek conversations with science colleagues where you begin to probe the potential for 'learning from' science. How might lessons on cell division or forces or chemical bonding contribute to a pupil's wider thinking about meaning and significance in life? This need not require a lot of additional planning. Are the deeper convictions and passions of scientists ever talked about? Often just the willingness of a teacher to be open to expressing their own thinking is enough to set the tone. An occasional pause for thought in a lesson can send a powerful signal.

2   Seek opportunities for collaboration, either through shared reference to topics in the discrete subjects or through integrated approaches. Given the inexperience of many science teachers in handling controversial material, more success is likely if we come out of the RE bunker and offer to engage with science content in RE lessons. But there has to be a quid pro quo. There has to be active acknowledgement of the importance of worldview discussions in science if religion is to escape its 'clutter image'.

3   Encourage an awareness of diversity in how science is thought about from within different worldviews. What are the overlaps? Are there conflicts? How do we react to discovering that a scientist is religious?

Worship in school

RE teachers are often reluctant to be identified with worship in school, fearing that the perceived coercive nature of compulsory worship will tar the reputation of RE. This is understandable, but the danger is that by not being involved we allow an unhelpful message about the nature of religion to be perpetuated. This can be illustrated from the debates that took place at national level.

In the last 25 years there has only been one concerted attempt to amend the complex regulations that govern school worship in England and Wales (Culham College Institute 1998). The aspiration was to develop an approach that ensured that all pupils and staff 'are able to share in good conscience' and was 'as inclusive as possible' (ibid.: 18). In particular, a way forward was considered that it was suggested might replace the stipulation that schools conduct a daily act of worship of a 'wholly or mainly broadly Christian character' as the law then required; and still does. It was:

> a statutory requirement for regular assemblies of a spiritual and moral character, with the present requirement for collective worship being withdrawn. The main focus of these gatherings would be the promotion of reflection on values, beliefs and the spiritual dimension of life.
>
> (Culham College Institute 1998: 19)

In Scotland a similar formula was adopted. Religious observance, as school worship is called in Scotland, was redefined as 'community acts which aim to promote the spiritual development of all members of the school community and express and celebrate the shared values of the school community' (Scottish Government 2004b:25).

The point of interest is that both initiatives adopt the strategy of removing explicit reference to religion as the means of making the acts more inclusive. However two things stand out when the Scottish documentation is compared to that considered by the consultation for England and Wales.

First, both expressed concerns about the appropriateness of worship in schools. However in the Scottish context this was not because worship itself might be considered to be an anti-educational activity. The report stated that acts of worship were entirely appropriate in a faith school where the religious character of the school was known to everyone who became part of that community. But it was not considered an appropriate activity for schools that did not have a designated religious affiliation (2006b:16). However, the English and Welsh proposed revision seemed to assume that religious worship was, in itself, *an inappropriate activity in any educational context, even faith schools.*

Second, both grappled with the appropriateness of explicitly mentioning the Christian heritage that shaped the legislation being reviewed. The Scottish document encouraged schools 'to use the rich resources of this tradition when planning religious observance' (Scottish Executive 2005: paragraph 8), taking account of the need to respect the integrity of pupils and staff. The English and Welsh documentation pointedly made no specific reference at all to Christianity in its recommendations, nor indeed to any faith.

This is very significant. One of the recurring concerns expressed about the English and Welsh proposals was that the new, 'inclusive' way forward would become a Trojan horse, effectively promoting the secularisation of school assembly. The impression given was that for education to be inclusive in a plural society, religion has to be banished to the private realm. Instead the focus is on the shared, apparently objective, characteristic of spiritual development. The underlying message is that religion, particularly Christianity in this case, is an irrelevance and that its exclusion will be to the educational benefit of all. An inclusive approach to assemblies seemed to assume that religion is clutter.

The point of this somewhat intricate discussion is to highlight the importance of alertness to the epistemological implications of policy discussions. Too often school leaders will resort to treating religion as problematic clutter and relegate it to the RE slot as the strategy for being inclusive. The RE teacher should certainly support sensitivity to diversity in whole school policy, but not at the expense of reinforcing the impression that 'it's religion that's the problem'. Rather we must continually remind our colleagues that everyone perceives life through a worldview, be that religious or non-religious. To attempt to overcome the challenge of diversity by simply removing the religious worldviews from the equation solves nothing. It merely masks the influence of one or more secular, and controversial, worldviews in the name of objectivity.

In relation to school worship I suggest this has one main implication for RE teachers. We should take an active interest in what happens in school worship and seek to ensure that a range of religious and non-religious worldviews are drawn upon in ways that respect the integrity of all involved. To be educational, school worship needs to make a contribution to helping pupils understand and participate in interpretation, the process of constructing meaning, as a defining human activity. We should resist the suggestion that this can be achieved by excluding religions.

Conclusion

Curiosity cupboard or kitchen? What is the position of RE in the curriculum? Is it the place where the bric-a-brac collected from the past and on exotic holidays is preserved for weekly viewing? Or is it at the hub of school life, leading thinking on what it means to learn?

As RE teachers, part of our professional role is to promote and defend our subject. We have a choice as to how we do that. We can be precious about our content and seek to build walls around our special place in the curriculum. If we do this, the danger is that we are reinforcing the perception that religion is irrelevant clutter. Or we can develop an outward looking subject that promotes hermeneutical learning throughout the school. It all depends on your epistemology.

Questions

What evidence is there for and against the suggestion that it is a significant threat to RE if religion is thought of as clutter in human knowledge?

To what degree is the skill of interpretation at the heart of RE?

What, if any, role should an RE teacher play in shaping the whole school culture in relation to attitudes to religion?

Further reading

Cooling, T. (2010) *Doing God in Education*, London: Theos. A short report written for policy makers arguing that religion ought to be taken seriously in public policy in education and not treated as irrelevant and unhelpful clutter.

Erricker, C. (2010) *Religious Education: A Conceptual and Interdisciplinary Approach for Secondary Level*, London: Routledge. A stimulating and provocative example of hermeneutical thinking about RE.

Grimmitt, M. (2000b) *Pedagogies of Religious Education: Case Studies in the Research and Development of Good Pedagogic Practice in Religious Education*, Great Wakering: McCrimmons. A classic of RE literature that advocates a constructivist pedagogy and reviews influential approaches to the subject.

Thiselton, A. (2009) *Hermeneutics: An Introduction*, Grand Rapids, MI: Eerdmans. An introduction from a leading theologian covering the fundamental characteristics of hermeneutical thinking.

Chapter 7

Faith schools

J. Mark Halstead

Few debates in education raise such strong feelings in Britain as faith schools. In a recent television documentary on More 4, Richard Dawkins lambasted faith schools as a 'menace', engaged in the 'wicked' practice of 'forcing religious beliefs on their pupils' (Leach 2010). Elsewhere he has described them as a location of 'real child abuse' (Dawkins 2002a: 9). Others have dismissed them as 'causing apartheid' (Toynbee 2001), 'brainwashing' children (Grayling 2007a) and 'helping to foster terrorists' (David Canter, quoted in MacLeod 2008). Despite such heated opposition the British government continues to invest in faith schools, apparently in the belief that they deliver what parents want: high levels of academic achievement, and coherent and effective moral guidance. Faith schools are generally popular with parents and many are oversubscribed. Public opinion polls confirm the strength of feeling about faith schools, but give mixed messages. In a *Guardian* poll in February 2009, 60 per cent of respondents agreed that 'children benefit from a faith-based education' and 69 per cent of those with school-age children supported 'a religious ethos at school' (Curtis 2009), but an earlier poll for the same newspaper found 64 per cent of respondents agreeing that 'the government should not be funding faith schools of any kind' (Taylor 2005).

Behind the strong passions and emotive language lie deep questions about the nature and purpose of education itself and about the principles on which basic educational decisions are made. Do faith schools indoctrinate children, undermine community cohesion and discourage personal autonomy, as their opponents claim? Or is it oppressive to deny parents the freedom to bring children up in line with their own beliefs and values? Is it in the best interests of children to attend a school whose values are broadly in line with those of the home, or to be set free from the constraints of their current cultural environment? Who makes the decisions anyway about the best interests of children – the government, the parents, the 'experts', the taxpayers or the children themselves – and on what basis?

The aim of this chapter is to explore some of the deeper issues that emerge in discussions and arguments about faith schools. It begins with a clarification of the concept of 'faith school' and the numbers of pupils attending such schools. The next section summarises the history of faith schooling in Britain, refers to current policies and recent legislation and makes brief international comparisons. The nature of the academic and political arguments about faith schools is then explored, and four different but intertwined debates are identified. Finally, the arguments and counter-arguments are examined directly: seven main arguments in support of faith schools are identified and evaluated, and seven main arguments against.

Definitions and demographics

The term 'faith school' has come into widespread use in Britain only recently, replacing the older term 'church schools' in recognition of the fact that schools belonging to world faiths such as Islam and Sikhism are now being accorded maintained status alongside the longer established Catholic, Protestant and Jewish schools. The term covers a wide diversity of provision. In particular, faith schools may differ in terms of

- their founding religious denomination or faith
- their underlying mission or philosophy
- the type of school (voluntary-aided, voluntary-controlled, special agreement, academies, foundation schools and a wide variety of private and independent schools)
- practical matters such as the admission of pupils and employment of teachers not belonging to the faith
- their compatibility with liberal democratic values
- the amount of time spent on religious education and the kind of religious education offered.

An important distinction can be made between 'old' and 'new' religious schools (Halstead 2002). 'Old' religious schools are generally large, well-established schools which are either members of the Independent Schools Council or voluntary aided, voluntary controlled or otherwise state funded; 'new' religious schools are generally much smaller, more recently founded private schools often with a much stronger religious vision. However, this distinction is becoming increasingly blurred as the first 'new' religious schools have obtained maintained status and the government has expressed its intention to encourage more independent faith schools to move into the maintained sector.

A more fruitful distinction is one between schools which see it as their mission to cater primarily for the children of a faith community, and those which seek to provide an education with a religious ethos and based on religious values for the benefit of the broader community. Catholic, Jewish, Muslim and Sikh schools exemplify the first category: although they are generally willing to accept children from other backgrounds, they are centrally concerned to nurture children from their own faith community. Church of England schools, on the other hand, exemplify the second category. In the words of the Church Schools Review Group (2001), they seek to 'nourish those of the faith; encourage those of other faiths; challenge those who have no faith'. Of course, the distinction is not clear-cut. There are some Catholic schools which welcome large numbers of pupils from other faiths, just as there are some Anglican schools where admissions policies are linked to church allegiance.

Nearly one-third of all publicly funded schools in England have a religious foundation and character. Of these, according to figures for 2009, 4,627 are Church of England (including the Church in Wales) (4,422 primary and 205 secondary), 2,019 are Catholic (1,685 primary and 334 secondary), 26 are Methodist, 38 are Jewish and a small number are other Christian or mixed denomination. There are a further 263 maintained faith schools in Wales and 395 in Scotland. In the last ten years, eleven Muslim schools, three Sikh, one Hindu, one Greek Orthodox and one Seventh Day Adventist have been granted public funding (Bolton and Gillie 2009). There are also community schools where as a matter of fact though not of policy the pupils are virtually exclusively from a single faith background (such as Belle Vue Girls' School in Bradford, which is 99 per cent Muslim). Outside the maintained sector, there are just over 950 religious independent schools (40 per cent of all independent schools); four-fifths of these are Christian and one-eighth Muslim. Significantly fewer than one per cent of all maintained faith schools in England are non-Christian, though such schools receive prominent attention in many of the debates about faith schools. Faith schools are more likely to be found in towns and cities than in rural locations, and there are substantial regional variations in numbers (without any consistent pattern emerging: see Bolton and Gillie 2009: 3–4).

In terms of student numbers, faith schools tend to be somewhat smaller than schools with no religious character, and about 24 per cent of all children in England attend maintained schools of a religious character. Of these 945,610 attend Church of England schools, 720,500 attend Catholic schools, 64,420 attend other Christian schools, 15,460 attend Jewish schools and 4,230 attend Muslim schools. The percentage of children attending faith schools in England is thus very similar to the percentage of people who attend church as least once a year (26 per cent according to Tearfund 2009), though the English Church Census found that only 6.3 per cent of the population of England attended church on census day (8 May 2005, see Evangelical Alliance online n.d.).

Background to faith schools

The current situation of faith schooling in England and Wales has more to do with historical compromise than with principled rational planning (Chadwick 1997). A 'dual system' of co-existing faith schools and non-faith schools (originally called 'board schools', later 'county schools' and later still 'community schools') has operated ever since the 1870 Education Act established universal schooling. The 1944 Education Act increased public funding for church schools, which were given the option of becoming 'voluntary controlled' (in which case all their costs would be met by the state but they would be under local education authority control) or 'voluntary aided' (in which case they would have to pay a fixed percentage – initially 50 per cent, but reduced to 15 per cent in 1975 – of building costs and external maintenance but would retain the right to appoint their own teachers, fix their own admissions policies, teach their own RE syllabus and hold acts of collective worship in accordance with their own traditions). Most Church of England schools chose the former option, while Catholic and Jewish schools chose the latter.

Since 1998 England has seen significant changes in policy towards faith schools in the maintained sector. Eighty-four new faith schools had been accepted for state funding by 2008, including non-Christian schools for the first time. In 2001 the government expressed its intention to allow voluntary and faith groups to sponsor new schools within the City Academy programme (DfES 2001). In 2007 the government allocated additional money to help private faith schools to move into the maintained sector, subject to certain conditions (for example, at least half the admissions to faith-sponsored Academies would have to come from other faiths or none: DCSF 2007a: 15, 18). The establishment of faith schools was made easier by a further reduction in the financial commitment of the sponsoring group to 10 per cent of the capital costs of the new school. A report produced by Lord Dearing for the Church of England in 2001 recommended the opening of a further 100 Church of England secondary schools (Church Schools Review Group 2001), though less than half of this number have been set up so far. The possibility of establishing a faith-based school serving different faiths has also been explored (Wittenberg 2002), though this has not yet come to fruition. It seems likely that the number of faith schools will continue to grow under David Cameron's government, particularly through the new legislation on Academies and 'Free Schools'. Currently, 1 per cent of faith schools have either Foundation or Academy status (Bolton and Gillie 2009).

In order to qualify for state funding, faith schools must teach the National Curriculum, employ qualified teachers and (according to the Education and Inspections Act 2006) actively promote community cohesion. In other respects, however, they are subject to different legal requirements than non-religious schools. In particular, they have exemption from some sections of the equality law banning discrimination on the grounds of religion: they are still allowed to take an individual's faith and ability to support the school's religious ethos into consideration when appointing teaching or other staff, and while many faith schools do not refuse entry to pupils from other faiths or none, they can still (under the Equality Act 2006) apply religious criteria in the selection of pupils if the school is oversubscribed.

The nature of the relationship between religious faith and public schooling is a matter of debate in many parts of the world, involving questions of freedom of choice, curriculum content and the control of the educational system, and is capable of being resolved in a number of different ways (Tulasiewicz and To

1993). In many Muslim and some Catholic countries, the faith of the majority is taught to all children in public schools as a regular part of the curriculum: all schools are effectively religious schools. At the other extreme, countries such as the United States and France observe a strict separation between religion and state-funded schooling, and see education in any faith as a matter for the religious community rather than the state. In between, there are countries like Denmark, where secular schools, religious schools and those based on any other distinctive shared conviction have an equal right to state funding.

History of the debate

The debate about faith schools is one that surfaces from time to time in British society, as it did after publication of the *Swann Report* (DfES 1985; see Halstead 1986; CRE 1990; Honeyford 1992), but it has been going almost constantly since the planned expansion in the number of faith schools in 2001. This year coincided with serious disturbances outside Holy Cross School in Belfast, race riots in several cities in the North of England and the 9/11 attacks in America, and many people began to question the wisdom of allowing faith groups an increased role in any public institutions, let alone educational provision. Official reports into the north of England riots drew attention to the segregated lives of many ethnic minority groups, and expressed the fear that increasing the number of faith schools would exacerbate this trend (Cantle 2001; Ouseley 2001). Their findings were picked up by the opponents of faith schools who argued that faith schooling is socially divisive and against the best interests of children (Humanist Philosophers' Group 2001). Claims that creationism was being taught in science lessons at Emmanuel College, a Christian City Technical College in Gateshead, as well as in some Muslim schools, provided further occasion for Dawkins and others to pour scorn on faith schools (Dawkins 2002b).

A number of academic publications have made further contributions to the debate since 2001, some historical (Chadwick 2001; Kay 2002), some policy-oriented (Walford 2000; Halstead 2002), some in support of faith schools (Chesters 2001; Short 2003; Wright 2003), and some opposing the expansion of faith schooling (Harris 2002; Humanist Philosophers' Group 2001) or at least the provision of public funding to faith schools (Underkuffler 2001).

There are in fact a number of different intertwined debates about faith schools and it is important to try to disentangle these in order to avoid confusion and arguing at cross-purposes. First, there is the debate between those who think that religion and education should be kept separate since the process of religious nurture and the process of education are conceptually different, and those who claim that religion is an overarching concept that affects every aspect of life. Second, there is the debate between those who claim pragmatically that since faith schools provide a high quality education in a caring atmosphere the number of faith schools should be increased in line with demand, and those who claim that however popular faith schools are they should not be permitted *in principle*, either because they privilege certain sectors of society over others or because – to put it bluntly – they teach things that are not true (or not demonstrably so). Third, there is a debate between those who would like to extend the right to establish faith schools to all minority faiths in the country, and those who believe the social costs of so doing (in terms of the non-integration of minorities) would be too high. Finally, there is the debate about public funding: some claim that refusing to fund faith schools would be unjust, while others claim that although parents have the right to educate their children in whatever religious schools they choose, they do not have the right to expect public funding for their choice. These different debates often draw on related arguments, and so the next section reviews in turn each of the main arguments that have been put forward both for and against the establishment of state-funded faith schooling.

The main arguments

Arguments for faith schools

There are seven main arguments in favour of faith schools:

1   Minorities have the right to maintain their cultures, beliefs, practices and ways of life and avoid cultural absorption by the majority, and faith schools play an important part in this process. By establishing schools with a distinctive religious ethos or value system, religious groups are able to preserve their faith by transmitting it to the next generation and ensuring that children from their own communities develop an enriched understanding of the place of religion in their lives. Opponents of faith schools respond to this argument by claiming that it is not the role of a publicly funded school to preserve religious faith. On this view, the task of cultural maintenance and transmission belongs to the home, not the school, since the latter should extend rather than narrow children's horizons and should teach values shared by all citizens.

2   The right of parents to choose a form of schooling that is in line with their own beliefs is enshrined in Article 2 of Protocol 1 of the European Convention on Human Rights. Faith schools allow religious believers from different faiths the freedom to choose a school whose values are broadly consistent with those of the home. Opponents would argue, however, that parental rights are constrained by the right of children to an open education which leaves them free to make their own choices in life and liberates them from the cultural constraints of the home environment.

3   Faith schools offer students from different religious backgrounds the freedom to develop their own identity and self-esteem in a supportive environment, free from racism, discrimination and expectations of cultural conformity. They remove some of the barriers to faith that are often found in the common school, such as the promotion of relativism, neutrality and secular values.

They provide cultural stability, continuity and security for children from faith backgrounds, in a way that common schools, even if they make strenuous efforts to avoid exerting de facto secularist influence, cannot do. By helping students to develop a strong self-concept and a positive faith identity for themselves, such schools also help them to develop tolerance and respect for others and play a worthwhile role in the broader multicultural society. As well as giving opportunities for children from religious families to explore and reflect on their own beliefs and those of others (because they take faith itself seriously), faith schools also offer their students a sense of belonging and common purpose. Opponents argue that schools must develop children's critical faculties as well, and make it easier for them to leave cultural or religious environments that they find claustrophobic.

4   A plural society requires recognition of group rights and a plurality of structures. Faith schools represent a symbolic step towards a fairer and more inclusive society and are an embodiment of the values of tolerance, respect for diversity and mutual understanding that liberal societies claim to value. Treating children equally does not require that all children are educated in an identical fashion, because the uniform provision for all children that is embedded in the common school system can be oppressive for those children whose values and way of life are different from those of the majority. A diversity of educational provision is thus essential to a successful multicultural society. Negative attitudes are more likely to develop among minorities where there is a perception that they are not being treated equally either in community schools or in relation to requests for their own schools. Opponents may respond by claiming that respect for diversity is best learned by being educated alongside others from different backgrounds in a context where all faiths are studied in an open and neutral way.

5   Faith schools have a coherent framework of moral values grounded on their own religious teaching, and this helps to create an ethos in which children develop good behaviour, positive attitudes and a clear understanding of right and wrong. Faith schools also often have a reputation for encouraging a spirit of caring and service, as well as personal responsibility and self-discipline, and they can thus make a positive contribution to life in the broader society. Opponents respond that moral values have no necessary connection with religious beliefs, and in any case a school's ethos depends more on the quality and vision of leadership than on the school's religious affiliation.

6   Faith schools on average have higher academic standards and get better results than non-religious schools. They usually top the school league tables, and in 2008, for example, 71.3 per cent of students at faith schools got five or more good GCSEs, compared to 65.6 per cent of students at non-religious schools. Many reasons may be put forward for this success rate. It is claimed that faith schools provide an environment with positive role models in which students can become well motivated and overcome low aspirations. Students may see it as their religious duty to work hard and to support fellow students

who find the work difficult. Critics respond that the differential levels of achievement can be explained entirely by the background of the children, parental self-selection and the schools' own selection methods: faith schools have a significantly lower proportion of pupils receiving free school meals, fewer pupils who do not speak English as their first language, and a significantly lower percentage of pupils with Special Educational Needs (Bolton and Gillie 2009). This clearly does not apply to the 'new' faith schools, however, which tend to serve inner-city communities, to have higher rates of free school meals and to be comparatively poorly resourced. Nevertheless, Muslim schools have topped the Contextualised Value-Added league tables in recent years, and girls educated in Muslim schools are twice as likely as those educated in community schools to go on to higher education (Marley 2008).

7   Faith schools provide an environment where the spiritual side of life is valued and taken seriously, so that children have more chance of developing this side of their personality. This may include a fuller appreciation of the links between religion and other areas of human achievement, including art, music and literature. Opponents may respond that faith schools are less likely than non-religious schools to help their students to appreciate links between the arts and faiths other than their own, and in any case their approach to the spiritual dimension is not open to a diversity of understandings.

Arguments against faith schools

There are seven main arguments against faith schools:

1   Faith schools make it more difficult for children to grow into autonomous adults (a central aim of liberal education) because they do not encourage children to think for themselves in an open way. Dawkins says that they treat children as though they are already believers, which implies that children are no longer free to make up their own minds about religion (2008: 25 and 379–383). Faith schools fail to respect children's right to an open future and they do not adequately respect the children's rights such as the right to have their horizons extended beyond their present, particular circumstances and to escape from the community into which they were born. In response, supporters of faith schools argue that the development of a cultural or religious identity through faith schooling can be a stage on the way to personal autonomy (McLaughlin 2008: 189–193), and that children benefit from the security and stability of a clear framework of belief and guidance until they have the necessary knowledge and maturity of judgement to step out on their own.

2   Faith schools indoctrinate children, either explicitly or implicitly, and are therefore using anti-educational methods to develop faith. It is not the role of the publicly funded school to advocate any particular religious position or

seek to instil unprovable knowledge such as religious beliefs in children. In response it is claimed that no schooling can operate in a cultural vacuum, and that the aim of faith schools is not to indoctrinate children or imprison them within a particular faith or culture, but to provide them with a rounded education that includes a fuller understanding of the beliefs and values that their parents and faith community take seriously.

3   Faith schools may encourage children to develop certain fundamentalist or extremist views that are not shared by the broader society and that may potentially be harmful. This applies particularly to 'new' faith schools, which have been accused of encouraging extremist attitudes that endanger civil liberty and security; of supporting beliefs that undermine the democratic values of the broader society, such as the unacceptability of homosexuality; and of teaching beliefs that lack scientific credibility, such as creationism. However, faith schools deny any link to political extremism or civil unrest and any teaching of inappropriate content, though they may claim the right to teach creationism as an alternative religious perspective on the origins of life and to teach their traditional beliefs about sexuality to children so long as they make it clear that not everyone agrees with them and the civil rights of those with different beliefs and practices (including homosexuals) are respected.

4   Faith schools are divisive in two distinct ways. 'Old' faith schools privilege white middle-class parents who may choose such schools for non-religious reasons; the divisiveness here is to do with social class, though it may have ethnocentric undertones. 'New' faith schools, especially Muslim schools, encourage a kind of educational 'apartheid' by exacerbating existing community segregation and encapsulating their pupils in particular neighbourhoods and particular cultural traditions rather than preparing them for life in the broader multicultural society. In response, supporters of faith schools argue that all schools allow admission to children from outside the faith, though if they are oversubscribed they may give priority to children from within the faith. This may be an argument for increasing the number of faith schools to a level where the demand is fully satisfied, so that those from other faith backgrounds or none are never turned away if they apply to a faith school.

5   Faith schools do not do as much as the common school to encourage civic virtues or community cohesion, because they prevent different groups from having much contact with each other. On this view educating children together is the best way of promoting mutual understanding and tolerance. However, a recent study has shown that faith schools tend to be rated higher on community cohesion than other schools by Ofsted inspectors (Harrison 2009). In any case, the 'contact hypothesis' masks a number of theoretical and practical difficulties, not least the problem of desegregating schools when there is continuing residential segregation in local communities and when racism and Islamophobia are still rife.

6   Faith schools use covert selection practices that may lead to social segregation or privilege certain sections of the population. However, supporters will argue that equity, not social privilege, is at the heart of the mission of faith schools, and that the principle of equity is best served by funding a range of different schools to meet a range of different needs and backgrounds. In any case, the government is taking substantial steps to ensure that covert selection is not practised (Bolton and Gillie 2009: 11–25), and many faith schools – both Christian and Muslim – in fact serve the most deprived inner-city communities.

7   The public funding of faith schools is an unjustifiable violation of conscience for taxpayers who are non-believers. Supporters of faith schools, however, point out the inconsistency of this frequently repeated argument, which can be taken either as a case of special pleading for atheists or as a principled claim that allows all taxpayers the right to say what kind of schools they want their taxes to be spent on. In the former case, the offence to atheists must be balanced by the violation of conscience felt by believers when *their* taxes are spent on schools promoting a secular framework of values. In the latter case, the fact that many faith schools are oversubscribed suggests that if taxpayers were free to specify what type of schools their taxes were spent on, the number of faith schools would go up.

Conclusion

If the central question about faith schools is whether parents who wish to do so should continue to be free to send their children to state-funded faith schools, then a dispassionate review of the arguments and counter-arguments set out above probably leads to the conclusion that there are not good enough reasons to deny them this freedom. However, the arguments themselves may not be the deciding factor. Some people may find religious schools unacceptable simply because they find religion unacceptable. People approach the debate with preconceived sets of beliefs, values and commitments, and those who prioritise social integration over cultural preservation, or political over religious identity, or education in civic virtue over spiritual and moral development, will be unlikely to favour faith schools. However, different people have different views about the relationship between religion and education, and their needs can be best met through a range of options that includes faith schools. This does not imply, however, that there is no room for improvement in the vision and provision of faith schools. The recommendations in a recent Runnymede Trust report may suggest a sensible way forward: they re-emphasise the need for faith schools to serve the most disadvantaged, to value all young people and to allow a greater say to children themselves in how they are educated (Berkeley 2008).

Questions

Is the promotion of a set of religious beliefs in faith schools compatible with the principles of liberal education, particularly the development of personal autonomy?

Should public funds be used to support and expand faith schools if parents want these?

What are the strengths and weaknesses in the provision of any one faith school with which you are familiar, and what factors might influence parents who do not share its underlying beliefs to send their children there?

Further reading

Gardner, R., Cairns, J. and Lawton, D. (eds) (2005) *Faith Schools: Consensus or Conflict?* Abingdon: RoutledgeFalmer. A detailed analysis of the current British and international situation, and a balanced, generally sympathetic evaluation of key issues.

Haydon, G. (ed.) (2009) *Faith in Education*, London: University of London Institute of Education. Philosophical perspectives on religious upbringing, autonomy and the place of faith schools in a liberal society.

McKinney, S. J. (2010b) *Faith Schools in the Twenty-first Century*, Edinburgh: Dunedin Academic Press. An examination of the future of faith schooling and particularly Catholic schooling in the light of current British, American and Australian thinking.

Parker-Jenkins, M., Hartas, D. and Irving, B. A. (2005) *In Good Faith: Schools, Religion and Public Funding*, Aldershot: Ashgate. A combination of empirical evidence and discussion of broader themes including race, gender, community and human rights.

The National Secular Society's website *Learning Together* (http://www.angelfire. com/nb/lt) provides detailed background information and resources for the campaign against faith-based schools.

Chapter 8

Citizenship and human rights

Mark A. Pike

> We hold these truths to be self evident, that all men are created equal, that they are endowed by their Creator with certain inalienable Rights, that among these are Life, Liberty and the pursuit of Happiness.
>
> (*The Unanimous Declaration of the Thirteen United States of America*, 1776)

> Render unto Caesar the things which are Caesar's; and unto God the things that are God's.
>
> (*The Bible*, Matthew 22: 21)

> Democracy is more than a form of government; it is primarily a mode of associated living.
>
> (Dewey 1966: 101)

Citizenship and religious education

What has religious education (RE) got to do with rights and citizenship? The short answer, with regard to schooling, is that both RE and citizenship education in the UK aim to promote understanding and tolerance of religious and cultural difference and diversity (although there are competing interpretations of 'tolerance' which are addressed later in this chapter). Children and young people need to have a good understanding of religious beliefs and practices not only to be informed citizens but also to be active and respectful citizens. Clearly, 'religious education should make a vital and distinctive contribution to education for citizenship' (Jackson 2002: 162) as it can enable young citizens to recognise 'the complex interrelationships between faith, religious identity, ethnicity and citizenship' (Baumfield 2002a: 82). It has even been suggested that if 'Citizenship' is the 'new RE' it is distinctly 'confessional' as it seeks to nurture children in a particular belief system and way of life. Arguably, citizenship education teaches people to 'believe in' and to subscribe to the values of a liberal democracy. Citizenship education in England does not simply entail learning *about* citizenship; it is *for* active citizenship as it aims to produce citizens who have specific beliefs and commitments (Pike 2008).

The mandatory citizenship curriculum in England does not only aim to teach skills and convey civic information, it is designed to influence young citizens' values and actions. The 'idea of citizenship-as-outcome reveals a strong instrumental orientation in the idea of citizenship education' (Biesta and Lawy 2006: 72) and this can be appreciated when the nature of the change to be achieved in young citizens is understood. The 'transformative' aims of the citizenship curriculum are, in McLaughlin's (2000) terms, 'maximal' not 'minimal'. Children and young people are not only to be taught *about* liberal democracy but are, in a very real sense, taught to 'believe in' such a way of living and the curriculum can be seen as a means to this end. This should not surprise us for in *Education and Democracy*, John Dewey observed that 'democracy is more than a form of government; it is primarily a mode of associated living' (Dewey 1966: 101).

In this chapter it will be argued that citizenship and RE should foster reflection upon the beliefs and assumptions that underpin our particular 'mode of associated living' and should enable learners to explore different interpretations rather than legitimating an uncritical allegiance to secular, liberal, democratic values (Pike 2008).

In liberal democracies the freedom exists to 'read' beliefs and practices in different ways and this is what makes the combination of RE and citizenship so fascinating and so important. An example of two contrasting 'readings' of a religious practice are those of President Sarkozy of France and President Obama of the USA when each addressed the issue of some Muslim women wearing the burqa and hijab in public. Last year President Sarkozy stated, 'We cannot accept to have in our country women who are prisoners behind netting, cut off from all social life, deprived of identity' and explained, 'That is not the idea that the French republic has of women's dignity. The burka is not a sign of religion, it is a sign of subservience. It will not be welcome on the territory of the French republic' (BBC 2009). President Obama, on the other hand, stated that 'freedom in America is indivisible from the freedom to practice one's religion' and explained, 'That is why there is a mosque in every state of our union, and over 1,200 mosques within our borders. That is why the U.S. government has gone to court to protect the right of women and girls to wear the hijab, and to punish those who would deny it' (*New York Times* 2009). The burqa can be interpreted as a symbol of the repression of women or of the freedom to practise one's religion and citizens will often disagree on such matters. Clearly, different 'religious and secular traditions offer contested accounts of the good life' and it has been argued that the unity of RE lies in its search for 'an understanding of ultimate reality' (Hella and Wright 2009: 58). Citizenship, which addresses how such issues are played out in public, should be an integral part of such a search.

Liberal values underpin citizenship education in England (Pike 2007) and although the conventional wisdom is that 'no one conception of the good life is favoured in liberalism, and a vast range of lifestyles, commitments, priorities, occupational roles and life-plans form a marketplace of ideas within the liberal society' (Halstead and Pike 2006: x), liberalism is often much less accommodating to those who do not fully subscribe to liberal values. Approving of a 'vast range of lifestyles' rather than advocating a particular way of life is a specific vision not a neutral one. Indeed 'the claim to be culturally neutral or to be a meeting ground for all cultures, which is sometimes made on behalf of liberalism, is itself a cultural stance' (Halstead 1995: 268). Yet, if schools 'promote the adoption of secular core values on the basis that they constitute a common denominator, to which religious and secular people alike can subscribe' but fail to grasp that if values are limited to the secular 'they are in practice anti-religious since they leave religion out' (Copley 2005: 109–110) this may well result in tolerance of secular perspectives but intolerance of religious perspectives (Pike 2009).

Tensions necessarily arise when it is asserted that freedom can be experienced by a society, 'only when a nation state is unified around a set of democratic values' (Banks *et al.* 2005: 7). Citizenship education in the secular state schools of liberal democracies often views the beliefs of those who do not share its values 'through the lens of an illicitly comprehensive liberalism' (McLaughlin 1995: 251) and some may see citizenship education as the 'neo-colonial imposition of majority liberal values on minority non-liberal religious communities' (Wright 2003: 142). Of course, as Rawls points out, the

> danger of disintegration in societies that can no longer be forced into unity around a shared religious faith has haunted the liberal tradition since its inception, and comprehensive liberalism may be thought to exacerbate the danger by attempting to ground legitimacy in a divisive secular analogue to religious faith.
>
> (Rawls 1993: 37–38)

RE and Citizenship lessons should not just help young people to consider how religious practices are viewed but should encourage them to look at different religious responses to *liberal and secular values*. To fail do so would be tantamount to RE ignoring the dominant state-sponsored 'religion'.

Reading liberal values in citizenship and religious education

If 'liberal values permeate the curriculum of the common school generally, and the subject of citizenship in particular' (Halstead and Pike 2006: 23) then students need to be able to critically evaluate these values. After all, to seek to educate a child without disclosing the values upon which his or her education is based is to behave as if he or she was a 'subject' rather than a 'citizen' (Pike 2007). Core liberal values are generally considered to be liberty, equality and rationality but these are not interpreted in the same way by everyone and are sometimes regarded quite differently by citizens of faith to their secular compatriots. In a secular age, faith is increasingly put in human rights legislation to protect our freedom and yet even the notion of 'rights' is variously interpreted. Core liberal values will be considered here in relation to education and schooling, before turning briefly to the notion of rights.

Liberty in education and schooling

It was not so much *freedom from* religion but *freedom to* practise religion (which generally meant one's specific version of Christianity at the time) that led to *The Unanimous Declaration of the Thirteen United States of America* in 1776. The American Revolution was largely fought by Protestant settlers and, significantly, *freedom from* religion versus *freedom to* hold religious views is at the centre of the new tolerance debate. We are currently seeing 'the emergence of an increasingly powerful form of secularism that is not only intolerant of religion but also of its embodiment in particular ways of life' (Almond 2010: 139). Almond asks two important questions: 'How is it that the generalized principle of toleration of diversity (non-discrimination) can result in criminalizing religious and moral objections to a practice?' and 'How can this have happened in countries like Britain and the USA in which tolerance and liberty, especially freedom of religion and freedom of thought and of speech, are amongst their highest political ideals?' (ibid.: 139). Religious views of homosexual practice are a case in point: many Jews, Muslims and Christians sincerely believe that such practice is sinful on the basis of their readings of sacred texts which they believe to be authoritative for living. Such religious believers should not be persecuted or considered bigoted or intolerant; the tolerance and respect they exercise is rooted in profound disagreement. According to Almond, the new code of conduct for teachers (GTC 2009) 'poses a challenge for any teachers who have a principled objection to homosexuality as a practice' and suggests that for Christian teachers in particular, 'this could have the effect of forcing them to choose between their profession and their conscience' (Almond 2010: 138).

In a liberal society individual liberty is generally regarded as entailing the freedom to pursue *one's own* interests and desires. Yet for many committed religious believers this may not be considered to be freedom at all but the very opposite. Indeed, the pursuit of one's own desires might be regarded as evidence of a lack of *freedom from* such desires and as bondage or enslavement to a sinful nature. For many Christians, for instance, genuine freedom can only be found in exercising the choice to follow God's ways as communicated in Scripture. In Islam, according to Halstead, 'personal and moral autonomy ... is a kind of nonsense' (Halstead 2007: 289); the word 'Islam' means 'submission' and no body of work exists that is 'comparable to that of Bentham, Mill, Kant or Rawls in the West in the sense of seeking to provide a framework for moral decision-making without any necessary link to religion' (Halstead 2007: 284).

For John Stuart Mill (1909) in *On Liberty*, 'He who does anything because it is the custom makes no choice' (see Callini 1995: 59) and for Joseph Raz, autonomy entails 'choosing between goods' which is of value to people living in the kinds of society 'whose social forms are such that they are based on individual choice' (Mulhall and Swift 1996: 325–326). Yet in a pervasively secular society we need to consider the freedom some children and young people actually have to learn from religion or to choose commitment to a particular religion. The freedom they have to lead a religious life rather than a secular one may be significantly curtailed if 'religious adherence is one of the most "uncool" social activities one could imagine, especially for the young' (Copley 2005: xiii). Indeed, then one might argue that young people were well on the way to being indoctrinated *against* religion and the possibility of aggressive secular indoctrination needs to be taken seriously.

We should consider children 'raised by atheists, in a neighborhood in which few people openly discuss what religious commitments they have, and in a public culture which privatizes religious commitments and practices' and ask 'how are they going to learn about spiritual life in a way that is sufficiently meaningful that embracing it autonomously could be a real possibility for them?' (Brighouse 2008: 22). Schools with a pervasive secular ethos, that 'maintain a deafening silence about spiritual or anti-materialist values' (Brighouse 2005: 85), are not a neutral alternative to many faith schools; neither may they be best placed to foster students' autonomy. Religious beliefs *or* secular liberal beliefs that limit the exercise of choice militate against freedom. According to Mill, 'a general State education is a mere contrivance for moulding people to be exactly like one another: and as the mould in which it casts them is that which pleases the predominant power in the government … it establishes a despotism over the mind' (Mill 1962: 239). Such a state education is likely to be a powerful secularising force in the UK and if secularisation in our culture stops many young people taking religious truth claims seriously there are important implications for RE. If only 'economic independence allows an education not controlled by Government' and yet 'equality' is only gained when 'the State is everyone's schoolmaster and employer' (Lewis 1996: 180) we will not be free at all. When the State claims to know best and terrorist and economic threats mean greater control is exerted over our lives, we might well ask: 'Are not these the ideal opportunity for enslavement?' (Lewis 1996: 181).

Equality in education and schooling

Equality also tends to be viewed in different ways by 'believers' and 'non-believers'. Certainly many religious parents do 'not want parity of treatment with other groups but the freedom to bring up their own children in line with their own religious commitments' (Halstead 1995: 264). If the recommendations of Badman's (2009) *Review of Elective Home Education* (EHE) had been implemented (Clause 26 of the recent Children, Schools and Families Bill), this would have fundamentally shifted the primary responsibility for the education of children from parents to the state and would have been regarded by many, quite rightly, as a gross intrusion of the state into family life. In the UK, parents currently have the primary responsibility for their child's education and can choose to provide this at school 'or otherwise' so long as this is 'suitable' and 'efficient' (Section 7, Education Act 1996). It is important to note that a 'suitable' education is one which equips a child 'for life within the community' of which he or she is a member and not necessarily for 'the way of life in the country as a whole' providing the child's freedom to 'adopt some other form of life' is not infringed (Section 7, Education Act 1996). This last condition is crucial, however, for we need to ensure that children are protected and that they are supported in their growth towards normal rational autonomy.

The sensitivities surrounding Elective Home Education (EHE) highlight the ways in which the competing rights of children, parents and state are balanced in a liberal democracy. Children's rights to be safe and to receive an education are to be balanced with the religious rights of parents and families and the need to foster community cohesion. The Human Rights Act 1998, which gives effect to the European Convention on Human Rights (ECHR), provides that 'the State shall respect the right of parents to ensure such education and teaching is in conformity with their own religious and philosophical convictions' (UK Parliament 1998 Schedule 1 Part 2 Article 2 Protocol 1) and we need to consider whether the current form of schooling in general, and RE in particular, does this. The Universal Declaration of Human Rights (United Nations 1948) allows parents 'the right to choose the kind of education that shall be given to their children' (Article 26/3) and we must be wary of

> claiming for the state a right to replace parental values, which may favour traditional family life, with an approach to children's moral education that is directed by its own experts and ethical advisors and based on quite contrary ethical assumptions.
>
> (Almond 2010: 139)

Schools with a comprehensively liberal ethos are not a neutral alternative to schools with a distinctly religious one. In a sense, all schools are 'faith' schools because schooling necessarily teaches children to 'believe in' something and cannot be value-neutral (Pike 2007). Indeed, all teachers and parents might be considered 'indoctrinators' because they lead children into certain doctrines or truths. We would quite rightly expect children to be indoctrinated in 'tolerance' but if children are taught that they must *approve* of conduct with which they disapprove, we must use the term 'indoctrination' in its common, pejorative sense rather than in any literal sense. The freedom to engage in dialogue concerning the customary beliefs and practices of one's group, whether secular or religious, is a hallmark of life in a liberal democracy. I would argue that if any parental organisation, claiming adherence to any faith, wished to run a school (I am writing at the time of the launch of 'free schools' by Michael Gove, the Schools Secretary) we would need to know whether the freedom of students in matters of faith would be respected. We would also need to know whether students were encouraged to make ethical choices and the extent to which they would be encouraged to choose to respect those with whom they disagree.

Legal equality is necessary to protect the most vulnerable from exploitation and it was the Protestant belief in the 'priesthood of all believers', asserted at Reformation, which emphasised the equality before God of ordinary people. This can, however, be traced even further to the Judeo-Christian teaching that human beings are 'made in the image of God' (Genesis 1: 26) and, therefore, 'that every person has intrinsic dignity and value' (Lickona 2004: 140). In a liberal democracy, the professor of politics is not awarded more votes than the cleaner of her office on the basis of superior knowledge and this might be regarded as being largely due to the influence of the Judeo-Christian belief in equality in the sight of God. Yet, as we have seen, equality does not mean that everyone is the same or has the same needs, wishes, priorities and values in life. It has been plausibly suggested that:

> The demand for equality has two sources; one of them is among the noblest, the other is the basest, of human emotions. The noble source is the desire for fair play. But the other source is the hatred of superiority.
>
> (Lewis 1996: 40)

Appreciating difference and diversity is better for democracy than promoting a 'democratic education' where egalitarianism ensures that no one is any 'better' at anything than anyone else.

Autonomous rationality in education and schooling

The twin values of 'liberty' and 'equality' need to be mediated and this mediation is generally provided in our society by recourse to the third core liberal value of 'rationality'. In a secular liberal democracy, decisions tend to be made on the basis of rational justification and while this seems entirely reasonable to most secular people the *exclusive* reliance upon this approach may well be contested by religious people for whom many decisions should not be made only on the basis of reason. The view of individual autonomy as a primary right above those of parents or community is a presupposition derived from a liberal perspective. Unsurprisingly, the 'liberal state based on propositions about the desirability of individual autonomy is bound to be committed to educational programmes which are incompatible with the beliefs and values of parents from non-liberal religious and cultural minorities' (Burtonwood 2000: 269). Many religious believers would object to the view that a person 'ought to act autonomously when it is *reasonable* to act autonomously' simply on the basis that 'what *reason* demands on any given occasion will vary between persons depending on their circumstances, spheres of expertise and organisational roles' (Hand 2006: 538, my italic). Autonomy has been challenged as an educational aim not least by those who advocate teaching for commitment and the importance of Christian nurture in children's lives

(Thiessen 1993). Certainly many parents appreciate that it is not always in their children's best interests to exercise autonomy all the time.

Even adults do not exercise autonomy in every situation they encounter in life and many parents consider it to be important for their children to accept guidance as well as to be able to make their own decisions. Many believers make decisions in the light of readings of sacred texts which are regarded as authoritative for living. This is not to suggest that religious people are irrational but simply to draw attention to the incompatibility between religion and narrow definitions of autonomous rationality. To see reason and revelation as incompatible has been comprehensively challenged by authors such as Sampson (2000) and we are more aware now than ever that living by reason alone is inadequate given the nature of our lives. Even though rationality involves the giving of reasons for beliefs held, any assessment of whether a reason is good or not is made by people who hold beliefs and have presuppositions. The Western, secular, liberal tradition of education is prone to overemphasise the rational and often forgets that commitments are held by individuals who are not entirely rational and emotionless any more than they are completely solitary and autonomous. A more holistic approach acknowledges that 'our rational nature is intimately bound up with the emotional, physical, moral and spiritual dimensions of our being' (Thiessen 2001: 139).

Rights, citizenship and religious education

There appears to be a 'growing consensus internationally that human rights principles underpin education for citizenship in multicultural democracies' (Osler and Starkey 2005: 6) but the result of this is that tensions between worldviews can all too often remain unacknowledged. Although there are 'supposedly universal human rights, defined by the international community as accepted by all' there is unmistakably 'a tension between cultural and religious tradition on the one hand and universal notions of rights' (Gearon and Brown 2003: 205) on the other. For instance, many Christians believe that citizenship 'does not begin with inalienable rights but begins with lives of service' (van Geest 2004: 118) and we should remember that the Good Samaritan was not obliged to behave as he did.

When the 'ethic of contract becomes more and more the pervasive ethic of society' (Wolterstorff et al. 1994: 91) our human capacity to choose to volunteer may be diminished. Certainly, 'dignity does not depend solely on individual rights' (Burtonwood 2000: 281, my italic) and the emphasis upon children's rights can even destroy dignity and militate against proper reverence and respect being shown towards responsible parents and authority figures at home and at school. The culture of children and young people asserting their rights can be a legitimate 'area of anxiety for teachers' (Hudson 2005: 128) and for many parents. Indeed, 'Every intrusion of the spirit that says "I'm as good as you" into our personal and spiritual life is to be resisted just as jealously as every intrusion of bureaucracy or privilege into our politics' (Lewis 1996: 31). Children and young people face life from a position of dangerous inexperience and need to be able to heed good advice. Ensuring young people assert their rights to 'equality', which they believe ensures their freedom, while at the same time increasing regulation and control in schools, ensures less freedom is enjoyed. It was suggested at the beginning of this chapter that citizenship has a strong instrumental orientation and seeks to change children and young people; the same point can be made about human rights. Arguably, the modern state 'exists not to protect our rights but to do us good or make us good – anyway, to do something to us or to make us something' (ibid.: 179). We need to consider whether the current emphasis upon 'rights' is protecting or manipulating us. In a society where human relations are increasingly regulated, autonomy necessarily diminishes. Paradoxically, insisting upon our 'rights' can result in our enslavement both spiritually and materially.

Conclusions

Just as notions of 'equality' or 'rights' have been secularised, so too has the concept of 'citizenship' itself. Stories of profound religious significance are all too often secularised (Copley 2001; Pike 2006) and the story of citizenship is no exception and has become inaccurately secular. In the UK, the 'historiography of Citizenship often neglects to provide a detailed analysis of Christian conceptions of Citizenship' which are 'frequently treated as archaic precursors to the "real" secular version' (Freathy 2004: 2). Children and young people should certainly be helped to understand that 'for a considerable proportion of English history and for a considerable proportion of the population, consideration of social and moral responsibilities and community involvement would have been inconceivable without reference to Christian beliefs and ethics' (ibid.: 21) and before the Second World War there was a 'common belief that British citizenship was aligned to membership of the Christian faith' (Thompson 2003: 171.)

Young people need to be well informed about the place of religion in the past in order to understand the foundations and development of liberal democracies and they need to understand complex religious issues in the present if they are to be young citizens who participate wisely and well. The influence of Christianity on liberalism is well documented and it has been plausibly suggested that the concept of democracy is 'fed from two sources' in the Christian faith: 'first, the dignity of man, as possessor of freedom and reason; and second, his propensity for evil, as inheritor of original sin'; the first 'makes democratic government possible' and the second 'prompts arrogance and conceit, thereby making it a necessary source of restraint' (Haldane 1986: 176). Indeed the sort of 'critical openness which flows from Christian faith has many links with the secular educational ideal of autonomy' (Hull 1984: 220). Christianity is important to citizenship education because 'notions of freedom, moral equality and social responsibility which feed into Law and Government through concepts of Justice and Democracy, themselves derive both meaning and justification from Christian doctrines' (Haldane 1986: 176).

It is all too easy for secular educators to forget the contribution faith can make to citizenship. A way forward may be to view citizenship education in common schools as 'an opportunity for young citizens to reflect on issues, on their own beliefs and values and on the society in which they wish to live' (Halstead and Pike 2006). One of the most quoted religious texts regarding citizenship is: 'Render therefore unto Caesar the things which are Caesar's; and unto God the things that are God's' (Matthew 22: 21) and this is often read as an endorsement of the separation of state and religious belief. Yet a different interpretation may be suggested: that bringing moral and religious conviction to readings of the state's values can render vital service to Caesar (Pike 2009). Young citizens may engage in reflection upon their citizenship from a committed and faith-based perspective or from a liberal and secular one. Such an approach respects young citizens and may help them to respect their own inheritance as well as the beliefs of those who do not share their faith. The exchange of their interpretations could prove liberating and Citizenship and RE lessons can provide an excellent context for such liberation.

Questions

Why is tolerance not the same as agreement and how can RE foster tolerance of legitimate religious perspectives on controversial issues in civic life?

How might some religious and secular citizens interpret 'freedom', 'equality', 'reason' and 'rights' differently?

How do you see the relation between citizenship and Christianity in the UK and why is it important for young citizens to learn from Christianity in RE and Citizenship?

Further reading

Almond, B. (2010) 'Education for tolerance: cultural difference and family values', *Journal of Moral Education* 39: 131–143. Very important article that explains the new tolerance debate and shows how the notion of 'toleration as celebration' is not only wrongheaded but also dangerous. This is essential reading for all religious educators.

Halstead, J. M. and Pike, M. A. (2006) *Citizenship and Moral Education – Values in Action*, London: Routledge. The first part of the book lays the philosophical foundations which are subsequently exemplified by practical lessons across the curriculum. Chapter 7 is on RE.

Lewis, C. S. (1996) 'Equality', 'Democratic education', and 'Willing slaves of the welfare state', in *Compelling Reason – Essays on Ethics and Theology* (ed.) Walter Hooper, London: HarperCollins. Very short and thought provoking; astonishingly prescient and relevant to the twenty-first century.

Pike, M. A. (2009) 'Religious freedom and rendering to Caesar: reading democratic and faith-based values in curriculum, pedagogy and policy', *Oxford Review of Education*, 35: 133–146. Here I try to show why it is so important for learners to be liberated to bring legitimate moral and religious conviction to their reading of state-sponsored values.

Pike, M. A. (2008) 'Faith in citizenship? On teaching children to believe in liberal democracy', *British Journal of Religious Education*, 30: 113–122. Short and provocative critique of the 'confessional' citizenship curriculum.

Chapter 9

Spiritual and moral development

Tony Eaude

Current debates regarding spiritual and moral development in English education can only be understood in relation to legislation and policy both within and beyond religious education (RE), especially since 1988, and recent social and cultural changes.

The 2002 Education Act (Section 78) requires schools to provide a balanced and broadly based curriculum which:

- promotes the spiritual, moral, cultural, mental and physical development of pupils at the school and of society; and
- prepares pupils at the school for the opportunities, responsibilities and experiences of later life.

The emphasis on spiritual and moral development, among other aspects, reflects a long tradition in British education involving other aspects than the cognitive. For instance, moral education in its broadest sense has been a stable element in education, with both the 1918 and 1944 Education Acts concerned with re-building civilisation and character in the aftermath of world wars. While the exact wording has changed, spiritual and moral development have remained central to the stated aims of education in the 1988 Education Reform Act and in subsequent legislation.

This chapter discusses how social and cultural change has affected the landscape within which children grow up, before outlining how spiritual and moral development have been understood in educational policy and practice, and how these 'fit in' to the broader pattern of educational provision and the specific issues raised for religious educators. It concludes by considering the current position and key debates.

The changing landscape of spiritual and moral development

Recent social and cultural change is complex, with the following list far from exhaustive. Societies, in Britain as in other Western countries, have become more diverse in terms of culture, religion and family structure, especially in urban areas. Growing, but unevenly distributed, wealth has led to a greater level of consumerism. Access to television, computers, the Internet and other forms of information technology has made global communication and culture widely available. And there has been a growing emphasis on both choice and accountability. What constitutes success is defined increasingly in terms of tangible possessions and measurable outcomes.

Patterns of religious affiliation and attendance are discussed elsewhere in this volume, but two trends are evident, a decline in numbers of children brought up actively within a faith tradition, especially among the ethnic majority, and the practice of a wider range of religious traditions. Society has become increasingly secular with religious belief seen as a private matter, and often an area where teachers are concerned at causing offence, but with religion remaining significant for a minority. Therefore, children's knowledge of religion and religions is on a wide spectrum from those with little knowledge of, or interest in, organised religion to those for whom it forms a central part of their lives, identity and framework of belief.

Paradoxically, the situation, as described by Andrew Wright (1999), is one of 'declining religion, persistent spirituality'. David Hay (2006) and David Tacey (2004), in English and Australian contexts respectively, identify a move away from religion, but a growing interest in, and search, for something more intangible. Tacey describes this as a 'spirituality revolution', relating this to a fascination with something beyond the material world and a need for the sacred, a need previously met by organised religion. Tacey (2001: 92) writes 'this new spiritual movement ... is not primarily anti-religion nor targeted against the churches ... (but) a desperate attempt by youth culture to counter the advances of a profane and secular society'. The huge number of courses, events, books and websites associated with spirituality suggests that this search is common to many different age groups and cultures. However, it is usually individualised and eclectic, a pick-and-mix approach rather than one of commitment.

The landscape of morality has many similarities. The role of religion as the traditional basis of morality has been challenged, although the appeal of Judaeo-Christian principles remains strong. The older generation, especially, express a widespread concern that the absence of the old certainties provided by religion and community leaves young people at risk of moral relativism, where 'anything goes'. A similar concern about the morals of the young is a recurrent historical theme, but events such as the murder of James Bulger by two boys of primary school age in 1993 and the attack on the World Trade Center in September 2001 led to soul searching, reflecting a state of moral panic, fuelled by the media. These concerns resulted in debates and policies, in which schools were expected to play a large part, to promote citizenship and community cohesion.

Public issues loosely associated with morality, such as those related to the environment, climate change and poverty, arouse considerable interest, especially among adolescents, although the systematic injustice of the world order or how business should be conducted continues to attract little discussion, in moral terms. However, questions of personal morality are increasingly regarded as matters of individual choice, but in White's words (1997: 19), 'the problem is not moral decline, but a certain *lack of confidence* about how we should behave and what we should believe'.

Spiritual and moral development in education therefore must be understood in the light of (at least a perceived) fragmentation of structures which previously provided the basis for these, but a fascination with some, but not all, aspects of these and a greater expectation that these are matters of personal choice. Moreover, the growth of global culture and the instant access to information seems to make any return to old certainties impossible.

Spiritual and moral development in education after 1988

Prior to the 1988 Education Act, there was little debate on what spiritual development, especially, entailed, apart from a growing disquiet, especially in secondary schools, about the requirement for a daily act of collective worship. The Act, as such, did not change this. However, the creation of Ofsted, following the 1992 Act, meant that, since inspection reports were publicly available, including a judgement on the provision for spiritual, moral, social and cultural development (SMSC), the pressure for a common language and understanding and criteria by which to judge this became intense, among both schools and inspectors. The Ofsted Framework for Inspection, in its original form and subsequent revisions, attempted to grapple with this, as did a succession of discussion documents, notably Ofsted (1994), SCAA (1995; 1996) and QCA (1997).

These are not described in detail (for this, see Barnes and Kay 2002: 27–37, and Erricker 2000, in relation to spiritual education), though the key points of SCAA (1995) are considered below, but two main issues, apart from their number and frequency, are noteworthy, namely the focus on provision and types of activity rather than outcomes and the raising of further questions rather providing definitive answers.

Debates in spiritual development

One key debate about spirituality is that of definition. Jack Priestley (1996) suggests that spirituality in the modern context should be seen as:

- encompassing a broader domain than that of religion
- dynamic
- related to being and becoming
- utopian
- communal as well as individual
- holistic.

Many religious traditions, notably Catholicism, Islam and Judaism, see belief, public worship and spirituality as inseparable, in contrast to those who see spirituality as universal. David Carr (1996) argues that the link between spirituality and religion is so close that spirituality makes no sense without engagement in a religious tradition. He suggests that 'spiritual experience is not primarily, if at all, a matter of detached empirical observation but of practical engagement; (…) only really possible from the inside' (1996: 167), making the analogy (1996: 175) that 'we may reasonably suppose that the best way to learn a human language is to be initiated into some particular language (rather than no language at all)'. Blake argues that the concept of spiritual *education* is flawed, writing (1996: 444) that 'outside the most specific religious traditions and religious institutional contexts, spiritual education is almost a contradiction in terms'.

David Hay (1985; 1998 with Nye; 2001; 2006), in contrast, argues for spirituality as a universal human trait, an inclusivist view which seems to accord with the expectation to make provision for all pupils. This reflects Priestley's call for spirituality being dynamic and holistic, adapting to different circumstances and dealing with the whole person. Much recent work on children's spirituality, especially empirical studies of young children, or their teachers (e.g. Erricker and Erricker 2000b; Hyde 2008; Eaude 2005), takes a similar view of spirituality as not necessarily linked to religion. Metaphors such as spiritual *dimension* (Priestley 2001) help to suggest that this involves a process embedded in, but at times transcending, everyday experience and drawing on approaches and qualities rather different from those currently valued most in school and society.

The subtitle of Brendan Hyde's *Children and Spirituality* (2008), 'searching for meaning and connectedness', captures three central elements of an inclusivist view. First, there is the sense of search, of trying to make sense of existential questions such as who am I, where do I fit in, why am I here? – related to identity, place and purpose. Second, this involves attempting to create a coherent narrative, a process of making meaning. Finally, this search is, always, constructed within a culture and a tradition and is both individual and social. In MacIntyre's words:

> the story of my life is always embedded in the story of those communities from which I derive my identity. I am born with a past; and to try to cut myself off from that past, in the individualistic mode, is to deform my present relationships. The possession of an historical identity and the possession of a social identity coincide.
>
> (MacIntyre 1999: 221)

Hyde's subtitle highlights that this search is for meaning and connectedness. We understand events, if at all, only with hindsight. So meaning is constructed in response to, and to make sense of, experience, whether or not within an explicit religious framework. Spirituality is seen as affecting, and affected by, one's view of fundamental questions, with gaining, or regaining, a sense of perspective, one reason why experiences of 'awe and wonder' are often associated with spirituality.

Hay with Nye (1998) present what they call 'relational consciousness' as central to children's spirituality. They break this into four elements:

- awareness of self
- awareness of others
- awareness of the environment
- (for some people) awareness of a Transcendent Other.

This is linked to an emerging sense of identity, where children, often centred on their own needs, learn over time how they fit into a 'bigger picture' and recognise both their independence and interdependence, reflecting many religious traditions' emphasis on being less obsessed with oneself. John Hull's (1996b; 1998) sociological approach where values are expressed in social as well as individual terms rejects a view of spirituality as just interior or individual, expressed as 'spirituality exists not inside people, but between them' (1998: 66).

While there is a broad consensus that spirituality deals with matters of profound importance, there is less about how it should be enhanced. Terence Copley argues that the secular language of spiritual development is cut adrift from spirituality as understood by world religions and that, while remaining a potentially viable and valuable goal, it is 'in dire need of balance and enrichment from the religious language of spiritualities' (2000: 142). Wright (2004: 206) highlights that SCAA (1995) 'offers no more than a generalised account of spirituality', with many examples of activities which may contribute to spiritual development. Policy and practice to enhance spiritual development have emphasised types of activity and experience, such as reflection or, especially in primary and early years, experiences of 'awe and wonder', or more intangible aspects such as relationships and creativity. Even though such activities may be loosely associated with religious traditions of spirituality, such a link is somewhat tenuous, although many would regard this as beneficial in a pluralist society. However, Carr (1996: 168) states that

> effective initiation of young people into ... moral, religious or spiritual enquiry ... presupposes ... substantial acquaintance with ... specific traditions of reflection – rather than training in repertoires of abstractly-conceived critical or problem-solving skills.

He dismisses the notion that 'awe and wonderment' at the idea of infinity, for instance, has anything to do with spirituality.

There is no shortage of specific programmes claiming to enhance spirituality, most of them relying on detachment from one's current concerns, usually emphasising individual happiness or well-being. However, as David Smith (1999: 4) writes: 'it seems more helpful to think in terms of how we can create opportunities for growth than ... how we can move pupils through a programmed sequence', going on to suggest thinking 'in terms of creating spaces where spirituality is affirmed and spiritual growth can happen'.

David Lambourn (1996) argues that an inclusivist view of spiritual development does not relate to anything separate from social, religious, moral, aesthetic or other forms of development – that it is an empty category. However, although these categories overlap, to conflate them all into a general category such as personal development makes it harder to examine and draw on specific, often difficult, messages from previous traditions and discussions of what contested, but important, terms such as spiritual and moral mean.

Wright (2000a: 75–77) warns against an inclusive understanding of spiritual development if this implies a rejection of tradition, an abandonment of critical reflection and a concentration on 'inner' emotional experience, or what he calls (2000a: 76) 'the possibility of a spiritual emotivism detached from critical reflection'. He, and many others, such as Adrian Thatcher (1991), Carr (1996) and Eaude (2008a), express concern at a view of spiritual experience being individualistic or self-authenticating, where one can choose what makes one feel good and call it spirituality.

Hay's (2001: 115) suggestion that 'the insights of spirituality are always likely to be counter-cultural' raises the question whether policies on spirituality have been, and should be, conservative or radical. Nigel Blake (1996) is wary of the whole debate on spiritual education because it has been championed by the political right and concentrates on transcendence rather than the everyday. However, Jacqueline Watson (2007) argues that the notion of spiritual development as broader than religion was, as conceptualised, an attempt to re-institute progressive pedagogical values after the 1988 Act; but that it proved to be insufficiently robust to withstand other curricular pressures, so that spiritual development came to be located mainly within RE, with other areas left free for a more outcome-based approach.

In contrast to Watson, Wright (2004: 206) sees the discourse exemplified in SCAA (1995) as 'deliberately disengag(ing) spiritual education from religious education, presenting spirituality as a cross-curricular theme which should permeate the life of the whole school', based on its 'broad non-committal description ... (which) clearly leaves room for educative engagement with a broad range of specific spiritual traditions, both religious and secular'.

Debates in moral development

Terence McLaughlin and Mark Halstead (1999) describe two main traditions of moral education, which they call non-expansive and expansive. The former emphasises:

- a set of core, or universal, values
- a specific programme to introduce and reinforce them
- a process of values being internalised more by repetition and habit than by conscious reasoning, at least with young children.

An expansive approach highlights that values:

- vary between cultures
- are internalised more through the hidden curriculum and modelling than direct teaching
- often conflict, such that children need to learn from a young age how to resolve such conflict by moral reasoning.

These are not mutually exclusive. Any one approach is likely to adopt aspects of each, but both emphasise the inadequacy of an approach that 'anything goes'. In Amy Gutmann's words, (1987: 62) 'moral education begins by winning the battle against amoralism and egoism'.

The National Forum for Values in Education and the Community in the mid-1990s (see Talbot and Tate 1997) was based on a search for universal values. As discussed in Eaude (2008a), such a search, in a pluralist society, will work only at a minimalist level, because values differ legitimately in important respects. Despite this, the Forum reflected a change from the situation where most debate on moral development was based on a 'duty ethics' approach framed mostly in terms of knowing right from wrong, reflecting Kohlberg's (for example 1987) emphasis on rational decision making. However, as McLaughlin and Halstead (1999: 136) argue, 'all conceptions of "character education" [emphasise] that adults, in particular teachers, have duty not merely to teach children *about* character [and virtue more generally] but also to *develop* qualities of character and virtue'. Moral development is about what one does, not just what one ought to do. Children need to experience what values entail and to practise them, as well as reflect critically on them; and, given the importance of example, adults need not just to 'talk the talk, but walk the walk' if children are to internalise values.

Duty ethics tends to be normative, that is to encourage conformity with other people's expectations, which accords with the current approach to behaviour management. However, as West-Burnham and Huws-Jones suggest (2007: 38), 'morality that is based on obedience, compliance and the threat of sanction will always be fragile because it is based on external, negative compulsion'. A more formative approach is that of virtue ethics, described by Alasdair MacIntyre (1999) as having a long pedigree, back to Aristotle, but largely forgotten since the Enlightenment. This is concerned with the cultivation of the virtues to enable someone to lead the good life, based on what it is to be a good person, associated with the unfashionable ideas of virtues and character (see McLaughlin and Halstead 1999, for a good discussion of these). Although virtue ethics can be challenged as too individualistic, MacIntyre stresses that virtues depend on what it is to lead the good life in any particular society. A holistic approach such as virtue ethics – what McLaughlin and Halstead (1999: 134) call an 'ethics of aspiration' – may be more likely to encourage engagement and intrinsic motivation, in a less deferential society where young people expect to make their own decisions.

Richard Pring (2001: 102) argues that the practice of education has become detached from a moral perspective, 'with no driving and unifying ideal, no coherent set of values', going on that educational practice should '[bring] together a wider range of activities which *embody* the values and the moral aims which they are intended to promote'. So, moral education is not just part of, or a subject within, education, but education is itself a moral enterprise. This echoes Jackson *et al.*'s (1993) findings that the most important messages in terms of moral development are often the least obvious, with any action having the potential to influence this. So, unconscious messages and belief systems, demonstrated through everyday, apparently trivial, practices are likely to matter at least as much as programmes of conscious instruction. Moral education is therefore not primarily about programmes designed for moral – or wider aspects of personal – development but a dimension to be taken seriously in every aspect of provision.

The implications are well captured by the Archbishop of Canterbury's words:

> [moral education] is neither the imparting of rules in a vacuum nor the discussion of how young people [think they] decide issues, but is bound up with the roles and responsibilities actually learned in the corporate life of an institution … It is no use at all to pontificate about the need for 'values' to be communicated if the entire style and pace of an institution allow no room for understanding of learning in their diversity, or … if the institution sees its task as the – increasingly hurried and anxious – job of passing on quantifiable information and measurable outcomes at the expense of reflection on the character of its common life as educative.
>
> (Williams 2000: 92)

While the term 'spiritual' is often viewed with suspicion, moral education is often linked to other (often broad and loosely defined) agendas and enlisted as one, albeit often ill-defined, way of achieving broader social goals. Examples include personal, social and health education (PSHE), with citizenship added later, and a growing concern with emotional intelligence, resulting in the widespread adoption in primary schools of circle time and recently Social and Emotional Aspects of Learning (SEAL) and programmes such as healthy schools or eco-schools. Citizenship, introduced as a foundation subject in secondary schools in 2002, has clear overlaps with moral education but, as Halstead and Pike (2006, especially Part 1) discuss, each has distinctive elements which makes the relationship complex. Similar debates apply to community cohesion, with schools from 2007 expected to promote this, although what this entails remains very broad and is, arguably, made more difficult by policies which emphasise parental choice.

Where do spiritual and moral development fit in?

While personal, social, health and citizenship education is usually addressed separately, spiritual, especially, and moral development are all too easily seen as the preserve of RE, especially in non-faith schools. If spiritual and moral development are to be central to the life of the school, this requires a chance to search and engage critically with questions related to meaning, identity and purpose and what it is to live the good life, both in theory and practice, across the whole of school life; and indeed beyond. This requires, ideally, a pedagogy across the curriculum which encourages engagement with controversial and difficult issues, whether personal, social or global. All children are faced with what is hard to comprehend, and will continue to be so throughout life, whether the frustration of not getting one's own way or more severe concerns such as those about parental arguments or separation from those whom one loves; or in moral terms, how to conduct oneself or behave faced with personal choices to do with behaviour and relationships, or the ethics of science or business. In avoiding such questions, providing over-simple answers or failing to help children recognise that some questions do not have easy or definitive answers, adults may discourage them from continuing to ask such questions.

Since 1997, despite the relatively short-lived debates about citizenship and community cohesion, there has been little policy consideration of issues explicitly related to spiritual and moral development, in contrast to the mid-1990s. For example, Ofsted has only produced one substantial publication on this (Ofsted 2004a) in the last decade. This may result from continuing uncertainty about what these entail and how to address them in a curriculum arranged largely in terms of subjects. However, a more cogent reason is that the dominant discourse has related especially to standards of attainment within core subjects. This has made success largely dependent on outcome measures in literacy and numeracy, tending to marginalise aspects such as spiritual and moral development which are less open to such judgements.

It is therefore uncertain where spiritual and moral development 'fit in'. They need to permeate the life the whole school, but a curriculum – and a timetable – which divides learning into discrete subjects presents a dilemma. Given a particular 'slot', they will tend to be seen as not the concern of other subjects. Without such a slot, they are too easily overlooked.

What is the distinctive contribution of RE?

Spiritual and moral development are matters for the whole school, but RE (and collective worship, despite this chapter's lack of discussion of this) has a distinctive contribution to make. This is especially in relating the role of religion and different religious traditions to the wider school and social context, especially in secondary schools, where religion may be marginalised or seen as a private matter.

Ofsted, in reporting RE as of uneven quality, states (2010: 6) that 'RE made a positive contribution to key aspects of pupils' personal development, most notably in relation to the understanding and appreciation of the diverse nature of our society. However, the subject's contribution to promoting pupils' spiritual development was often limited', with relatively little mention in the whole report of moral development, despite praising RE's contribution to community cohesion. One recommendation is that 'schools should ensure that RE promotes pupils' spiritual development more effectively by allowing for more genuine investigation into, and reflection on, the implications of religion and belief for their personal lives' (2010: 8).

The nature of the school is likely to affect substantially how RE can best contribute to spiritual and moral development. In faith schools, the challenge may be to introduce children to the insights and beliefs of a wide range of religions, or even to persuade colleagues that this is appropriate. In schools without a religious foundation, the challenge may be to highlight religion's contribution to spiritual and moral development, or even that spiritual and moral development, or religion itself, matter. However, the growing popularity of RE in secondary schools and the enduring interest in it, when well taught, in primary schools provides a source of hope. For instance, a primary school visit to a place of worship or a consideration of the stories of faith can provide the chance for engagement with issues of belief and meaning; and a comparison of beliefs and responses on universal themes across, and beyond, religions can enrich the understanding of older students in a way unlikely to be achieved by a non-specialist. Moreover, such approaches can help to affirm the importance of religion in how fundamental questions are, and can be, addressed, whether or not individual students belong to any faith community.

Recent developments and contemporary debates

Elsewhere in this volume, the place of RE in the curriculum and whether it should be statutory or not and its content locally or nationally determined, is discussed. The QCA/DfES *Non-Statutory Framework for Religious Education* (2004) highlights three elements of the RE curriculum – religions and beliefs, themes and experiences and opportunities – with many locally agreed syllabuses emphasising both experience and content, for example Birmingham's (2007) 'learning from faith' and 'learning about religious traditions'. This reflects the importance of RE involving process as well as content, with Michael Grimmitt (2000b) providing a useful discussion of how RE was affected by the wider curricular assumptions in the 1990s. The place of RE, somewhat surprisingly given the situation in the 1990s, seems secure, although this is a wider debate, with, for instance, the Cambridge Primary Review (Alexander 2010: 268) proposing that one of the eight 'domains' of learning should be that of 'faith and belief', implying that RE should be replaced by a broader, and statutory, domain, and Ofsted (2010) supporting the call for a statutory, less locally determined approach to RE.

However, the place of spiritual and moral development is less secure, at least in practice. Despite their importance in legislation, they are no longer widely discussed in policy and practice, in contrast to the 1990s. This is evident in the lack of policy documents and, more worryingly, reference to spiritual, moral, social and cultural education in mainstream policies, apart from more general terms such as 'social and emotional'. For instance, the Rose Review of the Primary Curriculum (Rose Review/DCSE 2009: paragraph 1.3) dismissed the wording of 'spiritual, moral, social and cultural' as 'somewhat clumsy', preferring personal, social and health education. Most obviously, this results from the emphasis on standards of attainment, especially in English and Maths, but also uncertainty about what spiritual development, especially, entails and where spiritual and moral development 'fit in' to a curriculum based largely on discrete subjects. The 'system' struggles to deal with such areas where questions may be uncomfortable and outcomes uncertain.

For RE teachers, especially, this poses the problem of how to ensure that spiritual and moral development is addressed, and what the distinctive contribution of RE is, especially in helping children engage with how religious traditions have understood these and continue to do so; but without this becoming seen as the sole preserve of RE. Many adolescents, especially, are interested in spirituality and issues associated with morality, but less so than previously in the context of religious belief or belonging and, as always, not in the context of being told what to believe or to think. RE teachers have an important contribution in raising, and encouraging critical engagement with, such issues. Doing so across the curriculum may be easier in primary schools, despite a lack of specialist expertise in RE, but specialist RE teachers in secondary schools can draw on a greater breadth and depth of knowledge to place such discussions within a context of religious belief. The challenge is therefore to develop a pedagogy which provides a framework for discussion and exploration, allowing for and respecting, but not expecting, affiliation to a particular set of beliefs; so that the individual search is informed by the wisdom of traditions without demanding allegiance.

Questions

How can religious educators ensure that RE makes a distinctive contribution to children's spiritual and moral development *and* that this does not just become the preserve of RE?

What contribution can RE teachers make to ensure that worldviews based on religion which have been and, despite secularisation, remain influential are taken seriously?

How can RE teachers contribute to a school ethos which recognises the centrality of religious identity and affiliation to the lives of many people, including students, so that both they and others feel 'comfortable' in practising and discussing religion or not?

Further reading

Eaude, T. (2008b) *Children's Spiritual, Moral, Social and Cultural Development – Primary and Early Years,* Exeter: Learning Matters. An overview, designed for teachers in training, of philosophical and practical issues related to SMSC with young children.

McLaughlin, T. H. and Halstead, J. M. (1999) 'Education in character and virtue', in J. M. Halstead and T. H. McLaughlin (eds) *Education in Morality,* London: Routledge. A good discussion summarising different approaches to moral education.

Tacey, D. (2004) *The Spirituality Revolution – The Emergence of Contemporary Spirituality,* Hove: Brunner-Routledge. A commentary from an Australian academic on why so many young people continue to search for the spiritual without commitment to religious affiliation.

Wright, A. (2000a) *Spirituality and Education,* London: RoutledgeFalmer. A thoughtful book, primarily from a Christian perspective, about the dilemmas of educators working within the current educational and social context.

Chapter 10

Community cohesion

Rosemary Woodward

It ticked all the boxes! They were teaching the same year group; the mother in a large inner city school, the daughter in rural East Anglia. What could be easier than starting a school partnership? The children were excited, the link developing well, and the daughter spent an evening putting up a display about her class's new friends. Next morning, as her pupils came in, she was horrified to hear the comment 'Look, we've got a picture of the poor children that we sent our harvest gifts to!'

For these children brown skins were equated with poverty and the new school links had not yet had enough impact to break down the stereotypes already imprinted on these six-year-old minds by parents, experience and the media. It is a desire to counteract such divisive misunderstanding within the multi-racial Britain of the twenty-first century that prompted the launching of the community cohesion agenda.

What is community cohesion?

The widely used definition of community cohesion is

> working towards a society in which there is a common vision and sense of belonging by all communities; a society in which the diversity of people's backgrounds and circumstances is appreciated and valued; a society in which similar life opportunities are available to all; and a society in which strong and positive relationships exist and continue to be developed in the workplace, in schools and in the wider community.
>
> (DCSF 2007b: 30)

The community cohesion agenda values diversity and accepts all regardless of race, belief, gender, disability, sexual orientation or age. It recognises that, for society to be fully cohesive, all members must feel that they belong, can achieve their full potential and can contribute at local, national and global level. Within schools pupils should also engage with controversial issues such as bullying or homophobia and be equipped to identify and challenge extremist narratives.

Guidance suggests that giving everyone 'the opportunity to interact and make a contribution to their community can also build bridges, dispel myths and develop a shared sense of belonging' (QCDA 2010b: 2). Since 2007 English schools have had a legal duty to promote community cohesion, and embed it within teaching and learning across all curriculum areas. Whatever its future legal status, community cohesion is likely to remain an objective within British education.

Modern British culture has been enriched by contributions from the many groups that have come to the United Kingdom throughout its history. Multicultural education has featured in British schools for many years, alongside government initiatives to support more isolated groups within the community. Yet, the terrorist attacks of 9/11 and 7/7 and race riots in Bradford and Oldham highlighted divisions that still exist between ethnic and faith groups. 'Mistrust of different groups, particularly those new to the community; a perception that local authorities are giving others special treatment; and a lack of spaces for meaningful interaction' were among the principle barriers to building cohesion (DCSF 2007b: 4).

The community cohesion agenda seeks to reshape a deeply ingrained way of thinking, as all individuals exist within their own culture. 'Culture is a gift to every person from his society. The ideas, values and assumptions which make up a worldview are a precious heritage from previous generations which seeks to enable the individual to cope successfully with their present day environment' (Burnett 1990: 250). Kraft suggests that 'we all exist within culture much as fish exist in water. Totally immersed in it from soon after conception until death, human beings cannot live outside of culture or think except in cultural categories' (1989: 274). Cultural pride or 'ethnocentrism', which assumes that one's own culture is best and sees those outside as 'illogical' is common across all societies (Burnett 1990: 21). The community cohesion agenda does not deny the importance of culture, but rather seeks to ensure that the diversity found within British society is celebrated as positive. 'Cohesion is therefore about how to avoid the corrosive effects of intolerance and harassment; how to build a mutual civility among different groups, and to ensure respect for diversity alongside a commitment to common and shared bonds' (DCSF 2007b: 4).

Individuals bring their own values and priorities to every interaction, so all inter-personal relationships encapsulate something of the community cohesion agenda. Each child is growing in a world rich in diversity, and Nesbitt suggests that pupils already have many of the skills needed to relate from their own cultural position to that of others because they 'are mixing with people, and so talking, listening, participating in activity, and observing it, noticing patterns of behaviour and anomalies, forming and revising judgements and reporting to others, in ways they can relate to, what we have experienced' (Nesbitt 2002: 113). Daily interaction provides a foundation for understanding cultural diversity, but this must be fostered if individuals are to contribute positively to a cohesive neighbourhood, region or country.

An example of the way in which shared experience can unite is seen whenever football enthusiasts meet with ball and open space. Their common interest allows them to share a game regardless of divisions of language, culture or faith. It is only when a player is excluded or their contribution questioned, that conflict occurs. Problems will then be greater if language differences prevent discussion, allowing misunderstandings to deepen. In the same way within society it is when shared points of common understanding cannot be found that divisions develop.

Maintaining the football analogy, a tournament such as the World Cup is, in part, a global celebration of 'the beautiful game'. This diversity of participating countries provides the positive expectation of a global party. It is when the mutual love of sport is overwhelmed by national pride or disappointment, and others become 'the opposition' that the celebration aspect disappears and divisions surface, creating an 'us and them' mentality. In the same way, within society, when differences are highlighted as negative and 'other', stereotyping and prejudice result. A fully cohesive society has no place for 'us and them'. Everyone is accepted as having a positive part to contribute. In order to achieve this, it is essential to celebrate diversity, approaching it with an open mind and seeing it as rich and positive, while allowing prejudices to be challenged within a safe environment. Although community cohesion should be embedded across all areas of school life, 'RE makes an important contribution to a school's duty to promote community cohesion. It provides a key context to develop young people's understanding and appreciation of diversity, to promote shared values and to challenge racism and discrimination' (DCSF 2010:7).

The role of RE within community cohesion

The duty of community cohesion empowers RE to consider issues of identity and diversity in a way not always reflected in past teaching. It plays a significant part in

> developing pupils' knowledge and understanding about the diversity of national, regional, religious and ethnic identities in the United Kingdom and the need for mutual respect and understanding; enabling pupils to think about topical spiritual, moral, social and cultural issues including the importance of resolving conflict fairly [and] exploring the rights, responsibilities and duties of citizens locally, nationally and globally.
>
> (QCA 2004: 17)

In order to achieve these important roles all study of religion must be clear and unbiased. Respect and understanding have been key aims of RE since it adopted a multi-faith approach during the 1970s. However, like much multi-cultural work across the curriculum, RE has often considered each faith as a self-contained entity within British society, thus highlighting difference.

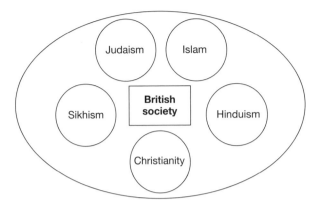

Figure 10.1 The multi-faith approach – distinct religions existing within British society

Community cohesion calls for the identification of common ground. RE should equip pupils to act as detectives searching for answers to the life questions humanity has grappled with for millennia. Pupils need to explore and interpret the 'evidence' offered by major faiths and worldviews. Knowledge of the concepts at the heart of each religion enables learners to form their own opinions on factual knowledge rather than uninformed prejudice or stereotypes. It is not enough to know that Sikhs wear turbans and carry a kirpan. These symbols mark individuals as different. In order to understand why these articles are important to Sikhs it is essential to explore the teaching of Guru Gobind Singh that Amritdhari follow when they adopt the five Ks. However, to give these relevance and meaning to pupils they must also explore the themes of dedication, self-respect and justice that lie behind the articles' symbolism. These shared values may help them relate Sikh beliefs to their own experience.

All attempts to promote community cohesion through RE must be relevant and meaningful. Jackson suggests that 'one problem for religious education (RE) is that "religions" and "cultures" are rarely presented in a vibrant, flexible and organic way' (1997: 47). Giles recounts discussions with pupils who all believed that they did not have a culture, but were just 'normal', and that 'we learn too much about other cultures. It is not important – I am not a Muslim. I don't even know any Muslims, so why should I have to know about their culture?' (2006: 28). Teaching had failed to engage the pupils, because, as they neither understood the meaning of culture nor recognised their place within it, they could not find any areas of shared contact with Muslims. Only by exploring their own position within the local community could these pupils begin to identify interests they shared with their Muslim neighbours. Giles, explaining the importance of learning from religion, states 'if we, as teachers, cannot identify the relevance ourselves and transmit this to students in some way which links to their own lives and is therefore clear to them, then the subject will feel irrelevant and boring' (2006:

29). Only when pupils are engaged and interested are they ready to explore the attitudes and values that unite or divide individuals or communities.

Good RE encourages pupils to share and investigate their questions, explore and discuss possible answers, and formulate their own informed opinions. However, pupils must remain open-minded, reviewing their opinions in the light of the new experiences they meet on their life journey. They must understand that all viewpoints are to be considered seriously and be treated with respect, and that every individual has something positive to contribute to discussion. Two attitudes essential for good learning within RE are respect for all and open mindness (QCA 2004: 15). 'Religious Education also recognises the changing nature of society … and the influence of religion in the local, national and global community' (ibid.: 10) and so can contribute positively to each level of community cohesion.

Equipping the individual with strong roots

Community cohesion begins not with interpersonal skills, but when individuals develop confidence in their own position within society.

> A central concern of religious education is the promotion of each pupil's self-worth. A sense of self-worth helps pupils to reflect on their uniqueness as human beings, share their feelings and emotions with others and appreciate the importance of forming and maintaining positive relationships.
>
> (QCA 2004: 11)

Pupils need to develop understanding and pride in their own cultural heritage and to value their place within it before they can begin to consider the position of others. Those belonging to a faith tradition should be confident that their beliefs will be respected and not compromised. All should be enabled to share their own opinions confident that they will not be embarrassed or ridiculed.

Once pupils are confident in their right to make a positive contribution within society they can begin to examine the opinions and beliefs of others without feeling threatened. Self-esteem is a prerequisite for debating wider issues, handling disagreement and acknowledging other viewpoints.

Demolishing the walls: 'experienced-near' in the school and local community

School is where most children are introduced to community life. Here inclusion, the 'Every Child Matters' agenda and celebration of achievements underpin the community cohesion agenda. Every school consists of individuals who bring their own strengths and challenges and learn to work and play together in harmony, developing a unique community. Geertz calls such interaction 'experiencing-near', a concept which someone 'might himself naturally and effortlessly use to define what he or his fellows see, feel, think, imagine and so on, and which he would readily understand when similarly applied to others' (1983: 57).

Within school pupils may encounter those from other social groups for the first time. As pupils formulate their own opinions they should learn to consider the viewpoints of others, explore the concepts of rights and responsibilities and develop the skills needed to resolve conflicts, laying the foundations for all wider community interaction. By modelling how different ideas can be listened to and valued the teacher can embed attitudes important for community cohesion.

> The aims, curriculum, resources and pedagogy of RE embrace the values at the heart of inclusion, notably respect for all. The teaching of religions in itself does not promote respect, but when teaching exemplifies openness and sensitivity to differences in beliefs and practices then RE plays a part in creating an open and accepting atmosphere in the school.
>
> (Ofsted 2003: 5)

Children should learn from an early age how to handle disagreements, bullying, verbal abuse and prejudice as many issues that provoke arguments between individuals mirror those that cause fights between rival gangs or wars between countries. Strategies for reconciliation and peace may also be the same. Each school needs to establish

> a set of school values that show respect for all but challenge unfairness and discrimination. RE can therefore have a strategic impact on any divisive issue affected by faith – because it is the precise place where young people can have their prejudices challenged and their positive values affirmed in guided discussion.
>
> (Hudson 2008: 11)

Schools model community cohesion within their unique local setting. For some the school catchment may include a wide variety of faith or cultural groups, while others are situated within rural all-white British community. Every school should examine its own context, identifying strengths and weaknesses. For example, there may be persistent underachievement within one pupil group whose parents are less engaged within the life of the school. The school can be proactive in involving them; exploring why divisions exist, how barriers can be removed and which shared values can provide a basis for developing understanding. Schools 'need to find out more about the diversity of beliefs, religious or otherwise, among their pupils and their families, so that these can be acknowledged and valued through the subject and in the wider life of the school' (Ofsted 2010: 48).

RE as a subject is in a unique position to relate to local issues because its locally determined syllabus allows investigation of religions as they are lived out within the local community. Visits to places of worship and visitors from local faith groups can enrich teaching and learning and allow pupils to develop an understanding of diversity within their local religious heritage. Opportunities for pupils to relate to local faith leaders should enable trust to develop and areas of shared belief to be explored.

> The very fact that these religiously-motivated activities tend to focus on shared ethical objectives – educating children, treating addictions, uniting families, protecting the elderly, building community life – means that, if anything, such religiously-inspired work unites rather than divides religious groups ... it is not uncommon to see faith groups working together towards shared objectives.
>
> (Spencer 2006: 47)

RE can provide explicit opportunities to discover shared values and teaching between faiths, while modelling positive ways of resolving conflict. For example, the hopes and fears associated with birth, marriage and death are shared by many of every faith or none, and experienced by pupils. Understanding that these emotions are held in common may enable pupils to relate the diverse ceremonies and beliefs with which the rites of passage are surrounded to their own experience.

Building national and global bridges to 'experience-distant'

Pupils should '[u]nderstand, meet and engage with people from different faiths, cultures and social backgrounds in ways that promote common values while recognising diversity within communities' (QCDA 2010b: 8). The high levels of global interaction and interdependence resulting from modern advances in communication mean that pupils must be equipped to become citizens of the world as well as their own community.

Differences between cultures must not be underestimated. Pupils are being asked to 'experience-distant' (Geertz 1983: 58). Every individual has, and must have, a worldview, a 'shared framework of ideas held by a particular society concerning how they perceive the world' (Burnett 1990: 13). The greater the separation of geography, language and religion, the fewer the points of contact between worldviews, yet many diverse cultures live side by side within the cities of modern Britain, while the internet links homes and classrooms across the 'global village'.

Individuals around the world share emotional, biological, psychological and spiritual needs providing a common focus for bridging cultural divisions. Comparisons of household pets, love of sport and relationships at home and school can lead to the discovery of further shared interests, and the growth of deeper understanding and friendship. It is when differences are highlighted that misunderstanding and prejudice result. The gaps between cultures can be crossed, and must be if different societies are to co-exist in harmony.

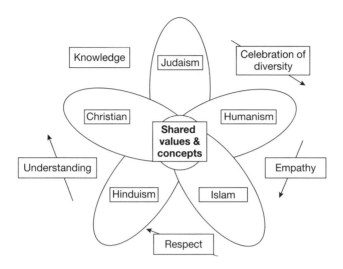

Figure 10.2 The community cohesion approach centred on shared values

   This need to bridge cultural divides prompted the initiative to build partnerships between schools in different British settings and with those overseas. For pupils growing up within all-white rural areas there is much to learn from meeting peers whose classes encompass a wide range of cultural and faith groups. Pupils from urban schools may not realise that there are children in Britain who have not yet met anyone with a dark skin. Individuals may not question their own perceptions until confronted with someone from a differing culture.

   As the opening example shows, simply introducing individuals or allowing an exchange of e-mails does not ensure that meaningful and positive friendships will result. For school partnerships to be successful they must incorporate shared curriculum projects, which may have an RE focus. For example, a comparison of the places of worship of each community can form the basis for shared work within a real-life context. It is the task of teachers to ensure that cross-cultural interaction is relevant and positive, allowing pupils to find enough points of contact with their new friends to discuss their differences openly and respectfully.

   International partnerships are particularly dependent on well-planned curriculum projects based on shared values and interests if stereotyping is to be avoided. They must not be seen as synonymous with charitable giving, important though that is, because an 'us and them' mentality of rich aiding poor will undermine efforts to create an equal partnership. It would be equally irresponsible to ignore problems of unemployment, over-population and under-resourcing where these exist. 'Young people need a balanced range of images, stories and authentic voices from the majority world, and, where possible, opportunities to build real relationships' (Bradford and Ripon and Leeds Diocesan Education Team 2008: 14). Once friendship and understanding are established the real

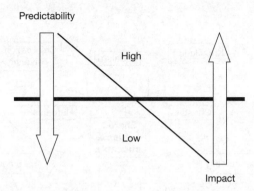

Figure 10.3 See-saw diagram showing relationship between predictability and impact (following Kraft 1979: 160)

concerns of both schools can be shared, and partners can work together in an informed way on sustainable and relevant projects.

In the same way the requirement for schools to develop international partnerships can enrich work in RE. Pupils are more likely to be challenged by material which is unfamiliar and outside their own experience, as this will be less predictable (King 2001: 8). This can be shown in diagrammatic form, suggesting that there is a direct link between the two elements of impact and predictability.

'A message has greatest impact if it is not a stereotyped message and it is presented in very life-related fashion' (Kraft 1979: 159). Introducing a global perspective to RE offers potential for using unfamiliar material, making lesson content less predictable and so increasing the impact of the resulting learning experience, especially as 'one of the key aims of RE is concerned with helping pupils to reflect on their studies of ways of life that are different in some respects from their own' (Jackson 2000: 135). There is then an increased likelihood that pupils will consider the issues raised, promoting learning skills such as questioning, researching, reasoning and evaluating as well as embedding the attitudes of community cohesion.

Moreover the faiths studied in RE are global and must be understood as such. Christianity, for example, is neither British nor European. The British church is a small part of something far greater. Sadly some elements within Britain's heritage can portray a negative image of Christianity; and if more positive models of Christianity can be found within the churches of other countries, these should be explored. Adding a global perspective to teaching not only increases the relevance of the subject matter and helps understanding of the concepts at the faith's heart; it also overcomes any claims of superiority by British Christianity. The church can be seen as international, including the traditions of all believers, from whatever culture.

Other major world faiths have also evolved through history. None began in Britain and yet all are now an integral part of British culture. An exploration of the way each faith is lived out across the world can increase understanding of underlying concepts. For example, teaching about Hinduism that focuses on one Indian cultural group by using the Hindi symbol for Aum excludes many British Hindus who use other representations of this important sound. Exploring such diversity within the Hindu faith can enrich, rather than detract from, understanding of the sound of creation used in Hindu worship and uniting believers separated by geography, ethnicity and language (Woodward 2006: 5). History, cultural variety and differences of interpretation give every community its own unique position. There is a danger that if this diversity is not recognised all those connected with one faith will be associated with the failings of some of its members. On the other hand, using global perspectives can bridge cultural divisions by enabling pupils, whatever their background, to illustrate how their distinct heritage plays an important role within the rich wider picture of world faith as lived out today.

Moreover, asking pupils to build bridges with those whom they experience-distant may provide a secure environment in which to explore issues that cause misunderstanding or prejudice within their local community. The causes of gang warfare or racism may be explored within an impartial context, and possible ways of resolving conflict explored. Topics such as gender issues or roles in marriage may also be diffused and enriched through study in a wider and less immediate context.

Hurdles to community cohesion

Although RE has much to contribute towards community cohesion, the topic is not without debate. One hurdle to promoting community cohesion is that of parental pressure. Many pupils enter school already holding prejudices learned from parents. If the school challenges these pupils may be torn between the values of home and of school. The community cohesion agenda also encourages local communities to come together for dialogue and interaction. Where there are few points of contact, this has to be facilitated. RE teachers are often better informed about the diverse religious groups in their area than are members of these groups about each other. By taking an active part in creating opportunities for positive engagement between groups RE teachers may confront community misunderstanding. However, it must be realised that many prejudices are deep rooted and not easily overcome.

Faced with the on-going problem of religious fanaticism some would argue that the study of religion is best confined to the private sphere, as highlighting the diversity of religious faith within society prevents community cohesion from taking place (e.g. National Secular Society spokesperson, BBC Breakfast News 6 June 2010). However,

Religious belief and adherence is in good health around the world. This alone suggests that religion will play some part in future public debates about British identity, unless the nation desires to seal itself off from the globalising trends that now shape the world. Even if British-born citizens are less overtly religious, foreign-born citizens are unlikely to be.

(Spencer 2006: 62)

If this is the case, it cannot be ignored. Rabbi Sacks suggests that 'if religion is not part of the solution it will certainly be part of the problem' (2002: 9).

It would be facile to pretend that all difference in society can be overcome through discussion and identifying shared values and concepts, even if the community cohesion agenda allows groups to 'agree to disagree agreeably'. It requires a readiness to dialogue and respect that does not always exist. Some viewpoints are fundamentally opposed, and areas of commonality are not readily found. Other divisions are based on very good understanding and resulting distrust of another point of view. Moreover it could be argued that some stereotyping is essential in order for pupils to feel safe and secure within the community. Some viewpoints are not acceptable, and children need to learn from a young age that a minority within society may seek to harm or abuse them. Not all conflicts can be resolved even by using all the tools they have been taught, and not all groups do contribute in a positive way to society. The issues of religious and political extremism and radicalisation remain and, in a postmodern age in which all viewpoints are to be valued, pupils may question who has the right to decide what is or is not acceptable.

Many RE teachers find the topic of Islam difficult to teach due to public perception of extremism within the faith. This may lead to factual teaching about the religion with few opportunities to learn from it. Yet, if pupils are not shown that values, heritage and teaching are shared between Islam and other faiths there will be fewer opportunities to break down the walls of misunderstanding which surround this diverse religion. Only if teachers are proactive in helping pupils to explore the issues that have led to the radicalisation of some members of the faith can they suggest alternative outcomes.

The community cohesion agenda is based on the premise that all cultures be valued and respected, but there is a danger that a focus on shared concepts may narrow content within RE. Pupil-led questioning and cross-curricular work, alongside a search for commonality between faiths, could herald a return to the comparative mishmash sometimes experienced within 1980s' RE. The very real differences between faiths must not be overlooked. 'People may hold different beliefs and opinions, it is important that these values can be shared, practised and upheld by different groups of people' (DCSF 2010: 2). The subject must be taught in a way that honours the beliefs and practices of believers in order for shared concepts within religion to be understood. All religions celebrate festivals, but a study of Easter, for example, is little more than an exploration of hot cross

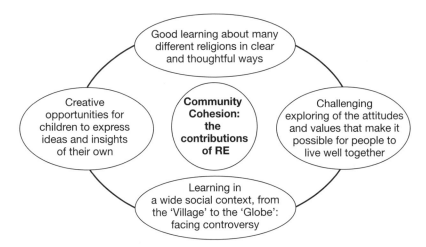

Figure 10.4 RE Today Services day course:'Community Cohesion through Primary RE'

© RE Today, course materials on respect for all in primary RE, http://www.retoday.org.uk

buns and chocolate eggs without some understanding of the Christian concept of a divine Christ offering grace, forgiveness and salvation.

Yet this belief in Jesus' divinity can alienate those of other faiths. It is exclusive, as are many truth claims, and community cohesion is explicitly inclusive. Every world faith makes truth claims that are not mutually compatible. Common value systems may enable conflicting beliefs to be considered without the need for a hostile reaction, but community cohesion should not provide an excuse for advocating syncretism or a search for a *Real an sich* existing only within shared faith experiences (Hick 2004). Community cohesion may encourage dialogue and respect, but it cannot be denied that belief in the truth claims of each religion continues both to be powerfully held, and to prompt misinterpretation, division and fear. The community cohesion agenda assumes that society values equality, and yet the majority of the world's population do not have equal opportunities and their rights are not respected or listened to. In many societies religions are divisive as the truth claims do conflict. Even within Britain it would be wrong to assume that all share the desire to achieve community cohesion.

Conclusions

RE can make a significant positive contribution to community cohesion by allowing young people to build their own self-esteem and confidence, take ownership of their own views and ideas and develop confidence in their own community roots. They can then explore the common values and emotions that enable individuals to find their own answers to life questions and to understand their own place in society. Using shared concepts as a basis to understanding RE can provide opportunities for clear, thoughtful exploration of different religions. As pupils learn to relate the views of others to their own and develop an informed understanding of different religious worldviews, the barriers of difference should be demolished and areas of commonality provide a foundation for understanding. Within the safe and affirming environment of school, discrimination, unfairness and prejudice can be challenged, while pupils explore ways of handling controversy and conflict. As pupils develop confidence in their own place within the local community, RE can also help them to build bridges of understanding with others who may live in other cities or countries, but with whom they share interests, values and friendship. Community cohesion is not easily achieved, but RE has a great deal to contribute to attempts to bring it a little more into reality within twenty-first-century Britain.

According to Ofsted,

> RE cannot ignore its role in fostering community cohesion and in educating for diversity. This goal has never been far from good RE teaching but the current changes in society give this renewed urgency. Pupils have opinions, attitudes, feelings, prejudices and stereotypes. Developing respect for the commitments of others while retaining the right to question, criticise and evaluate different viewpoints is not just an academic exercise: it involves creating opportunities for children and young people to meet those with different viewpoints. They need to grasp how powerful religion is in people's lives. RE should engage pupils' feelings and emotions, as well as their intellect.
>
> (Ofsted 2007: 40–41)

Questions

It is widely accepted that RE is not a platform for indoctrination. How can schools promote community cohesion with pupils from prejudiced or intolerant homes without seeming to undermine parental authority?

Are the opinions of all groups to be treated with equal respect? Is all stereotyping to be avoided? Are there groups or characteristics within society which pupils should be taught to see as dangerous? If so, how do teachers decide which groups these are?

If community cohesion is to be achieved it is essential that highly sensitive and contentious topics such as those used to justify violent extremism be discussed. How should teachers who lack confidence in tackling such issues prepare? How can they ensure that broaching such issues will not either heighten interest or increase prejudice?

Further reading

Bradford and Ripon and Leeds Diocesan Education Team (2008), *Every Child of God Matters Everywhere*, Bradford and Ripon and Leeds Diocesan Education Team. An extensive and very practical guide to building sustainable global partnerships.

Jackson, R. (2004b) *Rethinking Religious Education and Plurality*, London: RoutledgeFalmer. Excellent resource that relates the need for a cohesive community to issues of methodology within RE.

Hudson, C. (2008) *We and They – Using RE to Support Community Cohesion*, Nottingham: Stapleford Centre. A simple and practical guide to community cohesion within RE for teachers.

Wingate, A. (2005) *Celebrating Difference, Staying Faithful*, London: Darton, Longman & Todd. A fascinating study of community cohesion in action within an inter-faith setting.

Related websites

http://www.re-silience.org.uk
http://www.cohesioninstitute.org.uk

Both are useful web resources.

Chapter 11

Secular humanism

Marius Felderhof

Defining secularity

Religion as a description of a particular system of thought and practice, separable from the secular sphere, is a relatively recent phenomenon in the Western world. Prior to the modern period, religion was simply what everyone did, i.e. it was how they lived. To think there was a sphere of life that was simply outside the religious sphere was inconceivable. Dividing the world into the religious and the secular was therefore alien to traditional thinking. Something like the distinction first made its appearance in the Middle Ages, when they sought to distinguish those clergy who lived under a monastic rule, the regular clergy, from those who lived in the wider world, the secular clergy. It was a distinction which effectively contrasted those who were supposedly solely living in and for the eternal versus those who were living in the present age (*saeculum*).

Gradually, following the Reformation, new concerns emerged which gave the distinction between religion and the secular new nuances. In Reformation polity there was an increasing separation between civic and ecclesial authority. Many of the dissenting and Puritan struggles focused on establishing this separation of civil and ecclesial authority, primarily in order to eliminate state interference from the life of the church, not to stop religious people and institutions from having a role in society's collective life. However, not everyone wished to cut the link between the state and the church, hence today we have an *established* church in Britain which until recently largely articulated and represented the values of the state. But we also have 'free churches', i.e., churches largely free of state control.

More recently, secularisation refers to the process whereby the wider society and various social institutions (e.g. universities) gained an increasing autonomy and independence, escaping from ecclesial control and influence. In some circles this process of secularisation has taken the yet further step of actively seeking to limit the contribution of religious institutions to collective life more generally, relegating religion and faith to the sphere of private life of the individual and minimising all public expression of religious life. An extreme version of this in Britain has been the phenomenon of preventing any public show of religious allegiance and adherence. Such public show is regarded as being either divisive or 'offensive'.

Given the above, there can be some confusion on what is meant by the 'secular' world. It can refer to one of three basic but very different socio-political conditions. First, it might refer to collective life outside the monastic walls, i.e. to a civil society where the church or religious institution normally operates, applying its canons and rules through ecclesial courts alongside and through the state's civic laws and courts. Second, it might refer to the world where people can live their lives free from direct ecclesial influence or control but where religious faith could nevertheless freely express itself and where religious individuals and institutions are active and contribute to public debate and decisions about society's collective life. Third, it could refer to a situation where the state has devised an independent value system that impinges on religious life so that individuals and institutions are constrained, or straightforwardly prevented, from operating according to their own standards and purposes in the public square. A prime example of the latter was the way in which adoption agencies of the Roman Catholic Church were prevented from giving preferential treatment to heterosexual couples seeking to adopt children. The government's justification was that the interest of equality (of the adopting individuals) was deemed to override the RC judgement that the interest of children made the church's preferential social policy not only desirable but right. This is not pluralism, this is secularism.

Defining faith

The earlier reference to 'faith' generates yet other questions. Today when some people in the context of religious education speak of children 'without faith' or of children of 'non-faith', one wonders what can be meant by it. To what kind of creatures are they referring? One can begin to guess: perhaps they are speaking of youngsters who do not adhere to certain social institutions or engage in certain identifiable and traditional ritual practices that are called 'religious' in the more contemporary use of the term. The situation is far more complex than that. In its widest meaning to have faith is to live relatively purposefully, confident that world has some kind of meaning and sense. So to live without faith is effectively to be in despair, i.e. to have no overarching sense of purpose.

One can see that the claim to have faith is not yet to say very much. One must still enquire into *what kind of faith* it is; what is its nature and object, or what is the sense that underwrites, or is expressed in, what people do and how they act. To speak of implicit religion in this context, as some people do, is to recognise that there is normally some overarching sense to what people say and do, though this sense is not always articulated, acknowledged or thought about in any detail. In so far as people have thought clearly and deliberately about the sense of their life we might be able to classify these patterns of thought and practice as either theistic or non-theistic. But for most people this sense of life is neither sufficiently systematic nor deliberate, though some have the benefit of its having been loosely derived from a tradition of thinking.

It may be observed that many lack this deliberate rootedness in a tradition except for what happens to be generally embedded in our language and culture. Such people arrive at their sense of life only indirectly through the character of shared activities enjoyed in the wider community. If we speak of Britain as a 'Christian' society it is something of this nature; there are continuing traditions of shared living, many of which have their roots in Christianity. Simply to describe pupils as being of 'non-faith' may, therefore, be far from accurate; they participate in this shared communal life; they certainly seldom suffer from despair, a condition found more frequently among adults rather than children.

Given this situation one should not accept the claim sometimes made by British Humanists or by the National Secular Society that they represent or speak for the purported 'non-faith' majority of people in this country. The organisations in question are small groups who, contrary to the majority, do have a deliberate and relatively coherent view of life that incorporates an opposition and antipathy to theism and traditional forms of religious life. This is not the position of most people who when questioned will admit to some belief in the transcendent or in God and unlike the National Secular Society (NSS) they are often indifferent to the church(es). They do not have sufficiently considered views to share the antipathies of the NSS, but if they do have views, they react negatively to the hostility and antipathy expressed by the NSS.

It is also necessary to admit that even without a conscious participation in the traditions of philosophy and theology the implicit faith that informs life may be dynamic and emotionally mature but not necessarily very coherent and cohesive. In fact, the sense of life embraced by many can be contradictory, eclectic, ragged and utterly lacking in an overarching 'narrative'. Some embrace this latter condition willingly and even thoughtfully. In academic circles this is sometimes described as 'post-modern' and taken to be the prevailing condition of our age, or at least in Western societies. But generally, via educational processes, people do look for some intellectual and emotional integration, at the very least, to order their actions. This leads to the formation of what is sometimes referred to as a 'life stance', a loose but comprehensive term for the diverse intellectual and emotional constructions which inform what people do and how they live in pursuit of the good.

The impulse to form such an integrated construction arises from a basic human desire for a happy, ordered life. It leads people to consider the various obstacles and dissonances that life throws up. The urge is especially acute for those who encounter problems that challenge the sense of their overarching narratives which serve to draw together the diverse experiences in day-to-day life since a fractured overarching narrative leads to the most fundamental existential dis-ease. A compulsion to some sort of resolution is a welcome commitment to being self-critical of their ultimate loyalties but this self-same compulsion may also lead to the temptation to oversimplify. Evidence of this temptation is the popularity of reductionisms of various kinds, e.g. where human behaviour is deemed to be determined by genes rather than thought, or where religious inclinations are 'explained away' as 'nothing but' expressions of sexual desire or where religious inclinations are solely thought to serve certain psychological or social functions. Integration is achieved through an oversimplification.

Nevertheless, the critique of any faith is important if this faith is not to suffer from an ill-considered emotionalism, from intellectual fads and fashions, or from inertia. Criticism is particularly important if the faith, which informs what people *do*, leads them inadvertently to hard heartedness, to immoralities or to intellectual delusions. This can happen when people are driven by ideals which overlook other considerations. Arditti explores this possibility in his novel, *The Enemy of the Good* (2009). Citing Voltaire's observation, 'the best is the enemy of the good', he examines the human capacity to hold high ideals whilst overriding ordinary human decency. And who can deny that there is an element of truth in the provocative claim that religion 'appeals to all that is noblest, purest, loftiest in the human spirit, and yet there scarcely exists a religion which has not been responsible for wars, tyrannies and the suppression of the truth' (Wilson 1991: 1)? The same could be said of communism or of other ideologies, including secular humanism. Despite the benefit of purification provided by the criticisms of religion and ideologies, the criticisms are not always welcomed because they disturb our sense of life and meaning. At a social level they have the power to undermine collective certainties and weaken community solidarity.

Whilst criticism is not only necessary and indicative of a healthy community, one must not assume that every criticism is either warranted, or constructive. Criticisms may equally be ill-informed, misguided and serving to confuse rather than to clarify. Any critic of faith, religious or otherwise, should not necessarily be seen as contributing to the common good. In fact it is part of the theological complaint that much atheistic critique of religious faith is misplaced and misleading, as for example Richard Dawkins' attempt to see religious life as a kind of scientific theory that fails scientific scrutiny (see Dawkins 2006). However, maintaining free expression and resisting censorship is vital where we cannot always determine decisively as to which criticisms lead to better understanding and which do not, which criticisms contribute to the common good and which do not. Maintaining open discussion, testing opinions and experiments, looking for further evidence, information and thought is central to the scientific enterprise and to the growth in human knowledge generally. However, openness cannot be judged by admitting antagonists to criticise on every possible occasion or in every situation.

One should conclude from the above that talk of religions or 'life stances' can be misleading if one conceives of them as clearly defined entities or as comprehensive systems of thought; more frequently they are not. One might equally describe them as a mood, a general disposition in life that is more or less self-critical, more or less open, and more or less coherent. However, there is an underlying drive to create a systematic whole. In this endeavour criticism has an important role in developing a more coherent, more cohesive, more ethical and, dare I say, a more spiritual form of life.

Secular humanism

Humanism is encountered most frequently in the contemporary world as a supposed alternative 'life stance' to religious life. It was not always thus. In the fifteenth and sixteenth century humanism referred to the revival of interest in the classical world, in the languages of Greek and Latin, in Greek and Roman writers and thinkers. A particular feature of this classical world was its interest in the nature and destiny of human beings, in ethical reflection. The Christian tradition has been open to this influence from the classical world from its very beginning. This is most evident from the influence of Plato and Neo-Platonism on St Augustine in the fourth and fifth century, and of Aristotle on the thought of St Thomas Aquinas in the thirteenth century. Not only the Christian tradition but also the Islamic tradition is imbued by this classical influence. Indeed, it is well known that the revival of Aristotelianism within Christian theology in the thirteenth century is largely attributable to increased contact with Islamic scholars who were the main transmitters of Aristotle's writings. It is therefore not at all strange given its syncretistic history that during the Renaissance period Greek and Roman culture once again became a focus of attention and a source for what is known as Christian humanism.

Contemporary humanism, however, has its roots in the eighteenth- and nineteenth-century European intellectual history. Some of the main contributors are the following. In the eighteenth century, Thomas Paine wrote *The Age of Reason* (1794) which was a powerful political attack on ecclesial and class privilege. In the meantime David Hume from within the empiricist tradition attempted to undermine philosophical foundations for religious belief with his *Dialogues Concerning Natural Religion* (1779), whilst on the Continent early in the nineteenth century, Ludwig Feuerbach in *The Essence of Christianity* (1848), reacting to Hegel, emphasised the importance of religion but saw God as a human projection, as part of a process through which human beings came to know themselves. The main burden of eighteenth- and nineteenth-century philosophical reflection was that religious life is intimately related to the definition of our humanity but no longer necessarily as the ultimate expression and guarantor of human dignity. Instead, religion was treated by some as the obstacle to the realisation of mankind's final destiny, as something to outgrow, as a source of false-consciousness (Marx) or as a neurosis (Freud). Much of this is doctrinaire and fanciful speculation.

Human self-understanding was challenged still further by the emerging science of geology, and later by biology. The first undermined traditional biblical historical perceptions by greatly enlarging the age of the earth and the universe, the second by demonstrating the close interrelationship of all animal life. This too has consequences for human self-understanding. In the nascent biological sciences in particular, human beings appeared to be the product of a-moral, impersonal processes. These processes were deemed to be wasteful, competitive and dependent on killing. The implication was clear. They seemed self-evidently to subvert the dignity of human life as maintained by religious traditions by suggesting that human beings *should* behave like that. Religious traditions had relied on there being something fundamentally distinctive about human life, such as an eternal soul or in having been made by a personal, creative act 'in the image and likeness of God' that required love and collaboration. The images and metaphors of religious traditions were too intimately tied to human self-understanding and too obviously at variance with the apparent implications from scientific descriptions to allow the developing scientific picture to be accepted as a simple growth in understanding of how the world works. Work needed to be done on how descriptive enquiries of science relate to our moral and spiritual life.

The stories of conflict between religion and science that were cultivated later had distinct ideological roots that were hardly warranted by the nature of either. More impartial histories of science would demonstrate a more intimate and supportive link between religion and modern science in its earliest stages (Jaki 1979; Hooykaas 1973). The point at issue is not on differences in the valuation of knowledge or on scientific methodology but on the most responsible way of being human. This was all too evident from the great Oxford debate (1860) between Huxley (Darwin's bulldog) and Samuel Wilberforce, the bishop of Oxford. There was no great triumph either way on scientific grounds as the scientific evidence at that stage was far from conclusive; if anything, it was claimed that the bishop had the better argument scientifically. However, Bishop Samuel's famous jibe reportedly made about Huxley's ancestry and its retort uncovered the real Victorian anxiety, namely, that the link to a simian ancestry undermined human dignity.

There were other forces at work in the emerging friction. Personal and social reactions to ecclesial authority and control played their part. Many of the early secular humanists were alienated clergyman or disaffected church members (see Budd 1977); the quest of scientists to become members of a recognised profession in a context where one could not have a university post without belonging to the established church and taking holy orders was yet another factor in secularisation; also industrialisation was transforming society and unsettling the traditional social relationships in which the church had its place. The experiments in science were a further stimulus to experimenting in establishing what some deemed to be a more rational religion (as pursued by Comte and by Kant) or to exploring other ways in which human beings might pursue the good and discover the authority of the rules that prescribe what is right and just. Contemporary British Humanists have their roots in ethical societies and in worshipping communities that redesigned liturgies and rewrote hymns. Modern penchants for naming and marriage ceremonies, and secular humanist burial services, have very little to do with science but demonstrate that traditional religious ritual could not simply be discarded in its entirety.

Etsi deus non daretur ('As if God did not exist')

Without its interest in ritual and its attempt to redefine the nature and basis of human moral life, secular humanism might simply comprise the range of human activities on which religious practices and conceptions have little or no direct bearing and as such would be religiously indifferent. Such indifference would also ensure that it had little to contribute to those aspects of life which are the particular concerns of religious life. The human capacity to imagine and enlarge such secular spheres of human life has grown significantly with the developments of science and technology. Technology is a preoccupation with *the means by* which people live rather than with *the ends for* which people live. Secularity in this sense complements religious and ethical life rather than providing an alternative to it.

This complementarity between science and religion is also evident in their respective interests. The scientific world investigates causal relationships largely on the assumption that there are clear boundaries within which the investigation operates. The consequent scientific methodology does not admit the possibility of a change in categories, e.g. from causes to intentions, or to reasons. This axiomatic procedure of limiting the scope of the enquiry in scientific investigations is known in theological circles as 'methodological atheism' or, more accurately, it is a methodology that works on the basis that a reference to God would change the terms of the investigation and hence the basis of the discussion i.e. it would no longer be scientific. This scientific methodology is a self-limitation adopted for heuristic or practical reasons. There is no reason to accept claims that this is the *only* method of enquiry worth pursuing except for doctrinaire reasons encountered in the various guises of reductionism mentioned above.

It is only when science becomes self-evidently a human activity for which human beings might be held responsible, individually and collectively, that it once again comes within the purview of a religious world. On such occasions we seek a rationale for the pursuit of science or of knowledge more generally. In and of itself science does not encourage the adoption or the abandonment of religious practices and beliefs whereas religion does encourage or fail to encourage the pursuit of science and its causal enquiries. These observations are important since secular humanism is sometimes presented as an alternative life stance to the religious life on supposedly scientific grounds. If it is wholly grounded in science and complementary, it cannot be a genuine alternative for it would belong to a sphere of human activity that has little bearing on anything resembling religious interests.

Secular humanism and religious education

The role of secular humanism in religious education is affected by confusion on its precise nature and origin. Is it genuinely an alternative to religious faith or is it a range of intellectual activities using a methodology 'etsi deus non daretur'? If the latter, might one say secular humanism dominates the school curriculum since nearly all the curricular subjects pursue knowledge precisely with such a methodology? The one subject where this approach would be inappropriate is precisely the subject which considers humanity as existing 'before God', a condition which requires a very different methodology and which engages with people on a very different basis.

When in 1974 the City of Birmingham took legal advice on the proposal from its agreed syllabus conference that Marxism and Secular Humanism be included in its RE provision, the response was that these could only be included as *critiques* of religion but not 'in their own right'. Existing 'before God', or belief in God with its methodology was taken to be definitive of anything that could be called *religious* education. Criticism of religion from whatever perspective, as argued earlier, has an important role in religious life and for that reason alone the critiques offered by Marxism and Secular Humanism must be considered.

From the point of view of defining a subject area and enquiry, its methodology is important though boundaries are often blurred. In the case of RE the fact that Marxism and Secular Humanism offer critiques of religion contributes to the blurring of its boundaries. Whilst apparently being about religion their methodology demonstrates that, fundamentally, they do not think or enquire religiously. Apart from their critiques of religion, they are therefore best excluded from RE, in that by their nature, they have no bearing on religious interests and on religious approaches to these interests.

The issue is further confused by the history of RE which has in recent decades increasingly relied on Religious Studies as a discipline. Religious Studies, like Marxism and Secular Humanism, relies on a methodology that could readily belong to that characterised as 'etsi deus non daretur'. The exclusive reliance on such a methodology also means that it too does not understand religious life religiously. RE that has become nothing but Religious Studies has effectively ceased to be religious by being a secular study of religion. Indeed some have described RE precisely in these terms so that in its methodology RE becomes a form of history of religion, psychology of religion, sociology of religion or philosophy of religion. Those who do not welcome the secularisation of RE have every reason to exclude Marxism and Secular Humanism (apart from their critiques of religion) from RE. They will be seen as distractions and as a potential source of confusion about methodology, since such secular disciplines do not seek to learn or to teach what it might mean to understand oneself and the world religiously, i.e. as an agent 'before God' or 'before the transcendent'.

Some of the confusion might also stem from the universal desire to be inclusive and to offer everyone access to education, as for example expressed in the Jomtien Declaration, 1990. But giving everyone access to education is not quite the same as saying that a particular school subject should include every topic and methodology. Further, Article 2 of the protocols to the European Convention of Human Rights states that

> no person shall be denied the right to education. In the exercise of any functions which it assumes in relation to education and to teaching the State

shall respect the right of parents to ensure such education and teaching in conformity with their own religious and philosophical convictions.

This too might be thought to require secular humanist convictions to be included in the school curriculum and that therefore RE should include Marxism and Secular Humanism 'in their own right' within its remit. But this conclusion is also a confusion. First, the argument presumes that secular humanist convictions are not already reflected in the school curriculum. The points made above suggest that the methodology of much of the school curriculum reflects precisely secular humanist convictions and where it does not, e.g. in RE in Britain, pupils may be exempted by their parents.

Moreover, a secular system of values is most likely to be found in subjects like Citizenship Education or in Personal, Social and Health Education. Where this is the case it cannot be argued that secular humanist pupils are not receiving an education in conformity with secular humanist convictions. So the question remains: must secular philosophies be included in RE 'in their own right'? The answer would appear to be that it cannot do so legally but more importantly it cannot do so constitutionally, without RE ceasing to be characteristically religious. The only parents being denied access to an education according to their convictions where RE has become entirely a secular teaching about religion are religious parents. What may redeem this situation somewhat in Britain is access to faith schools or access to a form of RE in community schools that is explicitly religious in content and method.

In the *Toledo Guiding Principles about Religions and Beliefs in Public Schools* (ODIHR 2007) we find the European Council of Ministers adopting a language which is not only confusing but deceptive. First, the reference to 'beliefs' (alongside 'religions') might refer to any claim made and the way it is supported but it is evidently more restrictive than that. If what is intended is something like Marxist and Secular Humanist philosophies then they should say so because many people with religious convictions are used to thinking of 'beliefs' as having to do with religious life and not with claims, e.g. about the presence of water on Mars. Second, the *Toledo Guiding Principles* represent Marxism and secular philosophies as alternatives to religious beliefs and practices rather than as social theories or theories about e.g. human nature that are subject to quite different criteria.

Because the draft guidance for RE created by the Department for Children, Schools and Families in 2009 echoed these references to 'religion and belief', where belief was a clear code for secular philosophies, the City of Birmingham's Solicitor's Office sought further legal advice from a London QC. It had been suggested by the draft guidance that the Human Rights Act and the Equalities Act required that Marxism and Secular Humanism in the guise of 'belief' be included in RE. This proved not to be the case. Where 'belief' refers to secular philosophies the earlier advice from 1974 still stood. It is evidently problematical for the British Humanist Association to argue both that its life stance is not religious and to insist it should be included in RE. The only possible justification is that somehow religions and secular philosophies belong to the same category. This, despite some family resemblances, is contentious.

It might be argued that secular philosophies and religions are all 'life stances' and therefore should be treated equally under a common (possibly new) subject heading as competing hypotheses about human beings and the nature of the world. To think in this way is already to adopt a secular point of view. Competing hypotheses suggest that you are in control, free to make judgements about 'beliefs'. But within religious life, God and his commands do not present themselves as a hypotheses about which one might make a judgement. To illustrate this point I have argued elsewhere that 'respect for all' is not received by a religious person as a hypothesis, i.e. as something to take or leave depending on the evidence, instead one may obey or disobey. Invariably religious life is not primarily about subscribing to a set of beliefs for indifferent or insubstantial reasons.

Conclusion

A tolerant and open society will normally admit religious people on their own terms and give them space to live as they see fit. Secular interests and enquiries are normally shared by religious people and complement religious life and interests rather than present themselves as alternatives. These secular interests are well represented on the school curriculum where nearly all disciplines pursue a line of enquiry 'etsi deus non daretur'. RE is designed to represent religious interests and religious forms of understanding that are marked by a decentring from the self, and focus on a form of human flourishing uniquely occasioned by existing 'before God' or before the transcendent. This demands from the human person certain dispositions, virtues or strengths of character. One creates confusions about what it means to educate religiously by including secular philosophies in RE as 'alternatives' to religious faith. RE is about the endeavour to learn what religious life has to contribute by seeing oneself as a responsible self rather than as a spectator devising theories about human nature and the world. By all means criticise religious life but do not misrepresent it as if it were a theory.

Questions

Are secular views of life oversimplifications?

Do school curricula accommodate or reflect secular philosophies? If so, where and how?

Should RE give time to secular philosophies? If so, on what basis?

Further reading

Budd, S. (1977) *Varieties of Unbelief, Atheists and Agnostics in English Society 1850–1960*, London: Heinemann. A good discussion of the rise of cultural unbelief in England.

Ferguson, D. (2009) *Faith and its Critics: A Conversation*, Oxford: Oxford University Press. A theologian engages with the 'new atheism'.

Haldane, J. (2010) *Reasonable Faith*, London: Routledge. Sophisticated discussion of religious themes in relation to scepticism.

Shaw, D. W. D. (1978) *The Dissuaders, Three Explanations of Religion*, London: SCM. Short discussion of three influential critics of religion: Freud, Marx and Durkheim.

Chapter 12

Empirical research

Leslie J. Francis

The aim of this chapter is to provide a broad introduction to the development of empirical research in religious education (RE) in the United Kingdom during the 50-year period from 1960 until 2010. The focus will be limited to published qualitative and quantitative studies concerning the religiosity of young people and relevant to school-related RE.

Research in RE in the UK during the twentieth century was not shaped by a central initiative, a major research institute, or a powerful funder. In one sense, these are major weaknesses which have resulted in the failure to generate and to train a wide pool of highly skilled researchers. In another sense, the vacuum has allowed space for private initiative to take root and sometimes even to flourish. In the absence of central co-ordination, the story of the four decades between 1960 and 2000 becomes a story written around individual researchers. Nevertheless, the story conveniently divides into three phases: the period of the pioneers; the period of quantitative studies; and the period of qualitative studies. In the next decade (2000–2010) a new mood emerged with a period of consolidation.

Phase one: the pioneers

The new impetus for empirical research in RE which emerged in the UK during the early 1960s was heralded by six key figures: Harold Loukes, Violet Madge, Ronald Goldman, Kenneth Hyde, Edwin Cox and Colin Alves, all of whom published a major study between 1961 and 1968. Each of these authors seemed to have worked independently and established a precedent that others followed.

Harold Loukes (1961), in *Teenage Religion*, drew on two research methods. In stage one he arranged for six schools to record discussions held by 14-year-old pupils. In stage two he selected a number of typical quotations which were then submitted to 502 pupils for their written comments. A decade later Loukes employed the same methodology to produce his book *Teenage Morality* (1973). Between these two studies, Loukes (1965) employed a more quantitative approach in his *New Ground in Christian Education*.

Violet Madge (1965), in *Children in Search of Meaning*, employed a less systematic and less disciplined method to data generation than that employed by

Loukes. She drew heavily on her personal experience and observation to generate rich illustrative materials. In her second book, Madge (1971) examined children's statements about Jesus.

Ronald Goldman (1964), in *Religious Thinking from Childhood to Adolescence*, drew on a recognised research methodology and a recognised theoretical framework grounded in Piagetian psychology. Piaget distinguishes between three sequential developmental stages in thinking which are characterised as pre-operational, concrete operational and formal operational thinking. Goldman detected evidence for these stages on the basis of clinical interviews conducted among a sample of 200 pupils, 10 boys and 10 girls within each year group between the ages of 6 and 17, treating 15-, 16-, and 17-year-olds as one age group.

Goldman's research was the most influential of the era. It influenced the RE curriculum and shaped the research agenda for other researchers, including Bull (1969), Greer (1972b), Whitehouse (1972), Richmond (1972) and Morley (1975).

Kenneth Hyde (1965), in *Religious Learning in Adolescence*, brought quantitative methods to research in RE. He developed four tests, concerned with God images, religious concepts, religious knowledge and attitude towards religion, applied among more than 3,500 pupils. Hyde's instruments were subsequently employed by others, including Richmond (1972).

Edwin Cox (1967), in *Sixth Form Religion*, also employed quantitative methods to explore the following issues: existence of God, Jesus, life after death, Bible, church, RE, personal religious behaviours and moral behaviours, among 2,276 sixth-form pupils. Further analysis of Cox's data were provided by Wright and Cox (1967a, 1967b).

Colin Alves (1968), in *Religion in the Secondary School*, reported an ambitious project conducted among 14- to 16-year-old pupils in 526 schools. The questionnaire contained a test of pupils' knowledge of the New Testament, pupils' insight into the meaning of New Testament quotations, belief and attitude items about Jesus, the bible and the church, items relating to moral choices and questions about personal religious identity and practice.

Phase two: quantitative studies

The 1970s saw the development of a concern to apply psychometric theories and techniques to research in RE, reflected in two initiatives building on Ronald Goldman's work. The first initiative concerned measuring religious thinking. The second initiative concerned measuring attitudes towards religion.

In terms of religious thinking, John Peatling (1974, 1977) designed the test known as *Thinking about the Bible*. Although Peatling's work originated in the USA it had significant influence in the UK, where Peatling's instrument was employed and significantly criticised (see Greer 1983a; McGrady 1983). After reviewing Peatling's attempt to measure religious thinking, D. Linnet Smith (1998) proposed a different solution, in which she was careful to distinguish between theological content and operational level. Smith's test of religious thinking concentrated on one biblical narrative used by Goldman, the burning bush, and identified six distinct scales from the pattern of pupils' responses to Goldman's questions.

In terms of attitude toward religion, Francis (1979) recognised that, while a series of studies had explored aspects of pupil attitudes towards religion, the problem of integrating and synthesising the findings from these studies resulted from the diversity of measuring instruments used. In a paper entitled 'Measurement reapplied', Francis (1978) invited other researchers to collaborate with him in using the Francis scale of attitude towards Christianity. The scale has also been subjected to significant scrutiny and criticism, for example by Greer (1982, 1983b) and Levitt (1995). The scale is not recommended for use among young people under the age of eight years. The initial studies employing the Francis scale of attitude towards Christianity began to provide a cumulative picture of the personal, social and contextual factors relating to attitudes towards Christianity during childhood and adolescence. These studies fall into seven main groups (Francis 1993). First, a series of descriptive studies charted how attitudes towards Christianity change as children grow up, how attitudes differ between boys and girls, and how the situation varies between different cultures (Francis 1989a; Francis and Greer 1990a). Second, a series of studies were conducted throughout the same schools at four-yearly intervals since 1974. Such replication allows careful monitoring of how the young person's response to Christianity is changing over time (Francis 1989b, 1992a). Third, several studies concentrated on identifying the character and influence of denominational schools, at primary (Francis 1987) and secondary level (Francis and Carter 1980; Francis and Greer 1990b). Fourth, a group of studies focused specifically on the influence of home and parents, including social class (Gibson, Francis and Pearson 1990) and the relative influence of mothers and fathers on sons and daughters at two different stages in development (Francis and Gibson 1993a). A fifth set of studies modelled the influence of personality on individual differences in religious development, including the function of neuroticism (Francis and Pearson 1991), extraversion (Francis and Pearson 1985) and psychoticism (Francis 1992b). A sixth set of studies explored the relationship between attitudes towards Christianity and attitudes towards science, giving particular attention to the ideas of scientism and creationism (Fulljames, Gibson and Francis 1991; Francis, Fulljames and Gibson 1992; Fulljames 1996). A seventh set of studies explored issues like the impact of popular religious television (Francis and Gibson 1992), the influence of pop culture (Francis and Gibson 1993b), the contribution of religious experiences (Greer and Francis 1992), and the relationship between religion and just world beliefs (Crozier and Joseph 1997), schizotypal traits (Diduca and Joseph 1997), altruism (Eckert and Lester 1997), intelligence (Francis 1998), happiness (Robbins and Francis 1996), gender orientation (Francis and Wilcox 1998), social desirability (Gillings and Joseph 1996), self-esteem (Jones and Francis 1996), and life satisfaction (Lewis 1998).

Legacy from the quantitative studies

The foundation studies in quantitative methods published by Greer and by Francis in the 1970s have continued to be influential in the contemporary landscape of research in RE. Greer's (1972a) original study on sixth-form religion, using Cox's (1967) questionnaire in Northern Ireland, had been conducted in 1968. Greer (1980) reported on the first replication in 1978, and Greer (1989) reported on the second replication in 1988. Already this careful programme of replication was able to point to important aspects of continuity and of discontinuity in the ways in which sixth-form pupils in Protestant schools in Northern Ireland view matters of religion and matter of morality. After Greer's untimely death in 1994, his colleagues continued with his research plans by conducting the third replication in1998, and this time extending the research to include sixth-form pupils attending Catholic schools in Northern Ireland. Drawing now on four waves of data spanning 30 years, Greer's colleagues discussed the findings in a series of six papers. Francis, Robbins, Barnes and Lewis (2006a) discussed the four profiles of Protestant pupils generated in 1968, 1978, 1988, and 1989. Francis, Robbins, Barnes and Lewis (2006b) compared the new data among sixth-form pupils with data collected by Greer in 1984 among fourth-year pupils in both Protestant and Catholic schools. Francis, Robbins, Lewis, Barnes and ap Siôn (2007) found that, while males attending Catholic schools maintain a more positive attitude towards Christianity than males attending Protestant schools, females attending Catholic schools report a less positive attitude towards Christianity than females attending Protestant schools. Francis, ap Siôn, Lewis, Barnes, and Robbins (2006) linked with two of Greer's studies conducted in 1981 and 1991 on religious experience; and ap Siôn (2006) analysed the content of the reported religious experiences of the pupils within nine descriptive categories. Francis, Robbins, ap Siôn, Lewis and Barnes (2007) demonstrated that there was no evidence to associate a positive view of Christianity with poorer levels of psychological health among adolescents in Northern Ireland, and some evidence to associate a positive view of Christianity with better levels of psychological health.

Francis' original study was published in 1978, inviting colleagues concerned with empirical research in RE to allow their findings to be co-ordinated through agreement as a common measure, the Francis Scale of Attitude towards Christianity (Francis 1978). By the mid-1990s, Kay and Francis (1996) identified over one hundred studies that had used the measure and were in a position to begin to construct a co-ordinated tapestry of findings. An overview of subsequent studies has been provided by Francis (2009).

Two interesting developments have occurred in this research tradition. The first development concerns the translation of the Francis Scale of Attitude towards Christianity into more than ten other languages, including Arabic (Munayer 2000), Chinese (Francis, Lewis and Ng 2002), Dutch (Francis and Hermans 2000), French (Lewis and Francis 2003) and German (Francis, Ziebertz and Lewis 2002).

The second development concerns collaboration with colleagues working within other faith traditions in order to create comparable measuring instruments, including the Sahin-Francis Scale of Attitude towards Islam (Sahin and Francis 2002), the Katz-Francis Scale of Attitude towards Judaism (Francis and Katz 2007), and the Santosh-Francis Scale of Attitude towards Hinduism (Francis, Santosh, Robbins and Vij 2008). As a consequence of these two developments, a research tradition begun in England and Wales has fostered comparable studies in a number of contexts.

Phase three: qualitative studies

During the 1990s a new interest emerged in qualitative studies in RE, as reflected in the Children and Worldviews Project at Chichester, the Children's Spirituality Project at Nottingham and the work of the Warwick Religions and Education Research Unit. The Children and Worldviews Project was established to examine the ways in which children think, learn and view the world in which they live. The project set out to listen to children in settings where they feel at ease. The project approached listening to children through the use of story, poetry and the discussion of themes. The children themselves set the agenda. At each stage the project team discussed with teachers what children were saying. Drawing on this research method, in *The Education of the Whole Child*, Erricker *et al.* (1997) illustrate the findings of their research by exploring six topics: children's experience of conflict and loss; children's religious and scientific thinking; the identity of 'Asian' children; taking children's stories to other children; children and parental separation; and religious identity and children's worldviews. Other findings from the Children and Worldviews Project have been published in the following studies. Erricker and Erricker (1995) draw on the research to identify the ways in which children's story telling can be understood, addressed and valued by taking into account its ontological significance. Erricker and Erricker (1996) drew on the research to illustrate children's spirituality. Ota (1997) draws on the research to discuss the experience of Muslim and Sikh children coping with different value systems. Ota *et al.* (1997) draw on the research to profile the 'secrets' of the playground. Erricker (1998) draws on the research to examine the effect of death, loss and conflict on children's worldviews.

The Children's Spirituality Project grew out of the concerns of the Alister Hardy Religious Experience Research Centre. In *The Spirit of the Child*, Hay and Nye (1998) pose two key problems: what conceptual boundaries can be set to the term 'spirituality' and how can we identify categories of children's experience which belong to this realm? In addressing the first question, Hay and Nye conceive of an innate spiritual capacity in childhood, but recognise that this may focus in particular ways and take different and changing forms as children's other capacities develop. In addressing the second question, Hay and Nye propose a set of three interrelated themes or categories of spiritual sensitivity, which they define as: awareness sensing; mystery sensing; and value sensing.

In the course of their project a total of 38 children were interviewed on a one-to-one basis by Nye. The data generated by these interviews were approached in two ways. The first approach resembled that of case studies. Nye interrogated the transcripts of individual children in order to identify each child's individual spirituality. Here she spoke in terms of a kind of personal 'signature' for each child. The second approach tried to identify patterns or conclusions which were common across the individual children. In this connection Nye identified two different kinds of conversation which were of particular relevance: dialogue that employed religious ideas and language; and non-religious dialogue that implicitly conveyed that the child was engaged in something more than the casual or mundane.

The Warwick Religions and Education Research Unit, under the directorship of Robert Jackson, employed ethnographic research to underpin curriculum development in RE. Helpful introductions to both the research and the curriculum development are provided by Jackson (1996a) in an essay entitled 'Ethnographic research and curriculum development' and by Jackson (1997) in his book *Religious Education: An Interpretive Approach*. Jackson's argument is that RE should present religions as they are perceived and lived by their adherents, rather than as reified belief systems. Ethnographic research, he argued, provides the method for uncovering how it is that adherents perceive and live their faith.

The Warwick Religions and Education Research Unit integrated a series of studies conducted throughout the 1980s and 1990s among children from different religious communities in Britain. The projects focused on children in the 8–13 age range, using participant observation, informal and semi-structured interviews, documentary analysis and photography. Robert Jackson and Eleanor Nesbitt initiated this research tradition in 1984, in a study exploring formal religious nurture among Hindu children in different parts of England. This was followed by a second much larger study of Hindu children in Coventry (Jackson and Nesbitt 1993) and by a third study, among children from two Punjabi caste-based movements with an ambiguous identity as either Hindu or Sikh.

Other findings from the Religious Education and Community Project are presented in a series of articles and chapters. For example, Jackson (1989, 1996b) focuses on aspects of Hinduism; Nesbitt (1990) examines the Valmiki community in Coventry; Nesbitt (1992) focuses on issues raised by ethnographic studies of children's participation in worship; Nesbitt (1993) examines children's views on life after death; Nesbitt (1995) examines the cultural history and cultural choices of Punjabis in Britain; Nesbitt (1997a, 1997b) focuses on aspects of the experience of young Sikhs; Nesbitt (1998a) explores the self-understanding of young British Hindus as 'British', 'Asian' and 'Hindu'; Nesbitt (1998b) explores the relationship between young Hindus' and Sikhs' experiences of their faith tradition outside school with its presentation in school; Nesbitt and Jackson (1992) compare the perceptions held by Hindu and Christian children of each other's religion; Nesbitt and Jackson (1993) explore cultural transmission in a Diaspora Sikh community; Nesbitt and Jackson (1995) concentrate on Sikh children's use of 'God'.

Legacies from the qualitative studies

The foundation studies in qualitative methods published by Jackson and by Nesbitt in the 1990s have continued to be influential in the contemporary landscape of research in RE through the pioneering work of the Warwick Religions and Education Research Unit. A series of studies reported on pupils experiencing values education informed by religious principles. For example Nesbitt and Arweck (2003) and Arweck and Nesbitt (2004) reported on ethnographical research among pupils experiencing a values education programme known as 'Living Values: an educational program' developed in association with a Hindu-related religious organisation, the Brahma Kumaris World Spiritual University. Arweck and Nesbitt (2007) reported on ethnographic research among pupils experiencing the Sathya Sai Education in Human Values programme. In a more broadly based study, Nesbitt and Henderson (2003) reported on ethnographic research among pupils experiencing one of three different values education programmes made by religious organisations. In addition to the Brahma Kumaris and the Sathya Sai programmes, the third programme was developed by the Religious Society of Friends (Quakers).

A three-year ethnographic study investigated the identity formation of young people growing up in mixed faith families in the UK. Arweck and Nesbitt (2010a) explored to what extent and in what way religious values are transmitted from generation to generation, taking into account the parents' background in terms of faith tradition, ethnicity and culture. Arweck and Nesbitt (2010b) presented a case study to examine what kind of cultural repertoire young people could draw on and whether this fostered 'multiple cultural competence' in them. Other analyses from these data are presented by Arweck and Nesbitt (2010c), and Nesbitt and Arweck (2010).

Other published studies have employed ethnographic methods: to examine the delivery of RE to Muslim pupils (Ipgrave 1999); to examine motivation in RE (O'Grady 2003); to explore religious diversity, and inter-ethnic relations within a Catholic primary school (Breen 2009); to explore reflexive self-assessment in RE (Fancourt 2010); and to explore pupils' perspectives on the purpose of RE, resourcing RE, and ways in which religions are presented in curriculum materials (Jackson *et al.* 2010).

Phase three: consolidation

During the first decade of the twenty-first century the culture underpinning empirical research in RE in the UK began to move from individual to institutional initiatives, from independent UK to European initiatives, and from marginal concern to research council priorities. During the first decade of the twenty-first century religion reasserted itself as a matter of public concern and social significance (see Francis and Ziebertz in press). Four examples of this major transition are provided by: The Teenage Religion and Values Survey (TRVS) at the Welsh National Centre for Religious Education; the Religion and Life Perspectives Project (RaLP) at Würzburg University, involving Bangor University; the project 'Religion in education: a contribution to dialogue or a factor of conflict in transforming societies of European Countries' (REDCo) at Hamburg University, involving the Warwick Religions and Education Research Unit; by the Religion and Society Programme jointly sponsored by two Research Councils (AHRC and ESRC).

The Teenage Religions and Values Survey was designed to provide a valuable and unique source of data about the place of religion in the lives of young people throughout England and Wales at the close of the twentieth century. Drawing on a large sample of 33,982 young people between the ages of 13 and 15, the survey was able to profile the range of religious traditions visible within England and Wales, including representatives from the major world faiths (e.g. Hindus, Jews, Muslims and Sikhs), the smaller Christian denominations (e.g. Baptists, Methodists and Presbyterians), and other sects (e.g. Jehovah's Witnesses). The first overview of the study was published by Francis (2001a) in *The Values Debate* and a recent overview of the many focused analyses, distributed across a range of edited volumes or journals, has been provided by Robbins and Francis (2010).

The second book to emerge from the study, *Urban Hope and Spiritual Health* (Francis and Robbins 2005), was offered as a contribution to the work of the Commission on Urban Life and Faith. This book draws on the model of spiritual health proposed by John Fisher (2001, 2004) who maintains that good spiritual health is reflected in positive relationships within four domains: the personal domain (concerned with relationship with self); the communal domain (concerned with relationship with others); the environmental domain (concerned with relationship with the wider world); and the transcendental domain (concerned with relationship with matters of ultimate concern however these are conceived).

Studies from the Teenage Religions and Values Survey examined the association between affiliation to the world faiths and personal, family and social values (Francis 2001b), and attitudes towards school, sex, alcohol, environment and leisure (Francis 2001c), and between the different denominations, distinguishing between Anglicans, Baptists, Catholics, Methodists, Pentecostals, Presbyterians, and Jehovah's Witnesses (Francis 2008a, 2008b). Francis and Robbins (2004) undertook a comparison between two groups: those who do not believe in God and claim no religious affiliation and those who do not believe in God but describe themselves as Anglicans. Robbins (2000) compared the profile of four groups of young people: those who attended church regularly at the time of completing the survey (attenders); those who used to attend church regularly, but now do so only occasionally (partial leavers); those who used to attend church regularly, but now no longer attend church (total leavers); and those who have never attended church regularly (non-attenders). Three studies examined the association between pupils' values and beliefs and attendance of schools with a religious character: Anglican schools (Lankshear 2005), Catholic schools (Francis 2002a) and the new independent Christian schools (Francis 2005a).

The Teenage Religion and Values Survey has enabled a number of other issues concerning the place of religion in the lives of young people to be examined in depth. Detailed studies have been offered on the influence of religion on attitudes towards smoking (Robbins 2005), on attitudes towards RE and school assemblies (Kay and Francis 2001), on attitudes towards science (Astley 2005), on attitudes towards abortion (Francis 2004), on suicidal ideation (Kay and Francis 2006). More complex multi-variate analyses have been employed to identify and isolate the influence of bible reading (Francis 2000a, 2000b, 2002b); the influence of prayer (Francis 2005b; Francis and Robbins 2006), and the influence of God images on personal well-being and moral values (Francis 2001d).

The Religion and Life Perspectives Project was designed to facilitate a comparative study of the life orientations, values, religion and institutional trust at the upper end of the secondary school age range across nine countries: Germany, the UK, Poland, the Netherlands, Sweden, Finland, the Republic of Ireland, Croatia and Israel. Subsequently Turkey also joined the project (see Kay and Ziebertz 2006, for an introduction). All told 9,852 young people participated in the project. The project was first conceived in a way that would allow the individual young person to be located within a socio-demographic context. For this reason, the variables used within the questionnaire were related to concepts at the *micro*-level: these were concerned with personal life planning. Then there were variables at the *meso*-level which included trust in organisations and issue-related groups; and finally variables were grouped at the *macro*-level and dealt with the arena of public life, political parties and willingness to undertake political or parliamentary action. In relation to religion two other analytic measures were introduced. The first concerned the contrast or connection between the religious beliefs and practices of the parents and the religious beliefs and practices of the young person. A fourfold classification was constructed: young people from a practising religious home who were themselves practising believers; young people from a practising religious home who were not believers; young people from secular homes who were believers; and young people from secular homes who were themselves secular. The second was more directly concerned with RE. Here the presumption was that pupils might adopt a mono-religious approach to RE (where only one religion is thought to be true), a multi-religious RE (where all religions may be equally true) and an inter-religious RE (where each religion is seen in the light of others) (Ziebertz 2005).

The main findings from the Religion and Life Perspectives Project were published in the three-volume series *Youth in Europe*, edited by Ziebertz and Kay (2005, 2006) and by Ziebertz, Kay and Riegel (2009). Two chapters are of particular significance for research in RE in the UK. In volume one, Kay (2005a) characterises the responses of the sample of 1,083 young people in England as one of cautious optimism. He suggests that these young people are oriented toward career success and family life, and are generally neutral towards Europe. He concludes that they are generally apathetic towards politics and inclined to turn to their private and social worlds for solace and satisfaction in the face of their alienation from the political process. He demonstrates that religion, personality and gender remain important factors in shaping values. In volume two, Kay (2006) concentrates specifically on analysing the religious worldview of three young people. Other analyses are reported by Kay and Ziebertz (2008, 2009).

The Religion in Education Project (REDCo) was designed to establish and compare the potentials and limitations of religion, in the educational systems of selected countries, for transforming societies, including: Germany, Norway, the Netherlands, England and Wales, France, Spain, Russia and Estonia. Alongside theoretical and conceptual analyses, the REDCo project employed a rich variety of qualitative and quantitative empirical methods to examine the perceptions of 14- to 16-year-old pupils across the participating countries. Here is a comparative research project on young people's views on religion, religious diversity and possibilities of dialogue with implications for future research in RE. Main findings from the REDCo project were published in volumes in the Waxmann series, *Religious Diversity and Education in Europe*, including Jackson, Miedama, Weiße and Willaime (2007), Knauth, Jozsa, Bertram-Troost and Ipgrave (2008), Valke, Bertram-Troost, Friederici and Béraud (2009), Jackson, Ipgrave and O'Grady (2009) and Schihalejev (2010).

Key conclusions from the empirical data provided by the young people include the following: the majority of students appreciated the religious heterogeneity in their societies although a range of prejudices were expressed; irrespective of their religious positions a majority of students are interested in learning about religions in school; students are well aware of and experience religious diversity mostly in, but also outside school; students are generally open towards peers of different religious backgrounds, although they tend to socialise with peers from the same background as themselves, even when they live in areas characterised by religious diversity; students often express a tolerant attitude more at an abstract than a practical level, the tolerance expressed in classroom discussion is not always replicated in their daily life-world; those who learn about religious diversity in school are more willing to enter into conversations about religions and worldviews with students from other backgrounds than those who do not have this opportunity for learning; students desire peaceful co-existence across religious differences, and believe that this is possible; students for whom religion is important in their lives are more likely to respect the religious background of others and value the role of religion in their world; students generally wish to avoid conflict on religious issues, and some of the religiously committed students feel especially vulnerable.

The Religion and Society Programme (AHRC and ESRC) sponsored in its first call a project entitled 'Does RE Work?' involving the University of Glasgow, King's College London and Queens University Belfast. The project included the voices of pupils (see Lundie 2010). The second call from this programme focused specifically on youth, and includes large projects with considerable potential for influencing research in RE: the project on 'young people's attitudes to religious diversity' directed by Professor Jackson at the University of Warwick; the project on 'negotiating identity: young people's perspectives on faith values, community norms and social cohesion' directed by Dr Madge at Brunel University; the project on 'marginalised spiritualities: faith and religion among young people in socially deprived Britain' directed by Dr Olsen at University of Edinburgh; the project on 'Religion, youth and sexuality: a multi-faith exploration' directed by Dr Yip at University of Nottingham. As the publications emerge from these projects they will help to reshape the way in which the story of research in RE in the UK can be told.

Conclusion

This chapter has provided an overview of the empirical research published in the UK between 1960 and 2010 concerning the religiosity of young people and relevant to school-related RE. Behind the published research there are a number of quality dissertations and other unpublished materials worth further investigation.

Questions

What are the distinctive strengths of the qualitative and the quantitative research traditions in RE?

How can individuals and groups of religious educators best build on the existing research traditions to extend knowledge in RE?

How can a productive research tradition in empirical research in RE be best supported?

Further reading

Collins-Mayo, S. and Dandelion, P. (eds) (2010) *Religion and Youth*, Farnham: Ashgate. This book presents an accessible guide to the key issues in the study of youth and religion, including methodological perspectives.

Francis, L. J., Kay, W. K. and Campbell, W. S. (eds) (1996) *Research in Religious Education*, Leominster: Gracewing. Invaluable review of historical and contemporary research in RE.

Francis, L. J., Robbins, M. and Astley, J. (eds) (2005) *Religion, Education and Adolescence: International Empirical Perspectives*, Cardiff: University of Wales Press. International review of adolescent views on a range of topics relevant to RE.

Smith, A. (2007) *Growing up in Multifaith Britain*, Cardiff: University of Wales Press. This book focuses on religious beliefs and practices of the Christian, Hindu, Muslim and Sikh communities in one of the most multicultural parts of Britain; it demonstrates that religion is a decisive factor in understanding communities and individuals.

Chapter 13

European developments

Robert Jackson

The European debate is very important to religious education (RE) in individual states. At the very least, the European discussion takes us from focusing on parochial issues and provides examples of different educational systems, traditions and approaches. Of the many developments in RE within public education that have taken place in Europe, three key areas are selected to explore. The first concerns important European institutions and their role in fostering particular rationales for studying religions in public education and in developing standard-setting policy recommendations. The second is the professionalisation of RE and related fields, through the formation of European professional organisations and through the establishment of the European Wergeland Centre, a European educational centre, based in Oslo, including religious diversity in its remit to cover human rights, citizenship and intercultural education. The third is European research on RE, with particular reference to the following: a European Commission Framework 6 project – the REDCo Project – conducted between 2006 and 2009; the growth of doctoral research in RE in Europe; and a European book series on 'Religious Diversity and Education in Europe' in which many publications on research and theory in RE in different parts of Europe appear, including books from the REDCo Project.

As a preliminary, it is important to recognise that the term 'religious education' is contested, and means different things in different national contexts (and sometimes within them); there is a range of terms used to identify the study of religions within public education. Thus, there are some very diverse understandings and approaches to 'religious education' across Europe, as well as some emerging patterns of overlap and commonality (Jackson 2007; Kuyk *et al.* 2007).

Issues about the study of religions in public education are being discussed at a European level and more widely internationally as never before. The discussions include specialists in religion and religious bodies, but also politicians, civil servants, non-governmental organisations (NGOs) and other groups within civil society as well as educators concerned with fields such as citizenship and intercultural education. This is partly due to the global attention given to religion as a result of the events of 11 September 2001 in the USA, their causes, on-going consequences and associated incidents that have affected people in many parts of the world. In Europe, it also relates to the challenge of transcultural diversities and the climate of racism in some states, much of it directed against Muslims, exacerbated by 9/11 and its consequences. These negative events have helped to push discourse about religions into the public sphere, even in countries like France where religion has been regarded strongly as a private concern. There are also some very positive reasons for studying religions in public education articulated in European discussion. For example, the Delors Report considers that education should include learning to know, learning to do, learning to live together and learning to be (UNESCO 1996). It is arguable that RE should be concerned with all of these, especially the fourth, although policy developed within some key European institutions has particularly focused on the third.

European institutions: the Council of Europe

The Council of Europe is an inter-governmental organisation founded in 1949 and based in Strasbourg, France. It comprises 47 member states currently and its aims include protecting human rights, pluralist democracy and the rule of law and seeking solutions to problems such as discrimination against minorities, xenophobia and intolerance. The Council's work leads to European conventions and agreements in the light of which member states may amend their own legislation. The key political bodies of the Council are the Parliamentary Assembly (made up of cross-party members of national parliaments from the member states), the Committee of Ministers (the Foreign Ministers of member states, each of whom has a diplomatic representative resident in Strasbourg) and various specialist conferences of Ministers, including one on education. The powers of the Parliamentary Assembly extend only to investigation, recommendation and advice.

The Council is organised under various administrative directorates, including the Directorate of Education, Culture and Heritage, Youth and Sport (the names and remits of the directorates are currently under review). Ideas for projects or results of projects are channelled by the Directorates, for consideration by the Parliamentary Assembly and the Committee of Ministers. There is also a Commissioner for Human Rights, who operates, organisationally, independently of the Directorates. Thus, the Council of Europe offers a structure which integrates the development of new ideas – from educational projects, for example – and political processes. Project proposals are approved by the Council's political institutions and project findings and ministerial recommendations are considered and eventually approved by them. They are then transmitted to the member states. There is an expectation that member states will consider them seriously in their own policy development at national level.

Intercultural education and the challenge of religious diversity and dialogue in Europe

In 2002 the Council of Europe launched its first project on teaching about religions in schools – 'The New Challenge of Intercultural Education: Religious Diversity and Dialogue in Europe'. The rationale for this was concerned with the relationship of religion to culture. It was argued that, regardless of the truth or falsity of religious claims, religion is a part of life and culture and therefore should be understood by *all* citizens as part of their education. This is essentially a *cultural* argument for the study of religions. However, human rights remain the bedrock of Council of Europe policy.

It was on the basis of the 'cultural argument' that the Council of Europe launched its project on the study of religions as part of intercultural education. There were several outcomes. One was the publication of a reference book for schools, aimed especially at those countries with little or no study of religions in public education (Keast 2007). But, most importantly, the Committee of Ministers agreed to a policy recommendation that *all* member states should include the impartial study of religions within the curricula of their schools (Council of Europe 2008a).

A team was brought together to draft the recommendation on behalf of the Committee of Ministers on the management of religious and 'convictional' diversity in schools, based on the project's approach, and incorporating ideas from the White Paper on Intercultural Dialogue (Council of Europe 2008b). The ministerial recommendation was adopted by the Committee of Ministers in December 2008, and provides a set of principles that can be used by all member states. The recommendation can be used as a tool in discussing policy in fields including RE and citizenship education. For reasons of space it is possible here to do no more than indicate the general 'flavour' of the document. For example, its underlying principles include the view that intercultural dialogue and its dimension of religious and non-religious convictions are an essential precondition for the development of tolerance and a culture of 'living together' and for the recognition of different identities on the basis of human rights.

Its objectives include:

- developing a tolerant attitude and respect for the right to hold a particular belief ... (recognising) the inherent dignity and fundamental freedoms of each human being
- nurturing a sensitivity to the diversity of religions and non-religious convictions as an element contributing to the richness of Europe
- ensuring that teaching about the diversity of religions and non-religious convictions is consistent with the aims of education for democratic citizenship, human rights and respect for equal dignity of all individuals
- promoting communication and dialogue between people from different cultural, religious and non-religious backgrounds.

Its educational preconditions include:

- sensitivity to the equal dignity of every individual
- recognition of human rights as values to be applied, beyond religious and cultural diversity
- communication between individuals and the capacity to put oneself in the place of others in order to establish an environment where mutual trust and understanding is fostered
- co-operative learning in which peoples of all traditions can be included and participate
- provision of a safe learning space to encourage expression without fear of being judged or held to ridicule.

With regard to teacher training, member states are requested to:

- provide teachers with the training and means to acquire relevant teaching resources with the aim to develop the ... skills (*for teaching about*) religions and non-religious convictions
- provide training that is objective and open minded
- develop training in methods of teaching and learning which ensure education in democracy at local, regional, national and international level
- encourage multiperspectivity in ... training courses, to take into account ... different points of view in teaching and learning.

Thus, both the 'intercultural' and 'human rights' ethos of the document are clear.

European institutions: the Organisation for Security and Co-operation in Europe

Independently from the Council of Europe, another major European institution concerned with human rights also considered the place of the study of religions and beliefs in public education. This is the Organisation for Security and Co-operation in Europe (OSCE), based in Vienna. The OSCE is the largest regional security organisation in Europe. Its 56 participant states include most European countries plus the United States and Canada. It was set up in the 1970s to create a forum for dialogue during the Cold War. The OSCE uses the concept of 'three-dimensional security'. Security is not only considered in politico-military terms but also through its human dimension and an environmental and economic dimension.

Because of the human dimension to security, OSCE has an Office for Democratic Institutions and Human Rights (ODIHR), which is based in Warsaw. As with the Council of Europe, the ODIHR conducted a project to identify principles on which participant states could develop policy and practice for teaching about religions and non-religious beliefs in schools across its huge geographical region. The result was the production of a standard-setting document, the *Toledo Guiding Principles on Teaching about Religions and Beliefs in Public Schools* (TGPs), named after the city in which the drafting team first worked on the text, and in recognition of Toledo's historical role in communication between those of different religions (OSCE 2007).

The Toledo Guiding Principles

The Toledo Guiding Principles (TGPs) were prepared in order to contribute to an improved understanding of the world's increasing religious (and philosophical) diversity and the growing presence of religion in the public sphere. Their rationale is based on two core principles: first, that there is positive value in teaching that emphasises respect for *everyone's* right to freedom of religion and belief, and second, that teaching *about* religions and beliefs can reduce harmful misunderstandings and stereotypes.

The primary purpose of the TGPs is to assist OSCE participating states whenever they choose to promote the study and knowledge about religions and beliefs in schools, particularly as a tool to enhance religious freedom. The TGPs focus solely on an educational approach that seeks to provide teaching *about* different religions and beliefs as distinguished from instruction in a specific religion or belief. They also aim to offer criteria that should be considered when and wherever teaching about religions and beliefs takes place (OSCE 2007: 11–12). The TGPs offer guidance on preparing curricula for teaching about religions and beliefs, preferred procedures for assuring fairness in the development of curricula, and standards for how they could be implemented.

The TGPs were developed by an inter-disciplinary team including members of the ODIHR Advisory Council of Experts on Freedom of Religion or Belief. The members were picked for their particular expertise. However, they happened to be from a cross-section of religious and philosophical backgrounds. Thus there were Christians, Jews, Muslims and Humanists plus one member of a 'new religious movement'.

In the TGPs, the underlying argument for the inclusion of the study of religions and beliefs in public education has a human rights emphasis. The first premise is that freedom of religion or belief predicates plurality: if freedom of religion or belief is a given for society, then society inevitably will be plural. The next premise is that, if society is to be cohesive, plurality requires tolerance of difference. The conclusion is that tolerance of difference requires *at least* knowledge and understanding of the beliefs and values of others. This would be so whatever the approach specifically taken to RE or intercultural education in particular countries. In other words, the document supports the inclusion of a just and fair approach to religious difference, whatever the system of RE or education about religion in particular states.

The TGPs include a substantial chapter on the human rights framework – including legal issues in relation to the state and the rights of parents, children, teachers and minorities, as well as chapters on preparing curricula and teacher education, plus conclusions and recommendations. The *Toledo Guiding Principles* were approved by the Ministerial Council and launched at the 15th OSCE Ministerial Council held in Madrid in November 2007.

In concluding this section, it should be clear that both the Council of Europe and OSCE documents are intended as tools for those discussing the place of religion in education within European democracies. They are not intended as finished programmes or syllabuses, and are expected to be adapted and developed in different ways within different systems of education.

The professionalisation of religious education

A second feature of the European RE scene is an increasing professionalisation of the subject and related fields, enabling international networking and professional contact, as well as collaborative development and application of ideas. This has happened especially through the formation of European professional organisations – in particular through their conferences, websites and publications – and through the establishment of the European Wergeland Centre, a European educational facility, based in Oslo, including religious diversity in its remit to cover human rights, citizenship and intercultural education. I will mention three professional associations whose work has a bearing on RE within public education and will make some remarks about the European Wergeland Centre.

The European Forum for Teachers of Religious Education (EFTRE)

The European Forum for Teachers of Religious Education brings together various national professional organisations in Europe. EFTRE is a non-confessional forum which represents the interests of RE teachers in Europe, aiming to serve and strengthen the work of national RE teachers' associations. EFTRE aims to contribute to the international co-operation of teachers of RE in theoretical and practical aspects of their work in order to strengthen the position of the subject in schools in the member countries and across Europe. Member organisations (including the National Association of Teachers of Religious Education (NATRE) from England and Wales) represent teachers in schools, colleges and universities and work together to provide a forum for the exchange of ideas and working methods. EFTRE holds conferences, with delegates attending from across Europe, and arranges seminars and teacher exchanges. EFTRE has an elected Executive which meets twice a year, a board which meets annually and a general assembly which meets every three years. Each member country is entitled to one member of the board and each institution is entitled to send a representative to the general assembly.

The Co-ordinating Group for Religious Education in Europe (CoGREE)

The Co-ordinating Group for Religious Education in Europe (CoGREE) brings together a range of European professional RE associations in the field, and includes both non-confessional and Christian organisations (http://www.cogree.com/). Member organisations share some common values (including embracing religious diversity in democratic societies, upholding the principle of freedom of religion or belief and regarding any education taking no account of religion and spirituality as incomplete). Its members include the European Forum for Teachers of Religious Education, the Inter-European Commission on Church and School, the European Association for World Religions in Education, the European Forum for Religious Education in Schools and the International Association for Christian Education. CoGREE holds conferences every three years, and engages in various development and publication projects.

The European Association for the Study of Religions (EASR)

The European Association for the Study of Religions (EASR) (http://easr.eu/) is a professional association which promotes the academic study of religions through the international collaboration of (mainly) European scholars working in the field of the study of religions. The EASR is affiliated to the International Association for the History of Religions (IAHR) which is active globally. The British Association for the Study of Religions (BASR) is affiliated to EASR. EASR includes a group of Religious Studies scholars who have a particular interest in education, and these researchers provide an important link between the worlds of academic religious studies and RE in Europe; for example, the link facilitates contact between academic specialists in particular religions, whose work is at the cutting edge of scholarship and research, and those preparing material on the religions for use by young people in schools. The 2007 EASR conference held in Bremen, Germany, was focused on education, and was entitled 'Plurality and Representation. Religion in Education, Culture and Society'. A selection of papers relevant to RE (including Jackson 2008) is available in a special double issue of the journal *Numen: International Review for the History of Religions* (volume 55, 2/3).

The European Wergeland Centre (EWC)

The European Wergeland Centre (EWC) (Henrik Wergeland was a nineteenth-century Norwegian poet who stood up for religious freedom) is a European resource centre on education for intercultural understanding, human rights and democratic citizenship, incorporating such cross-cutting topics as religion, history, language and gender. The idea for the Centre came from the Council of

Europe, where separate proposals for a European Centre concentrating on citizenship and another concentrating on religion and education were merged (Jackson 2007). The Norwegian government took up the opportunity to establish the Centre in co-operation with the Council of Europe. The EWC, which caters for all the member states of the Council of Europe, and uses English as its working language, is situated in Oslo and was opened officially in May 2009. The main target groups are teachers, teacher trainers, decision makers and multipliers within education for intercultural understanding, human rights and democratic citizenship.

From the point of view of RE, the EWC acts as a partner in European research projects and, via its website and through conferences and meetings, assists in the dissemination of research findings to users such as teachers. An important feature of the EWC is its 'Share and Connect' database through which teachers, teacher trainers and researchers can form networks and contact one another. Share and Connect provides various opportunities, including the facility to look for experts in particular specialisms throughout Europe and beyond, to explore potential co-operation and partnerships and to connect with peers from theory and practice, for example, forming networks on particular research themes, networks of PhD students, or partnerships between academic specialists and teachers to produce high quality materials (go to http://www.theewc.org for more information). By providing in-service training, carrying out and supporting research, creating networks, serving as a platform and disseminating information and good practice, the EWC is establishing itself as a leading professional body.

European research in religious education

Research networks

Empirical research has become increasingly important in informing the development of policy and practice in European RE (Jackson 2004a, 2004b). There are a number of international and European research networks in the RE field. The International Seminar on Religious Education and Values (ISREV) has met every two years since 1978 and now includes many empirical researchers in RE from around the world, including many from different European countries (http://www.isrev.org/). The European Network for Religious Education through Contextual Approaches is a specifically European network, having a particular interest in the relevance of 'context' to the development of RE (e.g. Heimbrock *et al.* 2001). Such networks have facilitated the assembly of cross-national teams to conduct research at a European level.

The REDCo project

There have been a number of collaborative European research projects in RE, and more are planned. However, the first to obtain substantial funding from the

European Commission for a major mixed methods study was the REDCo (*R*eligion, *E*ducation, *D*ialogue, *C*onflict) project, funded by the Framework 6 initiative (http://www.redco.uni-hamburg.de/web/3480/3481/index.html). REDCo was a three-year project (2006–2009) involving universities from eight European countries (University of Warwick, England; Universities of Hamburg and Münster, Germany; VU University, the Netherlands; University of Stavanger, Norway; Russian Christian Academy for Humanities, St Petersburg, Russia; Tartu University, Estonia; the Sorbonne, Paris, France and the University of Granada, Spain). The project aimed to establish whether studies of religions in schools could help to promote dialogue and reduce conflict in school and society. The main research focused on young people in the 14–16 age group, but there were also some studies of teachers, of primary pupils and of the place of religion in different educational systems. The key concepts of the interpretive approach (Jackson 1997, 2011) were used as a stimulus to method and theory. Core studies included a mapping exercise of religion and education in Europe (Jackson *et al.* 2007); a qualitative study of teenagers' views on religion in schools (Knauth *et al.* 2008); a cross-national quantitative survey of young people's views in the eight countries (Valk *et al.* 2009); studies of classroom interaction (ter Avest *et al.* 2009); and a study of teachers of RE (van der Want *et al.* 2009).

Several individual studies were also completed in the different countries. For example, the Warwick team produced action research studies, based in schools and teacher training institutes, applying key concepts from the interpretive approach (Jackson 1997). These were conducted by a 'community of practice' which included teachers, teacher trainers and a CPD provider (Ipgrave *et al.* 2009).

Selected findings from qualitative and quantitative studies

Each of the REDCo national studies gives a flavour of the particular national situation where it was located and needs to be examined in some detail. However, some broad trends emerged from the data. Qualitative questionnaires and interviews completed by 14–16-year-olds and a quantitative survey, conducted with the same age group in the eight countries participating in the REDCo Project, revealed some general trends that are of relevance to the evaluation and implementation of the policies advocated by the Council of Europe and the Office for Democratic Institution and Human Rights of the OSCE. These might be summarised very briefly as follows:

- Students wish for peaceful co-existence across differences, and believe this to be possible.
- For students peaceful co-existence depends on knowledge about each other's religions and worldviews and on sharing common interests /doing things together.

- Students who learn about religious diversity in school are *more willing* to have conversations about religions/beliefs with students of other backgrounds than those who do not.
- Students wish to avoid conflict: some religiously committed students feel vulnerable.
- Students want learning to take place in a safe classroom environment where there are agreed procedures for expression and discussion.
- *Most* students would like school to be a place for learning *about* different religions/worldviews, rather than for instruction *into* a particular religion/ worldview (respondents tended to support the system of which they had personal experience).

Having made these points, the various REDCo studies suggest that approaches to the study of religious diversity would need to be implemented differently in particular national contexts. For example, in some countries (e.g. England), religious diversity would be covered mainly in a *separate subject* devoted to the study of religion, while in others (e.g. France) religious diversity would be covered through *several* subjects, with none dedicated specifically to religion. In some countries, religious diversity could be linked to students' discussion of their *personal views* (e.g. Netherlands, Norway, England, Germany), while in others, this would be more difficult (e.g. France and Estonia). In some countries (e.g. Estonia, France, Norway) religious diversity would be covered in a non-confessional setting, while in others (e.g. Spain), religious diversity would be taught in a confessional context, and steps would need to be taken to ensure fairness, balance and objectivity in teaching and learning. In some countries, religious diversity would be taught in *both* confessional and non-confessional contexts (e.g. Netherlands, England).

Doctoral research

There has been a growth in doctoral research in Europe in RE over the last ten years or so, much of it directly relevant to the improvement of practice in schools. This is partly due to the growth of collaborative research projects in which PhD students have been able to participate as researchers. For example, several PhDs emerged from the REDCo Project (e.g. Schihalejev 2010; von der Lippe 2011b). Moreover, there has been an internationalisation of some of this research, with international collaboration in publications and with research students being based in universities in countries other than their own. Several Norwegian students have been based at the University of Warwick, for example, with one applying ethnographic methods used in the UK to the study of children from a religious minority in Norway (Østberg 2003), another pioneering a methodology for comparative RE, using Norway and England as examples (Braaten 2010) and a third analysing and comparing Norwegian policy and practice in RE in relation to issues of national identity (Eriksen 2010).

European book series

The development of research networks, research projects and doctoral research has also stimulated the publication of research, through books and journal articles. Academic journals such as the *British Journal of Religious Education* (http://www.tandf.co.uk/journals/bjre) have become international in outlook, and report a good deal of European research. One particular book series, *Religious Diversity and Education in Europe*, published by Waxmann, was initiated in 2006 and is now a major source of European research findings on RE. At the time of writing (July 2010), no less than 19 volumes have been published (http://www.waxmann.com/?id=21andcHash=1andreihe=1862-9547). The series publishes significant new research in RE in Europe, including revised versions of recent PhD theses. Recent titles include Jenny Berglund's book *Teaching Islam: Islamic Religious Education in Sweden*, which extends the range of research on Islam and education in Europe. Much of the REDCo Project's research is published through volumes in the Religious Diversity and Education in Europe series, the latest (volume 19) being *From Indifference to Dialogue? Estonian Young People, the School and Religious Diversity*, written by Olga Schihalejev.

Conclusion

The Europeanisation – part of a broader internationalisation – of debates and research about RE is to be welcomed. Its outcomes have been very positive, whether in opening up discussion about the rationale for the study of religions in public education, building networks of communication for exchanging ideas on pedagogy and policy and for collaborative research, fostering new, outward looking, doctoral research, or extending the publication of research on RE. These developments do not belong to a different world from that of the RE teacher in the UK; they are highly relevant to discussions at a national level, which are apt to become parochial and over-focused on particular issues. For example, research from REDCo and elsewhere on comparative RE (e.g. Braaten 2010; Knauth *et al.* 2008) shows that the relationship between theory, policy and practice in particular countries is highly complex; it is not simply 'top down', and also a range of both supra- and sub-national influences are part of the picture. This research shows that a particular trend in practice is very unlikely to be explained by a single 'top down' influence or factor: for example, does the influence of phenomenology of religion in the 1970s *really* account for the condition of RE in England and Wales today or is the situation significantly more complex?

Questions

How can UK students and teachers better access ideas and developments coming from Europe and participate in the discussions?

How far should human rights principles provide a rationale for RE in publicly funded schools?

How far and in what ways should religious organisations participate in designing curricula for the study of religions in publicly funded schools?

Further reading

Council of Europe (2008a) Recommendation CM/Rec(2008)12 of the Committee of Ministers to member states on the dimension of religions and non-religious convictions within intercultural education. Available at: https://wcd.coe.int//ViewDoc.jsp?Ref=CM/Rec(2008)12andLanguage=lanEnglish andVer=originalandBackColorInternet=DBDCF2andBackColorIntranet=FD C864andBackColorLogged=FDC864. This document – go to the appendix – is the list of recommendations from the 47 Foreign Ministers of the Council of Europe which is intended for use by governments, policy makers, NGOs and any other groups (e.g. teachers) as a tool in developing policy.

Jackson, R., Miedema, S., Weisse, W. and Willaime, J.-P. (eds) (2007) *Religion and Education in Europe: Developments, Contexts and Debates*, Münster: Waxmann. Outlines the REDCo Project, gives an overview of European RE and Citizenship issues and explains the national RE systems of the eight countries involved in the REDCo Project.

Knauth, T., Jozsa, D.-P., Bertram-Troost, G. and Ipgrave, J. (eds) (2008) *Encountering Religious Pluralism in School and Society: A Qualitative Study of Teenage Perspectives in Europe*, Münster: Waxmann. Reports of qualitative studies on RE in eight countries including England conducted as part of the REDCo Project.

OSCE (2007) *The Toledo Guiding Principles on Teaching about Religions and Beliefs in Public Schools*, Warsaw: Organisation for Security and Co-operation in Europe, Office for Democratic Institutions and Human Rights (full text available at http://www.osce.org/item/28314.html accessed 10 July 2010). This standard-setting document is intended as a tool for discussion and policy development in the 56 participant states of the Organisation for Security and Co-operation in Europe. It includes useful summaries of human rights codes in relation to freedom of religion or belief and education.

The European Wergeland Centre http://www.theewc.org/. Website of an important European resource centre on education for intercultural understanding, human rights and democratic citizenship, incorporating religion, as a cross-cutting topic. Search the library, teacher training and news, and especially the 'Share and Connect' database.

Valk, P., Bertram-Troost, G., Friederici, M. and Béraud, C. (2009) *Teenagers' Perspectives on the Role of Religion in their Lives, Schools and Societies: A Quantitative Study*, Münster: Waxmann. Reports of quantitative studies on RE in eight countries including England conducted as part of the REDCo Project.

Section III

Issues in teaching and learning in religious education

Chapter 14

Constructing religion

Roger Homan

This critical survey prompts the addressing of a number of questions:

- Can religious content be simplified without distortion?
- Is one constructed religious reality any better than another?
- What is wrong with religious controversy anyway?

This chapter is about the competition to define an objective reality of religion. It is, of course, elusive. All perceptions are mediated. Some are pronounced with a greater claim to authority than others. In particular, those uttered by faith leaders are calculated to sustain an orthodox account of their respective faith and the authors of educational texts have the sense of a political responsibility to do their little bit for social harmony. Again, there is pressure on curriculum-mongers to find content that can be assessed and this is a factor in the recent shift observed by *inter alia* Hayward (2006) and Grimmitt (2000a) from a process-oriented view of religious education (RE) to one that is content-centred or content-led. Following the classic work of Berger and Luckmann (1967), the mediation of experience or reality and its transmission as knowledge has been widely appreciated; the notion of 'social construction' may also be applied to the curriculum. Here we are vigilant of the measure of construction that is implicit in resources for teaching and suggest that RE is in its own way a deviation from what it purports to communicate.

In recent years the dominant paradigm in the delivery of RE has owed much to the work of Ninian Smart who developed an approach around the notional virtues of neutrality and dispassion. The plausibility of such virtues as a theoretical objective, let alone their achievement in classroom practice, has been frequently subjected to critical scrutiny. The study of religions by means of the dimensions widely attributed to Smart (but in fact derived from Glock and Stark 1965) deploys a battery of conceptual categories that make western sense of eastern faiths: Derrida (1982) refers to such preconceptions as 'white mythology' and I'Anson (2010) has explored the possibility of a neutral pedagogy. Here we examine some of the more concrete drivers that bear upon the construction of religion for classroom consumption. These include the rendering of content according to psychological notions of what pupils can bear, the claims of the faith communities to affect the accounts given of them and the embedding of distortions in syllabuses and texts.

The fallout from Piaget and Goldman

The legacies of Piaget and his follower Ronald Goldman have been, alas, pervasive in RE. Piaget's notion that intellectual development inclined teachers to think in terms of stages and to hold fire with abstract thinking until pupils had emerged from the concrete stage. Goldman then registered the principle of 'readiness' for religion. Concrete questions yielded concrete responses, as though to prove Piaget right. Teaching methods like story and the handling of artefacts lent themselves to this way of thinking. Piaget and Goldman were subsequently to be discredited on grounds of methodology as well as application (Howkins 1966; Gates 1976; Donaldson 1978; Minney 1985; Slee 1986; Petrovich 1989) but the doctrine of stages proved more durable than the critique. Petrovich discovered a capacity for abstract thought and the understanding of metaphor in children as young as three or four years and contended that literalism was a habit conveyed by adults rather than programmed by anatomy. As Elizabeth Ashton (1992: 169) has observed, the word so frequently on the lips of the young child is 'Why?' and yet the agreed syllabuses for the early key stages give little encouragement to reason, reflect and interpret. In its day Goldman's was the only or principal empirical research bearing upon RE and so it took root in the agreed syllabuses (Jackson 2004b: 146–149): there are suggestions in this chapter, however that Goldman's ghost has not been exorcised by persistent research findings to the contrary.

In a philosophical critique of the legacy of Piaget, Robin Minney (1985: 259–260) argued for the rehabilitation of experience and emotion in RE, the suppression of which in the quest for 'objectivity' he reasoned to be a factor in boredom across the curriculum.

In more recent years, the agenda of the subject in the later secondary years has increasingly embraced the kinds of issue for which Minney appealed (for example, issues of life and death, genetic intervention, reproductive technology). Simultaneously the subject has flourished in the popularity stakes and entries for public examinations in this subject have risen sharply.

To convey the nuances of this variety and the circumstances that bear upon it is rather more than we can expect of a teacher, let alone of a published resource. The personal – albeit distant – exchanges afforded by Julia Ipgrave's method therefore have distinctive merits. When teaching in a primary school in Leicester, she set up partnerships between a Roman Catholic primary school and a school with a predominantly Muslim population. Each of her pupils, aged nine to ten, corresponded by e-mail with a partner in the other school. The capacity of primary school children to surpass the passive digestion of 'subject facts' is evident in the dialogical approach. The uninhibited dialogues (Ipgrave 2001: 30) are illuminating for the proof of the way in which pupils can put ideas to immediate use, shift from passive to active modes of managing information, comprehend common and contrasting elements of belief, appreciate the relation of belief and celebration, use theological language, disagree respectfully:

Dear Nasim,

Christmas is the birth of Jesus! He gave his life for us on the cross at Easter which is sometimes in April. At Christmas we give gifts to each other like God gives his only son to us. On the 25th December Jesus was born and we go to church first thing...

I think you are right! The Holy Book is the holiest and most precious thing God has given us! For me the holy book is the Bible!

Hope to hear from you soon! From Benedict.

Dear Benedict,

Thank you for your email. I think Jesus is God's messenger and not god's son. I agree that the holy book is most precious. My holy book is the Quran because if you pray one word of it, it is 10 good deeds so you get saved at the end of the world. Do you think you get saved by the Bible?

From Nasim

Not only has Piaget inclined generations of teachers to reserve abstract questions for the later years of schooling, but there persists a protective disapprobation of debate and controversy as though they belong to the post-innocence stage of discourse, like sex and politics. Within RE, it is suggested (I'Anson 2010: 108) aversion to debate and to the recognition of conflict is inherent in a phenomenological and neutralising pedagogy.

Nevertheless, the desire to be 'positive' has inclined teachers to skirt around the embarrassment of history and to leave bad press to the media. Liam Gearon, much of whose work has had to do with the coming together of RE and citizenship (e.g. Gearon 2002, 2004), notes that religious educationists have seldom featured the role or complicity of the churches in colonialism and genocide: doubtless the cloud of paedophilia will not be darkly drawn. The assumption of a public relations role in the face of negative evidence can only diminish the credibility of the subject.

The 'constructivist' pedagogy commended by Michael Grimmitt affords the emancipation of the student in the process of evaluation and

would prevent RE from furthering the hegemony of cultural and social reproduction involving the perpetuation of injustice, inequality and oppression and would challenge concepts and practices which have become reified by tradition and which may no longer be worthy of support and toleration.

(Grimmitt 2000a: 225)

So we should be wary of the terms *respect* if it is to imply tolerance for injustice and of *negative stereotype* if what is meant is the discovery of an uncomfortable truth. Nor is it self-evident that 'resources for sensitive topics are best produced by/in association with members of the faiths concerned' (Inter Faith Network 2001: 7): they surely have no greater right than politicians to control their image and reputation in an age of access to information. Addressing the dilemma posed by Sarah Smalley (2005) on the need to be both positive and realistic, Julian Stern pleads that 'RE must be a gritty subject, and must not be a bland diet of "niceness"' (Stern 2006: 101).

There is a difficulty here in that transactions may be seen as positive at source but produce a negative stereotype when viewed in another cultural context. In the video series *Believe it or Not* (1991), the rabbi explaining the wedding custom in which the bridegroom treads on a wineglass says 'some people say it's the last chance he has to put his foot down'. We would be unlikely to find such an explanation in a textbook, nor would a teacher feel it appropriate. On the same cassette we view and hear the discomfort of a baby boy during the rite of circumcision. Pupils for whom this is not standard practice may not share the rabbi's view that 'altogether it's an extremely happy occasion'. The dilemma of teachers is whether to censure this clip, either to spare their squeamish pupils or because it may not be thought altogether happy in the judgement of the class.

By allowing the communities to speak for themselves, typically through the voice of faith leaders, we derive a party line, a theoretical truth about belief rather than an empirical insight of reality. Shazia Mirza, who is described on her website as the 'award winning British Asian Muslim comic', declares that while in Makkah walking round the *ka'aba* somebody pinched her bottom. This happened a second time and she subsequently featured the experience in her comedy act. Her doing so elicited two kinds of response. On the one hand there were those who thought she should not be publicising the fact or making jokes about what happened in the holy city; on the other, she received messages from women to whom the same had happened in that place (Mirza 2009). The expurgated version of religious practice is the less stimulating for the loss of observed or reported habits that may constitute negative images. This is the essence of the problem: should we in the school classroom tell the truth, the whole truth or the mediated truth which is elsewhere known as 'spin'?

Faith leaders and the faith community

RE is largely occupied with the beliefs and practices of the world faiths, particularly the big six (Buddhism, Christianity, Hinduism, Islam, Judaism and Sikhism). There is a notional entitlement of the faith communities to define their own beliefs and practices but this cannot be an exclusive right for religious organisations any more than it can be for political parties. In all cases there is an elusive reality and the capacity for spin is the measure of distortion. At the one extreme are the custodians of the party or faith and at the other are investigative journalists who have interests in financial irregularities, corruption and sleaze, sexual abuse, paramilitary activities, the role of women, kidnapping, brainwashing and so on. Teachers and the writers of textbooks tend to spare pupils the awareness of these distasteful possibilities and to stay safe.

Astley (1992) has drawn to the attention of educators the very heterogeneity of Christian belief and in particular of christological expressions. The figure of Jesus may be regarded by the faithful as a Saviour: or Jesus is a martyr. Or he is understood primarily as Messiah, as by N. T. Wright (1996). Or John Dominic Crossan (1991) has him as a rural revolutionary. So while Cooling (1994: 19) insists that theological foundations be laid at an early stage, Christology is all about constructions and the curriculum representation is yet another, adapted to the needs of little children who are supposed to require something safe and simple. What is at issue is whether these needs constitute a case for continuing to dispense to the primary school the cosy domesticated Jesus that has been around for more than a century.

Much debate rests on an estimation of whether Britain is a Christian society. For all that students of religion have come to view it in respect of several dimensions, it is frequently attendance that is taken as the measure. It happens that non-attenders are often more conventional in their belief than those who have adjusted to liberalising change or survived liturgical reform. The quest for some kind of evidence within each of the dimensions attributed to Smart leads to a stereotype of the adherent of any faith: such a person will hold seminal beliefs firmly, attend the place of worship on a weekly basis, participate in the rituals and celebrations of the faithful community and be bonded to a specified collection of artefacts. The risk of overload and confusion weighs heavily on the curriculum-mongers. So does the desirability of visual images, to the extent that those (like the Brethren) whose habits do not lend themselves to film and photography are unlikely to feature in the classroom. A still more conspicuous omission is that of those whose way of life in a secular society is loosely aligned with a particular tradition but who are not ritually engaged.

Teece's pocket guide (2001) is largely occupied with 'subject facts'. The series in which it appears purports to provide 'the knowledge you need to teach the primary curriculum'. The suggested activities then embed the knowledge by sweetened methods: visit a temple, construct and dedicate a classroom shrine, design a poster, learn particular prayers, investigate the three most important mosques. The practice which the pocket guide suggests is the banking and securing of subject facts with little opportunity for evaluation.

Occasionally in the excerpts recorded and published by Ipgrave there are representations of religious belief that do not quite accord with official formulations preferred by faith leaders or the sometimes anodyne accounts that appear in textbooks. This does not mean that they are less real. On the contrary, they are the more realistic for not having been stripped of subjectivity and for being thereby rather more intelligible within the experience and understanding of a peer. One mediation may be a political or diplomatic spin while that of a peer in an individual dialogue is innocent of the pressure to distort. A broad overview of the merits of forms of the dialogical approach is offered by Jackson (2004b: 109–125).

The hazards of affording faith leaders some ownership of curriculum materials was evident in the Model Syllabuses produced by the School Curriculum and Assessment Authority in 1994. These materials included a glossary of terms which was intended to be the basis of subsequent materials. In the event, definitions were formulated for learning and recitation in examinations but were not recognisable by university lecturers in Religious Studies. At a conference of such specialists the definition 'love in action, freely given of itself to serve and save' (School Curriculum and Assessment Authority 1994b: 3) was projected on the screen and participants wrote on slips of paper the term to which they supposed it referred. The most popular answers were *agape* with ten votes, *charity* with eight and *compassion* with seven. In the SCAA glossary the form of words displayed was presented as a definition of grace, which was recognised by only one participant (Homan 2004: 22–23). Thus teachers are authorised to settle for learning purposes at school level definitions that do not make sense among specialists.

'The syllabus'

Among the more potent constructions of faith and practice is that of the syllabus. Ofsted has it that two-thirds of primary schools are conforming to the agreed syllabus in their respective local authorities (Ofsted 1997: 5). The quest for the Jesus of history has given way to the Jesus of the classroom; thus Walshe and Copley (2001) conducted an analysis of 24 local authority syllabuses for RE in the earliest years of schooling. It is therefore appropriate that scholars are vigilant of the extent to which representations of faiths may be distorted by curriculum-mongers. So we find journal articles with titles like 'The Jesus of Agreed Syllabuses in Key Stage 1' (Walshe and Copley 2001) and 'Curriculum Christianity' (Hayward 2006).

The Office for Standards in Education (Ofsted 1997: 29) notes with implicit approval a task in which pupils represented at the end of a cartoon of the Creation an image of God resting in bed. It is of course a depiction that has been studiously avoided in Christian iconography in which God prefers to be represented by a single hand, as on the Sistine ceiling. Still less would a figurative image be entertained in Islam. Again, 'Pupils in a Devon school ... learnt the proper name for Shrove Tuesday' (Ofsted 1997: 34). One wonders what this 'proper' term might be: the last day before Lent? Pancake Day? *Mardi gras*? A diversity of nomenclature has been resolved for the sake of classroom learning. And such is the priority given to education that faith leaders yield to it.

It is a function of the curriculum version of Christianity that the notions of revelation and history are fragmented and the Old Testament is isolated from the New. Neither the medieval understanding in which one prefigures the other nor recent views of Judaism and Christianity as siblings (McDade 1991) is evident in accounts that at most make reference to Noah, Joseph and Moses as stories that Jesus would have known and do not feature Jesus' status as a prophet in the context of Islam (Walshe and Copley 2001: 33).

While the content of RE has largely been distilled by key words and dodgy definitions, its delivery has been popularly effected by the parading of physical objects plundered from the sacred domain via an educational supplier and redefined as 'artefacts'. As with the glossaries of terms, many items will be known only to committed members of the respective faiths: they represent an orthodox and possibly atypical sphere of practice.

The seductive capacity of 'artefacts' for teachers has four aspects. First there is a learning theory – not always appropriate in respect of religion – that pupils need to touch and feel. Second, there are educational suppliers who assemble kits with instructions. Third, the acquisition of some kind of subject specific hardware gives teachers of RE a sense of parity with other elements of the curriculum. And fourth, their notional authenticity (albeit some are manufactured specifically for the educational market) gives non-specialists confidence that they are doing the right thing. Thus the website of the supplier Articles of Faith invites teachers to click on 'RE: Solved' as though 'artefacts' were a panacea. 'Do you need to buy artefacts to teach about the 6 world religions…?' it asks. The truthful answer would be 'No' but it continues: 'Our comprehensive artefacts trolley provides a perfect storage solution and ideal display area. We are pleased to offer all of this for just £660.'

At that price they must earn their keep so we are encouraged to use them across the curriculum. Pupils can measure them, ponder design and construction, estimate commercial value and even prod them in a feely-bag. Gateshill and Thompson (1992: 5), for example, talk of 'hands-on experience'. Thus the effect of dislocating the apparatuses of devotion is to deprive them of the spiritual value with which they are properly invested. This value is commendably observed in the *Gift to the Child* approach from Birmingham (Grimmitt *et al.* 1991). In this approach the significance of what is more helpfully called a *numen* is discovered by a taboo on touching and even on going close and by an avoidance of affected rituals of reverence (Hull 1996a: 177; see also Hull 2000a).

There are several examples of the ways in which the definition of devotional objects as 'artefacts' misrepresents their significance. Within the sacramental traditions of the Christian faith there are many who would never touch the chalice with their hands and yet a convincing facsimile may be passed round the classroom. To group the Guru Granth Sahib (Shropshire Religious Education Artefacts Project 1992) or the *ikon* as artefacts is to ground understanding in the terms of human craft and not in those of divine visitation which is the basis of regarding them within our subject: it is not to appreciate but to divert from the principle of embodiment that makes these things what they are in the perception of the faithful.

The principle of the Birmingham approach to *numina* is to connect with original meaning and significance. The plundering of the means of devotion is to disconnect. It is to render the spiritual and the mystical as the concrete. That is not to represent religion but to misrepresent it (Homan 2000).

Perhaps as a function of the ease of assessing them, much store has been set by key words and definitions. In the Glossary of Terms produced by faith leaders and published with the normative *Model Syllabuses, jihad* was defined as a personal individual struggle against evil in the way of Allah and *fatwa* as 'a legal opinion in Islamic jurisprudence' (SCAA 1994a: 25 and 27). Both definitions are true but inadequate. *Jihad* is indeed an inner struggle but those who use it as a collective name for their activities in political conflict are not first and foremost mystics: Geoff Teece (2001: 185) gives a more comprehensive and accessible definition as 'struggle, both physical and moral'. *Fatwa* is indeed a judgment... but its definition needs some reference to its personalised expression if pupils are to understand why, for example, Salman Rushdie has needed to take special measures for his own security. Similarly the definition of euthanasia as 'a good and easy death' (possibly including a heart attack on the golf course) begs the question; what is significant in the context of ethics is that it is managed and the time for it is of human choosing. The author offered this observation to teachers adopting the Edexcel prescriptions who recognised the limitations of the definition but assured him that this was what the examiners wanted. The matter becomes still more serious in the following session when pupils are told that hospices do not believe in euthanasia. The inference is that hospices do not believe in comfort for the dying.

The hegemony of the syllabus was recently in evidence in the Warwick study. Faith members working as consultants observed a series of constructions and distortions of religions arising from syllabuses and examinations. A textbook was commended not for its integrity but as a good preparation for the examination: doubtless it had been written by the chief examiner (Jackson *et al.* 2010: 94).

Social cohesion

The potentially cohesive function of religious belief and practice was explored by Durkheim (1912), albeit within monocultural societies. The Office for Standards in Education has claimed this function as a primary purpose of RE (Ofsted 2007: 41).

Religious educationists and the authors of agreed syllabuses have assumed more than a marginal role in the aim of social cohesion. The expectation of such a pursuit creates a tension between non-confessionalists for whom the study of religion is a purely intellectual pursuit and neo-confessionalists who have taken on board the duty of anti-racist and anti-sexist education and willingly use their teaching to address issues of social and cultural divisions. Edward Hulmes (1992: 125) regards social cohesion to be the 'explicitly instrumental purpose of education'.

Having a particular focus on the contribution to community cohesion (Jackson *et al.* 2010: 1), the Warwick group examined classroom resources and the reviewers applauded positive images such as those of young Muslims and Muslim women (Jackson *et al.* 2010: 47). On the other hand, implausibly positive images may disaffect teachers: Donley (1992: 189) rejects the expectation that RE might be used as social engineering and Lawlor encounters teachers who are reluctant to embrace the cohesion agenda and who regard positive images as a distortion (Lawlor 2010: 167; see also Stern 2006: 81).

We have to decide whether to convey a notional reality, negative aspects of which may have reached pupils by means beyond our control, or aspire to an ideal. We cannot present the second as though it is the first. One of the principles periodically registered by Philip Barnes in his recent dispute with Kevin O'Grady is that the cosy ecumenical consensus emanating from Ninian Smart's influence and the durability of *Working Paper 36* (Schools Council 36) fights shy of dialogue and debate among the faiths: such a consensus, moreover, denies to religions their independent validity and to students the opportunity for discussion in a democratic manner (e.g. Barnes 2009b). The need is to face diversity honestly and to convey implausible and sanitised accounts in the hope that the prophecy will fulfil itself. Simplification for the sake of keeping things easy has serious consequences. Halliday (1999) observes simplification in mediated accounts of Islam as a condition of Islamophobia; affirming the analysis of the Runnymede Trust (1997) he notes the tendency to treat as a single denomination what spans many and diverse nations, cultures and dispositions on key issues such as human rights.

In the analysis of Syed Ali Ashraf (1992: 83) the evacuation of moral content is the consequence of a secular agenda. He affirms a 'religious sensibility' by which is meant 'that element in human nature that makes human beings aware of the transcendent selfless norms of Justice, Truth and all such values that pull the heart away from selfishness towards selflessness'. The prevailing secular regard for religion for its intellectual rather than its spiritual content inhibit teachers from connecting with or stimulating the religious sensibilities of their pupils. By that measure, Ashraf argues, RE is defective. The implication is that moral standards are offered for information rather than with anything as strong as a recommendation. And he is indignant that because there are atheists and agnostics about we should 'bow down' to them and teach religion in a secular manner (Ashraf 1992: 90).

Conclusion

This chapter has been about the seeming incompatibility of competing constructions and of the constituencies that promulgate them. The 'interpretive approach' to RE introduced by Robert Jackson is born out of his experiences within Hindu and other cultures and the realisation that academic accounts did not accord with these (Jackson 1997: 3). The mismatch of what we may observe at first hand and what we teach or are taught is prompted largely by the means of promoting and elevating learning. We reckon to stimulate the process of learning by finding things that are colourful, curious and provocative. References across the curriculum are thought to be a good thing. And teachers are urged to find opportunities within their subject to support various educational initiatives from literacy to anti-sexism and social cohesion. The dimensions of religion that Smart borrowed from sociology cut across discrete religions and lead to an emphasis on themes that may be found in most or all religious cultures, such as passage rites and festivals. When the faiths offer their own agenda, it leaves little room for these motives and obligations: rather, it is catechetical in scope and orthodox in tone. A function of the post-Enlightenment 'scientific' study of religion has been to turn faiths into *isms* and to impose names upon them (Jackson 1997: 57–59). In short, it is not what we as educationists can do for religions but what they can do for us. We have to find things to teach and activities that can be assessed and that will lead to extrinsic learning objectives like reflection and critical awareness.

So delivery is partly constrained by the trained habit of the teacher. It is also subject to the appetite of those who bear down upon education with their own prescriptions. On the basis of the irrefutable proposition that we cannot consume everything, indigestible morsels are left to the side of the plate: Aylett's *The Muslim Experience* (1991), for example, makes no mention either of *jihad* or of *fatwa*. On the advice of consultants from the faith communities, Jackson and his team (2010: 102) reckoned that excerpts from sacred texts were being chosen not for their authority or authenticity but for the convenience of an educational agenda. Religious conflict, associations with the mafia, flagellation, sexual and physical abuse and other sensations are left to the tabloid press to investigate and judge.

The good intention of religious educationists has been to offer teaching characterised by faithfulness to what is out there, engagement, moral responsibility and social sensitivity. The function of such circumspection is that it loses credibility and its construction is not plausible against the constructions received from other sources.

Questions

Is teaching about the faiths ideally delivered and documented by insiders?
Does religious education bear any more than its fair share of the social agenda?
Is religious education losing its credibility? What are the constraints upon being more responsive to images conveyed in the popular media?

Further reading

Walshe, K. and Copley, T. (2002) *The Figure of Jesus in Religious Education*, Exeter: University of Exeter. After the quest for the historical Jesus comes this research report as a quest for the Jesus of the classroom.

Grimmitt, M. (ed.) (2000b) *Pedagogies in Religious Education*, Great Wakering: McCrimmon. A collection of case studies in the research and development of innovative pedagogic practice in the delivery of the subject.

Ipgrave, J. (2001) *Pupil-to-pupil Dialogue in the Classroom as a Tool for Religious Education*, Warwick: Religious and Education Research Unit. From her primary classroom in Leicester, the author set up email partnerships with diverse schools enabling pupils to dialogue online with peers of different backgrounds. The paper includes recorded excerpts from their exchanges.

Jackson, R., Ipgrave, J., Hayward, M., Hopkins, P., Fancourt, N., Robbins, M., Francis, L. and McKenna, U. (2010) *Materials used to Teach about World Religions in Schools in England: Research Report DCSF-RR197*, Warwick: Department for Children, Schools and Families/University of Warwick. Reports on an extensive research project conducted in schools in England. It is not only of interest for its findings but of usefulness for its method in applying a wide range of criteria by which subject resources might be evaluated.

Stern, J. (2006) *Teaching Religious Education: Research in the Classroom*, London: Continuum. A closely informed overview of the current delivery of the subject with attention to critical issues and a number of exercises through which to explore them.

Chapter 15

Schemes of work and lesson planning

David Aldridge

The recent report, *Transforming Religious Education* (Ofsted 2010: 41) identified as one of the challenges facing religious education (RE) that 'there is uncertainty among many teachers' about 'the way to structure and define a clear process of learning in RE'. In addition, among the 'weaker aspects of teaching' in secondary schools, inspectors observed 'limitations in the structure and sequencing of learning, so that students were unable to see the connection between tasks and the overarching purpose of the lesson', as well as 'a lack of clarity about what constituted making progress in RE' (20). These problems were attributed in part to a 'lack of clarity about the core purpose of RE' (41). While it was acknowledged that this lack of clarity made for 'stimulating and lively debate within the subject community' it was found to inhibit 'the effectiveness of classroom practice'. Inspectors observed that 'teachers were often working with a variety of different perspectives about the basic purpose of the subject. Teachers were often very unsure how these perspectives could be combined or prioritised to promote coherence and progression in RE programmes' (41–42). The report indentified a number of objectives to which the *Non-Statutory Framework*, most agreed syllabuses and other RE policy statements refer but found that 'many teachers remain unclear how to prioritise and organise them within a coherent RE curriculum and the teaching of the subject. As a result, much of the work observed in the RE visits lacked a clear focus and structure' (42).

Where curriculum design was judged successful, the report focused on the use of concepts and investigative questions in units of work. A section devoted to whether an 'enquiry-based approach to learning' could help to improve the quality of religious education (Ofsted 2010: 44–46) discussed in detail the need for 'a clear model of how pupils learn that matched the nature of the subject' (45). In general practice was judged strong in some departments but far from universally so. Lesson planning in the worst cases took on a piecemeal structure, where text books supported by a range of different projects or methodologies were dipped into, pedagogical approaches to the nature and aims of the subject were treated as toolkits to be applied as the occasion seems to demand, and the resulting unit of study lacked overall coherence or a sense of progression; in the best cases attempts to draw on a clear model of learning were based on an integrated pedagogical approach but were perceived to be hindered by the constraints of the design of the locally agreed syllabus.

While not necessarily concurring with Ofsted's assessment of the state of RE teaching in the UK, this chapter aims to engage with the problems of offering a coherent theoretical description of what constitutes 'well-structured and sequenced teaching and learning' in RE (Ofsted 2010: 6) and the obstacles faced by teachers in attempting to implement such a structure in their planning. It will begin by identifying a number of possible entry points into the planning process and assess the implications that their prioritisation can have for the resulting learning experience. A number of these starting points are often experienced as 'given' by the professional teacher, and recognition of this will illuminate the gap that is often acknowledged between the theoretical and pedagogical discourse of religious education and the practical situation of classroom practitioners. This will be followed by an exploration of the most recent work of RE theorists toward establishing an 'integrated' approach to planning learning, focusing due to the limitations of space on Erricker and Wright; the chapter will conclude with a call to recognise and embrace the dialectic or creative tension at play in the planning process.

The search for a starting point

Curriculum

RE teachers will embark on the lesson planning process at different points or with differing amounts of autonomy, and the length or size of the units of learning under consideration will vary, but all will experience some sort of guidance – or alternatively constraint – from a curriculum; this operates differently on a number of strata.

At the highest level, there is no centralised curriculum in RE. In the most recent National Curriculum, RE was described as a statutory subject with a non-statutory programme of study, which broadly incorporates and refers to the *Non-Statutory Framework* for RE (QCA 2004). Ofsted observes that most (but not all) locally agreed syllabuses make explicit use of the *Non-Statutory Framework* (2010: 9) but also that the existence of a centralised document, given that statutory requirements continue to be decided at the local level, can serve to confuse planning at the classroom level (Ofsted 2010: 27).

The *Framework* is intended to be 'of interest to' teachers (QCA 2004: 5) but is not written specifically for them; it is rather intended to inform SACREs and LEAs in planning local syllabuses, providing a guideline statement of the importance of religious education, a description of the subject's attainment targets and key skills, guidance on which religions should be covered and a corresponding description of a student's developing understanding at each key stage. The label of 'Framework' recalls Grimmitt's early influential attempt to formulate a structure for the implementation of his approach to RE; he writes that 'unlike a syllabus a framework does not dictate actual subject-matter but rather serves to indicate when and where certain *types* of content may appropriately be introduced, depending, of course, on the teacher's knowledge, expertise and objectives' (Grimmitt 1978: 49). Charles Clark's observation that the *Framework* 'had to be robust enough to define and defend the knowledge, skills and understanding that is the entitlement of every pupil' and at the same time 'flexible enough to give religious education syllabus providers the scope and creativity to enhance teaching and learning in religious education' resonates closely with Grimmitt's explanation of the greater flexibility of a Framework rather than a syllabus (QCA 2004: 3; Grimmitt 1978: 49). While Grimmitt's 'conceptual framework' was supported by a detailed discussion of the conceptual development of students drawing on the developmental work of Piaget and Bruner, it is not explicitly stated, and not otherwise clear, which theories of learning underpin the *National Framework*. Although the *Framework* is not intended to be prescriptive, there is certainly the possibility for it to be viewed this way by a teacher, especially if adopted in large part by a locally agreed syllabus. While much of the *Framework* is oriented towards describing the levels of a student's understanding, directions such as 'It is important that ASCs and schools ensure that by the end of key stage 3 pupils have encountered all of these five principal religions in sufficient depth' (QCA 2004: 12) add to the long-running tension often acknowledged by RE teachers between focusing on developing subject-specific concepts and delivering essential content (see Ofsted 2010: 43).

Statutory guidance in RE is implemented at the level of the locally agreed syllabus. Although the model syllabuses (SCAA 1994b) and later the *National Framework* have encouraged a greater degree of uniformity, syllabuses vary significantly from one LEA to another not only in terms of the content specified for study but also in terms of their length and detail, the amount of guidance on the planning and delivery of the learning experience, and additional support in the form of teaching resources. Some classroom teachers and even departments disregard their agreed syllabus entirely (as observed in the preliminary unpublished findings of a major report described in Lundie 2010), however it is the finding of this writer, working with teachers as part of the Forum for Religious and Spiritual Education at King's College London, that the agreed syllabus is often experienced as a hindrance to the attempt to implement a particular set of pedagogical objectives, due to the predominant focus on prescribing particular content. Erricker remarks that no other curriculum subject retains the word 'syllabus', which focuses entirely on the prescription of content, preferring instead 'the more multi-layered word "curriculum"' (Erricker 2010: 27).

At the most local level, teachers will inevitably deliver a departmental curriculum. While this may not affect planning for a subject leader, for other department members this can mean in some cases that they feel that they (for better or worse) have limited input into the planning process, and in others that planning takes on a collaborative dimension, which will be further discussed below.

Pedagogy

Grimmitt offers as a working definition of a pedagogy 'a theory of teaching and learning encompassing aims, curriculum content and methodology' (Grimmitt 2000c: 16). Specific debates about the appropriate theoretical description of religious education are discussed elsewhere (see Chapter 19); the more general observation to be made at this point is that although pedagogical theory would seem to be the most important starting point in the planning process, classroom teachers often experience questions about the aims and curriculum content of their lessons as having been foreclosed in advance, because the three aspects of the pedagogical question are inextricably linked: certain aims can only be achieved by a focus on certain content in conjunction with a certain methodology. The selection of particular content for teaching (such as may be imposed by a locally agreed syllabus) will therefore entail certain judgements about the appropriate aims of the subject. Such judgements are often not made explicit in an agreed syllabus, and may only have played an implicit or arbitrary part in its formulation. However, a teacher bringing to the planning process a certain set of judgements about the aims of RE may experience them as incompatible with the content specified in the agreed syllabus. The inclusion or exclusion of humanism or atheism on an agreed syllabus is an excellent example of this. A teacher whose primary aim is to promote tolerance for the ancient religious faiths of the world may find this difficult to reconcile with the need to devote significant classroom time to a discussion of atheism, whereas a teacher who aims to encourage students to grapple with questions about the ultimate nature of reality might find this difficult to do if they have to spend so much time on delivering particular content from all of the major world religions that they are not able to adequately address atheistic answers to these questions.

Teachers might experience themselves as most autonomous in the sphere of methodology – as experts in the field, they are best placed to judge 'what works'. However, the question of what works cannot be separated from the question of 'to what end'? It has already been noted that Ofsted observed that where teachers took a pick and mix approach to resources and methodologies that appealed to them, students were left uncertain as to the nature of their subject and confused by the sequencing of units of study (Ofsted 2010: 27–28). The close link between assessing the effectiveness of a methodology and the pedagogical aims towards which the methodology is being directed has not always been acknowledged even by academics in the field: one study, for example, (Kay and Smith 2000) assesses the effectiveness of systematic, thematic or 'mixed' approaches to the teaching of religion by comparing the number of mistakes that students make when using religious terms. While the use of vocabulary is undoubtedly important in RE, this choice of a single success criterion ignores the fact that integrated pedagogical theories that justify either a systematic or a thematic methodology will carry their own concomitant picture of what successful learning in the subject looks like, and must therefore be assessed for effectiveness on their own terms. Two competing methodologies cannot be judged without also judging the decisions about the aims and content of the subject that they imply.

Implicit pedagogical assumptions may also operate at the departmental level; this 'collaborative' aspect of the planning conducted by many classroom teachers has already been noted. Stern's adaptation (Stern 2006: 73–78) of Blaylock's description of a range of RE pedagogies (2004) offers a model for 'diagnosing' the pedagogical priorities at play in a particular department or scheme of work. While Blaylock is not intending to describe accurately the formation of a scheme of work, the narrative concerning Miss X's treatment of Easter demonstrates how a gradually developed or collaborative scheme could arrive at a piecemeal set of pedagogical assumptions, and thus – although this is not Stern's or Blaylock's point – lack clear progression and a coherent overall approach to the nature of the subject. Miss X initially adopts a phenomenological approach and then supplements and extends her scheme as she is exposed to new methodologies. What might be considered a toolkit approach to the methodologies offered by the different pedagogies fails to take account of the fact that each methodology is situated within a specific account of the aims and content of religious education, and thus carries its own set of planning priorities and its own picture of what the final unit of study should look like. This toolkit approach is further encouraged when university departments produce resources intended to be immediately accessible to time-pressed teachers or non-specialists rather than engaging teachers in the pedagogical debate which underpins them (see Rudge 2000: 106).

Progression

While every beginner teacher knows that progression is an integral concern in the sequencing of a unit of study, this is an area where little specific guidance has been offered in the RE context. The *National Framework* offers in the eight-level scale a picture of how a student's skills are expected to progress throughout their school experience (although it has been noted that the grounding of this picture in specific learning theory is unclear) but does not touch at all on the issue of how progression is supposed to factor into the sequencing of particular content or concepts. This will be seen to be a key point of dissonance between the two 'integrated' approaches to planning discussed later in this chapter. A teacher planning a lesson within a scheme of work (or in some cases an agreed syllabus) that has prescribed the order in which content is to be addressed will find much of this particular discussion foreclosed. This will constitute a limiting factor in terms of their possibilities for understanding the nature of the particular subject matter: the Hajj, for example, will lend itself to being explored in a particular way if it is addressed as part of a sequence of lessons on 'pilgrimage' (implying a phenomenological pedagogy) and in another if it is addressed as part of a unit on 'Are all human beings equal?' (implying a conceptual enquiry or critical realist pedagogy).

Assessment

A unit of study must be designed with on-going and ultimate assessment objectives in mind. The current prevailing paradigm for assessment in educational policy documents remains the competencies and standards-based model introduced under conservative government in the late twentieth century (see Grimmitt 2000c for a particularly scathing account of this initiative). Many RE teachers find themselves under pressure in their school context to assess learning using an eight-level scale of attainment in line with other national curriculum subjects, regardless of whether or not they are required to do so by their agreed syllabus. The widespread adoption of the *National Framework*'s two RE attainment targets in departments throughout the country (much recent guidance on lesson planning, such as Backus (2008) simply accepts them as a ubiquitous given) can be attributed in large part to the fact that they are attached to a ready-made eight-level scale of assessment; this is ironic given that Grimmitt feels that his initial conception of *Learning About* and *Learning From Religion* as a pedagogical strategy has been hijacked and misinterpreted within an educational context for which it was never intended (Grimmitt 2000c). The assessment criteria of national Religious Studies examinations at Key Stage 4 and Key Stage 5, developed in isolation from the *National Framework* and locally agreed syllabuses and with therefore very little likelihood of assuming closely matched pedagogical principles, add to the general mélange and further limit the possibility of clear progression from Key Stage 3 to Key Stage 4 (Ofsted 2010: 6).

Teachers prioritising a skills-based model of assessment in the planning process will naturally find that the development of certain skills will take priority over the delivery of particular content. The issue of whether a skills-based model is the picture of assessment best suited to RE will be seen to be an implicit point of contention between the two 'integrated' approaches discussed later in the chapter.

The experience of students

Since the iconoclastic work of Harold Loukes in the 1960s, RE theorists have acknowledged the need to engage in their planning with the real needs and level of religious understanding that students bring to their classroom (Loukes 1961; Copley 2008: 69–71; Wright 1997). In RE this issue entails more than simply the recognition of a dialectical relationship between intended learning outcomes and a student's prior learning (see for example Marton and Booth 1997); it is tied up fundamentally with questions about the aims and content of the subject. Students are likely to find certain content more engaging and relevant – it will resonate more directly with questions that they are already asking about religion or the world and they will thus be more motivated in their learning; on the other hand, there may be certain questions which they are not asking which they need to be encouraged to ask, if the chosen pedagogical aims of the subject are to be met. This tension partly underlies the debate over the extent to which humanist or other non-religious worldviews have a place in what has traditionally been called 'religious' education, given that so many students will identify with a non-religious worldview and understand their identity in secular terms. This debate also serves to show how – unlike, perhaps, in other subject areas – the proper subject matter of religious education, rather than being the fixed starting point for lesson planning, remains an issue for ongoing discussion (Aldridge 2011).

Integrated approaches

While the growing importance of centralised statements of the nature and importance of RE, such as the *National Framework*, have served to defend the entitlement of students to religious education, they have also widened the gap between the academic discourse of the subject and the experience of classroom teachers. Erricker (2010: 67–68) identifies a 'systemic malfunction' that has opened up a fissure between theory and classroom practice. Certainly, the time that teachers, already hard-pressed, might have been inclined to devote to reading RE theory has been squeezed by the need to engage with an increasing number of generic policies such as ECM; however, more importantly, the more documents such as the *National Framework* have served to consolidate the inflexible 'givens' with which RE teachers feel themselves to be presented, the less academics have engaged with these givens. Prior to the existence of the model syllabuses or the *National Framework*, Grimmitt for example would devote half of his classic texts to pedagogical theory and the other half to detailing how this should be realised in the classroom (see Grimmitt 1978, 1987). Goldman pushes for a 'total view' that will allow his developmental account of RE learning to inform the construction of agreed syllabuses from the bottom up (Goldman 1964: 192–219). The effect of the production of centralised documents is to effectively take such considerations 'off the table', causing academics to address more abstract issues and withdraw from the daily experience of classroom teachers. There follows a discussion of two academics who have realised the need to address this situation, Erricker explicitly and Wright as an implicit aspect of his overall approach.

Interpreting worldviews

Although no explicit reference was made, the structure of a conceptual enquiry offered in the Ofsted report as a model of good practice drew directly from the Hampshire 'Living Difference' agreed syllabus, developed under Erricker's supervision (Hampshire County Council 2004). Erricker's recent work constitutes a distinct shift in emphasis from his earlier writing on pedagogy (see Erricker 2000). While he still draws on a constructivist model of learning, he now presents a model that does not rely on the postmodern form of constructivism with which he has been associated in the past (Erricker 2010: 77–80). He attributes this change in emphasis to his work as lead inspector in Hampshire, where he observed that students tended to have a limited grasp of core concepts and were unable to make critical judgements about religion – they were unable to 'read' the religious texts with which they were presented (Erricker 2010: 34).

Erricker in the Hampshire Syllabus seeks to provide teachers with a 'methodology' or 'procedural instrument' (Erricker 2010: 82). He pushes for an 'integrity' in lesson planning (81) and acknowledges that skill-based assessment is a central aspect of the practice of contemporary teachers. He then composes his own eight-level scale corresponding to the skills central to making a 'conceptual inquiry'. These five skills are integrated into lesson planning by themselves becoming the structure for a sequence of learning, thus 'changing RE from a subject that is not skills based to one that is' (98). Students always move in turn from *enquiring* to *contextualising* to *evaluating* to *communicating* to *applying*, although the skills are connected in a circular relationship, and a particular enquiry might begin at a different part of the circle. In lesson planning, this five-part structure is wedded to a particular concept 'related to the religious tradition you have decided to engage with' (101). Following Grimmitt, concepts of increasing levels of sophistication are thought to be appropriate to different stages of a student's development, moving from type A concepts that are common to religious and non-religious experience through to type C concepts that are particular to specific religions. Thus progression is conceived of (again following Grimmitt) as a 'spiral curriculum' where five skills are rotated with increasing sophistication, enabling students to engage with more sophisticated concepts as they progress through their school experience. Independent research suggests that Erricker's five-stage model is proving a very effective way for teachers to relate pedagogical principles to the realities of classroom practice (Wedell 2010).

Critical religious education

In the applications of Andrew Wright's critical realist pedagogy developed by Susanna Hookway (Hookway 2002, 2004) there is a similar emphasis on enquiry-based learning and a circular sequence, although more explicit theoretical use is made of the hermeneutics of Hans-Georg Gadamer than of constructivism or the language of levels of attainment. A sequence of learning for Hookway seeks to enable the student to answer a 'key question' about the nature of reality, such as 'What happens to us when we die?' The student's horizon of understanding is acknowledged as the point of departure for the sequence of learning; in an initial 'mirror' phase the students have an opportunity to articulate their answer to the key question. This is followed by the rigorous study of appropriate theological content from an alternative worldview (the 'window' phase), followed by the 'conversation', the reflective moment to which the learning sequence intends, which corresponds to Gadamer's moment of understanding, the 'fusion of horizons' (Gadamer 2004) although Wright prefers the language of 'engagement' rather than fusion (Wright 2000b).

Wright makes increasingly explicit use of the critical realist philosophy of Roy Bhaskar (Wright 2007) and the Variation Theory of Learning (Marton and Booth

1997; Marton and Tsui 2004). This leads to an emphasis on engagement with reality that is not present in Erricker's work. Whereas Erricker describes progression in terms of the development of a particular set of skills which are applied to increasingly complex concepts, Wright's model is quite different. The phenomenographical research methods employed by Marton describe levels of understanding in terms of a 'widening of awareness' of an aspect of reality (see Hella 2008) and what constitutes wider awareness will depend on the nature of the subject matter being taught, so that assessment criteria cannot be separated ultimately from the way the world is. Whereas Erricker's model of progression has at its apex the most complex concepts through which religions comprehend reality, Wright's model argues that although such concepts are an aspect of reality, ultimately they are not themselves the subject matter of RE. Although he has been associated with a 'conceptual' approach (see, for example, Stern 2006: 77) and is a defender of religious literacy, Wright urges that encouraging students to live truthfully in accordance with the nature of ultimate reality is the primary aim of religious education (Hella and Wright 2009), so his model for progression focuses on attaining a 'deeper' understanding of the way the world is, rather than specifying in advance the particular skills that will be required to do this; his success criteria will ultimately be transformational rather than epistemic.

Towards a 'total view'

Although they have a similar focus on an enquiry-based, hermeneutic model for religious education, Wright and Erricker present significantly different attempts to engage with the givens experienced by teachers in the planning process. Erricker's model is more explicitly radical; although he devotes some time to explaining how his model interacts with the language of the *National Framework*, the 'integrity' of his learning sequence relies on his having replaced the *Framework*'s eight-level scale with an alternative that corresponds to his five-stage learning sequence, and in perhaps the most obviously controversial aspect of his work he rejects the two-fold attainment target. He also binds his integrated approach to a particular agreed syllabus design that conceives of learning in terms of increasing levels of conceptual complexity; it is thus not be intended to be compatible with other agreed syllabuses built on different pedagogical principles. However, in terms of core educational principles he embraces a focus on levels of attainment and thus conforms to the political ideology that Grimmitt so scathingly rejected.

Wright's engagement is superficially more conservative; he makes little reference to the *National Framework*, and when he does so it serves to justify his approach (Wright 2007: 141). Recently he has argued that the critical realist approach is compatible with the two attainment targets, and in fact provides an additional insight into how they relate (Hella and Wright 2009). The implication of his own brief example of how a sequence of learning can be designed (Wright 2007: 254–259) is that his pedagogical method can be applied to whatever content a teacher finds herself faced with, although this may be somewhat neglectful of the question touched on above concerning the extent to which the prescribed order of a given scheme of work can serve to constitute the nature of the subject matter studied. More controversially, Wright's critical realist take on variation theory suggests that if assessment (hitherto not addressed by Wright in detail) is to be made an integrated aspect of his approach, this will need to be in a very different form from the skills-based 'levels of attainment' provided by the *National Framework*.

While Wright and Erricker both present an approach to lesson planning that seeks not only to integrate the three aspects of Grimmitt's account of pedagogy but also to integrate these pedagogical principles with the other competing priorities in the lesson planning process, such as the various policy documents and the horizon of understanding of the student, they do so in distinct ways, and theirs are not the only attempts at such an endeavour. The time has come to locate the classroom teacher within this debate. Are we any closer to establishing a 'starting point' or a first priority in the planning process, from which other considerations can be determined? Grimmitt, in a discussion of the formation of any curriculum, likens the prerequisite ideological assumptions about knowledge, values and the child as the sides of an equilateral triangle, held together in a dialectical or creative tension (Grimmitt 1987: 15–17), and calls teachers to be aware of the extent to which they are always already 'situated' in this dialectic. A similar model could perhaps be applied to the planning process in religious education, where the various priorities, rather than competing, might be held in a hermeneutic or circular relationship. Whilst the initially more fixed 'givens' such as the agreed syllabus or departmental scheme of work might offer a preliminary purchase on the planning process and help to initially define other aspects such as the nature of assessment or the progression of content, they themselves should not be seen by classroom teachers as immune from possible revision in the light of decisions made on the other points of the compass.

Questions

Identify what has been your main 'starting point' in the planning process to date. Why have you prioritised this particular aspect?

What in your view are the main obstacles hindering the realisation of an 'integrated' approach to sequencing lessons?

Evaluate the models for sequencing lessons provided by Clive Erricker and Susanna Hookway. Which approach is more consistent with your understanding of the aims, content and method of RE?

Further reading

Erricker, C. (2010) *Religious Education: A Conceptual and Interdisciplinary Approach for Secondary Level*, London: Routledge. Explains in detail the pedagogical principles underpinning the Hampshire approach to planning a unit of study.

Grimmitt, M. (1987) *Religious Education and Human Development,* Great Wakening, Essex: McCrimmons. The classic attempt at an 'integrated' approach to lesson planning and pedagogy which defines much of the language of subsequent debate.

Hookway, S. (2002) 'Mirrors, windows, conversations: religious education for the millennial generation in England and Wales', *British Journal of Religious Education* 24: 99–110. An exceptionally clear attempt to base a model for sequencing learning on sophisticated pedagogical principles.

Chapter 16

Pedagogy

Vivienne Baumfield

> The fundamental factors in the educative process are an immature, undeveloped being and certain social aims, meanings, values incarnated in the mature experience of the adult. The educative process is the due interaction of these forces.
>
> (Dewey 1956: 4)

The concern of all teachers is to create experiences that provide encouragement for students to learn something that is meaningful to them in the here and now and an interest in continuing to learn in the future. Pedagogy is the 'art of knowing' as a teacher how to conduct intentional and systematic intervention in order to influence the development of the learner; it is a cultural activity that is never neutral (Olson and Bruner 1996). In religious education (RE) we find two recurring themes in the debate about learning and teaching; the first of these is the nature of RE as a subject in the school curriculum, is it the study of religion as a cultural phenomenon, the study of what it means to belong to a religious tradition or the personal, spiritual development of the learner, and, second, what kind of learning experiences are required in order to promote understanding? The attention of researchers and policy makers has been focused on attempts to resolve these fundamental issues through establishing agreed understandings of the content and purpose of RE in schools and less consideration has been given to the question of developing an understanding of pedagogy. This has left teachers to face difficult choices in their daily practice in the classroom without recourse to the means by which to make professional judgements in complex and contested situations.

Pedagogy: what is it and why is it important?

The 'paidagogus' was the slave who led a child to school and pedagogy retains this sense of the teacher as both the guide and the servant of the learner. Pedagogy is concerned with the interactions through which knowledge is shared between generations through formal education, making it an activity with the potential to preserve or subvert cultural values and one that is never neutral (Nyborg 1993; Olson and Bruner 1996). It is a term that is not used very much in the UK where the dynamic relationship between teaching, learning and culture it signifies is frequently underplayed in restricted definitions of teaching as instruction (Simon 1981).

In *The Child and the Curriculum* (Dewey 1956), pedagogy is described as building a bridge between the world of the child and the intellectual, cultural life of the community, a task that requires a deep understanding of both the logical structure of subject knowledge and of the learner's psychological development. For the child, informal learning outside the classroom is a continuous, integrated process with no conscious division between experience, inquiry and knowledge where interest is assured and relevance can be taken for granted. However, the range of experience may be idiosyncratic and it is through formal education that children can participate in the wider cultural and social life of the community. Understanding and maintaining the balance between the interest of the learner and the requirements of the subject to be studied makes great demands on the teacher, who faces the challenge of achieving the same integration when learning in school settings as would occur outside the classroom.

Curriculum, pedagogy and assessment

Pedagogy is described by the sociologist of education Basil Bernstein as forming, with curriculum and assessment, one of the three 'message systems' by which educational knowledge is organised, transmitted and evaluated (Bernstein 1971). Education policy in the UK, at least since the Education Reform Act of 1988, has focused on determining the curriculum and the nature of assessment and, with the exception of the literacy and numeracy strategies in England, has not intervened directly in the area of pedagogy. However, the close, interdependent relationship between the three 'systems' leaves little room for manoeuvre in a culture of accountability through performance measured by test results. Schooling is a social, cultural activity and teachers do not work in isolation; even without direct intervention from policy makers, scope for individual choice is circumscribed by the expectations for education in the wider society. In the case of RE, the role of religion in an increasingly secular and multi-cultural society is controversial leaving the subject open to different, often conflicting, interpretations and its place in the curriculum contested. Awareness of the role of pedagogy as not simply the act of teaching but also as the 'theories, beliefs, policies and controversies that inform and shape it' (Alexander 2001: 540) can help teachers to understand that '[d]ifferent purposes ... will be served by different types of process and call for different types of interaction, which in turn, will yield different types of understanding (Grimmitt 1981: 42).

We need not suspend attention to pedagogy until the place of RE in the curriculum is resolved; not least because it is doubtful that this would ever happen in a subject which is not only controversial but which deals with controversy. Pedagogy articulates the complexity of teaching and highlights the need for teachers to be professional in their selection of strategies to build a bridge between the learner and the curriculum in order to educate rather than coerce or merely entertain the students in their charge. Teachers as pedagogues rather than instructors have more command over the way in which they approach learning and teaching based on their rich, contextual knowledge of learners in classrooms. They must also take responsibility and become what has been described as 'extended professionals' (Stenhouse 1975) by continuing to develop their knowledge, understanding and skills.

Learning about and learning from religious education

Although the specific content and purpose of RE has been debated since the establishment of a state funded school system in the UK, there is a consensus in key curriculum policy documents since the 1944 Education Act that it should play a dual role whereby young people will have a better understanding of religion as well as of themselves (Watson and Thompson 2007). The phrase 'learning about and learning from' to describe this dual role for RE was first used in the late 1970s (Grimmitt and Read 1977). In its original formulation, the construct was intended as a pedagogical principle to demarcate the content and process of RE in schools as distinct from Religious Studies or religious nurture (Grimmitt 1981). According to this principle, RE differs from Religious Studies in its concern for the personal development of the learner through the encounter with religious traditions and from religious nurture as its primary purpose is to serve educational rather than religious goals. It is this interactive relationship between the two aspects of learning, to promote evaluation of the learner's understanding of religion in personal terms as well as understanding of self in religious terms, that could provide a basis on which to develop pedagogy in RE. Unfortunately, the dynamic tension of the original formulation was lost in the incorporation of 'learning about and learning from' as the two attainment targets in the Model Syllabuses for RE (Grimmitt 2000d: 37).

Whilst the dissemination of a simplified version of 'learning about and learning from' following the publication of the Model Syllabuses undermined its potential to furnish a basis for pedagogy in RE, even in its original form the concept presented some difficulties. Developers of leading approaches to RE in the UK, who were well aware of the dynamic, interactive aspect of the construct, still had concerns regarding its potential to support educative experiences. Contributors of essays in *Pedagogies of Religious Education* (Grimmitt 2000b) question the extent to which 'learning about' would 'penetrate beyond the external core of religious expression and embrace its inner experiential heart' (Wright 2000b: 173) and whether 'learning from' could be separated from the framework of a particular religious tradition in order to provide 'material for promoting personal development' (Cooling 2000: 162). Also, the identification of two different aspects, no matter how dynamically they are supposed to interact, suggests a separation that many people would say was impossible as 'successful learning always requires the learner to engage with and not just learn about' (Brown 2000: 67). More fundamentally, 'learning about and learning from' gives weight to the existence of a body of knowledge external to the narrative of the process of knowing by the individual learner that is open to challenge (Erricker and Erricker 2000a).

The Constructive Pedagogies of RE project (Grimmitt 2000b) addresses some of the criticisms of the human development approach of 'learning about and learning from' religion through its emphasis on the learners' construction of understanding by an inter-subjective and intra-subjective search for meaning. Grimmitt outlines a process by which the teacher begins with a generic principle and then finds a means of expression in terms specific to RE from which to develop a pedagogical strategy. However, this description of the process still underplays any negotiation with the constraints imposed by the wider social, cultural context more usually associated with the exercising of pedagogical judgement. Grimmitt's review of contemporary pedagogies of RE is the most systematic attempt to address the issues but falls short of providing a secure rationale on which to make professional choices, as the diverse approaches and the use of the plural 'pedagogies' indicates. We are still left with a sense that teaching may be a case of exercising preferences regarding methods rather than having a secure grasp of the 'art of knowing' how best to approach learning in RE. The need for a more robust basis on which to advance debate about pedagogy in RE is recognised by Grimmitt himself in his call for more research into the impact of particular interventions on learners in classrooms to underpin advocacy of an approach.

Research as pedagogy/pedagogy as research in RE

Pedagogy's role as both the constructor and mediator of educational experience means that it can never be a neutral or 'innocent' activity (Bruner 1996; Olson and Bruner 1996) but it can be authentic. Authenticity is achieved when the teacher is willing to make their intentions explicit, is able to demonstrate coherence between theories held about learning and their practice and is open to challenge from different perspectives, including those of the learners themselves, on the effective mediation of learning. This orientation towards pedagogy is closely aligned with a commitment to inquiry as the foundation of learning and teaching (Dewey 1933) and can be located within the tradition of teacher development through their involvement in curriculum development (Stenhouse 1975). For the RE teacher, a commitment to authentic pedagogy has the advantage of providing a means of developing professional judgement that need not assume mastery of a well-defined body of agreed subject content:

> Either the teacher must be an expert or he [sic] must be a learner along with his students. In most cases, the teacher cannot in the nature of the case be an expert. It follows that he must cast himself in the role of a learner. Pedagogically this may in fact be a preferable role to that of the expert. It implies teaching by discovery or inquiry methods rather than by instruction.
>
> (Stenhouse 1975: 91)

The alternative, according to Stenhouse, is to manufacture a simplified, agreed version of a complex field of knowledge as a curriculum 'subject' of which it is possible for a teacher to be the master but which has little purchase on the world outside the school.

Julian Stern has worked with practitioners and researchers who attended a series of seminars funded by the Westhill Trust to promote dialogue about future directions in RE. The outcomes of the seminars have been published in a series of books and articles (Stern 2006, 2010) in which he sees a close connection between the future of research in RE and the future of RE in schools. Stern describes research as the most appropriate pedagogy for RE, especially in contested social circumstances, as it allows for negotiation between modernist school definitions of the subject on the one hand and on the other, the deconstruction of all content within a post-structuralist paradigm dominant in current undergraduate courses in theology and religious studies. The type of research advocated by Stern is practitioner inquiry, a form of action research by teachers with an explicit focus on the development of their classroom practice (Baumfield *et al.* 2008), with direct links to the development of authentic pedagogy as conceived by Dewey and with Stenhouse's promotion of teachers as researchers. Teachers researching what is happening in their classrooms when they are teaching RE are able to experiment with different methods, as suggested by Lat Blaylock's playful demonstration of 'Six ways around Easter: a pedagogical fantasy' (Stern 2006), whilst also working towards the evaluation of what could constitute a coherent pedagogy for RE.

Teachers who engage in systematic inquiry into their practice benefit from a progressive increase in understanding of their work and so become more able to make good pedagogical decisions (Stenhouse 1975). If they include the students they teach in the practice of co-inquiry in RE, they can accrue even greater benefits as members of a community of learners developing the reflexive knowledge of self, each other and the subject that is necessary if the bridge between the child and the curriculum is to be constructed: 'Teaching RE, with teachers and pupils as researchers in the classroom, can bring people and communities together' (Stern 2010: 112).

One of the classic problems of philosophy is that of 'other minds', that is the question of how we understand the relationship between what we think and experience in terms of what other people may be thinking and experiencing. It has been demonstrated that consciousness of 'other minds' is a distinctly human trait and closely connected with another human characteristic, teaching; an activity that assumes the possibility of one mind being able to influence, educate, another. Even before the study of cognition could provide insight into the processes of thinking, learning and teaching people had ideas about the mind that have been described as 'folk pyschology', which informed a 'folk pedagogy' (Olson and Bruner 1996). Taking an inquiry stance in teaching enables teachers to gain insight into the beliefs about learning that are implicit in their current practice and subject them to critical appraisal; it also has the added advantage of making the students' beliefs about learning explicit and amenable to change. Making the transition from folk pedagogy to an understanding of pedagogy which retains a close integration with practice but which can also provide a basis for the development of theory is essential if teaching is to be a progressive and professional activity. Practitioner inquiry in RE has contributed to the development of pedagogy through initiatives such as the collaboration with Newcastle University on thinking skills (Baumfield 2002b) and with the University of Warwick on the interpretive approach to RE (O'Grady 2010). The work of practitioners supported by fellowships awarded by the Farmington Institute at Harris Manchester College, University of Oxford has also contributed to the development of research as pedagogy in RE (http://www.farmington.ac.uk/fellowships).

Debating pedagogy in RE

It is encouraging to find, after a long period of relative neglect in the UK, signs that pedagogy is becoming a focus of attention in the RE community. However, we must guard against simplistic or reductive uses of the term, particularly by policy advisers, that uncouple it from interaction with the wider socio-cultural context so that it comes to mean simply the selection of effective teaching methods (Baumfield 2010). Ignoring this wider context undermines the power of pedagogy to transform learning and teaching by increasing the demands on the RE teacher to focus on the faithful implementation of a particular method or approach rather than on being an extended professional.

Another area where caution is needed if confusion is to be avoided when debating pedagogy in RE is in maintaining its distinction from another, related, important process in learning and teaching: didactics. If, as we have seen, pedagogy is concerned with taking account of the dynamic interactions between the learner, the subject matter and the implications of the wider socio-cultural interpretations of the purpose of education, then didactics shifts the emphasis to the implications of the way in which knowledge is structured in the context of a particular subject. Both didactics and pedagogy involve dynamic processes of interpretation and reinterpretation but consideration of didactics can anticipate the act of teaching whereas pedagogy also has an immediacy requiring decisions to be made as particular teaching moments arise in the classroom (Banks et al. 2005). Pedagogy is the means by which the teacher takes hold of the 'moments of contingency' (Black and Wiliam 2009), the teachable moments, which arise in the classroom. In Europe, where both the study of pedagogy and didactics forms part of teacher education, these distinctions are better understood than in the UK. We need to guard against the unintended consequences of seizing upon pedagogy as a means of achieving a more sophisticated understanding of teaching whilst ignoring its companion in the teachers' lexicon, didactics. If this seems rather abstruse and remote, we need only look at a statement in the most recent report from Her Majesty's Inspectorate on the current state of RE in schools to see how understanding the difference between pedagogy and didactics could have an immediate impact on teachers in classrooms. The point is made that what 'limited the effectiveness of both secondary and primary teachers was their understanding of subject pedagogy' (Ofsted 2010: 44). What is crucial here is deciding what is meant by 'subject pedagogy'. The diagnosis of the problem and consequently the recommendations for its solution will depend on what it is we think that RE teachers lack understanding about.

Subject knowledge is an important part of teaching and we would expect teachers of RE to be versed in both pedagogy and didactics. The changing name for the subject in the curriculum from 'Scripture' to 'Religious Instruction' and latterly 'Philosophy and Ethics' in some English schools charts the crisis of identity that has dogged the development of RE. Until recently, debate in RE has focused on definitions of the content and on who should have a role in defining the content, rather than looking at the processes of learning in classroom contexts. Persuasive cases have been made for adopting a phenomenological stance whereby religion is regarded as a social phenomenon (Smart 1973), the study of which requires us to be prepared to suspend pre-conceptions so that we do not rush to conclusions based on our unexamined prejudices. Unfortunately, much of the subtlety of such approaches is lost in translation into the classroom so that comparative description becomes dominant: 'RE is about observing differences and similarities in religious systems and noting recurring common themes' (Hay and Hammond 1992: 149).

Equally, keeping an open mind in some expressions equates to relativism and the conclusion that any belief is just as good as any other. However, these failings are as much a sign of a failure to consider the implications for pedagogy as to any necessary flaw in the original ideas. Similar arguments could be presented for the gap between the hermeneutics of the interpretive approach (Jackson 1997) and the implementation of the resources in the classroom or of the critical realism underpinning the religious literacy approach (Wright 1993) and its enactment in classrooms. Whilst some theorists of RE have paid some attention to the implications of their ideas for the classroom teacher, others did not as the observation that Ninian Smart had little to say about practice illustrates (O'Grady 2005). It is a truism to say that understanding the nature of the subject and understanding the 'art of teaching' go hand in hand, as 'in order to learn about something you have to have some idea of what it is you are learning about' (Marton and Booth 1997: viii). Unravelling the complex dynamics of didactics and pedagogy is more a question of where weight and emphasis should be given in the development of the professional teacher's repertoire. The argument presented in this chapter is for the insights of the teacher and their students to be given more prominence. Attention needs to be paid to the requirement for learning to be meaningful not just in terms of the requirements of the school curriculum or of the faith communities but for the learner and the teacher here and now.

Debate as to what constitutes 'educative process' in RE will continue and should be welcomed; we would not want it to be otherwise in such a controversial and contested aspect of the school curriculum. At the same time, we need to find ways of enabling learning and teaching to develop and to do this must give the teachers and their learners the freedom to construct, share and evaluate RE in their classrooms. Pedagogy is the means by which we can understand, challenge and improve what actually happens in the RE classroom.

Questions

To what extent do you think that consensus on the purpose of RE is essential for effective pedagogy?

How much flexibility can and should individual teachers have in determining the balance between content and process in RE?

What kind of learning opportunities need to be included in the initial and continuing education of teachers in order to promote the development of pedagogy?

Further reading

Alexander, R. J. (2000) *Culture and Pedagogy: International Comparisons in Primary Education*, London: Blackwell. Whilst this is a long book, it is written in a clear and engaging style and the final section includes a useful review of difficult concepts such as the relationship between pedagogy and didactics.

Dewey, J. (1956) *The Child and the Curriculum; and the School and Society*, London: University of Chicago Press. Although this short essay was first published early in the twentieth century, it remains one of the clearest accounts of the challenging task of the teacher in making connections between the world of the child and the cultural values of society as embodied in the content and processes of formal education.

Grimmitt, M. (ed.) (2000b) *Pedagogies of Religious Education*, Great Wakering: McCrimmons. This edited collection of case studies in the research and development of good pedagogic practice in RE includes contributions from the developers of the most influential approaches to learning and teaching in RE.

Stern, J. (2010) 'Research as pedagogy: building learning communities and religious understanding in RE', *British Journal of Religious Education*, 32: 133–146. This article explores the relationship between practitioner inquiry, research and pedagogy in an accessible manner, which is grounded in the practical experience of a group of teachers with whom the author was working over a period of time.

Chapter 17

Differentiation

Nigel Fancourt

Differentiation is simply the straightforward principle that teachers should adjust their teaching to ensure that the varying needs of different pupils are met, yet paradoxically it is highly contentious. Almost everyone has a strong view on it: teachers, parents, politicians. It will have been part of your education; perhaps it helped you or perhaps you bitterly resented it. This chapter will outline some of the debates surrounding differentiation; it is neither a general guide (see O'Brian and Guiney 2001; Capel *et al.* 2005: 133–283) nor a practical guide for differentiation in religious education (RE) (see Cappleman 2003).

To some extent differentiation overlaps with other important educational principles, notably inclusion. This is the policy of catering for the needs of those with special educational needs, including severe learning difficulties, in mainstream schools rather than in special schools. Some aspects of inclusion, for instance ensuring that a school site has wheelchair access, are unlikely to be the responsibility of an individual teacher. However other aspects of it may impinge on the teacher's usual routines, such as accommodating a wheelchair user in the classroom, or including pupils with Autistic Spectrum Disorder (e.g. Horsfield 2005). This chapter will focus more specifically on differentiation in terms of pupils' mental processes, rather than their physical needs. It is also linked to the demands for 'personalised' learning: that pupils' education should be more individually tailored (DfES 2006a). This is the recognition that some pupils will need a modified curriculum, for instance work-based learning, but will also affect decisions about how they are taught in lessons.

There are three sections. First, the nature of pupils' differences is considered, i.e. the range of intellectual and other attributes that may affect attainment. Then the detection of these differences is briefly explored, and some of the related problems. The third section reviews arguments about strategies for dealing with these differences. While most practical guides to differentiation focus on the last issue, the debates generally arise out of the first two.

What are the differences between pupils?

There are several ways of explaining and identifying differences in pupils' performance in RE. One of the most commonplace explanations for the difference in pupils' performance in any subject is that it is due to innate 'intelligence' (e.g. Jensen 1973); in short, that some pupils are naturally 'bright' and others 'dim'. This is a view commonly held across the population. It assumes that intelligence is fixed, and if there are some students who succeed, there are others who cannot. It is however strongly contested (e.g. Gilbourn and Youdell 2001). The problems are that intelligence is hard to define, and identifying it seems to deny the value of education, except merely to gain knowledge. The rival view, that everything can be learnt, suggests that, given enough time, any learner can achieve. Studies have shown this to be effective, but the issue is in creating enough time to ensure this (Kulik *et al.* 1990).

Alternatively, educationalists recognise generic skills and attitudes that run through a range of subjects, such as literacy or numeracy. This allows for a more nuanced approach to individual learning needs. The role of learning support in many schools will therefore be to ensure that pupils who struggle with these wide ranging skills have the opportunity to develop, e.g. the case of dyslexia (Alborz *et al.* 2009). Rather than attributing pupils' lack of success in literacy to their general intelligence, recognising the difficulties with the processes of reading and writing is now taken for granted as a possible explanation of low achievement. By diagnosing and overcoming one generic strand of learning, pupils can be helped in many subjects. However, within these skills, the same question arises as to whether they are innate or not, and therefore how to resolve them; thus there is an argument as whether dyslexia is innate or the result of other factors (see Poole 2010).

A third rather obvious strategy is to attribute pupils' performance in RE to their abilities in that subject itself. Thus RE has its own particular set of knowledge, understanding and skills, and the pupils' performance is not related to their performance in other subject areas (Fancourt 2003). For instance, guidance on 'gifted and talented' students explains how these qualities will be manifested in particular subject areas (Blaylock 2001): even if there are similarities, to be 'gifted and talented' in art is not to be 'gifted and talented' in RE.

Fourthly, the pupil's own experience of religion can be a significant influence on their performance in RE. This is of course not to say that being religious automatically means success in RE. Nevertheless, pupils who have personal experience and awareness of particular religious beliefs, traditions and values may engage with some aspects of RE more effectively than their classmates (Jackson *et al.* 2010: 131). By contrast, pupils with little personal experience of religion may need different learning experiences in order to open this up to them. Furthermore, pupils who live in multi-religious communities, such as Sheffield, will have personal experience of a diversity of religious beliefs and practices, compared with those from mono-religious backgrounds, such as remote rural communities in Cumbria, for whom rural Christianity will probably be the default model (see

Ipgrave and McKenna 2008: 116–117); these raise different challenges for the teacher. Pupils' experiences of religion in school, whether faith schools or not, will also affect their perceptions.

Finally, there are other social factors linked to pupil attainment: gender, ethnicity and social class (Haralambos and Holborn 2004: 731–789). Gender is discussed in Chapter 5, but it is also an aspect of differentiation. Ethnicity is also significant. There has long been concern about the performance of black pupils, though currently the most successful pupils are Chinese and the least successful are Roma (DfES 2006b); these statistics raise questions about the reasons behind them. Some argue that black students are naturally less intelligent than white students, thus linking the idea of general intelligence with ethnicity (Eysenck 1971). This is hotly contested (Gould 1996). Social class is also critical – probably the major factor on pupil performance. Whatever schools seem to do, middle-class pupils generally do better than working-class pupils. The reasons for this are contested: is it because of material factors? Some suggest that working-class pupils lack the requisite home context to succeed: their own bedroom, computers and books. Or are schools inherently middle class, so that middle-class pupils have the upper hand (Wilby 2010)? Bourdieu famously argued that the education system prioritises a certain set of knowledge, skills and values, such as 'good manners' and knowledge of high arts; middle-class pupils have this 'cultural capital' and therefore succeed, whereas working-class children do not and therefore fail (e.g. Bourdieu 1973). It may also be a combination of material *and* cultural factors (Sullivan 2001). Furthermore, it may be that the differences between pupils are not due to one factor but to a combination of different factors: ability, religiosity, class, ethnicity and gender.

How are the differences detected?

Some differences are obvious, e.g. gender and ethnicity. Others will be harder to detect. For the teacher, differences in pupils' performance will be evident from their work, and teachers can identify individual strengths and weaknesses. However this raises issues about the role of assessment and testing. A good example is the IQ test, which is often seen as the classic way to detect innate intelligence. It consists of a series of short numerical, spatial and verbal problems, and allows a pupil's 'intelligence quotient' to be measured. Clearly, this kind of test is only useful if innate intelligence exists, but it also assumes that IQ is essentially fixed. Thus someone who has an IQ of 125 when they are 12 years old should have roughly the same IQ later in life. This approach is critiqued; the focus of educational psychology should not be on 'how the child came to be what he is' but on 'how he can become what he not yet is', as the Russian psychologist Leont'ev observed (Bronfenbrenner 1977: 528). It runs counter to an educational system in which pupils are supposed to *improve*: assessment levels are intended to identify progress, not static ability (QCA 2004). IQ tests are also criticised for an implicit ethnic and social bias (Gould 1983); for example their expectations of language may reflect white middle-class speech, rather than allowing for the diversity of linguistic ability (Cline and Shamsi 2000).

The commonest method of detecting differences is through classroom assessment. The general issues surrounding this are discussed in Chapter 19. Here, the *diagnostic* role of assessment is important, i.e. using assessment to identify pupils' strengths and weaknesses, and thereby informing lesson planning and delivery. However, to do this effectively the criteria for measurement need to be accurate. The *National Framework*'s eight-level scale is supposed to provide this (QCA 2004), but this is contested. Is it really a model of intellectual development in the subject, or simply a set of tasks arranged in a rather haphazard order (Kay 2005b)?

What can be done about the differences?

The teacher's main challenge is to decide what to do: how can pupil X be helped to improve in RE? There are two important issues. The first is grouping: whether teachers, and more generally schools, should either group similar pupils together and teach them together, or instead teach mixed-ability groups but differentiate within that group. The second is the process of classroom differentiation, notably planning and the regulation of learning. Within these however lurks another argument about the role of education: whether the purpose of schooling is to develop students' particular strengths and skills, or whether to develop a broad range of skills and abilities in every pupil.

Grouping strategies

The classic debate on grouping is on the merits and drawbacks of streaming and setting versus mixed-ability teaching. Streaming is when, having (supposedly) identified pupils on the basis of intellectual ability, they are then placed together in one school for pupils of that ability. This is the approach adopted by grammar schools, and was the approach across the whole country from 1944 to 1965, under the tripartite system. In this system pupils would take a test at 11: the 11+. Those who passed went to a grammar school, at which there would be high expectations of success, for instance, going on to university. In some areas there were secondary technical colleges for more creative pupils. The rest would go on to a secondary modern school. The 11+ still operates in some local authorities, e.g. Buckinghamshire and Kent. The alternative was the development of comprehensive schools in 1960s, in which all pupils whatever their ability were educated together. Advocates of the selective system maintain that pupils are properly and appropriately differentiated, since the schools themselves are geared for pupils' particular needs. For them, the comprehensive system simply caters for the 'average' pupil, but the two extreme ends of the spectrum, high and low attainers, are ignored (Hillgate Group 1987). Advocates of the comprehensive system maintain that the selective system is based on a false notion of intelligence, and that all pupils can learn more effectively together.

Patterns are however even more nuanced, since in many comprehensive schools, pupils are 'setted'. This means that in particular subjects, pupils are put in classes according to ability. For instance, in mathematics, many schools will have 'top', 'middle' and 'bottom' sets. While this can prove effective in some subjects, there are concerns (Gamoran 2002). One is 'labelling'. If pupils are put in a 'top' set, they see themselves as 'bright', feel encouraged, and develop the self-confidence to work hard. Thus, they will often improve their attainment, confirming the label. By contrast, if a pupil is put into a 'bottom' set, they are likely to see themselves as failures, and therefore not to try. Thus they do not succeed, and the teachers' label is also confirmed, as a self-fulfilling prophecy (Ireson and Hallam 2005). Further, even if classes are setted, the lessons need to be altered accordingly, which is not always the case (Ofsted 2007: 21)

A further issue is subject difference. In more hierarchical subjects, for instance mathematics, it is easier to produce a linear measurement of attainment. In maturation subjects, for instance English literature or RE, it is less easy to be precise about the measurement of attainment. This is related to debates about assessment (see Chapter 19), but has implications for setting, since it is harder to draw clear lines between pupils. At a practical level, the issues for RE can be even more complicated because the subject will be timetabled against another subject; if it is science or mathematics, then the grouping is skewed. The final pattern is an eclectic mix, for instance to separate out a 'top' set, which is perhaps larger than other classes, and to maintain mixed ability groups with the remaining pupils.

The grouping argument is found in debates about gender, and indeed ethnicity. There are arguments for single sex education. It can also argued that pupils of different ethnic backgrounds should be educated separately, because they fail in white schools: e.g. African-centred schools (Sefa Dei 2008). An important facet to this debate is that streaming and setting tend to favour middle-class pupils; they pass the required tests, and they and their parents behave in ways that ensure that they are in the 'top' sets and selective groups, at the expense of pupils from less wealthy backgrounds (Ball 2002).

Setting can also be seen in relation to the pupils' religious background. For instance, faith schools can be seen as a form of streaming. In some schools, the nature of the RE that pupils receive can vary according to their religious background; for instance, a Jewish school with only a small percentage of Jewish pupils provided confessional RE to Jewish pupils, but a pluralistic approach for the non-Jewish majority (Jackson *et al.* 2010: 172). In other countries, pupils are setted for RE according to their religious or non-religious background. In parts of Germany, pupils are generally taught together, or at least 'setted' on ability, but for RE they have separate Catholic, Protestant and, more recently, Muslim classes (Knauth 2007). Until the late 1990s, Norwegian pupils either received Christian education or a secular ethics course, but the remainder of the time were in mixed-ability classes (Skeie 2007).

Classroom differentiation

The final area for consideration is classroom differentiation. This covers both planning and the regulation of learning. There are two topics relating to planning: choice of topic and pedagogical approach. The regulation of classroom learning includes task-setting, outcome, support and assessment; the term 'regulation of learning' is not widely used in English, but is drawn from francophone studies to describe the processes of guidance, adjustment and mediation (Allal and Mottier Lopez 2005; for French readers, Allal and Mottier Lopez 2007).

Choice of topic can be important. For instance, there is a trend in RE to focus on philosophical and ethical issues, particularly in secondary schools at A level and GCSE. This is considered to be valuable for 'gifted and talented' students (Whittall 2009); however lower-attaining pupils may struggle with the intellectual abstraction that this requires (Cappleman 2003). Topic choice can also be important in engaging with and challenging pupils from ethnic minorities. One of the explanations proffered for the lack of educational success of pupils from ethnic minorities is that the curriculum is ethnocentric, i.e. that it is too narrowly focused on white English culture, rather than reflecting the diversity of pupils' backgrounds. The content of RE can touch on the experiences of many non-white pupils (DfES 2006b: 22), indeed it is one of the commonest subjects for lower-attaining ethnic minority pupils, but not for white pupils (ibid.: 81). Nevertheless, as in any subject, there is a balance to be struck between relying on pupils' existing understanding and dispositions, and developing new ones. For instance, in one school, GCSE pupils, within the same class, study a second religion (after Christianity) according to their own religious background: Hindu, Muslim or Sikh (Jackson *et al.* 2010: 130); this was effective for the examination, but was it *learning*?

The next issue concerns pedagogical approaches. In RE, the arrangement of the attainment targets is often seen as suggesting that 'learning about religion', the factual content, should precede 'learning from religion', the pupils' reflections on this. However, some theorists suggest that learning in RE should start from pupils' own experiences and reflections, and then move into the more explicitly religious content (e.g. Grimmitt 2000a; see also Whittall 2009). The choice for the teacher may simply be a question of the pupils' personal experience of religion. For instance, in schools where few pupils come from explicitly religious backgrounds, or pupils have very little experience of religious diversity, teachers may adopt the policy of 'starting where they are at' (Jackson *et al.* 2010: 132). By contrast, other pupils may want to find out about religions: 'it's nice to learn about other people', 'it's from Ali's country and he's my friend' (ibid. 2010: 154).

The use of general pedagogical approaches is also debated. Many schools and teachers make use of the theories of 'multiple intelligences', developed by Gardner (1983), or 'learning styles' (Fleming and Mills 1992). Indeed, the use of learning styles is so prevalent that some pupils can identify their own, and expect to be taught in ways that are compatible with them (Jackson *et al.* 2010: 163). However, the psychological basis of the theories is questioned; to say that there are a number of 'intelligences' may simply multiply the problem of identifying intelligence, rather than resolving it (Klein 1997). Coffield *et al.* (2004) catalogued a range of theories of different types of intelligence and learning, identifying 71 in total! Further, one can argue that the purpose of education is for pupils to develop a number of different learning strategies, rather than simply relying on existing strengths. Pupils should be taught how to learn in different ways, rather than simply being categorised and channelled according to pre-existing strengths.

The third area is the regulation of learning. This covers the main headline terms of task, outcome and assistance. First, the nature of the task set is critical, to avoid being too demanding or not demanding enough, and is bound up in the notion of 'challenge'. Task-setting has been criticised in RE for not being challenging enough (Ofsted 2010: 20). One study compared it with English and history; for instance, in history, pupils in Year 7 are expected to describe the differences between Protestant and Catholic churches during the Reformation, but in their RE lessons, basic denominational differences may be ignored (Wintersgill 2000; see Rudge 2001). The development of the attainment targets in the *National Framework* has provided a structure that allows teachers to find the appropriate level of task for students (QCA 2004; Ofsted 2007: 21). Assessment also has a part to play in this. Formative assessment, especially feedback, can be seen as a way of providing pupils with appropriate guidance on how to improve, and is a vital part of the regulation of learning.

However, the question mentioned above as to whether the *National Framework* actually represents a genuine model of intellectual progression is relevant (Kay 2005b). Behind it lies a model of cognitive development which may be inappropriate, such as Bloom's taxonomy (Bloom 1956). This sets out a hierarchy of thinking processes, from basic questions (what? where? when?) to 'higher-order thinking', such as 'how?' and 'why?'. It underpins the eight-level scale in all subjects. Approaches such as accelerated learning presuppose that pupils progress in a linear way, and that some students can simply go faster along the track (e.g. Smith 2003). However, Bloom's constructivist model was not designed to deal with, e.g., ethical issues, to which pupils tend to react and reason differently. Bloom and his colleagues recognised this, attempting a different model of progression (Krathwohl *et al.* 1964); for instance, most pupils will have a view on stealing without having to work through a hierarchical set of questions. Secondly, a practical danger is that lower-attaining pupils will only be set basic questions rather than being guided to the more advanced questions, especially as each lesson may simply present them with more basic questions on a new topic, rather than being given the opportunity to analyse and reflect at a 'higher' level.

Other research has tested out different models of intellectual development, which suggest that learning is less sequential than Bloom and the *National Framework* might wish. One such tried to develop 'higher-order' thinking in lower-attaining pupils (Palinscar and Brown 2008) using Vygotsky's influential ideas of mental development. Vygotsky focused on the ways that children can learn with the help of a teacher, i.e. the role of teaching in cognitive development, such as learning activities, rather than simply the tasks which pupils can perform on their own (Vygotsky 1987). His social constructivist theory suggests that cognitive development was less hierarchical than Bloom concluded. This has implications for task-setting, and also for the role of teachers and indeed teaching assistants – how much help and guidance should they give and how? One issue with teaching assistants is that their understanding of their role, and their perception of differentiation, as well as of RE itself, may not match the teacher's (Alborz *et al.* 2009). Attitudes to task-setting also affect whole-class teaching. It would be an odd classroom in which pupils automatically divided off into smaller sub-groups for specific tasks without any whole-class teaching, yet this raises questions about how such whole-class teaching should be developed under this model of intellectual development (Fancourt 2003). This also links to the contentious issue of 'differentiation by outcome', which describes the process of giving all pupils the same task, and expecting some will produce higher quality work than others. It is often criticised by government agencies, who favour a more linear model of progression, and who are concerned that it becomes a justification for no planned structured differentiation (Ofsted 2004b). Nevertheless, while it is arguably not differentiation, it can be seen as recognition that the learning outcomes in RE are, like other subjects, not very hierarchical (Marshall 2004); the exploration of concepts is typically seen as open to all pupils, who can respond with increasing complexity (Teare 1997).

Finally, how radical do the changes to learning have to be? Some research suggests that varying the structure of the learning can make a significant difference to all pupils, for instance using a variety of media and activities (Muijs and Reynolds 2001). However, rather worryingly, an earlier review of research (Hattie *et al.* 1996) suggested that such modifications only benefited middle-attaining pupils, notably those who were underachievers, but that the genuinely low-attaining pupils (i.e., the lowest 20 per cent) did not benefit. They needed an even more radical approach, abandoning the usual forms of language and adopting new symbols and patterns unconnected with negative experiences of labelling and failure (Feuerstein *et al.* 1985). These radical approaches were effective, but the context of the research needs considering. It was based in Israel, which had a very test-driven, exam-focused educational culture, in which pupils were demotivated by their experiences. It might not be more effective than moderate approaches in more benign educational cultures. However, it stands as warning against being satisfied with strategies that ultimately simply amount to tinkering.

Conclusion

This chapter has not attempted to give practical advice on differentiation in RE, but instead has focused on the wider educational debate on differentiation as it relates to RE. In the first section, the possible factors that lead to differences in pupil attainment were considered. This explored ideas about innate intelligence, generic skills and subject specific issues, as well as wider social factors such as gender, race and class; further, the role of the pupils' religious background was reviewed. Second, the ways of identifying these differences were commented on, both generic tests of intelligence as well as the use of current assessment criteria. Finally, the potential strategies were considered, on both grouping, such as setting and streaming, and classroom differentiation, such as planning and the regulation of learning.

This has shown how quite fundamental assumptions about the nature of intelligence, the features that make pupils different and the role of education underpin classroom decisions about differentiation in RE; it is swept up in wider educational debates. If one considers that intelligence is generic and innate, it follows that it can be measured successfully, and that streaming and setting are appropriate. Others might argue that this has merely creamed off the white middle-class pupils, so that they benefit at the expense of working-class pupils. If one considers that pupil attainment in RE is subject specific and largely the result of teaching and collaborative learning, then mixed-ability classes with differentiation by outcome would be seen as suitable. Others might see this as merely catering for the middle-of-the-road pupil, and a failure to recognise the individual learning needs of both the highest and lowest attaining pupils; they would demand more structured interventions. The strength of the debate is because there are a series of assumptions about subjects and learning that are at stake.

These are all highly contested areas. Differentiation in RE is thus deeply affected by these general educational trends and assumptions, and the challenge is as much in identifying these trends and assumptions as in deciding what to in the classroom. Much of this chapter has alternated between subject-specific issues and the wider generic issues. This is because there is very little research on how these generic issues affect RE; research on this is vital both to ensure that the subject is less naively dominated by general educational trends, and to develop a more nuanced discussion about differentiation in RE.

Questions

What was your experience of differentiation at school?

Do you think there is general innate intelligence, and if so what part does it play in religious education?

Do you think that the best way to differentiate is to separate pupils of the same ability, or gender, or religion, do you think that they should all be educated together, or do you think that they can be separated on some criteria, but should be kept together on others?

Further reading

Fleming, N. and Mills, C. (1992) 'Not another inventory, rather a catalyst for reflection', *To Improve the Academy*, 11: 137–155; and Coffield, F., Moseley, D., Hall, E. and Ecclestone, K. (2004) *Learning Styles and Pedagogy in Post-16 learning. A Systematic and Critical Review*, London: Learning and Skills Research Centre. Both these works focus on learning styles.

Muijs, D. and Reynolds, D. (2001) *Effective Teaching: Evidence And Practice*, London: Sage. This book reviews much background research, showing how it can affect classroom practice.

Whittall, A. (2009) 'Developing principles and strategies for teaching gifted students of religious education', in J. Ipgrave, R. Jackson and K. O'Grady (eds) *Religious Education Research through a Community of Practice: Action Research and the Interpretive Approach*, Munster: Waxmann. A good example of teacher research into one area of differentiation in RE.

A number of research reviews on various topics can be found at the EPPI – Centre site: http://eppi.ioe.ac.uk

In RE, there are a number of papers dealing with specific issues, such as gifted and talented pupils, gender and ASD, at the Farmington website: http://www.farmington.ac.uk

Chapter 18

Thinking skills

Elina Wright and Andrew Wright

This chapter focuses on thinking skills in religious education (RE). In recent years, the topic of thinking skills in education in general (e.g. Higgins and Baumfield 1998; cf. Johnsson and Gardner 1999; see also McGregor 2007), and RE in particular (e.g. Kay 2007; Pike 2006, 2008), has been the subject of debate and controversy. We begin by providing an overview of current theory and practice, focusing in turn on the concept of thinking skills, the place of thinking skills in education in general and the place of thinking skills in RE in particular. We then go on to develop a critique of skills-centred approaches to teaching and learning in RE, focusing in turn on issues raised by philosophy, theology and pedagogy. Finally, we offer a modest proposal, namely that the cultivation of a set of pedagogic virtues – attentiveness, intelligence, reasonableness and responsibility – ought to take priority over the cultivation of specific thinking skills.

Thinking skills in religious education: current theory and practice

The concept of 'thinking skills'

'"Skills" usually refers to those specific competencies required for the successful completion of particular activities' (Pring 2004: 114). Thus, it takes skill to play football, read a book, cook a meal, comfort a friend in distress and perform open-heart surgery, and the more skilful we are, the better our ability to complete such tasks successfully. Thinking skills refer to cognitive processes – critical, rational, creative, empathetic, imaginative etc. – through which we engage with the world and live our lives effectively. Some skills may seem to be instinctive, while others appear to require focused thought and effort: an experienced driver will drive a car skilfully without much deliberate attention, whereas a learner drive will need to think carefully about their driving. It appears that some skills are genetically inherited (most of us breathe instinctively immediately we are born, without first going through the mental process of *deciding* to breathe); most however appear to be learned through experience. Since we don't normally speak of breathing as a 'skill', it could be argued that all skills must be learnt. It could also be argued that instinctive skills first need to be learnt through careful thought and attention before they can become instinctive (all experienced drivers were once learner drivers). 'A skilled person therefore has a range of competencies which are quite specific and which one can train a person to exercise through constant practice' (Pring 2004: 111).

Though the understanding of thinking skills outlined above is often taken for granted in ordinary everyday discourse, philosophers, psychologists and educationists have raised a range of important issues concerning them. What is the nature of thinking, and in what way can it be considered a 'skill'? Is it possible to identify different types of thinking skills? Are some thinking skills more important than others? What does it mean to be a skilful thinker? Is there a necessary link between thinking skills and critical thinking? What is the relationship between critical thinking and the emotions? Is creativity a 'thinking skill': what is the relationship between an artist's ability to transfer paint to a canvas and their creative vision? Are thinking skills generic or domain specific: either transferable from one subject area to another or intrinsically related to specific subject areas? What is the relation between critical thinking and autonomy? Is the skill of thinking normative for human beings, as opposed to animals? It is not possible to enter into these complex debates in any detail here, though at the end of this chapter we have suggested some key texts for further reading in this area. Educational policy tends to adopt particular assumptions about the *nature of thinking* and the *nature of learning* as these relate to thinking skills, and it is to these that we now turn.

Traditionally, education was seen as 'subject-centred'. The main role of the teacher was to impart packets of objective knowledge to pupils, and the primary task of the student was to assimilate and memorise that knowledge. This frequently led to forms of rote-learning, in which pupils absorbed knowledge in an uncritical and unreflective manner. It is now generally accepted that to learn facts without any depth of understanding and critical insight falls short of a full and rounded education and can, in instances where the knowledge being transmitted is contested and controversial, lead directly to indoctrination. Forms of 'student-centred' education arose in reaction to 'subject-centred' approaches. Here the emphasis was on the autonomy of the students, who were encouraged to explore the 'inner space' of their minds, express their feelings, attitudes and life-experiences in creative and imaginative ways. What mattered was not what the knowledge assimilated by the students, but the kind of people the students were becoming. Critics of student-centred education pointed out that this could leave students ignorant about issues beyond their immediate experience, and effectively trap them in their own limited experiences of life. It is possible to view 'skills-centred' approaches to education as attempts to mediate between these two extremes: on the one hand students need to have their horizons expanded by being introduced to new knowledge; on the other, they need to assimilate that knowledge in a manner that relates directly to their own concerns, interests and outlooks on life. By developing a set of skills students would be able to engage with the objective world beyond their immediate experience in a critical and imaginative way grounded in their own subjective experiences. Skills thus functioned to bridge the gap between the external world and students' inner life, thereby empowering them to engage in the world in more effective, efficient and creative ways.

Thinking skills in education

In the past few decades, a range of thinking skills programmes have emerged in education, grounded in the notion that a primary aim of education should be to foster students' ability to think critically, to reason and to use judgement effectively in decision making. Increasingly, the development of thinking skills is seen as a key feature of successful learning, whether this focuses narrowly on specific technical and vocational skills, or more broadly on the cultivation of confident individuals and responsible citizens. Phillips and Bond (2004) trace this movement back to John Dewey (1933), who argued that learning to think and reason were fundamental goals of education. Pring (2004) attributes the emergent focus on thinking skills in educational policy within the United Kingdom to increasing political concerns regarding the employment market and economic productivity. Hayward and Fernandez (2004) suggest that, despite a raft of policy initiatives over the past 25 years concerned with the teaching of such skills, there is no clear evidence of successful implementation. The earliest attempts resulted in long prescriptive lists of skills with little educational merit, which had the unintended effect of limiting rather than expanding opportunities for learners.

Thinking skills now constitute a central element in the National Curriculum for England and Wales (Glevey 2008). The Qualifications and Curriculum Authority (QCA) identifies, as part of the new secondary curriculum, a framework for Personal, Learning and Thinking Skills (PLTS). The Framework identifies a set of six generic skills, transferable across different subject domains and contexts, designed for 'supporting successful learners, confident individuals and responsible citizens' (QCA 2009). Students will learn to become:

- *independent enquirers*: able to 'process and evaluate information in their investigations, planning what to do and how to go about it'
- *team workers*: able to 'work confidently with others, adapting to different contexts and taking responsibility for their own part'
- *effective participants*: able to 'actively engage with issues that affect them and those around them'
- *self-managers*: able to 'organise themselves, showing personal responsibility, initiative, creativity and enterprise with a commitment to learning and self-improvement'
- *reflective learners*: able to 'evaluate their strengths and limitations, setting themselves realistic goals with criteria for success'
- *creative thinkers*: able to 'think creatively by generating and exploring ideas and making original connections'.

Such skill-based education programmes are inevitably open to a range of different interpretations and methods of implementation. Beyer (2008) offers one possible approach, in the form of a researched based framework for direct systematic instruction in thinking skills. The teaching of thinking skills begins with highly focused introductory instruction, designed to initiate students into step-by-step or rule-driven procedures for applying specific skills. This is then followed by repetitive practice of particular skills, in the form of on-going repetitions of the application of different skills, closely guided and supported by the teacher. Finally, students must be instructed by their teachers how to transfer skills across different subject domains. In the context of subject-focused teaching, the teacher's knowledge of the subject matter and its nature should inform selection and application of relevant thinking skills. Thinking skills then serve as tools for achieving subject matter learning goals, whilst, at the same time, exploration of the subject matter serves as a vehicle and context for applying thinking skills. Motivation to learn a new or complex skill improves when pupils recognise the importance of learning the skill in the context of subject-specific learning. Beyer presents research evidence in support of his claim that this method of direct systematic instruction positively improves thinking skills. Beyer's insistence on the importance of direct instruction and repetition appears at odds with the QCA PLTS Framework, with its stress on independent, reflexive and self-managed learning. It seems clear that a skills-centred approach to education can result in a range of significantly different learning experiences.

Thinking skills in religious education

Thinking skills have played an increasingly important role in recent locally agreed RE syllabuses. It is not possible, in the space available, to explore these in any detail, so we will focus instead on the approach to thinking skills promoted by the *Non-Statutory National Framework* for RE. The 'knowledge, skills and understanding outlined in the *National Framework* are designed to promote the best possible progress and attainment for all pupils' (QCA 2004: 8). The *Framework* reflects the aims of the National Curriculum: (i) to provide opportunities for all pupils to learn and achieve; (ii) to promote pupils' spiritual, moral, social and cultural development and prepare all pupils for the opportunities, responsibilities and experiences of life (8).

The *Framework* identifies subject specific 'knowledge, skills and understanding' that constitute key aspects of learning in RE. These are described as 'learning about religion' and 'learning from religion' (11). Learning about religion includes enquiry into, and investigation of, the nature of religion, its beliefs, teachings and ways of life, sources, practices and forms of expression. It covers pupils' knowledge and understanding of individual religions and how they relate to each other as well as the study of the nature and characteristics of religion. Pupils learn to identify and develop an understanding of ultimate questions and ethical issues, and communicate their knowledge and understanding using specialist vocabulary.

To achieve all of this, students must develop the *skills of interpretation, analysis and explanation*. Learning from religion is concerned with developing pupils' reflection on and response to their own and others' experiences in the light of their learning about religion. Pupils learn to develop and communicate their own ideas, particularly in relation to questions of identity and belonging, meaning, purpose and truth, and values and commitments (11). To achieve all of this, students must develop the *skills of application, interpretation and evaluation*.

The *Framework* also draws attention to the responsibility of RE teachers to promote cross-curricular generic skills. RE is seen to provide opportunities for pupils to develop the key skills of communication, application of number, information technology, working with others, improving own learning and performance and problem solving (15–16) Further, RE make 'an important contribution to pupils' skills in literacy and information and communication technology', promotes informed enquiry, enhances the capacity to think coherently and consistently, and enables students 'to evaluate thoughtfully their own and others' views in a reasoned and informed manner' (8).

Thinking skills in religious education: a critique

A philosophical critique

Earlier we suggested that skills-based educational programmes set out to bridge the gap between student-centred education and a subject-centred education, thereby giving proper weight to both the subjective experience of students and the objective reality of the external world. Though we welcome this aim, we want to suggest that skills-based approaches to education tend to fall short of their intended aims.

The dualistic assumption of a gulf between individual subjects and the external world has its roots in modern philosophy. Descartes, the 'founder of modern philosophy', set out on a journey in search of certain knowledge that led him to a deep suspicion of everything apart from his own self-conscious mind, as well as to the dualistic distinction between the inner space of his mind and the external world 'out there'. It was Kant who formulated the most influential account of how the gap between subjective mind and objective worlds could be bridged. He argued that we need to use our cognitive skills to impose order on an apparently chaotic external world: because we do not experience the world as meaningful in itself, we must accept the responsibility to construct meaningful patterns out of our experiences. The fact that different individuals skilfully construct different meanings leads directly to forms of postmodern relativism. At its most radical, constructivism maintains that knowledge is 'exclusively an order and organisation of a world constituted by our experience ... not a reflection of an objective ontological reality' (Grimmitt 2000a: 210, quoting E. von Glaserfeld). Skills-based educational programmes are often closely allied with the philosophy of constructivism. As a result, they run the risk of failing to do justice to the objectivity of the external world: students are encouraged to use their developing skills to organise and take control of their lives, but in so doing run the risk of losing touch with, or establishing a less than adequate relationship with, reality. Rather than seeking the 'truth out there', constructivists are content merely to construct their own subjective truths. At the end of the day, a skills-based constructivism does not make much sense: doctors are able to successfully perform open-heart surgery not because they skilfully construct some imaginary biological world, but because they have learnt to understand and penetrate deeply into the way things actually are; we condemn genocide not because we construct stories about such evil, but because we experience and discern the evil of genocide directly; we tell stories to ourselves about our friends, but if we ourselves are a true friend to them, we strive to ensure that the stories we construct are not merely useful to ourselves, but truthfully reflect the reality of our friends.

We are not dislocated spectators looking down on a world below us, but rather active participants in a reality we indwell. In order to understand our place in the world, we need to train our minds to penetrate deeply into its structures and seek to discern meaningful patterns inherent within it. Rather than force the world to conform to our own constructs, we need to find ways of bring our minds into conformity with the way things actually are. To understand the world and act appropriately within it requires wise discernment rather than rationalistic construction. This fits closely with Einstein's account of his work as a scientist: he set out to allow the world to transform his mind, and sought to resist the instinct to use his mind to transform the world. This is not to suggest that discernment is a purely passive process that requires no skill or active involvement on our part. It is, however, to suggest that a skills-centred education needs to beware of the dangers of constructivism, and ensure that students develop skills oriented towards the discernment, rather than the creation, of patterns of meaning in the world.

A theological critique

Such concerns about the dangers of skills-centred education failing to bridge the presumed gulf between the subjective mind and external reality effectively have increasingly exercised the minds of teachers and philosophers of education working in the tradition of critical realism. In this section we want to suggest that teachers of RE need to be especially wary of the dangers of a marriage between skills-based education and constructivism because of the nature of their subject matter. We will develop our argument with reference to the Christian tradition, though we believe that it can easily be transferred to most other religious traditions.

The skills identified by QCA's Personal, Learning and Thinking Skills Framework, which we discussed earlier, stress personal autonomy: students should become independent enquirers, self-managers, reflective learners and creative thinkers, and when working as team participants should take active responsibility for their own contributions. This, we suggest, reflects the modern ideal of individuals as autonomous thinkers, people with the courage to think for themselves and act freely, independently and rationally. One of the results of modern secularisation has been that we understand our humanity by relating ourselves to the natural order in general and the animal kingdom in particular. As a result, freedom for self-realisation has become a dominant modern value: we are different from animals by virtue of our greater cognitive abilities, and we are most truly ourselves when we act rationally without any external constraint.

The Christian tradition takes a significantly different stance. Christian revelation invites us to understand ourselves not primarily in terms of our relationship with the natural order, but more fundamentally in terms of our relationship with our creator. We are made in the image of God: since God is love, and that love is constituted by the reciprocal giving and receiving between the persons of the Trinity, so we are essentially relational creatures, created to enter into loving reciprocal relationships with other people and with our creator. What really matters is not our freedom and autonomy, nor our cognitive skills, but our ability to love and to be loved. This being the case, then the skills of rational autonomy valorised in Personal, Learning and Thinking Skills Framework would appear to rub against the grain of the Christian understanding of reality. For Christians selfless acts of charity (*agape*) and care for others take precedence over acts of self-determination; human duties take precedence over the assertion of our human rights; dying-to-self takes precedence over self-realisation. This does not free the Christian from the responsibility to fight for truth and justice and defend the rights of others; nor does dying-to-self imply self-harm – because love is reciprocal, we can only love others if we are able to receive the love of others directed to ourselves.

Two conclusions can be drawn from these observations. First, Christianity – in common with the vast majority of religious traditions – teaches the importance of submission and obedience to God, a task which requires an ongoing process of spiritual discipline in which the supplicant strives to allow God to transform and reshape their lives. This does not sit easily with the modern discourse surrounding the skills necessary for rational self-determination. This raises fundamental questions. Are such skills sensitive enough to respond appropriately to the self-understanding of most religious traditions? Might the cultivation of such skills in the RE classroom actually serve to restrict rather than enhance students' understandings of religion? Second, we have suggested that attempts to use a skills-based approach to bridge the gap between personal subjectivity and the external world tend to favour the student's horizon of meaning at the expense of the horizon of meaning ingrained in the external world. The cultivation of skills, that is to say, tends to lead to reality being manipulated to fit in with the prejudices of the mind, rather than the mind itself being transformed as it learns to discern patterns of meaning inherent in the external world. It may be that the Christian account of love as a two-way process of reciprocal giving and receiving offers a more powerful model to help guide our attempts to bridge the supposed gulf between mind and world. This would suggest that skills oriented towards rational self-determination, which support constructivist impositions of meaning on the world, need to be supplemented with a further set of skills oriented towards listening to, learning from, responding to and allowing oneself to be transformed by reality itself.

A pedagogical critique

The main pedagogical problem of a skills-centred education is the separation of thinking skills from the object of knowledge, leading to a focus on the thinking process *per se* without any necessary reference to the topic under investigation and its surrounding context. Thinking and learning are always about something; if the topic of investigation is dislocated from the thinking and learning process, then the process itself becomes the focus of learning. This means that RE students could spend more time learning-how-to-learn than actually investigating religious topics and themes. A further problem is the way in which skills tend to be broken down into different types, which produces a fragmentary approach to learning. Thus the *National Framework* separates 'knowledge, skills and understanding' from one another as different aspects of the learning process. Such fragmentation is increased once the distinction is made between 'learning about' and 'learning from' religion: the two modes of learning are seen as sequential and atomistic rather than simultaneous and holistic. Such analytical separation reflects different objects of knowledge and focuses on the process and nature of cognitive activity *per se* rather than on a holistic person–world relationship, in which changes in a person's understanding of religion are simultaneously changes in a person's self-understanding (see Hella and Wright 2009). The process of 'learning about religion' is broken down into different parts that relate to the learning activity itself, rather than to the object of learning. As a result, though different cognitive skills are seen as tools supporting the learning process, or as a means of developing students' understanding of religion(s), the ways in which different types of thinking skill relate to specific subject matter and to intended learning outcomes remain unclear. According to the *National Framework*, to learn about religion students must first develop the skills of interpretation, analysis and explanation. As a consequence, the object of learning shifts from an engagement with religion itself to an engagement with students' own learning experiences. A focus on different types of pre-defined thinking skill tends to isolate them both from the students' experiences and from the intended object of learning. For example, a focus on the abstract skills of interpretation, analysis and explanation may well bypass the concrete situation of students at the start of the learning process and ignore the ways they actually engage with the learning process. A skills-centred approach to education tends to focus on abstract skills at the expense of both the object of study and the actual experiences of the learners.

We suggest that the path from abstract learning skills to concrete objects of learning and actual learning situations is misconceived. Guiding student learning needs to start by identifying the object of learning as seen by the learner rather than reflecting on a list of abstract skills. Only by starting from the actual learning context will teachers be able to help students discern new aspects of the object in relation to their prior experiences, and identify the kinds of student capabilities that need to be developed in relation to the content of learning. Such close attention to the object of learning in relation to students' developing capabilities makes it possible for the teacher to discern qualitative changes between students' understanding of the object of learning, both prior to and after the learning process, and thus identify what the students have learned and what kinds of skills they have developed in relation to the object of learning. Close attention to the holistic relationship between context and content needs to take priority over abstract de-contextualised skills if students are to develop deeper understanding and knowledge of reality. Ference Marton (2006: 511) points out that in order to understand something as 'general' it first has to be discerned from the specific instance in which it is embedded. According to the Variation Theory of Learning developed by Marton and his colleagues (see Marton *et al.* 2004), the 'mother of learning' is not repetition but variation (Marton and Trigwell 2000): discernment of similarities and differences in any given situations is possible through variation; it is the contrast between different situations that allows similarities and differences to be identified. Therefore, learning is not a process of the application of abstract skills, but of discernment of differences and similarities in specific aspects of reality. The 'skill' of discernment is an intrinsic aspect of the students' engagement with a specific subject matter; it cannot be established in advance and brought to the learning situation from outside.

Thinking skills in religious education: a proposal

We have suggested that a skills-centred education that sets out to bridge the gap between the subjective self and the objective world is potentially flawed. Though the desire to achieve a synthesis between subject-centred and student-centred education is admirable in many ways, the focus on learning skills risks prioritising the subjectivity of the learner and marginalising the actual object of study. If learners focus on epistemic process at the expense of ontological reality they are in danger of squeezing the world into their ways of knowing and forcing reality into the procrustean bed of our prior epistemic assumptions, prejudices and ideologies. Logical Positivism offers an extreme example of this flawed process. The Positivists identified a set of basic learning skills: *observation* of empirical sense-data, *construction* of truth-statements informed by such observation, *verification* of such truth-statement by further empirical testing. A statement was deemed to be true if it could be verified by appeal to one or more of the five senses and false if verification failed. This meant that anything that could not, at least in principle, be directly observed was neither true, nor false, but rather quite literally meaningless. This led to the claim that all our moral, aesthetic and theological statements are simply nonsense statements. This rubs against the grain of our ordinary experience: we may disagree with the moral claims, aesthetic judgements and theological beliefs of others, but we do so because we disagree with them, not because we cannot understand them. In this particular case we have a set of skills – observation, construction and verification – that, however skilful the learner, will inevitably produce flawed results. Critical realists refer to the basic mistake of forcing knowledge to conform to our means of knowing as the 'epistemic fallacy'; it can be avoided if we allow the nature of the object of knowledge itself to shape the skills we utilise in our on-going search for knowledge. Just as tools are constantly modified in order to better serve the needs of the craftsman, so epistemic skills need to be adapted continuously if they are to fulfil their task of helping to enhance the deepening knowledge-relationship between the learner and the object of knowledge.

We want to suggest that skills should function as under-labourers rather than directors: what is needed is not a skills-centred education but a knowledge-centred education, in which knowledge is understood as the reciprocal relationship between knower and object known. It is standard practice in RE to distinguish between *learning from* and *learning about* religion: this assumes a basic dualism between the learner-learning-from and the object-learnt-about, and invites the notion that certain skills must be cultivated if the division between the two is to be overcome. However, if we indwell the world and thereby already participate in a range of different knowledge-relationships, then the task is not to find a set of skills whereby the learner can construct a bridge across the knowledge divide, but to seek ways of deepening and enhancing knowledge-relationships already in existence. The knowledge-relationship is reciprocal: to understand the world better is simultaneously to understand ourselves better, since to understand the world is necessarily also to understand our relationship to the world. However, within reciprocal knowledge relationships it is the objectivity of knowledge that must take precedence over the subjectivity of the learner. The world exists largely independently of our knowledge-relationships with it: if we were to drop dead tomorrow, nothing much of significance would change in the world. The cumulative knowledge established across the range of curricular disciplines exists independently of the understanding of any particular student. This is why we have suggested that to understand is to bring our minds into conformity with the world, rather than bring the world into conformity with our minds. The major problem with skills-centred education is that skills tend to function primarily as tools that enable us to construct our own accounts of reality and thereby empower us to manipulate and control reality. This is why we want to suggest, albeit tentatively, the possibility of a virtue-centred education, one designed to enrich our knowledge-relationships by empowering us, not to construct arbitrary accounts of reality, but to enter into deeper, more harmonious, more truthful, knowledge relationships. In this context Bernard Lonergan (1972: 20) has suggested four key virtues: attentiveness, intelligence, reasonableness and responsibility. These are not passive virtues, designed to enforce the passive reception of packets of knowledge through rote learning; neither are they skilful techniques, designed to enable students to construct imaginary realities without reference to the way things actually are in the world; rather, they constitute a moral and intellectual frame of reference, designed to cultivate a more truthful, less ideologically laden, knowledge-relationship between the knower and the object of knowledge. Skills have their place in such a relationship, but if such skills are allowed to dominate, then the learner as skilful practitioner will tend to dominate the knowledge-relationship. At the end of the day, we suggest, skill-centred education programmes tend to be merely student-centred education programmes in disguise. The alternative is not a reactionary return to a subject-centred education, but rather the cultivation of a virtue-centred education in which the developing knowledge-relationship between knower and object-of-knowledge is marked by attentiveness, intelligence, reasonableness and responsibility.

Conclusion

Our reservations about skills-centred approaches to RE have their roots in the model of critical RE (Wright 2007). Education, we suggest, should be concerned with the pursuit of ultimate truth, and the cultivation of truthful living in harmony with the ultimate order of things. The pursuit of truth and truthfulness must take account of variations between conflicting accounts of ultimate reality, and requires wise judgement and discernment in seeking to identify the most powerful and compelling accounts of the ultimate order of things. Such discernment requires the cultivation of appropriate levels of religious literacy, understood as the holistic capacity to think, feel, communicate and act wisely with regard to ultimate questions of meaning and truth. We have suggested reasons why a skills-centred approach to RE is unlikely to generate such religious literacy. This is primarily because the cultivation of thinking skills is unlikely to bridge the dualistic divide between subject-centred and student-centred education, and learning about and learning from religion, effectively; on the contrary, because skills tend to take priority over subject content, what comes to the fore is not a deeper understanding of reality, but a more powerful means of manipulating reality to one's own ends. The pursuit of ultimate truth and truthful living must focus on reality itself, and demands appropriate attitudes of attentiveness, intelligence, reasonableness and responsibility.

Questions

What are the strengths and weaknesses of skills-centred approaches to education?
What are the strengths and weaknesses of our counter-proposal?
How might the issues raised in this chapter impact on your own approach to teaching and learning?

Further reading

Baumfield, V. M (2002b) *Thinking Through Religious Education,* Cambridge: Chris Kington. Straightforward introduction to thinking skills.

Hella, E. and Wright, A. (2009) 'Learning "about" and learning "from" religion: phenomenography, the variation theory of learning and religious education in Finland and the UK', *British Journal of RE* 31, 1: 53–64. Applies phenomenography and the variation theory of learning to develop and enhance learning in religious education.

Kay, W. K. (2007) 'Can "skills" help RE?', in M. Felderhof, P. Thompson and D. Torevell, *Inspiring Faith in Schools: Studies in RE,* Aldershot: Ashgate. Important critique of thinking skills in religious education.

Wright, A. (2007) *Critical Religious Education, Multiculturalism and the Pursuit of Truth,* Cardiff: University of Wales Press. A constructive attempt to integrate critical thinking into religious education.

The Stapleford Centre's *REthinking Network* http://www.rethinking.co.uk/. Provides curriculum material to develop thinking skills in religious education.

Chapter 19

Assessment

Lat Blaylock

Assessment was also one of the weakest aspects of RE provision in the secondary schools. It was good or outstanding in just under a third and inadequate in three of 10 of the schools visited ... In both the primary and the secondary phases, most teachers were experiencing significant difficulties in using the levels of attainment set out in the locally agreed syllabus. This contributed to several problems.

(*Transforming Religious Education*, HMI Report, June 2010: 24)

The research evidence suggests that when formative assessment practices are integrated into the minute-to-minute and day-by-day classroom activities of teachers, substantial increases in student achievement – of the order of a 70 to 80 per cent increase in the speed of learning – are possible, even when outcomes are measured with externally-mandated standardized tests. Indeed, the currently available evidence suggests that there is nothing else that is remotely affordable that is likely to have such a large effect.

(Leahy and Wiliam 2009: 15)

Measuring achievement in religious education (RE) has been controversial among religious educators for decades. In England, the 1988 Education Reform Act omitted RE from the national curriculum, but not the basic curriculum. A negative consequence was that extensive investment in assessment theory was applied to all other subjects, but not RE. A positive consequence was that RE teachers were spared the highly contested contortions of other subjects around ten level scales, profile components and SATs. The history of the assessment of RE in England and Wales since then has been defined in relation to national curriculum assessment, with RE sometimes seeking to copy the National Curriculum models, and sometimes to march to a different drum.

Come forward two decades, and one of the last actions of the government's Qualifications and Curriculum Development Agency, in July 2010, was to publish online a collection of pupils' work for each subject of the curriculum, including RE, which intended to give definitive illustration to the meaning of levels 3–8 in secondary classroom terms (QCDA 2010a). The preparation of this guidance material used work from numerous pupils in four schools intending to clarify the meaning of the levels, to illustrate the kinds of learning activity that enable progression in learning and to suggest ways of assessing RE that are practical, valid and fair. These intentions arose in part from the demands of school assessment practice, commonly requiring a teacher in RE to record a levelled assessment of each pupil's achievement, based on evidence, every half term. For a teacher who works with 450 pupils per week – not uncommon in RE (or Music, Citizenship, PE or Art) this requires that they make over 8,000 judgements about pupils during Key Stage 3. It is questionable whether such numerous judgements, made so fast, can ever be done in ways that are fair, valid and manageable.

The aim of this chapter is to outline the positive possibilities of applying methods from Assessment for Learning (AfL) and from 'Assessing Pupils' Progress' (APP) to RE in ways that challenge RE professionals to be clear about their aims and learning intentions and about the kinds of evidence that demonstrate achievement in the subject. Examples from a primarily English setting are used to explore issues from the four UK nations. My argument is that RE's wide range of inter-disciplinary learning methods, including the conceptual, the creative, the spiritual and the phenomenological, all offer routes through which evidence of achievement can be gathered and weighed up. When this process is informed by the insights of assessment for learning, it not only measures achievement: it can enable higher achievement. For these reasons this chapter argues for carefully focused lightweight use of AfL methods in RE, and against comparability purposes in setting RE assessment. It argues for wide alertness to the range of inter-disciplinary learning opportunities RE offers (e.g. philosophical, creative, moral, spiritual, historical, personal), and for subjecting any assessment requirement to a rigorous questioning: is it fit for purpose in RE, fair, valid, manageable? The common current practice of RE assessment that is modelled on assessment structures designed for core subjects of the curriculum (English, Maths, Science) is rejected because it distorts the purposes of learning in RE as well as for practical reasons. One key plank of the model offered here is that teachers should set assessment tasks less often, but make them more effective in showing progress and delineating areas for improvement: RE needs to assess less but do it better.

What are the purposes of assessment in religious education?

While some subjects have used assessment information to distinguish between pupils, teachers and schools (comparability purposes), assessment in RE is formative. Most agreed syllabuses in England and Wales are explicit about this, and where SACREs collect data about performance, it is not to make comparisons between teachers or schools. Instead, RE uses assessment arrangements to improve the learning of individuals and groups. This point is significant because the purposes of assessment can have a significant impact on teaching and learning: RE needs assessment that serves good learning, rather than being driven by the (inadequate) goals of comparability. In practice, this argument leads away from SATs, summative assessment and league tables. It leads towards a clear focus on diagnosing what pupils have learned in RE, what is problematic for them, and on prescribing remedies, finding ways forward and improving learning. One example of this is wherever teachers use assessment information to plan improvements in students' grades in GCSE or Standard Grade RS examinations. Teachers are rightly suspicious of any assessment structure that is unwieldy, unmanageable or focused more on data collection than improvement. School inspectors are rightly interested in the use of assessment information to guide and improve teaching and learning. Any other use might be a waste of teachers' precious time.

This point leads to the idea that RE assessment should weigh up all the relevant achievements of pupils in relation to the learning outcomes that the subject seeks, and use the information to enable further learning. Thus, I contend that RE assessment should seek to relate to learning about religion and learning from religion, in English and Welsh settings.

Whilst the articulation of aims and objectives in RE is a subject of much critical debate in itself (including within the present volume), it is the full range of RE's aims that provide appropriate focus for assessment activity. One danger in RE assessment that inspectors confirm is a focus on collecting information, rather than on higher order skills of expression, evaluation, interpretation and creative thinking. This persistent difficulty was a part of the rationale for seeking to find new ways of articulating desirable and assessable outcomes in RE through the English QCDA's project on assessing pupils' progress in the foundation subjects (2007–2010).

Another issue for RE assessment involves the place of the subject alongside other subjects of the curriculum in legislation and guidance. Threats to the status of RE within the curriculum are a commonplace of RE professionals' discourse, and the virtues of being able to operate the same structures in, for example, planning, progression, curriculum organisation and assessment are often seen as providing a buttress to the subject, against the perception that RE is marginal in a secularising culture. So at a pragmatic classroom level some teachers have been happy to adopt assessment arrangements for the subject that give parity with history, geography or art, and at a political level, the inclusion of RE alongside other subjects in national initiatives and guidance is often welcomed (e.g. in the Learning and Teaching Scotland's *Curriculum for Excellence* (originally 2004), or the English QCDA's *New Secondary Curriculum*, 2008). In the field of curriculum research and development, RE has rarely been included in generalised research into assessment and achievement, but the need for application of national and research based models of assessment to RE has been recognised by RE advisers, inspectors and consultants.

What impact has national assessment policy had on RE?

In 1988, the Education Reform Act gave government ministers powers to determine patterns of assessment in the subjects of the National Curriculum. These powers did not extend to locally agreed syllabuses of RE, but the influence of National Curriculum assessment structures and practice was extensive, and led RE professionals to develop schemes of assessment for RE which were modelled on National Curriculum terminology and practice. The two foremost examples of such work undertaken at a level beyond a single agreed syllabus, both produced by consortia of local education authorities and academic institutions, were 'Forms of Assessment in RE: the FARE project' (Priestley and Copley 1991) and the Westhill Project 'Attainment in RE' (Westhill College 1989 and 1991). Many local agreed syllabus conferences incorporated ideas from the two projects into their syllabuses, establishing a pattern that has become familiar: national assessment work, adapted and reused in local syllabus making.

Two major RE attainment projects of the late 1980s and early 1990s, the FARE project and the Westhill Project, had followed the structures of the National Curriculum of 1988. For example, the Westhill approach of 1989 identified three profile components, 10 attainment targets and 146 attainment statements. This could require a secondary RE teacher with 400 pupils to make millions of judgements about pupils' achievements in RE. The Westhill scheme offers, potentially, a very fair, detailed and accurate description of a particular pupil's progress and learning. It has a certain purity and beauty, but seems to me to be of the Platonic kind, belonging to another world, not the world of classroom RE. The use of terminology from the 'first generation' National Curriculum (profile components, ten level scales and multiple attainment targets and a total of 146 attainment statements) is no longer relevant to the assessment needs of schools. The subsequent work of the Westhill project moved away from the complexity of the first versions of the National Curriculum, in directions which many teachers found more practical and helpful (Westhill 1991).

Bates (1992), in an astute review article of four publications on assessing RE, analysed the needs of RE professionals regarding assessment in the light of the FARE and Westhill projects, concluding:

> there is a pressing need for less complex more tightly structured syllabuses which make the task of teachers more manageable whilst doing justice to the key aspects of the subject ... Such is the burden on teachers, especially in primary schools, and such is the ambivalent status of RE in the basic curriculum that unless they are presented with sensible, concise, practical guidelines for RE little of value will be done in the subject at all.
>
> (Bates 1992: 59)

The passage of time has not blunted the point. Evidence and analysis from Her Majesty's Inspectors repeatedly suggests, generally, that standards of assessment in RE are particularly weak in comparison to other subjects of the curriculum (e.g. Ofsted 1998: 160). Pupils deserve coherent, clear, accurate and fair responses to the work they do in all subjects. In RE, good assessment practice is possible, but is too often encumbered by poor curriculum support, planning, or a low status for RE and misunderstood.

From an 8-level RE scale to assessment focuses for RE: what skills can RE assess?

In England, an 8-level scale of attainment for RE was published first by QCA in 2000. This work drew upon national work from the Association of RE Advisers, Inspectors and Consultants (AREIAC 1998), and paralleled the work of QCA in other subject areas such as music, geography or science. By providing a series of carefully worded statements about what might normally be expected of pupils through the years it reflected a learning model which included knowledge, understanding and skills, but required no particular knowledge of any pupil. The scale used a breakdown of the RE field of enquiry under six headings, grouped into the two attainment targets, learning about religions and learning from religion. This became the basis for a revised scale that was part of the DCFS non-statutory National Framework for RE in 2004, though it was adjusted quite substantially. In turn, the new Secondary Curriculum of 2008 copied the scale from the framework (see Table 19.1).

Table 19.1 Levels of learning about religion at AT1 and AT2

	Learning about religion and beliefs: AT1	Learning from religion and beliefs: AT2
8	Contextualising, analysing and synthesising their understandings of religion	Justifying their views with comprehensive and balanced conclusions
7	Showing coherent understanding and accounting for religion	Critically and personally evaluating religious questions using evidence
6	Explaining and interpreting religion in depth and diversity	Expressing their own insights into religious, spiritual and moral questions and issues
5	Explaining similarities and differences and the impact of religion in people's lives	Expressing their own views in the light of religious explanations
4	Using correct vocabulary to show understanding of religion	Applying religious and spiritual ideas themselves
3	Describing religious materials	Making links from religious materials to their own experience
2	Retelling religious stories, identifying religious materials	Asking questions, responding sensitively
1	Recognising and naming religious materials	Talking about religious materials

It is sometimes suggested that the interpretation of the meaning of these levels is too subjective to be helpful. This criticism can be answered by taking the teacher back to the full iteration of the scale, and noting that this shorthand homes in on a progression of skills. Criterion-referenced assessment always depends on the application of the criteria by the assessor, and the identification of the 'best fit' between a student's work and the scale is a professional skill developed through practice. To this end, many local authorities and SACREs have produced exemplification of standards materials in the last decade. Interesting examples include work done in Lancashire, Northamptonshire, Hertfordshire and Nottingham.

Can 'Assessing Pupils' Progress' pragmatically synthesise AfL and levelled assessment in RE?

In response to research findings about AfL's power to improve learning, and to professional and political pressure about national testing in core subjects, QCDA developed a new set of approaches to monitoring achievement, 'Assessing Pupils' Progress' (APP). My description of this project below is a case study in applied theory, through which I intend to illuminate the debate about key issues facing RE today with regard to assessment. The APP approaches were first developed in English and Maths, then, in a project running over three years, APP ideas were applied to Foundation subjects and RE. While in RE there is some practical threat from the application of assessment structures from subjects often taught for four or five hours every week, APP has, in my judgement, the potential in RE to clarify the use of levels, to sharpen the focus of teaching and learning on progress, and to provide teachers with tools that help pupils achieve high standards in RE. If this can be achieved in ways that are principled, manageable, administratively lightweight and clear, then the prize of better assessment in RE is achievable in many more schools, addressing the concerns that inspectors often raise.

Regarding both the politics of RE and the practice of RE, there is a benefit in the subject's inclusion in this initiative. QCDA consulted in depth with RE subject associations, advisers and with teachers of the subject in developing the assessment focuses and the standards files for levels 3–8 which were published in July 2010 (QCDA 2010a). These are positive examples of the assumption of inclusion that usually operates with regard to RE among the subjects of the curriculum in present times. This is a hard won benefit in RE's continuing struggle for status within the curriculum. The first idea I wish to consider is that a 'level' is a very large step in achievement in RE, so a focus within a level is often helpful to teachers in understanding pupil progress. The APP project identified the need for teachers to focus their attention on an aspect of a level, and following practice in Maths and English, a fresh iteration of the standards represented by the levels was produced.

How can an assessment focus clarify standards in RE?

An 'assessment focus' (AF) describes a part of the process of making progress in RE. The AFs make a precise and detailed connection to a pupil's skills. The APP project developed and used three AFs for RE and followed the work of a group of pupils in Key Stage 3 in four different schools over a period of 18 months, using the AFs to describe achievement, plan progression and feedback to students, and encourage high standards. The definition of these AFs is significant as it enables enable teachers – and pupils – to use a small part of the overall field of enquiry to focus on learning and assessment during a particular period of learning such as a unit of work or a term. Three assessment focuses were used in the project, and are offered here as an example of a way of describing achievements in RE.

Assessment in RE might focus upon three AFs

Thinking about religion and belief.

This focus attends to increasingly sophisticated use of religious vocabulary and concepts, and asks how effectively pupils handle questions about the nature, practice, teachings and beliefs of the religion they are studying. Learners show progress here if they can increasingly handle ideas and materials from the religions they study with thoughtfulness and understanding.

Enquiring, investigating and interpreting.

This focus explores how effectively pupils use the skills of investigation and enquiry in RE. By linking the two attainment targets of learning about religion and learning from religion, these process skills require learners to tackle provocative or challenging religious or spiritual questions with increasingly sophisticated investigative process of their own devising. The focus of the learning in this AF is on the skills of enquiry and sense-making or interpretation rather than upon amassing information or knowledge.

Reflecting, evaluating and communicating.

This assessment focus pays attention to activities in RE that move towards reflection, the application of understanding, and expressing insightful ideas evaluation. Handling questions of identity and diversity, meaning, purpose and truth, values and commitments, pupils will show progress by being increasingly able to handle questions about their ability to:

- suggest meanings in religion and life (L2)
- make links between religious materials and their own ideas and experiences (L3)

- apply ideas for themselves in fresh contexts (L4)
- express views about religions and beliefs, well informed by their study of religion (L5)
- develop insight of their own into human and spiritual questions (L6)
- engage in personal and critical evaluation of religious and spiritual issues and phenomena (L7)
- contextualise their learning about religions and synthesise it with their own view of the world (L8).

These three focuses intend to enable a teacher to plan work which pays close attention to one aspect of achievement in RE, then later in a course to attend to another. Further, rather than recording achievement for every pupil in 10 or 15 classes taught in a week, the APP approach asks teachers to sample the class's work. This is not a new idea – HMI strongly recommended sampled marking for RE teachers with large numbers of pupils in 2003. But if national government and agency guidance gives political support to processes where the teacher's knowledge of a class's progress is based on the very detailed analysis of a small sample of work, then the overall application of the levels of achievement to the skills in the class can be sharpened.

How do the QCDA APP standards files support better assessment practice in RE?

One example of a piece of work from the standards files (shown as Figure 19.1) suffices here to show how these materials are intended to work.

In this piece of writing, done towards the end of a unit of work on Buddhism, the 13-year-old student offers an interpretation of Nobel Prize winner Aung San Suu Kyi's decision in 1999 to remain in Rangoon under house arrest rather than accept the chance to leave and be with her dying husband and bereaved sons in Oxford. The student's insightful work uses religious and moral concepts from Buddhism and from religious study to explain her insights into the challenges of the dilemma. She refers to different viewpoints and explains some challenges to religious conviction in the contemporary world. The piece of work shows evidence of achievement at level 6, but of course does not meet every line of the level's requirements. The learner's ability to apply insights from sacred text and the noble eightfold path to her own vision of life and values, in the final paragraph, brings together her learning about an inspiring Buddhist leader and her personal reflection.

"May I be a protector of the
helpless"
Aung San Suu Kyi was a protector to the
helpless when she stayed in Burma to
fight for her country. She showed the
people she had courage when she stayed,
and she protected them by leaving her
own family and by not being scared,
everytime the army tried to put her down
by imprisoning her she always stood back
up and did what she said she would
which was fight for her country. I think
the buddhist teaching which inspired
her was from the eightfold path, which
was "you must think about the kind of
life you lead and make a commitment
to live in a caring and unselfish way".
She followed this because she definitely
was not selfish. She put everyone elses
needs before hers because she did not go
back to her family even though she
missed them so much. She felt she had
made a promise to the people of Burma
and she had to stay and keep her promise,
and also she wanted to keep her ~~from~~
beliefs of the buddhist rules.
I would like to be a protector to people
because I want people to not feel
scared and they should know they can
always come to me and know that I will
protect them.

Figure 19.1 Extract from pupil's work

In practice, what kinds of assessment activity in RE provide for fairness, validity and manageability?

Table 19.2 provides starting points which enact the principles discussed above, showing how RE teachers and learners might use the principles of APP and AfL to gather evidence of achievement, use it diagnostically and support better learning.

Table 19.2 Expressions of assessment focuses for three topics between levels 3 and 7

Level	Assessment Focus Example 1: Thinking about religion and belief in relation to celebration	Assessment Focus Example 2: Enquiring, investigating and interpreting in relation to religion in the community	Assessment Focus Example 3: Reflecting evaluating and communicating in relation to questions about God
3	I can describe what happens at Eid in a mosque, or at Christmas in a church. I can make links between the emotions of these festivities and some feelings and experiences that I share (e.g. feeling joyful, feeling excited, feeling sad).	I can examine some examples of funeral customs presented to the class and use the reflections these prompt to ask some good questions of my own about the topic of life after death. I can enquire into the links between some stories of the Buddha and Buddhist ideas about rebirth.	I can compare an idea of my own about what God is like with an idea from a different perspective, and communicate 'two sides of the question' simply in talk, image or writing.
4	I can show my understanding of words like 'celebrate', 'messenger', 'miracle' or 'revelation'. I can apply the idea of celebration to two religions and to my own life, answering the question: 'what's worth celebrating today?' thoughtfully.	I can gather information from two different religions or beliefs about questions of life after death for myself, and select from it the ideas which I find most interesting. I can suggest meanings in the funeral rituals I study, linked to beliefs about the next life. I can discuss some mysterious spiritual questions and describe my own view and the views of someone else.	I can apply some different ideas about God to the issue of 'how we know', reflecting on similarity and difference for myself. I can express my response in a work of art or poem under the title 'Where Is God?'
5	I can explain how and why Eid and Christmas are similar, and also explain 3 differences between them. I can explain the impact of practising the festivals on communal and spiritual life. I can express my view about whether religious people in the UK should be given a day off work for a major festival, in the light of religious teaching.	I can suggest lines of enquiry that address my own questions about belief in life after death, in the light of religions and beliefs, using different sources to suggest answers to my questions. I can discuss and explain what is similar and different between reincarnation and eternal life in Hindu and Christian traditions.	I can develop arguments and explanations of my own about the beliefs that God is unprovable, or loving, or omnipotent, or forgiving, or the creator, or a figment of human imagination, contributing explanations to discussions and creative images to reflective work.

Level	Assessment Focus Example 1: Thinking about religion and belief in relation to celebration	Assessment Focus Example 2: Enquiring, investigating and interpreting in relation to religion in the community	Assessment Focus Example 3: Reflecting evaluating and communicating in relation to questions about God
6	I can interpret the meanings of some sources (Qur'an, Hadith, Bible) for understanding two festivals for myself, referring to sacred texts thoughtfully. I can develop and express insights into what anyone could learn from the Muslims and Christians about celebration, remembrance and tradition.	I can develop insightful interpretations of my own from diverse sources within two different religions/beliefs into questions of meaning about life after death. I can enquire into the impact of belief about heaven or nirvana on life in Christian and Buddhist communities.	With regard to my own views about God, I can argue persuasively and express insights creatively to support the position I hold, while taking account of the views of others and the reasons, traditions and arguments that support them. I can balance different interpretations.
7	I can comprehensively understand and account for ways Christmas has become a kind of 'plural festival' and how and why Eid in the UK is different from Eid in Pakistan or Egypt. I can evaluate the contribution the festivals make to passing on the faith down generations, giving examples from Christianity and Islam.	I can initiate independent critical enquiry into how religions and beliefs approach the 'mystery of destiny' using reasoning and evidence, and analyse some related spiritual questions ('Do we have souls?' 'Does atheism make you live in the present?') using philosophical methods.	I can balance the conclusions I draw about the nature of God or ultimate reality by referring to the views and arguments of different religions, and I can critically evaluate the personal and communal significance of different views of God.

Conclusion

I suggest programmes of assessment activity like this demonstrate how RE can use the research insights of assessment for learning and the structures of assessing pupil progress to raise standards of achievement. For RE in the UK at present, the benefits of using the same assessment structures as other subjects of the curriculum are clear, though the teacher of RE may reasonably find the cost of such structures is high, where hundreds of pupils per week are taught. APP, with its sampling approaches to assessing classroom learning, provides a current example of the kind of approaches RE can adopt. These approaches intend:

- to raise pupil achievement in RE by using the methods of AfL, clarity about where learners are at, where they are going and the steps that will take them there
- to provide teachers with clear, level-based, criterion-referenced outcomes for particular pieces of work in a manageable way

- to encourage classroom task-setting (rather than testing) which enables learners to engage with their RE learning for themselves
- to use levels in ways that are both practical and manageable and also coherent and progressed
- to provide RE teachers with clear, evidence-based practical examples of the kinds of assessment questions and tasks that build up pupils' learning skills in RE-specific ways.

Questions

By what methods can the teacher of RE be sure that pupils are making the best possible learning progress in RE?

What do the terms 'assessment for learning', 'clear learning objectives', 'assessment task' and 'evidence of achievement' mean in the RE context?

In balancing the status value of alignment with national curriculum assessment with the particular demands of RE learning, is it usually better for RE to follow the assessment structures of other subjects, or do the specifics of RE require different models of assessment?

Further reading

Black, P. and Wiliam, D. (1998) *Inside the Black Box: Raising Standards through Classroom Assessment,* London: NFER-Nelson. One of the original publications that introduced the notion of assessment for learning – widely influential.

Draycott, P. (2006) *Assessed RE: Engaging with Secondary RE,* Birmingham: RE Today. This is a practical expression of good assessment practice in terms of the secondary classroom, full of examples.

Ofsted (2010) *Transforming Religious Education*, London: HMSO. This inspection report provides a benchmark description of the quality of RE, including assessment, in the context of the 2010 classroom.

Chapter 20

Information and communication technologies

Paul Hopkins

In *The Medium is the Message* (1967), Marshall McLuhan talked about how 'New technologies take the place of the old' (McLuhan and Fiore 1967: 14). School classrooms have always been places where technology has been used; it is very unlikely that you will not find a range of technologies in the religious education (RE) classroom. What has changed, over the last few years, are the kind of technologies that will be doing similar pedagogic or methodological tasks. Ten years ago it would have been common to have found a television, VCR player, CD player and an OHP in your RE classroom, with maybe a tape player and slide projector gathering dust in the cupboard. Now most of these will be redundant, replaced with a video projector and computer connected to the school network and to the wider internet. The questions that I will raise in this chapter are: 'What are you doing with these technologies, the technologies that students have in their pockets and schoolbags, that is methodologically different or which allows better RE to take place?', 'How is the technology in you classroom empowering learning as well as teaching?' and finally 'What core purposes for teaching RE are enhanced by the use of the technology?'

Technological hardware and software changes so fast, think of VHS to DVD to BluRay in the space of 10 years, that it is important that we focus not on these but on the underlying pedagogical principles that govern its use and how these can develop better learning, and teaching, in our subject. All the students we now teach, excepting possibly those who are recent arrivals in the country, have grown up in a rich technological environment. The Office for National Statistics data suggests that 90 per cent of children have a CD player, 85 per cent have a home computer, 95 per cent of secondary and about 50 per cent of primary children a mobile phone, about 70 per cent a portable digital music player and according to OfCOM (The Office of Communications) about two-thirds of UK households are now online via broadband. This rise in ownership of digital devices has caused alarm in some quarters. A *Daily Mail* headline claimed, 'Wrong sort of text: children of seven more likely to own a mobile phone than a book' (*Daily Mail* 2010). However the 'digital divide' that was a concern of politicians in the 1990s and 2000s has mostly gone away, though recent initiatives such as Becta's Home Access[1] initiative still recognised the disadvantage that students without access face.

McCormick and Scrimshaw (2001) posed three questions for the use of technology that are still key in this debate:

1   How does the use of technology make learning more efficient?
2   How does the use of technology make learning more effective?
3   How does the use of technology transform teaching and learning?

Above all the major change in the last few years has been the *convergence* of technologies into the online realm where access to the Internet is no longer, for the vast majority of people, a choice but a necessity. More and more information, communication, commerce and collaboration takes place in the online environment be this via the World Wide Web, e-mail, Facebook, Twitter, Amazon or other portals. There is an irony that you are reading this chapter in a paper book, though it may be that you are reading it on a screen on your desk or on a hand-held device. Data from OfCOM suggests that it is unlikely that you have not accessed the Internet today and almost certain that you have accessed it at some point this week; whether that be from your desktop computer, laptop computer or a mobile or handheld device.

In this chapter we will explore these questions and I will propose six ways in which using the technology in your school and in your classroom are now essential to give students access to high quality learning and to be able to honestly answer, 'yes' to the questions that McCormick and Scrimshaw pose.

How do we teach and learn with technology?

Governments have realised the increasing importance of competency in the use of ICT in the classroom. Between 1999 and 2003 a very large programme of Continuing Professional Development (CPD), the largest of its sort in UK Education, aided teachers already qualified to develop their ICT skills in teaching and learning. This New Opportunities Funded Programme (about £230 million) reached about 80 per cent of the 450,000 teachers in UK classrooms and, 'evidence suggests that the majority of teachers made progress by using the programme as a springboard for further development' (MirandaNet evaluation of the NoF programme, see Preston 2004).

Since the revision of the standards for Achieving Qualified Teacher Status (QTS) in 2002 and again in the revision in 2007 there have been standards requiring teaching to have facility and expertise with ICT. Standard 17 requires:

> trainees to demonstrate that they know how to use numeracy, literacy and information and communication technologies (ICT) skills to teach the relevant curriculum across the ability range in the age ranges they are trained to teach. They should also demonstrate that they know how to use the skills to support their wider professional role.
>
> (TDA 2011)

Standard 16 states that teachers cannot be recommended for QTS unless they have passed the ICT skills test (as well as those for English and Maths) emphasising the importance placed on facility with, and the use of, technology by all teachers. As the TDA website says 'The tests are designed to make sure all trainees have the knowledge, skills and understanding they need to carry out their professional roles as teachers effectively' (TDA 2011).

So, the vast majority of teachers now teaching in UK schools, and thus in RE classrooms, have a core competency in the use of ICT for teaching and learning and for their wider professional roles. Indeed in my own experience in running sessions on the use of ICT in many initial teacher training (ITT) establishments between 2006 and 2009 the level of competency amount trainees has risen year on year and it is rare now to find a trainee who does not feel competent in using core software packages (word-processing, desktop publishing, data processing, presentation), in using the WWW, and in using a range of communication (SMS, e-mail) or social networking tools (Wikis, Blogs, Facebook, Twitter) though the focus is still on the personal or the teacher use of the technology and not on facilitating the student use of technology.

In the last 15 years a huge amount of research has been carried out into effective use of technology in schools; from wider studies into impact (Condie and Munro 2007; Fullan 2005; Hughes 2005; Higgins 2008) to more targeted studies on specific subject areas and technologies; as well as many case-studies, evaluation studies and pilot projects. There has been some research specifically on the use of technology in RE classrooms (Hopkins 2004, 2009) and a number of Farmington Reports on ICT (Harrison 1998; Robinson 1999; Raine 1999; Coster 2000; Christodoulou 2005; Walker 2008; see http://www.farmington.ac.uk) and the recent Warwick report on resources included a considerable section on electronic resources (Jackson *et al.* 2010). Whilst it is not possible to report on all of these in the space here there are some key messages that come from these researches:

1   The use of technology must be embedded in the pedagogic and methodological processes of learning in the subject, not 'bolted-on' or used for the 'wow-factor'.
2   The use of technology must be a whole-school initiative with technical, curriculum, policy and financial support.
3   Technology must be used to engage and motivate students, not just be a tool for use by the teacher; teachers must know when using ICT enhances learning and when it does not.
4   The skills must be taught in parallel with the content.
5   Students should be allowed to use their own and creativity in the production of content.
6   Students' varied learning styles must be accommodated when using ICT.

It is rare now for classrooms not be equipped with a digital projector, a computer and access to the Internet; this is, in fact, a requirement for all new-build schools.

This puts into the hands of the teacher and possibly the students an incredibly powerful learning and teaching tool. Students' own personal access to technology has also increased dramatically and most secondary and a considerable proportion of upper primary students will now have access to a computer at home. The availability of OpenSource software now means that a suite of software programmes are available for free or minimal cost allowing students to have access to similar software as their teachers. (For more information about the software available see http://www.mmiweb.org.uk/mmisite/support.html.)

How do religious groups use technology?

At the core of RE is the study of religious groups and the beliefs of their adherents. Like nearly all organisations, religious groups have been keen to occupy their place in cyberspace, and as communities of practice (Wenger 1999) thrive on the Internet; you might consider the Internet as a natural home for religious groups. Enter any religious term into a search engine and the hits will rise into millions as the Warwick project on resources to support RE found (Hopkins and Hayward 2010). There are websites which are the official home in cyberspace of all the major, and many minor faith and belief groups; in fact the Internet has allowed many groups which struggled for a voice and a presence access to a wide audience. Then there are a growing number of religious groups and communities that only exist online; though some see this as an extension of earlier groups who existed as part of groups via radio or television. In May 2004 the first '3D church service in cyberspace' was reported on by Ruth Gledhill, the religion correspondent of *The Times* (Gledhill 2004) and Gledhill was quite complimentary about her experiences; this cyber chapel can be visited at http://www.churchoffools.com. An Internet search in 2010 brings up many hundreds of online churches, one interesting example of which is St Pixels (http://www.stpixels.com) and in the mainstream there is i-church, 'an online Christian community based on Benedictine principles' (http://www.i-church.org).

It is not only the Christian religion that has moved into cyberspace; looking online you can find virtual communities from major, minor and obscure groups and this has been greeted by the worshipping communities with a range of feelings. Commenting on the first cyber puja R. Banerjee commented,'one has to move with the times. Presumably, the pujas [worship/festival] will no longer be the same again' (Beckerlegge 2002).

Religious and faith groups are offering a number of things when using the Internet:

- access to information about the group both for members of the group and for visitors/enquirers. A website can easily contain images, sounds, texts and video to inform the visitor;

- a focal point for diverse communities engendering a sense of closer community. For example Hindus in the USA or Jewish groups outside the major cities in the UK;
- opportunities to participate in rituals and rites that otherwise would be difficult or impossible;
- contact for spiritual guidance, confession, inspiration or blessings;
- opportunities for questions to be raised which might be difficult in traditional communities or where there is no possibility of anonymity. Bunt talks of CyberIslamic chatrooms where questions of homosexuality and marriage may be raised (Bunt 2000);
- opportunities to explore one's own faith and the faith of others in a non-threatening manner, especially aspects which may not be available in one's geographic vicinity;
- access to the faith groups at a time that is suitable for the surfer.

It is not all positive news of course; the ability to hide in anonymity or behind cyberwalls also has made it easier for groups wanting to promote hatred, fundamentalism and looking to radicalise and proselytise. When exploring religion online one must tread with care.

Six ways of using technology for better teaching and learning in religious education

Having considered the nature of teaching and learning with the technology and had a brief glimpse into the ways the religions and belief systems portray themselves I would like to offer six ways in which RE teachers *must* incorporate technology into their classrooms.

Critical access to information held online

Due to the chaotic and anarchic nature of the web it is almost impossible to determine the number of webpages on the Internet. However, a 'ballpark' figure (taking data from Google, Yahoo and Netcraft)[2] gives us, in late 2010, about 125 billion webpages; an almost unimaginable amount of data. As we have seen, the information that is available via the knowledge depositories is incredibly valuable and rich. When was the last time you looked up something in an encyclopaedia rather than a wikipedia? The term 'Google' has come into common use as a verb – 'I'll Google that'.

However, children often come with an uncritical mind to the Internet so we must inculcate a critical realist approach to the information held online, getting them to offer an enquiring mind with questions such as 'who is writing this?', 'how do I know what is true?', 'what truth claims are they making', 'what is the foundation for these?'

For students of RE this should come as second nature, assuming that the teacher is adopting this kind of approach to their lessons as advocated by writers such as Wright, Cooling and others. This digging below the surface to ask about the nature of truth is both at the core of good RE and also at the core of good use of the information sources available online. The same skills that might be brought to textual exegesis are those that should be brought to online searches.

As the teacher might select carefully written resources that are suitable for a student given their cognitive abilities so the teacher can either use existing resources such as http://www.reonline.org.uk/ or http://www.bbc.co.uk/ religion to restrict the student to initially trusted sources or they can develop with the student their own webographies of materials, building up a trusted set of websites in the same way they might build up a trusted set of other resources. An example of this via a school website is at http://www.rsrevision.com/ where the RE teacher Paul Emerz has developed a fantastic resource.

Accessing the authentic voice and the diverse belief of the religious and belief communities

Whilst many of the UK's cities now have a rich and developing cultural and religious mix, this is not true of all of the UK's schools. Access to the authentic voice of the believer, and perhaps more importantly access to the range of beliefs within a single tradition, is very important. As Jackson (1997) would have us understand in his interpretive approach we must be aware of both the diversity of the tradition and the nature of reflexivity in the encountering of the tradition.

The online environment allows us access to the voice of the believer in a rich and varied way that would have been previously nearly impossible due to the twin restrictions of time and cost. This might be via the websites of the traditions (see above) or via forums, chat-rooms and social media. Sites like the National RE Festival database (http://www.natre.org.uk/db) or RE Online's People of Faith (http://pof.reonline.org.uk/) are a starting place but the web gives students access to forums, chat-rooms and via communication tools the opportunity to develop links with members of faith and belief groups different to the communities in which they live or belong. Julia Ipgrave's (2004; also Ipgrave and McKenna 2007) 'Building e-bridges' project is an important case-study of this. Growing numbers of Web 2.0 collaborative technologies such as blogs, Wikis and forums allow students to be in direct contact with members of other faiths, exploring and tackling questions of meaning and purpose and sharing their own ideas. Careful facilitating and guidance is needed to ensure that this is not a pooling of ignorance but the creation of activities allowing real interactions between real people rather than the more sterile receiving of passive information. CLEO (The Cumbria and Lancashire Education Online) (http://www.cleo.net.uk) have developed excellent resources showing this kind of practice.

Alongside this is the use of capture technologies (video and audio) which are now cheap and available, and quite possibly in the hands and pockets of the students, for gathering of data on the faith and beliefs of the people in the students' communities. Then students can analyse, interpret and evaluate these data and create their own understanding, giving them access to the higher-level cognitive skills (Anderson *et al.* 2000).

Access the richness of Digital Learning Artefacts (DLAs) (sound, image and video)

Alongside the huge amount of textual information that exists in the 'flat' web there is the growing archive of audio-visual materials from depositories all over the globe. These sound, image and video archives offer real richness for an encounter with the artefacts of religion. A simple place to start is the Shap Audio Glossary (http://www.shapworkingparty.org.uk/glossary.html) where you can hear members of the faith community speaking religious terminology. This is only the start of the developing archive materials that you can access; from facsimiles of beautiful texts at the British Library (http://www.bl.uk/onlinegallery/sacredtexts/) to high quality broadcast materials from the BBC (http://www.bbc.co.uk/religion/); to the anarchic but rich vein of resource on sites such as YouTube (http://www.youtube.com), British Pathe (http://www.britishpathe.com/) Google Video (http://video.google.co.uk/) and GodTube (http://www.godtube.com/). An on-going updated collection of resource sites for video, audio and images can be found at http://www.mmiweb.org.uk/publications/avresources.html.

Give students the ability to use the technology they have access to (including the opportunity to develop their creativity)

As software moves to open source and there are more and more free or cheap creative tools via the Web 2.0 community, such as Animoto (http://www.animoto.com), Bubblus (http://www.bubbl.us), Capzles (http://www.capzles.com/), Photostory 3 (http://photostory3.wikispaces.com/), to name but a tiny fraction (for details of more of these see http://www.mmiweb.org.uk/web20); then there are more and more opportunities for students to present their own understanding of knowledge in a variety of methods that allow them to learn, and express their learning in a variety of outcomes. So they might become filmmakers, animators, digital storywriters, cartoonists, documentary makers, radio programme makers, web developers and developers of interactive presentations as well as writers of text on the page.

How will you be able to facilitate this? The use of e-portfolios and digital archiving (see below in the section on VLEs) will allow you to store and access this material – as well as allowing the students to collaborate and communicate about work outside of the classroom with other members of their class, with members of the faith community and with the wider world. A way of developing this is to focus on the content and to allow the students to present work in a manner that most suits them.

The opportunities for drafting, re-drafting, amending and adapting as well as importing the DLAs mentioned above allow for a highly creative and adaptive approach to lessons and to assessment. Students themselves can use recording of their voice as staging posts for note-taking, brainstorming and developing ideas and tools such as GoogleDocs allow collaborative working. As Seymour Papert said, it is important that students are not just making meaning but making something, a knowledge artefact which develops the understanding of meaning (Papert 1982).

Using the technology to capture achievement in a creative manner

How often does the excellent work that your students do disappear into the ether because it is ethereal? Do you use still and video cameras to capture presentations or dramatic episodes? Do you use audio capture to get the key ideas of groups at the end of a discussion, debate or dialogue (the 3 'D's of the RE classroom)? So often we only assess written work, or work on paper.

The technological tools allow video, image and audio to be easily captured, stored and shared. So students can have access to materials that they have missed in class, or to extension and development materials via the schools VLE (see below); they can transport work from the classroom or have this available via the VLE or the cloud using DropBox or a similar mechanism (http://www.dropbox.com). Materials can be shared among students during the lesson using Bluetooth or Wireless encouraging collaboration and co-operation.

Using the school's VLE – the 'e-box' model of learning

All secondary, and the majority of primary schools, now operate a Virtual or Managed Learning Environment; this may be situated in the school, with a private contractor or via the support services provided the local authority. A requirement of the VLE/MLE is that students can access the materials on the VLE from outside of the school environs via a secure log-in. This means that the pupils can have access to the electronic support materials that you have produced or gathered from 'anywhere' at 'anytime'. This allows for the provision of quality support materials for students, which could be video, audio, podcasts, interactive quizzes, web links, classroom materials, extension materials, support materials for projects. VLE also allows this to be a two-way process where the students can contribute materials of their own to the repository. This online store or e-box allows a more flexible approach to learning and to encouraging independent enquirers, creative thinkers and reflective learners.

Communication tools such as Wikis, Forums and Blogs allow students to form communities of practice outside of the physical limitations of their classroom. It allows collaborative projects with other schools, communities and countries (see above). E-portfolios allow students to submit work electronically and for it to be assessed in the same manner as well as allowing access to the assessed work by parents and guardians.

Becoming e-mature

Technology has changed many areas of life, and will continue to do so. At the moment there is little impact on school-level education, though there has been more impact on the FE and HE sectors, but some of the technologies are beginning to challenge the classroom-based, age-related, information processing models (Fullan 2005). As technology becomes more personal, flexible and multi-tasking (think of the newest handheld 'phones' which have still and video capability, audio recording, internet access, e-reader capability and communication tools such as SMS, e-mail and social networking tools) and is situated in a school environment where information is stored centrally on the school hub/VLE, or in the cloud and the schools are wireless hotspots, then access to these learning artefacts truly becomes 'anytime, anywhere'.

Becta in 2004/5 were developing criteria for the e-confident school (http://www.becta.org.uk). We can look at these criteria with the aim of developing similar criteria for the e-confident teacher/learner. Placing these in a spectrum from e-naive to e-mature:

Table 20.1 From e-naive to e-mature

E-Naive	E-Mature
Focuses on the technology	Focuses on the religious education aims and objectives
Cannot identify how ICT can be used to develop RE knowledge, skills and deepen understanding	Is able to identify the appropriate ICT to use to develop RE knowledge, skills and deepen understanding
Is unable to show how the ICT makes learning more effective, efficient or transforms learning	Is able to show how the ICT makes learning more effective, efficient or transforms learning
Fails to use available or appropriate technology	Fully uses technology when appropriate and selects the most appropriate technology within the learning environment
Has difficulty with the technical aspects of the technology	Is able to use the technology with competence and solve technical problems
Is unable to persuade others to use the technology	Convinces others of the benefits of the use of the technology
Cannot differentiate between technology for personal use and for collaborative use	Is able to determine when technology is best used for personal learning and when best for collaborative learning
Does not recognise that technology changes over time	Recognises when e-maturity is threatened by technological development and takes steps to minimise this threat.

Using this matrix allows a reflective-practitioner approach to the use of the technology. As well as being aware of the elements of the matrix the e-mature teacher/learner must demonstrate abilities in the areas of competence, communication and confidence.

Competence: competence is used to mean an understanding of the subject content and the opportunities for ICT to aid in the delivery of subject objectives in a more effective, efficient or transformative way (McCormick and Scrimshaw 2001). It is also used to determine the level of competence in the use of the technology. It can be seen that both of these are time dependent.

Confidence: competence is not enough in itself; the e-mature teacher/learner also needs the confidence to seek and grasp opportunities to use technology where existing learning/teaching methods may seem sufficient and may be effective. The e-mature learner is willing to take risks and to see opportunities to be an innovator of new technologies.

Communication: the e-mature teacher/learner will need to be able to communicate with peers and non-peers over their use of the technology in developing subject achievement. This communication will be needed to explore when, and when not, to use technology and also how this is justified. They need to explain how the technology is as good as or better than non-technological methodologies in reaching given subject objectives and how they have utilised the technology so to do.

Only when a teacher/learner displays *confidence, competence* and *communication* can they be said to be e-mature. It is also not enough to become e-mature, one must remain so; as the technology changes there are new challenges to confidence, competence and communication and so the model is time dependent and the learning cycle of becoming competent with the technology, developing the confidence to use it and being able to communicate the effectiveness of the use all need to be re-developed.

Conclusion

Convergence into an online environment, the development of Web 2.0 and open source tools means that more and more tools and content are available at the touch of a button, or the click of a mouse, or the swipe of a finger. Also, as the hardware becomes cheaper and smaller more and more students will have access to powerful tools that allow them to learn in a smarter, more efficient, effective, transformative and creative manner. This ability to interact with the world beyond their physical boundaries, as well as express themselves in a growingly creative and skilled way, means that learning in general and learning about and from RE in particular is on the cusp of an enormous change.

In RE the concept of the mature learner is one who is a critically reflective thinker, aware of a range of learning methodologies, best able to choose the appropriate learning methodology for the task in hand and able to reflect on the effectiveness of the chosen methodology. The e-mature learner is no different but displays confidence, capability and communication skills about the technology and its use as well as its impact on learning in, and of, RE.

So, technology offers the student and teacher in RE an opportunity to reach out and touch an incredibly diverse, rich mix of people with all the inherent benefits and dangers of this. The teacher of RE must lose the idea of the role of the guru and adopt the role of the guide who journeys with the student offering support, advice and guidance in this brave new world.

Questions

What challenges to religious education are posed by the existent and emergent technologies?

How can we navigate the information provided by religious and belief groups online in a critical, evaluative method and make sense of the vast array of information provided?

What strategies do we need to develop in order to become and remain an e-mature RE teacher?

Notes

1 Becta (The British Educational Communications and Technology Agency) was responsible for the development and support of the use of technology in English schools.
2 From the data on the number of indexed pages last released by Google/Yahoo and multiplying this by the number of registered domains tracked by Netcraft for August 2010.

Further reading

Beckerlegge, G. (2002) *From Sacred Text to Internet*, Aldershot: Ashgate. Addresses two key issues affecting the global spread of religion: first, the impact of new media on the ways in which religious traditions present their messages, and second, the global relocation of religions in novel geographical and social settings.

Beetham, H. and Sharpe, R. (2007) *Rethinking Pedagogy for a Digital Age*, London: Routledge. This considers the whole nature of pedagogy and how the digital technologies challenge us to reconsider the educational process.

Warburg, M. and Hojsgaard, M. (2007) *Religion and Cyberspace*, London: Routledge. Explores how religious individuals and groups are responding to the opportunities and challenges that cyberspace brings.

Chapter 21

Science and religion

Michael Poole

The criteria for selecting topics for this chapter arise mainly out of a piece of research relating religious education (RE) to science (Bausor and Poole 2002, 2003). This involved a search of the English Local Education Authorities' Agreed Syllabuses for Religious Education for entries about science-and-religion. Much of this is reflected in the subsequent (2004) *Non-Statutory National Framework for Religious Education*. Topics that appear most relevant to education are:

- worldviews and the nature and scope of science; explanations; laws and the concept of miracles; relationships between science and religion
- creation and origins; big bang; young-Earth creationism
- evolution/chance/design and 'ID'
- language – models and metaphors, literary genre.

Worldviews and the nature and scope of science

A worldview is an interpretation of the world. At times the world has been seen, variously, as an *organism* or a *mechanism*. In ancient Greek science (600BCE–200CE) the organismic worldview, including the belief that nature was semi-divine, hindered experimental science. Performing experiments on a semi-divine nature seemed what the Greeks called *hubris* – insolence, an outrage. The mechanistic worldview, in which a founder member of the Royal Society, Robert Boyle, compared the world to a clock, resonated with Boyle's own Christian beliefs, by suggesting a 'clockmaker', God. Later this worldview backfired because the Deists argued that a clock, once made and wound up, doesn't need anything to keep it going. So that worldview seemed to offer partial support to both atheism and theism. Individual scientists work from within their worldview, atheistic or theistic, and this can colour their thinking. Richard Dawkins' view that science leads to atheism exemplifies the first: Francis Collins (2007: 3), leader of the Human Genome Project, the second, seeing the amazing structure of DNA as 'an occasion of worship'.

Additional, non-religious, ways of interpreting science raise questions like 'is science discovering truth about a real and orderly world?' (realism) or 'are we superimposing our idea of order on the random chaos of sense experience?' (idealism). Again, 'is the importance of science just that it "seems to work"?' (instrumentalism). The latter is exemplified, historically, by a claim that Copernicus' theory was just a convenient calculating device, rather than advancing a physical (true) theory, something which seemed likely to get him into trouble with the Roman Catholic authorities who then believed in an Earth-centred system. For the RE student, this instrumentalist 'bracketing out' of the importance of truth-claims about the world is significant. It finds a parallel with the way religious education has tended to 'bracket out' the truth-claims of individual religions by concentrating on religion as a phenomenon to be observed. This phenomenological approach bypasses the obvious pedagogical difficulties of handling truth-claims in a multi-faith society, but the cost is educationally high because, integral to religions is that they invite participation, not detached observation from the touchline. As Barnes (2001: 457) has put it, 'The study of religion in an educational context should involve not just knowing what religious people believe and do, and leaving it there, but should go on to investigate matters of religious truth and relevance.'

Science, too, can be studied phenomenologically, examining sociological factors influencing the choices of research topics, the effects of science on society and how checking the work of scientists by peer review can sometimes result in rejecting valuable work that strays too far from the current 'received view'. While the bracketing out of truth-claims is unexceptionable as a methodological principle, once it involves denying that truth-claims in science are an important and a legitimate area of study, it has overstepped its remit; so too in matters of religion.

Most practising scientists hold a *realist* position; they believe they are finding something out about a real world. But caveats are needed. How, for example, can we find out what actually exists if, say, we are looking through a telescope at a galaxy like Andromeda, two million light years away? We are looking into the past. It might not be there now. Then again, are the mysterious quarks 'things' that exist or just concepts to interpret sense data? 'Realism' needs qualifying and the term 'critical realism', in contrast to an implied 'naive realism', has gained currency.

Sometimes, however, more has been asked of science than it is in position to deliver. Then it can become a 'golden image' whose foundations cannot support its own weight. Such was the case in the early twentieth century with a movement called *positivism* which had a profound impact on religion. The movement had developed over a considerable period of time and worked from the assumption that the physical world is all there is and that direct sense experience enables verification of what is 'given', about which we can be positive. Invisible entities like atoms, although achieving economy of thought, were not regarded as having existential status. A group of philosophers in Vienna in the 1920s and 1930s applied principles of logic to positivist thought and developed what came to be known as *logical positivism*. Their crusade, for such it was, was directed against metaphysics, religion and aspects of ethics whose propositions were not considered empirically verifiable and therefore, in their view, meaningless. As Bertrand Russell (1972: 243) put it:

'Whatever knowledge is attainable, must be attained by scientific methods; and what science cannot discover, mankind cannot know.' The arguments which exposed the movement's Achilles' heel are too lengthy to spell out here (Poole 1995: 34–38) but in the mid-twentieth century they had a profound effect on religion. Finally, logical positivism's champion in England, Professor Sir A. J. Ayer, in a video interview with Bryan Magee posted on 17 March 2008, admitted that 'nearly all of it was false' (Ayer interviewed by Magee 2008).

This philosophical episode left an entrenched popular perception of antagonism between science and religion; long after most professional philosophers had abandoned this position. The view resurfaces whenever someone demands 'prove to me scientifically that God exists' and has echoes in Richard Dawkins' claim that 'religion is a scientific theory'. Such a demand has an odd ring since it runs counter to the nature of science itself. Science is a powerful tool for systematically studying the natural world. But for obvious logical reasons it cannot tackle religious questions like, 'is there anything *other* than the natural world (God?), to which the natural world owes its existence?' As recognised by *Science in the National Curriculum for England,* 'there are some questions that science cannot currently answer, and some that science cannot address'. The subject matter of science – nature – comes with a small 'n'. Sometimes, however, it appears as 'Nature' – or even Mother Nature – attributed with God-like powers to 'choose', 'build' and 'create'. Closer scrutiny reveals the oddity that nature, which is every physical thing there is, should be reified and treated as though it had the power to create every physical thing there is!

Explanations

Scientific explanations of objects and the actions of people (agents) are of different types. A scientific explanation of why the water in the tank is hot is that the burning of gas in the boiler transfers the chemical energy in the gas to heat energy. A non-scientific, but equally valid explanation is Tom wanted a bath. The second encapsulates explanations of both agency and purpose (Tom's). There is no contradiction between these explanations; they are logically compatible. Failure to recognise a plurality of compatible explanations causes unnecessary tensions between scientific and religious ones. The different types of explanations are not interchangeable, though. Where this goes unrecognised, serious philosophical misunderstandings can arise. When the action of gravity became accepted, some anxious theologians thought God's activity was being denied. So they pointed to things science had not yet explained, saying, 'that's God'. Subsequently each new thing that could be scientifically explained appeared to leave less room for God's involvement. This counterproductive, explanatory *type error* came to be dubbed the 'God of the gaps'. It encouraged scientific laziness; what was required was greater diligence to find a scientific explanation to fill the scientific gap; not an explanation concerning an agent, human or divine, which is outside the scope of science.

Laws and the concept of miracles

Can miracles happen? Do miracles happen? What is a miracle anyway? Wouldn't miracles 'break' scientific laws? The non-theist would probably answer 'no' to the first two questions and 'yes' to the last one, begging the question 'what is a scientific "law"?' Since 'laws' of the land are the means of establishing and maintaining order in society, the apparent orderliness in the way the world works led to adopting the term 'laws' of science, rather than, say, 'principles'. This was unfortunate because the unexamined difference between these two uses of 'law' frequently causes confusion, especially about miracles. Laws-of-the-land are *pre*scriptive and say what *must be* done to avoid penalties. Scientific 'laws', by contrast, are *de*scriptive and say what *is* done when, say, you double the pressure on a fixed mass of gas at constant temperature and its volume is halved (Boyle's 'law'). The only thing a scientific law *does* prescribe is our expectation of what is likely to happen, based on precedent. Scientific laws describe *normal* behaviour; they are like maps, human constructions resulting from carefully examining the way the world works. Scientific 'laws' are corrigible. If the 'laws' don't summarise the observations then the laws, like the maps, have to be changed. Scientific laws cannot be 'obeyed' or 'broken'. That is sloppy talk, a hangover from the forensic use of 'law'. Events can only 'conform' or 'fail to conform' to a scientific law.

Theologically, a miracle is more than an amazing happening, like a parachutist surviving a drop when the 'chute failed to open. A 'wonder' *is* involved but additionally it has significance, being a sign from God in its nature or its timing. So an answer of 'no' to the first question 'can miracles happen?' cannot be justified *a priori* from scientific criteria. Scientific laws are only expressions of the normal behaviour of the natural world and, by definition, miracles are not normal. Whether a particular miracle *has* happened must be decided by historical criteria rather than scientific generalisations.

From the theist's perspective 'laws' reflect the faithfulness of a non-capricious God who makes and maintains a world of regularities, rendering it liveable. The orderliness of the world – *cosmos*, not *chaos* – makes it possible to search for patterns, and encapsulate them in concise 'summary statements' called scientific laws. The belief that nature is orderly is one of the basic presuppositions (assumptions, beliefs) of science; such assumptions cannot be proved by science, but have to be made if science is to be pursued at all. This presupposition is often referred to as the *uniformity of nature*, the assumption that, even though the world changes, the underlying 'laws of nature' remain the same in time and space. An even more fundamental presupposition that has to be made is that of human rationality – the assumption that our thought processes make sense and are basically reliable. This belief underpins all branches of study, otherwise writing and talking would be just scribbles and sounds. We cannot even meaningfully argue whether rationality is a valid presupposition without assuming it is! One further presupposition is the *intelligibility of nature*; but whereas rationality assumes we can make sense of, and understand, things, intelligibility assumes the world itself is *capable* of being understood. Otherwise there would be no basis for science. That may seem obvious, but as Einstein commented, 'The most incomprehensible thing about the universe is that it is comprehensible' (Hoffman 1972: 18).

Relationships between science and religion

What kinds of relationships might there be between science and religion – or even 'are any interactions possible between them?' Aren't they so different as to be in 'watertight compartments'? A thorough and accessible analysis of the various positions held was undertaken by Austin (1976) while a more recent treatment by Barbour (2000) has been the subject of further discussion. According to popular perception, the view most likely to be encountered is what historians of science call the 'conflict thesis'. Also known as the 'military metaphor', it is a relatively recent phenomenon. It features all too often in some media portrayals of science-and-religion as a battleground, where confrontation, and consequent higher viewing ratings, seems at a higher premium than historical accuracy. This view runs counter to the understandings of academic historians of science who regard the notion of an enduring conflict between science and religion as an inadequate generalisation of the many different relationships which have, and do exist between them. Peter Harrison (2008: 9), Professor of Science and Religion at Oxford, comments that 'Those who argue for the incompatibility of science and religion will draw little comfort from history... the myth of a perennial conflict between science and religion is one to which no historian of science would subscribe.'

The persistence of the conflict thesis owes much to deliberate attempts in the nineteenth century, and in the present, to promulgate a 'warfare model'. Historical episodes like the Galileo affair and the Wilberforce/Huxley encounter of 30 June 1860 have been retold and rewritten in 'baddies' versus 'goodies' style with scant regard for history.

Creation and origins, big bang, young-earth creationism

Claims are sometimes made that there is a need to choose between 'creation' and the 'big bang' and 'creation and evolution'. Some people decide simply to reject both the big bang and evolution. Others show over-enthusiasm for science, imagining it dispenses with a Creator. Such putative choices raise philosophical and theological questions like 'could these be rationally conceived as two pairs of alternatives between which one has to choose?' Is 'both/and' more appropriate than 'either/or'?

The word 'creation' has fairly common, though misleading, currency in phrases like 'Agatha Christie was the creator of Hercule Poirot', for she brought this fictional character into being. These are derivative uses which can be traced back to theology, but remain theologically confusing. Within the Abrahamic religions of Judaism, Christianity and Islam, creation refers to God bringing-everything-into-being (*creatio ex nihilo*) and sustaining-everything-in-being (*creatio continua*). St Augustine argued that if God is the creator of everything, then time, too, must be part of the created order (Augustine 2004). For a different reason, modern physics concludes that space and time (space-time) came into being with the big bang. Ideas of timelessness and nothingness are very difficult to conceptualise when our only experience is of matter in space-time, so the word 'counterintuitive' is used increasingly in the vocabulary of science. Einstein's work on relativity helps in 'thinking outside the box', while space-fiction attempts to enlarge our imaginations. Creation is a timeless act, 'with time', but not 'in time'. It is also a free act of God. In philosophical terminology, it is *contingent* (could have been otherwise) not *necessary* (had to be). Moreover, it is the act of a supreme God, not of some Gnostic or Platonic Demiurge or lesser god who fashions pre-existing matter. Furthermore, and this is important, the theological concept of creation is independent of any particular processes involved in 'bringing-into-being'.

The physical origins of the universe, as distinct from the act of creation, are the subject matter of science, whether in a big bang or in a process of the 'continuous creation' of new matter appearing at a rate which just compensates for what is moving outwards in an expanding universe. This second, and discarded, view was published in a Steady-State Theory of the Expanding Universe, put forward by Bondi and Gold (1948). The authors, from their atheist perspectives, saw their theory as purging cosmology of metaphysical ideas. Calling their theory 'continuous *creation*' was puzzling in view of their rejection of divine creation, but as well as being theologically muddled, it was a misconception. A theologian, Professor Eric Mascall (1956: 156) remarked, with tongue in cheek, in his Bampton Lectures that, 'in the strict sense, this is not a doctrine of *continuous*, but rather of steadily and unendingly *repeated*, creation'. No matter of principle was changed. One 'big bang' was simply replaced by 'innumerable "little pops"' (Mascall 1956: 162).

This historical episode illustrates the earlier point that scientists, like others, work from within their particular worldviews – in this instance, atheistic ones. This may colour their interpretations of scientific discoveries, as exemplified by the resistance offered by some scientists to the displacement of the steady state cosmology by what Hoyle disparagingly dubbed the 'big bang', because it seemed to point to a beginning and perhaps a 'Beginner'. But it can also affect beliefs about the nature of science itself as was the case with the grandiose claims of logical positivism. More recently, those taking a non-theistic perspective have sometimes been more ready to enlist the idea of a multiverse to explain the *anthropic coincidences* than is warranted by the present state of science. Dubbed the *Goldilocks effect*, the apparent 'fine tuning' of our universe for life-as-we-know-it draws attention to the fact that if the constants of nature were infinitesimally different from what they are, carbon-based life would not be possible. To those who dislike any hint of design, or a designer, the multiverse theory may appear to justify making the anthropic coincidences very probable in a vast number of 'universes'. But it has also been pointed out that if the main motive is to avoid the conclusion that there is one universe designed by God, a multiverse seems a huge violation of Ockham's razor, which says 'It is vain to do with more what can be done with fewer'. But much of this idea is little more than speculative metaphysics at present since observers in different 'universes' would not be able to communicate. In any case a multiverse would not obviate a Creator, for the matter of the plurality of compatible explanations again comes into view. Scientists will nowadays (almost universally) agree that the physical origin of the universe lay in a big bang. But theists will also want to affirm that an act of creation was involved and that this is logically compatible with a scientific explanation of physical origins. The philosophically minded will recognise the Fallacy of the Excluded Middle if someone insists that a choice has to be made between the two; because a third possibility, *both,* is a logical option. Similar points can be made, *mutatis mutandis,* about 'creation and evolution', as will be seen later.

Creationism

Having made the distinction between the mechanisms by which the universe is formed and the *act* of creation, the waters have been muddied by the introduction of another, similarly sounding word, creation*ism*. Three versions of this are old-Earth creationism, progressive creationism and young-Earth creationism, all of which posit additional, non-natural acts of God. But since about 1980, the young-Earth version is popularly understood by the abbreviation 'creationism'. Creationism embraces two beliefs; an orthodox belief in 'creation' as above, plus the belief that the Earth is about 6–10,000 years old. As indicated above, science is incapable of telling us whether there is a Creator of the universe, but it can give strong indications, by agreements between many different dating methods, of the age of the universe. It is something like 13.7 thousand million years old and Earth is about 4.6 thousand million years old (White 2007: 1). Disagreements have arisen because some have argued that the 'days' of Genesis chapter one are to be understood in their common sense of '24' hours. Others, including Church Fathers like Origen and Augustine, have argued for a more careful reading of the text since the sun, moon and stars don't arrive until 'day' four; and without these, 24-hour 'days' as we know them don't exist. In the King James translation of the Bible Genesis 2: 4 includes the phrase 'in the day [singular] that the LORD God made the earth and the heavens'. This has made readers look more deeply for the author's intended meaning, despite Archbishop Ussher of Armagh's attempts to calculate the age of the Earth by adding together numbers from the incomplete biblical genealogies. Historian of science, Professor David Livingstone (1987: 27) summarises thus, 'by and large, Christian geologists had both encountered and accommodated the issue of the age of the earth long before the appearance of Darwin's theory'. Nevertheless, the idea of a young Earth underwent something of a resurgence in the mid-twentieth century.

Evolution/chance/design and intelligent design

The processes of (organic) evolution are not about everything there is, nor how life arises in the first place; only about how adaptive changes take place in existing living things. Richard Dawkins (2009) claims that 'Darwin has removed the main argument for God's existence' and again 'The theory of evolution by cumulative natural selection is the only theory we know of that is in principle *capable* of explaining the evolution of organised complexity' (Dawkins 1988: 317). But it remains unclear how this could necessarily remove divine activity from the equation as Dawkins appears to think. Let the sceptic momentarily suppose there is a creator God who brings everything into being, employing the chance/random processes of elementary particles colliding in stars to form the elements from which life will eventually appear. If the reproduction of that life transmits information about itself, then characteristics that favour survival and reproduction will tend to be preserved by a built-in process that Darwin labelled 'natural selection'. Add to that the changes, or mutations, in the DNA caused by residual radiation from the earlier big bang and there will be diversity. Cannot this be seen as a much more efficient way for a God to bring about adaptation to the environment than Paley's piecemeal view? Van Till (1996) sees this process as part of *Creation's Functional Integrity*; it has been created to work as a whole. It seems that here is yet another example of the Fallacy of the Excluded Middle – choose between God or evolution – when logically you can go for both. Dawkins (1988: 6) says that 'although atheism must have been *logically* tenable before Darwin, Darwin made it possible to be an intellectually fulfilled atheist'. That seems open to question. Put another way, an explanation of divine agency in creating is in a different category to explanations of the physical mechanisms involved. To take a simple example, scientific explanations of a hovercraft leave the agency and creativity of Christopher Cockerill intact. To claim that one must choose between agency and mechanisms involves what the philosopher Gilbert Ryle called a *category mistake*.

Traditionally, belief in a designed world has always been a feature of the Abrahamic religions. The world has a purpose in the economy of God. What these evidences of design are has been the subject of debates by philosophers. Knock-down proofs belong solely to formal logic and to certain branches of mathematics. The kinds of evidence envisaged here are more comparable to what happens in a court of law. Here many separate pieces of evidence, none of which by themselves may be sufficient to compel belief, may nevertheless collectively add up to a cumulative case, rationally based as well as sufficient for belief and action.

As with creation*ism*, the waters of this debate have been recently muddied by a newcomer to the scene, the *Intelligent Design (ID) Movement*. Its concern is to remove any idea of 'chance', even though it is common knowledge that human designers now use chance processes, like genetic algorithms (see Bartholomew 2008: 170–172). The ID position is that some living things exhibit such complexity that their existence cannot be accounted for by evolutionary processes but point to a designer. A much-cited example is the bacterium flagellum, a minute propeller that moves certain bacteria. The designer is not identified but it seems that God is in mind. Mathematical attempts have been made to stipulate a *specified complexity*, beyond which a designer has to be invoked.

A number of problems arise from this line of argument. What if the structure of some organism does not reach this specified complexity? On ID criteria, it would then seem that a designer is not needed. Although their supporters would not say this, this is where the logic of the ID position leads. But the Abrahamic religions see *everything* as the handiwork of God, not just the very complicated things, so it seems counterproductive as an apologetic device. Another fatal weakness seems to be that the complicated mathematical probability arguments for 'Intelligent Design' are rendered erroneous by overlooking the fact that the intermediate components of evolutionary processes serve different functions at different stages of those processes. In this way ID seems to score an 'own goal' in what it is trying to do, although it leaves the traditional grounds for believing in design unaffected.

Language – models and metaphors, literary genre

One unfavourable comparison which has been made between religion and science is to criticise God-talk about shepherds, kings, rocks and heaven-up-there. Why, it is dismissively asked, can't people stick to the plain, straightforward language of science? Surprisingly it turns out that science, too, has a similar problem of trying to speak about phenomena which are any or all of the following: (i) too complex to handle by other means; (ii) inaccessible to our senses; (iii) conceptually difficult; (iv) novel. As in other walks of life we resort to the it-is-as-if language of comparisons between the familiar and the unfamiliar. This analogical strategy makes the assumption that a similar structure is shared by both the known and the unknown (*isomorphism*) and that they show resemblances between corresponding parts. Similes, metaphors and (conceptual) models are employed. The latter may be broadly defined as systematically developed metaphors. The models which science uses, by contrast with the theological comparisons mentioned above, include waves (for sound and light), billiard balls (for gases), fields (for magnetism, electricity and gravitation), solar-systems (for atoms) and water flowing in a pipe (for electricity). On a theological note, which is also applicable to science, the philosopher of religion, Professor Ian Ramsey (1964: 14), saw the function of models 'as builders of discourse' which 'enable us to make sense of discourse whose logical structure is so perplexing as to inhibit literacy'.

On the matter of literary genre, the textual interpretations of Genesis chapters one to three are beyond the scope of this short overview of issues of science and religion. Nevertheless, it is worth remembering that, in the Bible alone there are many different examples of literary genres. Here are just 20 of them: allegory, apocalyptic writing, elevated prose, enigmatic saying, euphemism, history, hyperbole, irony, joke, letter, metaphor, parable, paradox, personification, poetry, prayer, prophecy, riddle, simile and song. To take them all at face value without identifying different literary genres is to fail to treat the text carefully enough. Like shadow boxing, it creates an imaginary 'enemy' that people then feel obliged to knock around. Furthermore, to try to treat any of these literary genres as a scientific text is to embark on an unfruitful journey.

In conclusion what our review of a range of scientific topics shows is that 'conflict' is not the best metaphor to characterise a relationship between science and religion.

Questions

Have cosmology and quantum mechanics, with their emphasis on chance processes, changed our understanding of science and religion and, if so, how?

Everybody knows about the Galileo Affair and the confrontation between Bishop Wilberforce and T. H. Huxley – or do they? Sketch out what you think are popular perceptions of these two events and then consult some professional historians' views of these episodes in order to evaluate your sketches.

Explore in detail two examples of ways in which linguistic devices like metaphors and models are employed, one in science and one in religion, to enable us to be articulate about what is novel, invisible or conceptually difficult. Identify positive and negative (helpful and unhelpful) features of your chosen examples and point out possible pitfalls in the use of such linguistic devices.

Further reading

Alexander, D. (2008) *Creation or Evolution: Do We Have To Choose?* Oxford: Monarch. A rigorous, detailed, but accessible examination of many of the issues concerning 'creation' and 'evolution'.

Brooke, J. H. (1991) *Science and Religion: Some Historical Perspectives,* Cambridge: Cambridge University Press. A scholarly study, which has become a standard text for a study of the interplay between science and religion.

Poole, M. W. (2007) *User's Guide to Science and Belief,* Oxford: Lion Hudson. An illustrated introduction, substantially rewritten, enlarged and updated from earlier editions, addressing key issues of science and religion, with wider applications than to Christianity alone, used in schools.

A longer list, including classroom resources, is provided on the government website for the CPD of RE teachers, available online: http://www.re-handbook.org.uk/section/curriculum/science-and-religious-education (accessed 30 June 2010).

Bibliography

Akenson, D. H. (1973) *Education and Enmity: The Control of Schooling in Northern Ireland 1920–50*, Newton Abbot: David and Charles.

Alborz, A., Pearson, D., Farrell, P. and Howes, A. (2009) 'The impact of adult support staff on pupils and mainstream schools: Technical Report', in *Research Evidence in Education Library*, London: EPPI-Centre, Social Science Research Unit, Institute of Education, University of London. Available online: http://eppi.ioe.ac.uk (accessed 21 June 2010).

Aldridge, D. (2011) "What is religious education all about? A hermeneutic reappraisal" in *Journal of Beliefs and Values*, 32: in press.

Alexander, D. (2008) *Creation or Evolution: Do We Have To Choose?* Oxford: Monarch.

Alexander, R. J. (2000) *Culture and Pedagogy: International Comparisons in Primary Education*, London: Blackwell.

Alexander, R. (2010) *Children, Their World, Their Education – Final Report and Recommendations of the Cambridge Primary Review*, Abingdon: Routledge.

Allal, L. and Mottier Lopez, L. (2005) 'Formative Assessment of Learning: a review of publications in French', in Organisation for Economic Co-operation and Development (ed.) *Formative Assessment: Improving Learning in Secondary Classrooms*, Paris: OECD.

Allal, L. and Mottier Lopez, L. (eds) (2007) *Régulation des apprentissages en situation scolaire et en formation*, Brussels: de Boeck.

Almond, B. (2010) 'Education for tolerance: cultural difference and family values', *Journal of Moral Education*, 39: 131–143.

Alves, C. (1968) *Religion in the Secondary School*, London: SCM.

Anderson, L. W., Krathwohl, D. R., Airasian, P. W. and Cruikshank, K. A. (2000) *A Taxonomy for Learning, Teaching, and Assessing: A Revision of Bloom's Taxonomy of Educational Objectives*, New York: Allyn and Bacon.

Anderson, R. (2008) *The History of Scottish Education, pre-1980*, in T. G. K. Bryce and W. Humes (eds) *Scottish Education (3rd edn) Beyond Devolution*, Edinburgh: Edinburgh University Press.

ap Siôn, T. (2006) 'Looking for signs of the presence of God in Northern Ireland: religious experience among Catholic and Protestant sixth-form pupils', *Archiv fur Religionpsychologie*, 28: 349–370.

Arditti, M. (2009) *The Enemy of the Good*, London: Arcadia Books.

Armstrong, D. (2009) 'Religious education and the law in Northern Ireland's Controlled Schools', *Irish Educational Studies*, 28: 297–313.

Arnot, M. and an Ghaill, M. (eds) (2006) *The RoutledgeFalmer Reader in Gender and Education,* London: Routledge.

Arthur, J. (2006) *Faith and Secularisation in Religious Colleges and Universities*, Abingdon: Routledge.

Arweck, E. and Nesbitt, E. (2004) 'Living Values: an educational program. From initiative to uptake', *British Journal of Religious Education*, 26: 133–149.

Arweck, E. and Nesbitt, E. (2007) 'Spirituality in education: promoting children's spiritual development through values', *Journal of Contemporary Religion*, 22: 311–326.

Arweck, E. and Nesbitt, E. (2010a) 'Young people's identity formation in mixed-faith families: continuity or discontinuity of religious traditions?' *Journal of Contemporary Religion*, 25: 67–87.

Arweck, E. and Nesbitt, E. (2010b) 'Close encounters? The intersection of faith and ethnicity in mixed-faith families', *Journal of Beliefs and Values*, 31: 39–52.

Arweck, E. and Nesbitt, E. (2010c) 'Plurality at close quarters: mixed faith families in the UK', *Journal of Religions in Europe*, 3: 1–28.

Ashraf, S. A. (1992) 'The religious approach to religious education: the methodology of awakening and disciplining the religious sensibility', in B. Watson (ed.) *Religious Education: A Model for the 1990s and Beyond*, London: Falmer.

Ashton, E. (1992) 'The junior school child: developing the concept of God', in B. Watson (ed.) *Religious Education: A Model for the 1990s and Beyond*, London: Falmer.

Ashton, E. and Watson, B. (1998) 'Values education: a fresh look at procedural neutrality', *Educational Studies*, 24: 183–193.

Ashworth, J. and Farthing, I. (2007) *Churchgoing in the UK*, Teddington: Tearfund.

Askew, S. and Ross, C. (1988) *Boys Don't Cry. Boys and Sexism in Education*, Buckinghamshire: Open University Press.

Association of Community Schools (1992) *Model Lease for Community Schools*, Dublin: Association of Community Schools.

Association of RE Inspectors, Advisors and Consultants (1998) *Towards National Standards in Religious Education*, Bury: AREIAC.

Astley, J. (1992) 'Will the Real Christianity Please Stand Up?', *British Journal of Religious Education*, 15: 4–12.

Astley, J. (2005) 'The science and religion interface within young people's attitudes and beliefs', in L. J. Francis, J. Astley and M. Robbins (eds) *Religion, Education and Adolescence: International Empirical Perspectives*, Cardiff: University of Wales Press.

Astley, J. (2007) 'Crossing the Divide?' in M. Felderhof, P. Thompson and D. Torevell (eds) *Inspiring Faith In Schools: Studies in Religious Education*, Aldershot: Ashgate.

Augustine (2004) *The Literal Meaning of Genesis, Vol. 1* (trans. J. H. Taylor), New York: Paulist Press.

Austin, W. H. (1976) *The Relevance of Natural Science to Theology*, London: Macmillan.

Ayer, A. J. in an interview with Bryan Magee (2008), posted on 17 March 2008 on YouTube. Available online: http://www.youtube.com/watch?v=4cnRJGs08hEandfeat ure=related (accessed 29 June 2010).

Aylett, J. F. (1991) *The Muslim Experience*, London: Hodder and Stoughton.

Backus, J. (2008) 'Developing Programmes of Study', in L. P. Barnes, A. Wright and A-M. Brandom (eds) *Learning to Teach Religious Education in the Secondary School* (2nd ed) London: Routledge.

Badman, G. (2009) *Report to the Secretary of State on the Review of Elective Home Education in England*, London: HMSO.

Baker, K. (1993) *The Turbulent Years: My Life in Politics*, London: Faber and Faber.

Ball, S. (2002) *Class Strategies and the Education Market: The Middle Classes and Social Advantage*, London: RoutledgeFalmer

Banks, C. A. M. *et al* (2005) *Democracy and Diversity: Principles and Concepts for Educating Citizens in a Global Age*, Seattle: Center for Multicultural Education.

Banks, F., Leach, J. and Moon, B. (2005) 'Extract from "New understandings of teachers' pedagogic knowledge"', *The Curriculum Journal*, 16: 331–340.

Barbour, I. G. (2000) *When Science Meets Religion*, London: SPCK.

Barley, L. (2007) 'Introduction', in J. Ashworth and I. Farthing (eds) *Churchgoing in the UK*, Teddington: Tearfund.

Barnes, L. P. (1997) 'Reforming religious education in Northern Ireland: a critical review', *British Journal of Religious Education*, 19: 73–82.

Barnes, L. P. (2000) 'Ninian Smart and the phenomenological approach to religious education', *Religion*, 30: 315–332.

Barnes, L. P. (2001) 'What is wrong with the phenomenological approach to religious education?', *Religious Education*, 96: 445–461.

Barnes, L. P. (2002a) '*Working Paper 36*, Christian confessionalism and phenomenological religious education', *Journal of Education and Christian Belief*, 6: 61–77.

Barnes, L. P. (2002b) 'World religions and the Northern Ireland curriculum', *Journal of Beliefs and Values*, 23: 19–32.

Barnes, L. P. (2002c) 'The representation of religion in education: a critique of John Hull's interpretation of religionism and religious intolerance', *International Journal for Education and Religion*, 3: 97–116.

Barnes, L. P. (2006) 'The misrepresentation of religion in modern British (religious) education', *British Journal of Educational Studies*, 54: 395–411.

Barnes, L. P. (2007a) 'Religious education in Northern Ireland', in E. Kuyk, R. Jensen, D. Lankshear, E. L. Manna and P. Schreiner (eds) *Religious Education in Europe*, Oslo: IKO.

Barnes, L. P. (2007b) 'The disputed legacy of Ninian Smart and phenomenological religious education: a critical response to Kevin O'Grady', *British Journal of Religious Education*, 29: 157–169.

Barnes, L. P. (2007c) 'Religious education and the misrepresentation of religion', in M. Felderhof, P. Thompson and D. Torevell (eds) *Inspiring Faith In Schools: Studies in Religious Education*, Aldershot: Ashgate.

Barnes, L. P. (2008) 'The 2007 Birmingham Agreed Syllabus for Religious Education: a new direction for statutory religious education in England and Wales', *Journal of Beliefs and Values*, 29: 73–81.

Barnes, L. P. (2009a) *Religious Education: Taking Religious Difference Seriously*, London: Philosophy of Education Society of Great Britain.

Barnes, L. P. (2009b) 'An honest appraisal of phenomenological religious education and a final, honest reply to Kevin O'Grady', *British Journal of Religious Education*, 31: 69–72.

Barnes, L. P. (2010) 'Enlightenment's wake: religion and education at the close of the modern age', in G. Durka, E. Engebretson and L. Gearon (eds) *International Handbook of Inter-religious Education*, Philadelphia: Springer.

Barnes, L. P. and Kay, W. K. (2002) *Religious Education in England and Wales: Innovations and Reflections*, Leicester: Religious and Theological Studies Fellowship.

Barnes, L. P. and Wright, A. (2006) 'Romanticism, representations of religion and critical religious education', *British Journal of Religious Education*, 28: 65–77.

Barnes, L. P., Wright, A. and Brandom, A. M. (eds) (2008) *Learning to Teach Religious Education in the Secondary School: A Companion to School Experience* (2nd edn) London: Routledge.

Bartholomew, D. J. (2008) *God, Chance and Purpose: Can God Have It Both Ways?* Cambridge: Cambridge University Press.

Bates, D. (1992) 'Reviews on assessment', *British Journal of Religious Education*, 15: 55–59.

Baumfield, V. (2002a) 'The need for religious education', *British Journal of Religious Education*, 24: 82–83.

Baumfield, V. (2002b) *Thinking through Religious Education*, Cambridge: Chris Kington.

Baumfield, V. (2010) 'Pedagogies of Religious Education for inter-communication and inter-cultural understanding: what are they? Do they work?' in M. Grimmitt (ed.)

Religious Education and Social and Community Cohesion: Challenges and Opportunities, Great Wakering, Essex: McCrimmon.

Baumfield, V., Hall, E. and Wall, K. (2008) *Action Research in the Classroom*, London: Sage.

Bausor, J. and Poole, M. W. (2002) 'Science-and-religion in the agreed syllabuses: an investigation and some suggestions', *British Journal of Religious Education*, 25: 18–32.

Bausor, J. and Poole, M. W. (2003) 'Science education and religious education: possible links?' *School Science Review*, 85: 117–124.

BBC (2009) 'Sarkozy speaks out against burka', 22 June. Available online: http://news. bbc.co.uk/1/hi/world/europe/8112821.stm (accessed 30 June 2010).

Beckerlegge, G. (2002) 'Computer-mediated religion: religion on the Internet at the turn of the twenty-first century', in G. Beckerlegge (ed.) *From Sacred Text to Internet*, Aldershot: Ashgate Publishing, in association with The Open University.

Beetham, H. and Sharpe, R. (2007) *Rethinking Pedagogy for a Digital Age*, London: Routledge.

Believe it or Not (1991) Video Recording, Cassette 3, Birmingham: Central Television.

Berger, P. and Luckmann, T. (1967) *The Social Construction of Reality: A Treatise in the Sociology of Knowledge*, London: Penguin.

Berkeley, R. (2008) *Right to Divide? Faith schools and Community Cohesion*, London: Runnymede Trust.

Bernstein, B. (1971) 'On the classification and framing of educational knowledge', in M. Young (ed.) *Knowledge and Control: New Directions for the Sociology of Education*, London: Routledge.

Beyer, B. K. (2008) 'What research tells us about teaching thinking skills', *Social Studies*, 99: 223–232.

Bickley, P. (2010) 'Darwin dissent: religious education and the problem of origins', *Resource*, 32, 2: 6–9.

Biesta, G. and Lawy, R. (2006) 'From teaching citizenship to learning democracy: overcoming individualism in research, policy and practice', *Cambridge Journal of Education*, 36: 63–79.

Black, P. and Wiliam, D. (1998) *Inside the Black Box: Raising Standards through Classroom Assessment*, London: NFER-Nelson.

Black, P. and Wiliam, D. (2009) 'Developing the theory of formative assessment', *Educational Assessment, Evaluation and Accountability*, 21: 5–13.

Blake, N. (1996) 'Against spiritual education', *Oxford Review of Education*, 22: 443–456.

Blaylock, L. (2001) 'Teaching RE to gifted, talented and exceptionally able pupils', *Resource*, 23, 3: 14–20.

Blaylock, L. (2004) 'Six schools of thought in RE', *Resource*, 2: 13–16

Bloom, B. (ed.) (1956) *Taxonomy of Educational Objectives: The Classification of Educational Goals*, Boston: Allyn and Bacon.

Bolton, P. and Gillie, C. (2009) *Faith Schools: Admissions and Performance,* Standard Note SN/SG/4405, London: House of Commons Library.

Bondi, H. and Gold, T. (1948) 'The steady-state theory of the expanding universe', *Monthly Notices of the Royal Astronomical Society,* 108: 252–270.

Bourdieu, P. (1973) 'Cultural reproduction and social reproduction', in R. Brown (ed.) *Knowledge, Education and Cultural Change*, London: Tavistock.

Braaten, O. M. H. (2010) 'A comparative study of religious education in state schools in England and Norway', unpublished PhD thesis, University of Warwick.

Bradford and Ripon and Leeds Diocesan Education Team (2008) *Every Child of God Matters Everywhere*, Bradford: Bradford and Ripon and Leeds Diocesan Education Team.

Bredin, K. (1998) 'Campaign to Separate Church and State Ltd and Jeremiah Noel Murphy v Minister for Education, the Attorney General, The Most Reverend Cahal Daly, The Most Reverend Desmond Connell, The Most Reverend Dermot Clifford and the Most Reverend Joseph Cassidy: Supreme Court 1996 No. 36', *Irish Law Reports Monthly*, 2: 81–101.

Breen, D. (2009) 'Religious diversity, inter-ethnic relations and the Catholic school: introducing the responsive approach to single faith schooling', *British Journal of Religious Education*, 31: 103–115.

Brighouse, H. (2005) 'Faith-based schools in the United Kingdom', in R. Gardner, J. Cairns and D. Lawton (eds) *Faith schools–Consensus or Conflict?* London: RoutledgeFalmer.

Brighouse, H. (2008) 'Liberal democracy and faith schools', in S. J. McKinney (ed.) *Faith Schools in the Twenty-first Century*, Edinburgh: Dunedin Press.

Bronfenbrenner, U. (1977) 'Towards an experimental ecology of human development', *American Psychologist*, 32: 513–531.

Brooke, J. H. (1991) *Science and Religion: Some Historical Perspectives*, Cambridge: Cambridge University Press.

Brown, A. (2000) 'The Chichester Project: teaching Christianity: a world religions approach', in M. Grimmitt (ed.) *Pedagogies of Religious Education*, Great Wakering, Essex: McCrimmon.

Brown, G. (2007) 'A statement on national security'. Available online: http://news.bbc.co.uk/2/hi/7094620.stm (accessed on 19 October 2010).

Bruner, J. S. (1996) *The Culture of Education*, Cambridge, MA: Harvard University Press.

Bryce, T. G. K. and Humes, W. (eds) (2008) *Scottish Education (3rd edn) Beyond Devolution*, Edinburgh: Edinburgh University Press.

Budd, S. (1977) *Varieties of Unbelief, Atheists and Agnostics in English Society 1850–1960*, London: Heinemann.

Bull, N. J. (1969) *Moral Judgement from Childhood to Adolescence*, London: Routledge and Kegan Paul.

Bunt, G. (2000) *Virtually Islamic: Computer-mediated Communication and Cyber Islamic Environments*, Cardiff: University of Wales Press.

Burnett, D. (1990) *Clash of Worlds*, Eastbourne: Marc.

Burtonwood, N. (2000) 'Must liberal support for separate schools be subject to a condition of individual autonomy?', *British Journal of Educational Studies*, 48: 269–284.

Butler, J. (1990) *Gender Trouble: Feminism and the Subversion of Identity*, London: Routledge.

Butler, R. A. (1973), *The Art of the Possible: The Memoirs of Lord Butler*, Harmondsworth: Penguin.

Byrne, G. and Topley, R. (eds) (2004) *Nurturing Children's Religious Imagination: The Challenge of Primary Religious Education Today*, Dublin: Veritas.

Caldwell, E. (1998) 'A little bit of Israel in Glasgow: opinion', *TES Magazine* (26 June 1998). Available online: http://www.tes.co.uk/article.aspx?storycode=301043 (accessed 16 August 2010).

Callini, S. (ed.) (1995) *J. S. Mill On Liberty and Other Writings*, Cambridge: Cambridge University Press.

Cantle, T. (2001) *Community Cohesion: Report of the Independent Review Team Chaired by Ted Cantle*, London: Home Office.

Capel, S., Leask, M. and Turner, T. (2005) *Learning to Teach in the Secondary School: A Companion to School Experience*, London: RoutledgeFalmer.

Cappleman, S. (2003) *Methods of Differentiation in Religious Education*, Oxford: Farmington Institute.

Carr, D. (1996) 'Rival conceptions of spiritual education', *Journal of Philosophy of Education*, 30: 159–177.

Chadwick, P. (1997) 'The Anglican perspective on church schools', *Oxford Review of Education*, 27, 4: 475–87.

Chadwick, P. (2001) *Shifting Alliances: Church and State in English Education*, London: Cassell.

Chesters, A. (2001) *Distinctive or Divisive? The Role of Church Schools*, Hertford: Hockerill Educational Foundation.

Christodoulou, C. (2005) *Recent ICT Advances in Education and their Application to RE*, Oxford: Farmington Institute.

Church Schools Review Group (2001) *The Way Ahead: Church of England Schools in the New Millennium (the Dearing Report)*, London: Church House Publishing.

City of Birmingham Agreed Syllabus Conference (2007) *The Birmingham Agreed Syllabus for Religious Education*. Available online: http://www.birmingham-asc.org.uk/agreedsyll.php (accessed 21 June 2010).

City of Birmingham (1975) *Living Together: Agreed Syllabus for Religious Education*, Birmingham: City of Birmingham Education Committee.

Clarke, L. (2002), 'Putting the "C" in ICT: using computer conferencing to foster a community of practice among student teachers', *Journal of Information Technology for Teacher Education*, 11: 163–179.

Cline, T. and Shamsi, T. (2000) *Language Needs or Special Needs? The Assessment of Learning Difficulties in Literacy Among Children Learning English as an Additional Language: A Literature Review*, London: DfES.

Coffield, F., Moseley, D., Hall, E. and Ecclestone, K. (2004) *Learning Styles and Pedagogy in Post-16 Learning. A Systematic and Critical Review*, London: Learning and Skills Research Centre.

Collins, F. (2007) *The Language of God*, London: Simon and Schuster.

Collins-Mayo, S. and Dandelion, P. (eds) (2010) *Religion and Youth*, Farnham: Ashgate.

Commission for Racial Equality (CRE) (1990) *Schools of Faith*, London: CRE.

Condie, R. and Munro, B. (2007) *The Impact of ICT in Schools – A Landscape Review*. Available online: http://publications.becta.org.uk/display.cfm?resID=28221 (accessed 23 October 2010).

Connell, R. W. (1995) *Masculinities*, Cambridge: Polity Press.

Constitution of Ireland (2004) *Constitution of Ireland Enacted by the People 1st July, 1937*. Available online: http://www.taoiseach.gov.ie/attached_files/Pdf%20files/Constitution%20of%20Ireland.pdf (accessed 31 January 2011).

Cooling, T. (1994) *Concept Cracking: Exploring Christian Beliefs in School*, Stapleford: The Stapleford Centre.

Cooling, T. (2000) 'The Stapleford Project: theology as a basis for RE', in M. Grimmitt (ed.) *Pedagogies of Religious Education*, Great Wakering, Essex: McCrimmon.

Cooling, T. (2010) *Doing God in Education*, London: Theos.

Copley, T. (1997) *Teaching Religion: Fifty Years of Religious Education in England and Wales*, Exeter: University of Exeter Press.

Copley, T. (2000) *Spiritual Development in the State School: A Perspective on Worship and Spirituality in the Education System of England and Wales*, Exeter: University of Exeter Press.

Copley, T. (2001) 'Children "theologising" in RE: the Joseph story as a case study in three religions and competing cultures', *Education Today*, 51: 3–7.

Copley, T. (2005) *Indoctrination, Education and God*, London: SPCK.

Copley, T. (2008) *Teaching Religion: Sixty Years of Religious Education in England and Wales*, Exeter: University of Exeter Press.

Coster, C. (2000) *Is There a Role for the Internet in Teaching RE?* Oxford: Farmington Institute.

Council of Europe (2008a) 'Recommendation CM/Rec (2008): 12 of the Committee of Ministers to member states on the dimension of religions and non-religious convictions within intercultural education', Strasbourg: Council of Europe Publishing. Available online: https://wcd.coe.int//ViewDoc.jsp?Ref=CM/Rec(2008)12andLanguage=lan

EnglishandVer=originalandBackColorInternet=DBDCF2andBackColorIntranet=FDC 864andBackColorLogged=FDC864 (accessed 10 July 2010).

Council of Europe (2008b) *White Paper on Intercultural Dialogue: 'Living Together as Equals with Dignity'*, Strasbourg: Council of Europe Publishing.

Cox, E. (1967) *Sixth Form Religion*, London: SCM.

Crossan, J. D. (1991) *The Historical Jesus: the Life of a Mediterranean Jewish Peasant*, San Francisco: Harper.

Croydon (2001) *Croydon Agreed Syllabus*, London Borough of Croydon. Available online: http://www.croydon.gov.uk/education/resources/religiouseducation/ (accessed 27 September 2010).

Crozier, S. and Joseph, S. (1997) 'Religiosity and sphere-specific just world beliefs in 16- to 18-year olds', *Journal of Social Psychology*, 137: 510–513.

Cruickshank, M. (1963) *The Church and State in English Education*, London: Macmillan.

Culham College Institute (1998) *Collective Worship Reviewed*, Abingdon: Culham College Institute). Available online: http://www.culham.ac.uk/Res_conf/cw_reviewed/index.html (accessed 23 October 2010).

Curtis, P. (2009) 'Labour policies unconvincing, says poll', *Guardian*, 2 March.

Curtis, S. J. (1961) *History of Education in Great Britain*, London: University Tutorial Press.

Cush, D. and Francis, D. (2001) 'Positive pluralism to awareness, mystery and value: a case study in religious education curriculum development', *British Journal of Religious Education*, 24: 52–67.

Daily Mail (2010) 'Wrong sort of text: children of seven more likely to own a mobile phone than a book', 28 May. Available online: http://www.dailymail.co.uk/news/article-1281978/Children-seven-years-old-likely-mobile-phone-book.html (accessed 4 August 2010).

Davie, G. (1994) *Religion in Britain since 1945: Believing without Belonging*, Oxford: Blackwell.

Davis, R. A. (2008) 'Futures of faith schools', in S. J. McKinney (ed.) *Faith Schools in the 21ˢᵗ Century*, Edinburgh: Dunedin Press.

Dawkins, R. (1988) *The Blind Watchmaker*, London: Penguin.

Dawkins, R. (2002a) 'Religion's real child abuse', *Free Inquiry*, 22, 4: 9–12.

Dawkins, R. (2002b) 'A scientist's view', *Guardian*, 9 March.

Dawkins, R. (2006) *The God Delusion*, London: Bantam Press.

Dawkins, R. (2008) *The God Delusion*, New York: Houghton Mifflin (American edition).

Dawkins, R. (2009) in 'God and the Scientists', *Christianity – A History*, Episode 7, Channel 4; broadcast on 22 February 2010.

Debray, R. (2002) *L'Enseignement du fait religieux dans l'école laïque*, Paris: Editions Odile Jacob.

DCELLS (Department for Children, Education, Lifelong Learning and Skills) (2008) *National Exemplar Framework for Religious Education for 3 to 19-year-olds in Wales: Guidance for local education authorities and agreed syllabus conferences*, Cardiff: DCELLS.

DCSF (Department for Children, Schools and Families) (2007a) *Faith in the System: The Role of Schools with a Religious Character in English Education and Society*, Nottingham: DCSF Publications.

DCSF (Department for Children, Schools and Families) (2007b) *Guidance on the Duty to Promote Community Cohesion*, Nottingham: DSCF Publications.

DCSF (Department for Children, Schools and Families) (2007c) *Guidance on the Place of Creationism and Intelligent Design in Science Lessons*, London: Teachernet. Available online: http://www.teachernet.gov.uk/docbank/index.cfm?id=11890 (accessed 23 October 2010).

DCSF (Department for Children, Schools and Families) (2009) *Religious Education in English Schools: Non-statutory Guidance 2009*, Nottingham: DCSF Publications.

DCSF (Department for Children, Schools and Families) (2010) *Religious Education in English Schools: Non-statutory Guidance 2010*, Nottingham: DCSF Publications.

DfE (Department for Education) (1994) *Circular 1/94: Religious Education and Collective Worship*, London: DfE Publications Centre.

DfES (Department for Education and Science) (1985) *Education for All: Final Report of the Committee of Enquiry into the Education of Children from Ethnic Minority Groups, Under the Chairmanship of Lord Swann*, London: HMSO.

DfES (Department for Education and Science) (1989) *The Education Reform Act 1988: Religious Education and Collective Worship (Circular 3/89)*, London: HMSO.

DfES (Department for Education and Science) (2000) *Junior Certificate: Religious Education Syllabus: Ordinary and Higher Level*, Dublin: The Stationery Office.

(DfES) Department for Education and Skills (2001) *Schools Achieving Success*, London: The Stationery Office.

(DfES) Department for Education and Skills (2006a) *2020 Vision: Report of the Teaching and Learning in 2020 Review Group*, London: DfES.

(DfES) Department for Education and Skills (2006b) *Ethnicity and Education: The Evidence on Minority Ethnic Pupils Aged 5–16*, London: DfES. Available online: http://publications.teachernet.gov.uk/eOrderingDownload/DFES 0208 2006.pdf (accessed 4 June 2010).

Department of Education (1979) *Circular letter No. 7/79: Religious Instruction in Vocational Schools*, Dublin: Department of Education.

Department of Education and Science (2000) *Junior Certificate: Religious Education Syllabus: Ordinary and Higher Level*, Dublin: The Stationery Office.

Department of Education for Northern Ireland (DENI) (2007) *Policy Paper 2: Sectoral Support Post RPA*. Available online: http://www.deni.gov.uk/policy_paper_21_sectoral_support_post_rpa.53_kb_.pdf (accessed 27 January 2011).

Derrida, J. (1982) *Margins of Philosophy*, Chicago: University of Chicago Press.

Dewey, J. (1933) *How We Think*, Boston: Heath and Company.

Dewey, J. (1956) *The Child and the Curriculum; and the School and Society*, London: University of Chicago Press.

Dewey, J. (1966) *Democracy and Education*, New York: Macmillan.

Diduca, D. and Joseph, S. (1997) 'Schizotypal traits and dimensions of religiosity', *British Journal of Clinical Psychology*, 36: 635–638.

Donaldson, M. (1978) *Children's Minds*, London: Fontana.

Donley, M. (1992) 'Teaching discernment', in B. Watson (ed.) *Priorities in Religious Education*, London: Falmer Press.

Donnelly, C. (2000) 'In pursuit of school ethos', *British Journal of Educational Studies*, 48: 134–154.

Draycott, P. (2006) *Assessed RE: Engaging with Secondary RE*, Birmingham: RE Today.

Durkheim, E. (1912) *Les Formes Elémentaires de la Vie Religieuse*, Paris: Alcan.

Eaude, T. (2005) 'Strangely familiar? – teachers making sense of young children's spiritual development', *Early Years*, 25: 237–248.

Eaude, T. (2008a) 'Should religious educators be wary of values education?' *Journal of Religious Education*, 56: 57–65.

Eaude, T. (2008b) *Children's Spiritual, Moral, Social and Cultural Development – Primary and Early Years*, Exeter: Learning Matters.

Eckert, R. M. and Lester, D. (1997) 'Altruism and religiosity', *Psychological Reports*, 81: 562.

Eisner, E. (1985) *The Educational Imagination*, 2nd edn, New York: Macmillan.

Ekklesia (2006) *Statement on Religious Education Opens Church Schools up to Accusation of Double Standards* (22 February). Available online: http://www.ekklesia.co.uk/content/news_syndication/article_060222faithschools.shtml (accessed 21 June 2010).

Emerson-Moering, A. (2007) *Another Brick in the Wall? QCA's Non-Statutory National Framework for Religious Education and its Philosophical Underpinnings*, Oxford: Farmington Institute for Christian Studies.

Engebreston, K. (2007) *Connecting: Teenage Boys, Spirituality and Religious Education*, Homebush: St Paul's Publications.

Eriksen, L. L. (2010) 'Learning to be Norwegian: a case study of identity management in religious education in Norway', unpublished PhD thesis, University of Warwick.

Erricker, C. (1998). 'Journeys through the heart: the effect of death, loss and conflict on children's worldviews', *Journal of Beliefs and Values*, 19: 107–118.

Erricker, C. (2000) 'A critical review of spiritual education', in C. Erricker and J. Erricker (2000) *Reconstructing Religious, Spiritual and Moral Education*, London: RoutledgeFalmer.

Erricker, C. (2010) *Religious Education: A Conceptual and Interdisciplinary Approach for Secondary Level*, London: Routledge.

Erricker, C. and Erricker, J. (1996) 'Where angels fear to tread: discovering children's spirituality', in R. Best (ed.) *Education, Spirituality and the Whole Child*, London: Cassell.

Erricker, C. and Erricker J. (2000a) 'The Children and Worldviews Project: a narrative pedagogy of religious education', in M. Grimmitt (ed.) *Pedagogies of Religious Education*, Great Wakering, Essex: McCrimmon.

Erricker, C. and Erricker, J. (2000b) *Reconstructing Religious, Spiritual and Moral Education*, London: RoutledgeFalmer

Erricker, C., Erricker, J., Ota, C., Sullivan, D. and Fletcher, M. (1997) *The Education of the Whole Child*, London: Cassell.

Erricker, J. and Erricker, C. (1995) 'Children speaking their minds', *Panorama*, 7: 96–109.

Evangelical Alliance (n.d.) *2005 Church Census*. Available online: http://www.eauk.org/resources/info/statistics/2005englishchurchcensus.cfm (accessed 28 January 2011).

Eysenck, H. (1971) *Race, Intelligence and Education*, London: Temple Smith.

Fancourt, N. (2003) 'Whole class strategies in religious education', *Support for Learning*, 18: 112–116.

Fancourt, N. (2010) 'I'm less intolerant: reflexive self-assessment in religious education', *British Journal of Religious Education*, 32: 291–305.

Felderhof, M. (2004) 'The new national framework for RE in England and Wales: a critique', *Journal of Beliefs and Values*, 25: 241–248.

Felderhof, M. (2005) 'RE: religions, equality and curriculum time', *Journal of Beliefs and Values*, 26: 210–214.

Felderhof, M. (2007) 'Religious education, atheism and deception', in M. Felderhof, P. Thompson and D. Torevell (eds) *Inspiring Faith in Schools: Studies in Religious Education*, Aldershot: Ashgate.

Felderhof, M., Thompson, P. and Torevell, D. (eds) (2007) *Inspiring Faith in Schools: Studies in Religious Education*, Aldershot: Ashgate.

Ferguson, D. (2009) *Faith and its Critics: A Conversation*, Oxford: Oxford University Press.

Feuerstein, R., Feuerstein, Y., Hoffman, M. and Miller, M. (1985) *Instrumental Enrichment: An Intervention Programme For Cognitive Modifiability*, Baltimore, MD: University Park Press.

Fisher, J. W. (2001) 'Comparing levels of spiritual well-being in State, Catholic and Independent schools in Victoria, Australia', *Journal of Beliefs and Values*, 22: 99–105.

Fisher, J. W. (2004) 'Feeling good, living life: a spiritual health measure for young children', *Journal of Beliefs and Values*, 25: 307–315.

Fitzpatrick, T. A. (1986) *Catholic Secondary Education in South-West Scotland before 1972*, Aberdeen: Aberdeen University Press.

Fleming, N. and Mills, C. (1992) 'Not another inventory, rather a catalyst for reflection', *To Improve the Academy*, 11: 137–155.

Francis, B. (2000) 'The gendered subject: students' subject preferences and discussions of gender and subject ability', *Oxford Review of Education*, 26: 35–48.

Francis, B. and Skelton, C. (2001) *Investigating Gender: Contemporary Perspectives in Education*, Buckinghamshire: Open University Press.

Francis, B. and Skelton, C. (2005) *Reassessing Gender and Achievement: Questioning Contemporary Key Debates*, London: Routledge.

Francis, L. J. (1978) 'Measurement reapplied: research into the child's attitude towards religion', *British Journal of Religious Education*, 1: 45–51.

Francis, L. J. (1979) 'The child's attitude towards religion: a review of research', *Educational Research*, 21: 103–108.

Francis, L. J. (1987) *Religion in the Primary School: partnership between Church and State?* London: Collins Liturgical Publications.

Francis, L. J. (1989a) 'Measuring attitude towards Christianity during childhood and adolescence', *Personality and Individual Differences*, 10: 695–698.

Francis, L. J. (1989b) 'Drift from the churches: secondary school pupils' attitudes toward Christianity', *British Journal of Religious Education*, 11: 76–86.

Francis, L. J. (1992a) 'Monitoring attitudes toward Christianity: the 1990 study', *British Journal of Religious Education*, 14: 178–182.

Francis, L. J. (1992b) 'Is psychoticism really a dimension of personality fundamental to religiosity?' *Personality and Individual Differences*, 13: 645–652.

Francis, L. J. (1993) 'Attitudes towards Christianity during childhood and adolescence: assembling the jigsaw', *The Journal of Beliefs and Values*, 14: 4–6.

Francis, L. J. (1998) 'The relationship between intelligence and religiosity among 15- to 16-year olds', *Mental Health, Religion and Culture*, 1: 185–196.

Francis, L. J. (2000a) 'Who reads the bible? A study among 13–15 year olds', *British Journal of Religious Education*, 22: 165–172.

Francis, L. J. (2000b) 'The relationship between bible reading and purpose in life among 13–15 year olds', *Mental Health, Religion and Culture*, 3: 27–36.

Francis, L. J. (2001a) *The Values Debate: A Voice from the Pupils*, London: Woburn Press.

Francis, L. J. (2001b) 'Religion and values: A quantitative perspective', in L. J. Francis, J. Astley and M. Robbins (eds) *The Fourth R for the Third Millennium: Education in Religion and Values for the Global Future*, Dublin: Lindisfarne Books.

Francis, L. J. (2001c) 'The social significance of religious affiliation among adolescents in England and Wales', in H.-G. Ziebertz (ed.) *Religious Individualisation and Christian Religious Semantics*, Münster: Lit Verlag.

Francis, L. J. (2001d) 'God images, personal wellbeing and moral values: a survey among 13–15 year olds in England and Wales', in H.-G. Ziebertz (ed.) *Imagining God: Empirical Explorations from an International Perspective*, Münster: Lit Verlag.

Francis, L. J. (2002a) 'Catholic schools and Catholic values: a study of moral and religious values among 13–15 year old pupils attending non-denominational and Catholic schools in England and Wales', *International Journal of Education and Religion*, 3: 69–84.

Francis, L. J. (2002b) 'The relationship between bible reading and attitude toward substance use among 13–15 year olds', *Religious Education*, 97: 44–60.

Francis, L. J. (2004) 'Empirical theology and hermeneutical religious education: a case study concerning adolescent attitudes toward abortion', in H. Lombaerts and D. Pollefeyt (eds) *Hermeneutics and Religious Education*, Leuven: Peeters.

Francis, L. J. (2005a) 'Independent Christians schools and pupil values: an empirical investigation among 13- to 15-year-old boys', *British Journal of Religious Education*, 27: 127–141.

Francis, L. J. (2005b) 'Prayer, personality and purpose in life among churchgoing and non-churchgoing adolescents', in L. J. Francis, M. Robbins and J. Astley (eds) *Religion, Education and Adolescence: International Empirical Perspectives*, Cardiff: University of Wales Press.

Francis, L. J. (2008a) 'Family, denomination and the adolescent worldview: an empirical enquiry among 13- to 15-year-old females in England and Wales', *Marriage and Family Review*, 43: 185–204.

Francis, L. J. (2008b) 'Self-assigned religious affiliation: a study among adolescents in England and Wales', in B. Spalek and A. Imtoual (eds) *Religion, Spirituality and the Social Sciences: Challenging Marginalisation*, Bristol: Policy Press.

Francis, L. J. (2009) 'Understanding the attitudinal dimensions of religion and spirituality', in M. De Souza, L. J. Francis, J. O'Higgins-Norman and D. G. Scott (eds) *International Handbook of Education for Spirituality, Care and Wellbeing*, Dordrecht: Springer.

Francis, L. J. and Carter, M. (1980) 'Church aided secondary schools, religious education as an examination subject and pupil attitudes towards religion', *British Journal of Educational Psychology*, 50: 297–300.

Francis, L. J. and Gibson, H. M. (1992) 'Popular religious television and adolescent attitudes towards Christianity', in J. Astley and D. V. Day (eds) *The Contours of Christian Education*, Great Wakering, Essex: McCrimmons.

Francis, L. J. and Gibson, H. M. (1993a) 'Parental influence and adolescent religiosity: a study of church attendance and attitude toward Christianity among adolescents 11 to 12 and 15 to 16 years old', *International Journal for the Psychology of Religion*, 3: 241–253.

Francis, L. J. and Gibson, H. M. (1993b) 'Television, pop culture and the drift from Christianity during adolescence', *British Journal of Religious Education*, 15: 31–37.

Francis, L. J. and Greer, J. E. (1990a) 'Measuring attitudes towards Christianity among pupils in Protestant secondary schools in Northern Ireland', *Personality and Individual Differences*, 11: 853–856.

Francis, L. J. and Greer, J. E. (1990b) 'Catholic schools and adolescent religiosity in Northern Ireland: shaping moral values', *Irish Journal of Education*, 24: 40–47.

Francis, L. J. and Hermans, C. A. M. (2000) 'Internal consistency reliability and construct validity of the Dutch translation of the Francis scale of Attitude toward Christianity among adolescents', *Psychological Reports*, 86: 301–307.

Francis, L. J. and Katz, Y. J. (2007) 'Measuring attitude toward Judaism: the internal consistency reliability of the Katz-Francis Scale of Attitude toward Judaism', *Mental Health, Religion and Culture*, 10: 309–324.

Francis, L. J. and Pearson, P. R. (1985) 'Extraversion and religiosity', *Journal of Social Psychology*, 125: 269–270.

Francis, L. J. and Pearson, P. R. (1991) 'Religiosity, gender and the two faces of neuroticism', *Irish Journal of Psychology*, 12: 60–68.

Francis, L. J. and Robbins, M. (2004) 'Belonging without believing: a study in the social significance of Anglican identity and implicit religion among 13–15 year old males', *Implicit Religion*, 7: 37–54.

Francis, L. J. and Robbins, M. (2005) *Urban Hope and Spiritual Health: The Adolescent Voice*, Peterborough: Epworth.

Francis, L. J. and Robbins, M. (2006) 'Prayer, purpose in life, personality and social attitudes among non-churchgoing 13- to 15-year-olds in England and Wales', *Research in the Social Scientific Study of Religion*, 17: 123–155.

Francis, L. J. and Wilcox, C. (1998) 'Religiosity and femininity: do women really hold a more positive attitude toward Christianity?', *Journal for the Scientific Study of Religion*, 37: 462–469.

Francis, L.J. and Ziebertz, H.-G. (eds) (in press) *The Public Significance of Religion*, Leiden, Boston: Brill

Francis, L. J., ap Siôn, T., Lewis, C. A., Robbins, M. and Barnes, L. P. (2006) 'Attitude toward Christianity and religious experience: replication among 16- to 18-year-old adolescents in Northern Ireland', *Research in Education*, 76: 56–61.

Francis, L. J., Fulljames, P. and Gibson, H. M. (1992) 'Does creationism commend the gospel? A developmental study among 11–17 year olds', *Religious Education*, 87: 19–27.

Francis, L. J., Kay, W. K. and Campbell, W. S. (eds) (1996) *Research in Religious Education*, Leominster: Gracewing.

Francis, L. J., Lewis, C. A. and Ng, P. (2002) 'Assessing attitude toward Christianity among adolescents in Hong Kong: the Francis scale', *North American Journal of Psychology*, 4: 431–440.

Francis, L. J., Robbins, M. and Astley, J. (eds) (2005) *Religion, Education and Adolescence: International Empirical Perspectives*, Cardiff: University of Wales Press.

Francis, L. J., Robbins, M., ap Siôn, T., Lewis, C. A. and Barnes, L. P. (2007) 'Psychological health and attitude toward Christianity among Protestant and Catholic sixth-form pupils in Northern Ireland', *Pastoral Psychology*, 56: 157–164.

Francis, L. J., Robbins, M., Barnes L. P. and Lewis, C. A. (2006a) 'Sixth-form religion in Northern Ireland: the Protestant profile 1968–1998', *British Journal of Religious Education*, 28: 3–18.

Francis, L. J., Robbins, M., Barnes, L. P. and Lewis, C. A. (2006b) 'Religiously affiliated schools in Northern Ireland: the persistence of denominational differences in pupils' religious and moral values', *Journal of Empirical Theology*, 19: 182–202.

Francis, L. J., Robbins, M., Lewis, C. A., Barnes L. P. and ap Siôn, T. (2007) 'Attitude toward Christianity among secondary school pupils in Northern Ireland: shifts in denominational differences', *Educational Research*, 49: 431–436.

Francis, L. J., Santosh, R., Robbins, M. and Vij, S. (2008) 'Assessing attitude toward Hinduism: the Santosh-Francis Scale', *Mental Health, Religion and Culture*, 11: 609–621.

Francis, L. J., Ziebertz, H.-G. and Lewis, C. A. (2002) 'The psychometric properties of the Francis Scale of Attitude toward Christianity among German students', *Panorama*, 14: 153–162.

Freathy, R. (2004) 'Religious education and education for citizenship: religious traditionalism versus secular progressivism', unpublished PhD thesis, University of Exeter.

Friesen, J. W. (1999) 'Christian schools in a pluralistic society: a reply', *Interchange*, 30: 235–240.

Fullan, M. (2005) *Leadership and Sustainability: System Thinkers in Action*, California: Corwen Press and Ontario Principals' Council.

Fulljames, P. (1996) 'Science, creation and Christianity: a further look', in L. J. Francis, W. K. Kay and W. S. Campbell (eds) *Research in Religious Education*, Leominster: Gracewing.

Fulljames, P., Gibson, H. M. and Francis, L. J. (1991). 'Creationism, scientism, Christianity and science: a study in adolescent attitudes', *British Educational Research Journal*, 17: 171–190.

Furedi, F. (2009) *Wasted: Why Education Isn't Educating*, London: Continuum.

Gadamer, H-G. (2004) *Truth and Method*, London: Continuum.

Gallup (2009) *Gallup Coexist Index 2009: A Global Study of Interfaith Relations with an In-depth Analysis of Muslim Integration in France, Germany, and the United Kingdom*, Washington: Gallup.

Gamoran, A. (2002) 'Standards, inequality and ability grouping in schools', CES Paper 25. Online. Available online: http://www.ces.ed.ac.uk/PDF%20Files/Brief025.pdf (accessed 6 June 2010).

Gardner, H. (1983) *Frames of Mind: The Theory of Multiple Intelligences*, New York: Basic Books.

Gardner, R., Cairns, J. and Lawton, D. (eds) (2005) *Faith schools – Consensus or Conflict?* London: RoutledgeFalmer.

Gates, B. (1976) *Religion in the Developing World of Children and Young People*, unpublished PhD thesis, University of Lancaster.

Gates, B. (2007) 'Religious education and change', *Resource*, 29, 3: 4–8.

Gateshill, P. and Thompson, J. (1992) *Religious Artefacts in the Classroom*, London: Hodder and Stoughton.

Gearon, L. (2002) 'Human rights and religious education: some post-colonial perspectives', *British Journal of Religious Education*, 24: 140–151.

Gearon, L. (2004) *Citizenship through Secondary Religious Education*, London: Routledge Falmer.

Gearon, L. and Brown, M. (2003) 'Active participation in citizenship', in L. Gearon (ed.) *Learning to Teach Citizenship in the Secondary School*, London: Routledge.

Geaves, R. (1998) 'The borders between religions: a challenge to the world religions approach to religious education', *British Journal of Religious Education*, 21: 20–31.

Geertz, C. (1983) *Local Knowledge*, New York: Basic Books.

General Assembly of the Presbyterian Church in Ireland (2008) *Maintain Church Interest in Schools Maintained Sector*. Available online: http://www.presbyterianireland.org (accessed 22 October 2008).

General Teaching Council for England (GTC) (2009) *Revised Code of Conduct and Practice for Registered Teachers, 1 July 2009*. Available online: http://www.gtce.org.uk/teachers/thecode (accessed 28 December 2009).

Gibson, H. M., Francis, L. J. and Pearson, P. R. (1990) 'The relationship between social class and attitude towards Christianity among fourteen- and fifteen-year-old adolescents', *Personality and Individual Differences*, 11: 631–635.

Gillbourn, D. and Youdell, D. (2001) *Rationing Education: Policy, Practice, Reform and Equity*, Buckingham: Open University Press.

Giles, C. (2006) 'Reflections from classroom and community', in *Faith, Identity and Belonging: Educating for Shared Citizenship*, London: Inter-faith Network for UK.

Gillings, V. and Joseph, S. (1996) 'Religiosity and social desirability: impression management and self-deceptive positivity', *Personality and Individual Differences*, 21: 1047–1050.

Gledhill, R. (2004) 'I attend first service of a church that casts its net in cyber sea', *The Times*, 12 May.

Glevey, K. E. (2008) 'Thinking skills in England's National Curriculum', *Improving Schools*, 11: 115–125.

Glock, C. Y. and Stark, R. (1965) *Religion and Society in Tension*, Chicago: Bland McNally.

Goldman, R. (1964) *Religious Thinking from Childhood to Adolescence*, London: Routledge and Kegan Paul.

Goldman, R. (1965) *Readiness for Religion*, London: Routledge and Kegan Paul.

Gould, S. (1983) *The Mismeasure of Man*, New York: Norton.

Gould, S. (1996) *The Mismeasure of Man* (2nd edn) New York: Norton.

Gove, Rt Hon M. (2010) *Open letter to Rt Hon Ed Balls MP, 7 July*. Available online: http://leavingcare.org/data/tmp/6082-12855.pdf (accessed 12 July 2010).

Government of Ireland (1937/1990) *Bunreacht na hÉireann/Constitution of Ireland*, Dublin: The Stationery Office.

Government of Ireland (1998) *Education Act* (Irish Statute Book). Available online: http://www.irishstatutebook.ie/1998/en/act/pub/0051/index.html (accessed 27 January 2011).

Grayling, A. C. (2006) *The Form of Things: Essays on Life, Ideas and Liberty in the 21ˢᵗ Century*, London: Weidenfeld & Nicolson.

Grayling, A. C. (2007a) 'Onward Christian teachers', *Guardian*, 12 November.

Grayling, A. C. (2007b) 'Philosophy and Public Understanding', in Baggini, J. and Stangroom, J. (eds) *What More Philosophers Think*, London: Continuum.

Greer, J. E. (1972a) *A Questioning Generation*, Belfast: Church of Ireland Board of Education.

Greer, J. E. (1972b) 'The child's understanding of creation', *Educational Review*, 24: 94–110.

Greer, J. E. (1980) 'The persistence of religion: a study of adolescents in Northern Ireland', *Character Potential*, 9: 139–149.

Greer, J. E. (1982) 'A comparison of two attitude to religion scales', *Educational Research*, 24: 226–227.

Greer, J. E. (1983a) 'A critical study of "Thinking about the Bible"', *British Journal of Religious Education*, 5: 113–125.

Greer, J. E. (1983b) 'Attitude to religion reconsidered', *British Journal of Educational Studies*, 31: 18–28.

Greer, J. E. (1989) 'The persistence of religion in Northern Ireland: a study of sixth form religion, 1968–1988', *Collected Original Resources in Education*, 13, 2: fiche 20, G9.

Greer, J. E. and Francis, L. J. (1992) 'Religious experience and attitude toward Christianity among secondary school children in Northern Ireland', *Journal of Social Psychology*, 132: 277–279.

Grimmitt, M. (1973 and 1978, 2nd edn) *What Can I Do in RE?* Great Wakering, Essex: Mayhew-McCrimmon.

Grimmitt, M. (1981) 'When is commitment a problem in religious education?' *British Journal of Educational Studies*, 29: 42–53.

Grimmitt, M. (1987) *Religious Education and Human Development*, Great Wakering, Essex: McCrimmons.

Grimmitt, M. (1991) 'The use of religious phenomena in schools: some theoretical and practical considerations', *British Journal of Religious Education*, 13: 77–88.

Grimmitt, M. (2000a) 'Constructivist pedagogies of religious education project: re-thinking knowledge, teaching and learning in religious education', in M. Grimmitt (ed.) *Pedagogies of Religious Education*, Great Wakering, Essex: McCrimmons.

Grimmitt, M. (ed.) (2000b) *Pedagogies of Religious Education*, Great Wakering, Essex: McCrimmons.

Grimmitt, M. (2000c) 'The captivity and liberation of religious education and the meaning and significance of pedagogy' in M. Grimmitt (ed.) *Pedagogies of Religious Education*, Great Wakering, Essex: McCrimmons.

Grimmitt, M. (2000d) 'Contemporary pedagogies of religious education: what are they?', in M. Grimmitt (ed.) *Pedagogies of Religious Education*, Great Wakering, Essex: McCrimmons.

Grimmitt, M., Grove, J., Hull, J. and Spencer, L. (1991) *A Gift to the Child: Religious Education in the Primary School: Teachers' Sourcebook*, London: Simon and Schuster.

Grimmitt, M. H. and Read, G. T. (1977) *Teaching Christianity in RE*, Leigh on Sea, Essex: Kevin Mayhew.

Gurian, M. (2002) *Boys and Girls Learn Differently!* San Francisco: Jossey Bass.

Gutmann, A. (1987) *Democratic Education,* Princeton, NJ: Princeton University Press.

Haldane, J. (1986) 'Religious education in a pluralist society', *British Journal of Educational Studies,* 31: 161–181.

Haldane, J. (2010) *Reasonable Faith,* London: Routledge.

Halliday, F. (1999) 'Islamophobia reconsidered', *Ethnic and Racial Studies,* 22: 893–902.

Halman, L. (2001) *The European Values Study: A Third Wave,* Tilburg: Tilburg University.

Halstead, J. M. (1986) *The Case for Muslim voluntary-aided Schools: Some Philosophical Reflections,* Cambridge: Islamic Academy.

Halstead, J. M. (1995) 'Voluntary apartheid? Problems of schooling for religious and other minorities in democratic societies', *Journal of Philosophy of Education,* 29: 257–272.

Halstead, J. M. (2002) 'Faith and diversity in religious school provision', in L. Gearon (ed.) *Education in the United Kingdom: Structures and Organisation,* London: David Fulton.

Halstead, J. M. (2007) 'Islamic values: a distinctive framework for moral education?', *Journal of Moral Education,* 36: 283–286.

Halstead, J. M. and Pike, M. A. (2006) *Citizenship and moral education – Values in Action,* London: Routledge.

Hammersley, M. (2001) 'Obvious, all too obvious? Methodological issues in using sex/gender as a variable in education research', in B. Francis and C. Skelton (eds) *Investigating Gender: Contemporary Perspectives in Education,* Buckinghamshire: Open University Press.

Hammond, J. *et al* (1990) *New Methods in RE Teaching: An Experiential Approach,* Harlow: Oliver & Boyd.

Hampshire County Council/ Portsmouth City Council/Southampton City Council (2004) *Living Difference: The Agreed Syllabus for Hampshire, Portsmouth and Southampton,* Hampshire: Hampshire County Council.

Hand, M. (2006) 'Against autonomy as an educational aim', *Oxford Review of Education,* 32: 535–550.

Hanlon, D. (2002) 'Not "either-or", more a case of "both-and": towards an inclusive gender strategy for religious education', in L. Broadbent and A. Brown (eds) *Issues in Religious Education,* London: RoutledgeFalmer.

Haralambos, M. and Holborn, M. (2004) *Sociology: Themes and Perspectives* (6th edn) London: Collins.

Hargreaves, D. (1994) *The Mosaic of Learning: Schools and Teachers for the New Century,* Demos Paper 8, London: Demos.

Harris, F. (2002) 'Do we really want more faith schools?', *Education Review,* 15: 32–36.

Harris, J. (2005) 'Our agenda for technology integration: it's time to choose', *Contemporary Issues in Technology and Teacher Education* (Online serial), 5. 2. Available online: http://www.citejournal.org/vol5/iss2/editorial/article1.cfm (accessed 2 April 2008).

Harrison, A. (2009) 'Faith schools "good on cohesion"', *BBC News/Education.* Available online: http://news.bbc.co.uk/1/low/education/8381090.stm (accessed 20 September 2010).

Harrison, M. (1998) *The Enhancement and Development of Learning Opportunities in RE using IT,* Oxford: Farmington Institute.

Harrison, P. (2008) *Christianity and the Rise of Western Science,* Farmington Paper, Oxford: Farmington Institute for Christian Studies.

Hartshorn, B. (2008) 'Religious and moral education', in T. G. K. Bryce and W. Humes (eds) *Scottish Education (3rd edn) Beyond Devolution,* Edinburgh: Edinburgh University Press.

Hattie, J., Biggs, J. and Purdie, N. (1996) 'Effects of the learning skills interventions on student learning: a meta-analysis', *Review of Educational Research,* 66: 99–136.

Hay, D. (1985) 'Suspicion of the spiritual: teaching religion in a world of secular experience', *British Journal of Religious Education*, 7: 140–147.

Hay, D. (2001) 'Spirituality versus individualism: the challenge of relational consciousness', in J. Erricker, C. Ota and C. Erricker (eds) *Spiritual Education – Cultural, Religious and Social Differences*, Brighton: Sussex Academic Press.

Hay, D. (2006) *Something There – The Biology of the Human Spirit*, London: Darton, Longman and Todd.

Hay, D. and Hammond, J. (1992) 'Response: when you pray, go to your private room', *British Journal of Religious Education*, 14: 145–150.

Hay, D. with Nye, R. (1998) *The Spirit of the Child*, London: Fount.

Haydon, G. (ed.) (2009) *Faith in Education*, London: University of London Institute of Education.

Hayward, G. and Fernandez, R. M. (2004) 'From core skills to key skills: fast forward or back to the future?' *Oxford Review of Education*, 30: 117–145.

Hayward, M. (2006) 'Curriculum Christianity', *British Journal of Religious Education*, 28: 153–171.

Heimbrock, H.-G., Schreiner, P. and Sheilke, C. (eds) (2001) *Towards Religious Competence: Diversity as a Challenge for Education in Europe*, Hamburg: Lit Verlag.

Hella, E. (2008) 'Variation in Finnish students' understanding of Lutheranism and its implications for religious education, a phenomenographic study', *British Journal of Religious Education*, 30: 245–257.

Hella, E. and Wright, A. (2009) 'Learning "about" and learning "from" religion: phenomenography, the variation theory of learning and religious education in Finland and the UK', *British Journal of Religious Education*, 31: 53–64.

Hick, J. (2004) *The Real and Its Personae and Impersonae,* revised version of an article first published in L. Tessier (ed.) *Concepts of the Ultimate*, London: Macmillan, 1989. Available online: http://www.johnhick.org.uk (accessed 23 October 2010).

Higgins, S. (2008) *Does ICT Improve Teaching and Learning in Schools? Review for BREA*, Cheshire: British Educational Research Association.

Higgins, S. and Baumfield, V. (1998) 'A defence of teaching general thinking skills', *Journal of Philosophy of Education*, 32: 391–398.

Hillgate Group (1987) *The Reform of British Education*, London: Hillgate Group.

Hirst, P. (1972) 'Christian education: a contradiction in terms?' *Learning for Living*, 11, 4: 6–11.

Hirst, P. (1974) *Moral Education in a Secular Society*, London: University of London Press.

Hirst, P. (1981) 'Education, catechesis and the church school', *British Journal of Religious Education*, 3: 85–93.

Hoffman, B. (1972) *Albert Einstein: Creator and Rebel*, New York: Viking.

Hogan, P. and Williams, K. (eds) (1997) *The Future of Religion in Irish Education*, Dublin: Veritas.

Homan, R. (2000) 'Don't let the murti get dirty: the uses and abuses of religious "artefacts" in the classroom', *British Journal of Religious Education*, 23: 27–37.

Homan, R. (2004) 'Religion and literacy: observations on religious education and the literacy strategy for secondary education in Britain', *British Journal of Religious Education*, 26: 21–32.

Honeyford, R. (1992) *State-Funded Muslim Schools: The Case Against*, London: Majority Rights.

Hooykaas, R. (1973) *Religion and the Rise of Modern Science*, Edinburgh: Scottish Academic Press.

Hookway, S. (2002) 'Mirrors, windows, conversations: religious education for the millennial generation in England and Wales', *British Journal of Religious Education*, 24: 99–110.

Hookway, S. (2004) *Questions of Truth: Developing Critical Thinking Skills in Secondary Religious Education*, Norwich: Religious and Moral Education Press.

Hopkins, P. (2000) *ICT and Religious Education*, London: Nelson Thornes.

Hopkins, P. (2004) *A Survey of 800 RE Teachers' Use of ICT*, Coventry: Becta Publications.

Hopkins, P. (2009) 'A survey of teachers' views on RE', *Resource* 32: 1.

Hopkins, P. and Hayward, M. (2010) *Resources for Teaching about World Religions in English Schools: An Audit*, London: HMSO.

Horsfield, S. (2005) 'Different views for autistic pupils in mainstream GCSE RE', unpublished Farmington Paper, Oxford.

Howkins, K. (1966) *Religious Thinking and Religious Education: A Critique of the Research and Conclusions of Goldman*, Bristol: Tyndale.

Hudson, A. (2005) 'Citizenship education and students' identities: a school-based action research project', in A. Osler (ed.) *Teachers, Human Rights and Diversity*, Stoke on Trent: Trentham Books.

Hudson, C. (2008) *We and They – Using RE to Support Community Cohesion*, Nottingham: Stapleford Centre.

Hughes, M. (2005) 'Reach to teach ICT: issues and compromises', *Education and Information Technologies*, 10: 263–276.

Hull, J. M. (1984) *Studies in Religion and Education*, Lewes, Sussex: Falmer Press.

Hull, J. M. (1989) 'The content of religious education and the 1988 Education Reform Act', *British Journal of Religious Education*, 11: 59–61.

Hull, J. M. (1991) *Mishmash: Religious Education in Multicultural Britain: A Study in Metaphor*, London: Christian Education Movement.

Hull, J. M. (1992) 'The transmission of religious prejudice', *British Journal of Religious Education*, 14: 69–72.

Hull, J. M. (1996a) 'A gift to the child: a new pedagogy for teaching religion to your children', *Religious Education*, 91: 172–188.

Hull, J. M. (1996b) 'The ambiguity of spiritual values', in J. M. Halstead and M. J. Taylor (eds) *Values in Education and Education in Values*, London: Falmer.

Hull, J. M. (1998) *Utopian Whispers – Moral, Religious and Spiritual Values in Schools*, Norwich: Religious and Moral Education Press.

Hull, J. M. (2000a) 'The gift approach to religious education', in M. Grimmitt (ed.) *Pedagogies of Religious Education*, Great Wakering, Essex: McCrimmons.

Hull, J. M. (2000b) 'Religionism and religious education', in M. Leicester and S. Modgil (eds) *Spirit and Religious Education*, London: Falmer Press.

Hulmes, E. (1979) *Commitment and Neutrality in Religious Education*, London: Geoffrey Chapman.

Hulmes, E. (1992) 'Unity and diversity: the search for common identity', in B. Watson (ed.) *Religious Education: A Model for the 1990s and Beyond*, London: Falmer.

Humanist Philosophers' Group (2001) *Religious Schools: The Case Against*, London: British Humanist Association.

Hyde, B. (2008) *Children and Spirituality: Searching for Meaning and Connectedness*, London: Jessica Kingsley.

Hyde, K. E. (1965) *Religious Learning in Adolescence*, University of Birmingham Institute of Education, Monograph No. 7, London: Oliver and Boyd.

I'Anson, J. (2010) 'RE: pedagogy – after neutrality', *British Journal of Religious Education*, 32: 105–118.

Inter Faith Network (2001) *Inter Faith Issues and the Religious Education Curriculum*, London: Inter Faith Network for the UK.

Ipgrave, J. (1999). 'Issues in the delivery of religious education to Muslim pupils: perspectives from the classroom', *British Journal of Religious Education*, 21: 146–157.

Ipgrave, J. (2001) *Pupil-to-pupil Dialogue in the Classroom as a Tool for Religious Education*, Warwick: Religious and Education Research Unit.

Ipgrave, J. (2004) *Building E-bridges: Interfaith Dialogue for Primary Children using Email: The Religious Dimension of Intercultural Education*, Strasbourg: Council of Europe Publishing.

Ipgrave, J. and McKenna, U. (2007) 'Values and purposes: teacher perspectives on the "Building E-Bridges" project for inter faith dialogue between children across the UK', in C. Bakker and H-G. Heimbrock (eds*) Researching RE Teachers, RE Teachers as Researchers*, Münster: Waxmann.

Ipgrave, J. and McKenna, U. (2008) 'Diverse experiences and common vision: English Students' perspectives on religion and religious education', in T. Knauth, D-P. Jozsa, G. Bertram-Troost and J. Ipgrave (eds) *Encountering Religious Pluralism in School and Society: A Qualitative Study of Teenage Perspectives in Europe*, Münster: Waxmann.

Ipgrave, J. and O'Grady, K. (2009) 'Reflecting on the case studies as action research issues and responses', in J. Ipgrave, R. Jackson and K. O'Grady (eds) *Religious Education Research through a Community of Practice: Action Research and the Interpretive Approach*, Münster: Waxmann.

Ipgrave, J., Jackson, R. and O'Grady, K. (eds) (2009) *Religious Education Research through a Community of Practice: Action Research and the Interpretive Approach*, Münster: Waxmann.

Ireson, J. and Hallam, S. (2005) 'Pupils' liking for school: self-concept, ability grouping and pupils' experience of teaching', *British Journal of Educational Psychology*, 75: 297–311.

Irish Catholic Bishops' Conference (2008) *Vision 08: A Vision for Catholic Education in Ireland*, Maynooth: Irish Catholic Bishops' Conference.

Jackson, P. W., Boostrom, R. E. and Hansen, D. T. (1993) *The Moral Life of Schools,* San Francisco: Jossey Bass.

Jackson, R. (1989) 'Hinduism: from ethnographic research to curriculum development in religious education, *Panorama*, 1: 59–77.

Jackson, R. (1996a) 'Ethnographic research and curriculum development', in L. J. Francis, W. K. Kay and W. S. Campbell (eds) *Research in Religious Education*, Leominster: Gracewing.

Jackson, R. (1996b) 'The construction of "Hinduism" and its impact on religious education in England and Wales', *Panorama*, 8: 86–104.

Jackson, R. (1997) *Religious Education: An Interpretive Approach*, London: Hodder and Stoughton.

Jackson, R. (2000) 'The Warwick Religious Education Project: an interpretive approach to religious education', in M. Grimmitt (ed) *Pedagogies of Religious Education*, Great Wakering, Essex: McCrimmon.

Jackson, R. (2002) 'Editorial: religious education and education for citizenship', *British Journal of Religious Education*, 24: 162–169.

Jackson, R. (2003) 'Should the state fund faith-based schools? A review of the arguments', *British Journal of Religious Education*, 25: 89–102.

Jackson, R. (2004a) 'Current issues in research in religious education', in R. Larsson and C. Gustavsson (eds) *Towards a European Perspective on Religious Education*, Stockholm: Artos and Norma, pp.19–35.

Jackson, R. (2004b) *Rethinking Religious Education and Plurality*, London: RoutledgeFalmer.

Jackson, R. (2007) 'European institutions and the contribution of studies of religious diversity to education for democratic citizenship', in R. Jackson, S. Miedema, W. Weisse and J.-P. Willaime (eds) *Religion and Education in Europe: Developments, Contexts and Debates*, Münster: Waxmann.

Jackson, R. (2008) 'Teaching about religions in the public sphere: European policy initiatives and the interpretive approach', *Numen: International Review for the History of Religions*, 55: 151–182.

Jackson, R. (2011) 'The Interpretive Approach as a Research Tool: Inside the REDCo Project', *British Journal of Religious Education*, 33:189-208.

Jackson, R. *et al* (2010) *Materials used to Teach about World Religions in Schools in England: Research Report DCSF-RR197*, Warwick: Department for Children, Schools and Families/University of Warwick.

Jackson, R., Ipgrave, J. and O'Grady, K. (2009) *Religious Education Research through a Community of Practice: Action Research and the Interpretive Approach*, Münster: Waxmann.

Jackson, R. and Nesbitt, E. M. (1993) *Hindu Children in Britain*, Stoke on Trent: Trentham.

Jackson, R., Miedema, S., Weisse, W. and Willaime, J.-P. (eds) (2007) *Religion and Education in Europe: Developments, Contexts and Debates*, Münster: Waxmann.

Jaki, S. (1979) *The Origin of Science and the Science of its Origin*, Edinburgh: Scottish Academic Press.

Jenkins, R. (1995) *Gladstone*, London: Papermac.

Jensen, A. (1973) *Educational Differences*, London: Methuen.

Johnson, S. and Gardner, P. (1999) 'Some Achilles' Heels of thinking skills: a response to Higgins and Baumfield', *Journal of Philosophy of Education*, 33: 435–449.

Jones, S. H. and Francis, L. J. (1996) 'Religiosity and self-esteem during childhood and adolescence', in L. J. Francis, W. K. Kay and W. S. Campbell (eds) *Research in Religious Education*, Leominster: Gracewing.

Kalve, P. (1996) 'Some aspects of the work of Michael Grimmit', *British Journal of Religious Education*, 18: 181–190.

Kay, W. K. (1997) 'Phenomenology, religious education, and Piaget', *Religion*, 27: 275–283.

Kay, W. K. (2002) 'Political perspectives on church schools and religious education: a discussion of the period from Thatcher to Blair', *Educational Studies*, 28: 61–75.

Kay, W. K. (2005a) 'England and Wales: cautious optimism', in H-G. Ziebertz and W. K. Kay (eds) *Youth in Europe 1: An International Empirical Study about Life Perspectives*, Münster: Lit Verlag.

Kay, W. K (2005b) 'A non-statutory framework for religious education: issues and opportunities', *British Journal of Religious Education*, 27: 41–52.

Kay, W. K. (2006) 'England and Wales: open theism and materialism', in H-G. Ziebertz and W. K. Kay (eds) *Youth in Europe 2: An International Empirical Study about Religiosity*, Münster: Lit Verlag.

Kay, W. K. (2007) 'Can "skills" help RE?', in M. Felderhof, P. Thompson and D. Torevell (eds) *Inspiring Faith in Schools: Studies in RE*, Aldershot: Ashgate.

Kay, W. K. and Francis, L. J. (1996) *Drift from the Churches: Attitude toward Christianity during Childhood and Adolescence*, Cardiff: University of Wales Press.

Kay, W. K. and Francis, L. J. (2001) 'Religious education and school assembly in England and Wales: what do religious minorities think?' in H-G. Heimbrock, C. Th. Scheilke and P. Schreiner (eds) *Towards Religious Competence: Diversity as a Challenge for Education in Europe*, Münster: Lit Verlag.

Kay, W. K. and Francis, L. J. (2006) 'Suicidal ideation among young people in the UK: churchgoing as an inhibitory influence?' *Mental Health, Religion and Culture*, 9: 127–140.

Kay, W. K. and Smith, D. L. (2000) 'Religious terms and attitudes in the classroom (Part 1)', *British Journal of Religious Education*, 22: 81–90.

Kay, W. K. and Smith, D. L. (2002) 'Classroom factors and attitude toward six world religions', *British Journal of Religious Education*, 24: 111–122.

Kay, W. K. and Ziebertz, H-G. (2006) 'A nine country survey', *British Journal of Religious Education*, 28: 119–129.

Kay, W. K. and Ziebertz, H-G. (2008) 'Attitudes and values of adolescent Europeans towards Europeanisation', *Journal of Empirical Theology*, 21: 209–239.

Kay, W. K. and Ziebertz, H-G. (2009) 'A key to the future: the attitudes and values of adolescent Europeans', *Globalisation, Societies and Education*, 7: 151–165.

Keast, J. (2006) 'An RE for Europe?', *Resource* 28, 3: 13–15.

Keast, J. (ed.) (2007) *Religious Diversity and Intercultural Education: A Reference Book for Schools*, Strasbourg: Council of Europe Publishing.

King, J. (2001) *Global Perspectives on Christianity*, Norwich: Religious and Moral Education Press.

Klein, P. (1997) 'Multiplying the problems of intelligence by eight: a critique of Gardner's theory', *Canadian Journal of Education*, 22: 377–394.

Knauth, T. (2007) 'Religious education in Germany: a contribution to dialogue or sources of conflict? Historical and contextual analysis of the development since the 1960s', in R. Jackson, S. Miedema, W. Weisse and J.-P. Willaime (eds) *Religion and Education in Europe: Developments, Contexts and Debates*, Münster: Waxmann.

Knauth, T., Jozsa, D-P., Bertram-Troost, G. and Ipgrave, J. (2008) *Encountering Religious Pluralism in School and Society: A Qualitative Study of Teenage Perspectives in Europe*, Münster: Waxmann.

Kohlberg, L. (1987) *Child Psychology and Childhood Education: A Cognitive-developmental View*, New York: Longman.

Kraft, C. (1979) *Christianity in Culture*, Maryknoll: Orbis.

Kraft, C. (1989) 'Gospel and culture', in R. Banks (ed.) *The Quiet Revolution*, Oxford: Lion Publishing.

Krathwohl, D. R., Bloom, B. and Masia, B. (1964) *Taxonomy of Educational Objectives. Handbook II: The Affective Domain*, Boston: Allyn and Bacon.

Krisman, A. (1997) *Speaking from the Heart: Exploring and Responding to RE in the Special School*, Oxford: Farmington Institute.

Kulik, C., Kulik, J. and Bangert-Drowns, R. (1990) 'Effectiveness of mastery-learning programs: a meta-analysis', *Review of Educational Research*, 60: 265–299.

Kuyk, E., Jensen, R., Lankshear, D., Manna, E. L. and Schreiner, P. (eds) (2007) *Religious Education in Europe*, Oslo: IKO.

Laborde, C. (2010) 'In defence of the secular state', *Royal Society of Arts Journal*, Summer: 10–14.

Lambourn, D. (1996) '"Spiritual" minus "personal-social" = ?: a critical note on an empty category', in R. Best (ed.) *Education, Spirituality and the Whole Child*, London: Cassell.

Lankshear, D. W. (2005) 'The influence of Anglican secondary schools on personal, moral and religious values', in L. J Francis, M. Robbins and J. Astley (eds) *Religion, Education and Adolescence: International Empirical Perspectives*, Cardiff: University of Wales Press.

Laura, R. S. (1983) 'To educate or to indoctrinate: that is still the question', *Educational Philosophy and Theory*, 15: 43–55.

Law, S. (2002) *What's So Wrong with Faith?* London: British Humanist Association. Available online: http://www.humanism.org.uk/about/philosophers/faq/whats-so-wrong-with-faith (accessed 23 October 2010).

Lawlor, C. (2010) *The Construction of Islam in Religious Education at Key Stages 3 and 4*, unpublished Ed D thesis, University of Brighton.

Leach, B. (2010) 'Richard Dawkins: faith schools should not be allowed to opt out of religious education', *Telegraph*, 18 August.

Learning and Teaching Scotland (2004) *Understanding the Curriculum*. Available online: http://www.ltscotland.org.uk/understandingthecurriculum/ (accessed 16 August 2010).

Leahy, S. and Wiliam, D. (2009) *Embedding Assessment for Learning – A Professional Development Pack*, London: Specialist Schools and Academies Trust.

Levitt, M. (1995) '"The church is very important to me." A consideration of the relevance of Francis' attitude towards Christianity scale to the aims of Church of England aided schools', *British Journal of Religious Education*, 17: 100–107.

Lewis, C. A. (1998) 'Towards a clarification of the association between religiosity and life satisfaction', *Journal of Beliefs and Values*, 19: 119–122.

Lewis, C. A. and Francis, L. J. (2003) 'Evaluer l'attitude d'étudiantes universitaires françaises à l'égard du Christianisme: L'Echelle de Francis', *Sciences Pastorals*, 22 : 179–190.

Lewis, C. S. (1996) 'Equality', 'Democratic education', and 'Willing slaves of the welfare state', in W. Hooper (ed.) *Compelling Reason – Essays on Ethics and Theology*, London: HarperCollins.

Lewis, P. (1978) *The Fifties*, London: Heinemann.

Lickona, T. (2004) *Character Matters*, London: Touchstone.

Livingstone, D. N. (1987) *Darwin's Forgotten Defenders*, Edinburgh: Scottish Academic Press/Eerdmans.

Lloyd, I. (2007) 'Confession and reason', in M. Felderhof, P. Thompson and D. Torevell (eds) *Inspiring Faith In Schools: Studies in Religious Education*, Aldershot: Ashgate.

Lonergan, B. (1972) *Method in Theology*, New York: Herder and Herder.

Loukes, H. (1961) *Teenage Religion*, London: SCM.

Loukes, H. (1965) *New Ground in Christian Education*, London: SCM.

Loukes, H. (1973) *Teenage Morality*, London: SCM.

Lucey, H. (2001) 'Social class, gender and schooling', in B. Francis and C. Skelton (eds) *Investigating Gender*, Buckingham: Open University Press.

Lundie, D. (2010) '"Does RE work?" An analysis of the aims, practices and models of effectiveness of religious education in the UK', *British Journal of Religious Education*, 32: 163–170.

Lundy, L. (2000) *Education Law, Policy and Practice in Northern Ireland*, Northern Ireland: SLS Legal Publications.

Maan, B. (1992) *New Scots*, Edinburgh: John Donald Publishers Ltd.

Maan, B. (2008) *The Thistle and the Crescent*, Glendaruel: Argyll Publishing.

MacIntyre, A. (1999) *After Virtue*, London: Duckworth.

MacLeod, D. (2008) 'Faith schools "help foster terrorists"', *Guardian*, 9 September.

Madge, V. (1965) *Children in Search of Meaning*, London: SCM.

Madge, V. (1971) *Introducing Young Children to Jesus*, London: SCM.

Marley, D. (2008) 'Muslim schools prove stars of the higher-performing faith family', *Times Educational Supplement*, 19 December.

Marsden, G. M. (1997) *The Outrageous Idea of Christian Scholarship*, Oxford: Oxford University Press.

Marshall, B. (2004) 'Goals or horizons – the conundrum of progression in English: or a possible way of understanding formative assessment in English', *Curriculum Journal*, 15: 101–113.

Martino, W. (1999) '"Cool Boys", "Party Animals", "Squids" and "Poofters": integrating the dynamics and politics of adolescent masculinities in school', *British Journal of Sociology of Education*, 20: 239–263.

Martino, M., Kehler, M. and Weaver-Hightower, B. (eds) (2009) *The Problem with Boys' Education: Beyond the Backlash*, London: Routledge.

Marton, F. (2006) 'Sameness and difference in transfer', *Journal of the Learning Sciences*, 15: 499–535.

Marton, F. and Booth, S. (1997) *Learning and Awareness*, London: Routledge.

Marton, F. and Trigwell, K. (2000) 'Variatio Est Mater Studiorum', *Higher Education Research and Development*, 19: 381–395.

Marton, F. and Tsui, A. B. M. (eds) (2004) *Classroom Discourse and the Space of Learning*, Mahwah, NJ: Lawrence Erlbaum Associates, Inc.

Marton, F. *et al* (2004) *Classroom Discourse and the Space of Learning*, Mahwah, NJ: Lawrence Erlbaum.

Mascall, E. L. (1956) *Christian Theology and Natural Science*, London: Longmans, Green and Co.

McCormick, R. and Scrimshaw, P. (2001) 'Information and communications technology, knowledge, and pedagogy', *Education, Communication and Information*, 1: 37–57.

McDade, J. (1991) 'The continuing validity of the Jewish covenant', *The Month* (September–October): 376–381.

McGrady, A. G. (1983) 'Teaching the Bible: research from a Piagetian perspective', *British Journal of Religious Education*, 5: 126–133.

McGrath, M. (2000) *The Catholic Church and Catholic Schools in Northern Ireland: The Price of Faith*, Dublin: Irish Academic Press.

McGregor, D. (2007) *Developing Thinking; Developing Learning. A Guide to Thinking Skills in Education*, Berkshire: Open University Press.

McKinney, S. J. (2008a) 'Do Catholic schools in Scotland cause or promote sectarianism?' in S. J. McKinney (ed.) *Faith Schools in the 21ˢᵗ Century*, Edinburgh: Dunedin Academic Press.

McKinney, S. J. (2008b) *Faith Schools in the 21ˢᵗ Century*, Edinburgh: Dunedin Academic Press.

McKinney, S. J. (2010a) 'Communicating faith through RE', in J. Sullivan (ed.) *Communicating Faith*, Washington DC: The Catholic University of America Press.

McKinney, S. J. and Conroy, J. C. (2007) 'Religious education in Scotland', in E. Kuyk, R. Jensen, D. Lankshear, E. L. Mann and P. Schreiner (eds) *Religious Education in Europe*, Oslo: Iko.

McLaughlin, T. H. (1995) 'Liberalism, education and the common school', *Journal of Philosophy of Education*, 29: 239–253.

McLaughlin, T. H. (2000) 'Citizenship education in England: The Crick Report and beyond', *Journal of Philosophy of Education*, 34: 541–570.

McLaughlin, T. H. (2002) 'Review: religious schools: the case against by the Humanist Philosophers' Group', *British Journal of Religious Education*, 2: 82–84.

McLaughlin, T. H. (2008) *Liberalism, Education and Schooling*, (ed D. Carr, J. M. Halstead and R. Pring), Exeter: Imprint Academic.

McLaughlin, T. H. and Halstead J. M. (1999) 'Education in character and virtue' in J. M Halstead and T. H. McLaughlin (eds) *Education in Morality*, London: Routledge.

McLuhan, M. and Fiore, Q. (1967) *The Medium is the Message*, London: Penguin.

Miller, P. (2000) 'Historiography of compulsory schooling', in R. Lowe (ed.) *History of Education Volume II*, London: Routledge.

Mill, J. S. (1962) *On Liberty*, Glasgow: Collins Fontana.

Minney, R. (1985) 'Why are pupils bored with RE? – The ghost behind Piaget', *British Journal of Educational Studies*, 33: 250–261.

Mirza, S. (2009) 'Between ourselves', *BBC Radio 4*, 5 August.

Mitchell, B. (1970) 'Indoctrination', *The Fourth R*, London: SPCK.

Mitchell, B. (1994) *Faith and Criticism*, Oxford: Clarendon Press.

Morley, H. C. (1975) 'Religious concepts of slow learners: an application of the findings of Ronald Goldman', *Learning for Living*, 14: 107–110.

Muijs, D. and Reynolds, D. (2001) *Effective Teaching: Evidence and Practice*, London: Sage.

Mulhall, S. and Swift, A. (1996) *Liberals and Communitarians: An Introduction*, Oxford: Blackwell.

Müller, M. (1873) *Introduction to the Science of Religion*, London: Longman, Green and Co.

Munayer, S. J. (2000) *The Ethnic Identity of Palestinian Arab Christian Adolescents in Israel*, unpublished doctoral thesis, University of Wales (Oxford Centre for Mission Studies).

Murphy, J. (1971) *Church, State and Schools in Britain, 1800–1970*, London: Routledge and Kegan Paul.

National RE Committee (1974) *The Approach to RE in the Catholic Secondary School*, Edinburgh: Scottish Catholic Bishops.

National Society for Promoting Religious Education (no date) *Guidance for Church of England secondary schools on Religious Education in light of the new secondary curriculum*. Available online: http://www.natsoc.org.uk/reresources/reguidancecheckedversion. doc (accessed 21 June 2010).

Nelson, J. (2004) 'Uniformity and diversity in religious education in Northern Ireland', *British Journal of Religious Education*, 26: 249–258.

Nesbitt, E. M. (1990) 'Religion and identity: the Valmiki community in Coventry', *New Community*, 16: 261–274.

Nesbitt, E. M. (1992) 'Photographing worship: issues raised by ethnographical study of children's participation in acts of worship', *Visual Anthropology*, 5: 285–306.

Nesbitt, E. M. (1993) 'Children and the world to come: the views of children aged eight to fourteen on life after death', *Religion Today*, 8: 10–13.

Nesbitt, E. M. (1995) 'Punjabis in Britain: cultural history and cultural choices', *South Asia Research*, 15: 221–240.

Nesbitt, E. M. (1997a) 'Splashed with goodness: the many meanings of *Amrit* for young British Sikhs', *Journal of Contemporary Religion*, 12: 17–33.

Nesbitt, E. M. (1997b) 'Sikhs and proper Sikhs: young British Sikhs' perceptions of their identity', in P. Singh and N. G. Barrier (eds) *Sikh Identity: Continuity and Change*, Delhi: Manohar.

Nesbitt, E. M. (1998a) 'British, Asian and Hindu: identity, self-narration and the ethnographic interview', *Journal of Beliefs and Values*, 19: 189–200.

Nesbitt, E. M. (1998b) 'Bridging the gap between young people's experience of their religious traditions at home and school: the contribution of ethnographic research', *British Journal of Religious Education*, 20: 102–114.

Nesbitt, E. M. (2002) 'Ethnography and religious education', in L. Broadbent and A. Brown (eds) *Issues in Religious Education*, London: RoutledgeFalmer.

Nesbitt, E. M. and Arweck, E. (2003) 'Researching a new interface between religions and publicly funded schools in the UK', *International Journal of Children's Spirituality*, 8: 239–254.

Nesbitt, E. M. and Arweck, E. (2010) 'Issues arising from an ethnographic investigation of the religious identity formation of young people in mixed faith families', *Fieldwork in Religion*, 5: 7–30.

Nesbitt, E. M. and Henderson, A. (2003) 'Religious organisations in the UK and values education programmes for schools', *Journal of Beliefs and Values*, 24, 75–88.

Nesbitt, E. M. and Jackson, R. (1992) 'Christian and Hindu children: their perceptions of each others' religious traditions', *Journal of Empirical Theology*, 5: 39–62.

Nesbitt, E. M. and Jackson, R. (1993) 'Aspects of cultural transmission in a Diaspora Sikh community', *Journal of Sikh Studies*, 18: 52–66.

Nesbitt, E. M. and Jackson, R. (1995) 'Sikh children's use of "God": ethnographic fieldwork and religious education', *British Journal of Religious Education*, 17: 108–120.

New York Times (2009) 'Text: Obama's speech in Cairo'. Available online: http://www. nytimes.com/2009/06/04/us/politics/04obama.text.html?_r=1andpagewanted=2 (accessed 30 June 2010).

Nixon, G. (2008) 'Religious and moral education', in T. G. K. Bryce and W. Humes (eds) *Scottish Education (3rd edn) Beyond Devolution*, Edinburgh: Edinburgh University Press.

Norman, R. (2004) *On Humanism*, London: Routledge.

Norman, R. (ed.) (2007) *The Case for Secularism: A Neutral State in an Open Society*, London: British Humanist Association.

Nyborg, N. (1993) *Pedagogy*, Haugesund: Nordisk Undervisningsforlag.

Oakley, A. (1972) *Sex, Gender and Society*, London: Temple Smith.

O'Brian, T. and Guiney, D. (2001) *Differentiation in Teaching and Learning: Principles and Practice*, London: Continuum.

O'Dell, G. (2009) 'Action research into teaching about religious diversity: pedagogical and gender issues in applying the interpretive approach', in J. Ipgrave, R. Jackson and K. O'Grady (eds) *Religious Education Research through a Community of Practice: Action Research and the Interpretive Approach*, Münster: Waxmann.

O'Donoghue, P. (2007) *Fit for Mission? Schools*, Lancaster: Roman Catholic Diocesan Trustees.

O'Grady, K. (2003) 'Motivation in religious education: a collaborative investigation with year eight students', *British Journal of Religious Education*, 25: 214–225.

O'Grady, K. (2005) 'Professor Ninian Smart, phenomenology and religious education', *British Journal of Religious Education*, 27: 227–238.

O'Grady, K. (2009) 'Honesty in religious education. Some further remarks on the legacy of Ninian Smart and related issues, in reply to L. Philip Barnes', *Journal of Religious Education*, 31: 65–68.

O'Grady, K. (2010) 'Researching religious education pedagogy through an action research community of practice', *British Journal of Religious Education*, 32: 119–131.

Office for Democratic Institutions and Human Rights (ODIHR) (2007) *Toledo Guiding Principles about Religions and Beliefs in Public Schools*, Warsaw: ODIHR.

Office of Public Sector Information (1980) *Education (Scotland) Act*. Available online: http://www.opsi.gov.uk/RevisedStatutes/Acts/ukpga/1980/cukpga_19800044_en_1 (accessed 16 August 2010).

Ofsted (Office for Standards in Education) (1994) *Spiritual, Moral, Social and Cultural Development*, London: Ofsted.

Ofsted (1997) *The Impact of New Agreed Syllabuses on the Teaching and Learning of Religious Education*, London: HMSO.

Ofsted (1998) *Secondary Education 1993–97: A Review of Secondary Schools in England*, London: HMSO.

Ofsted (2003) *Religious Education in Primary Schools*, London: Ofsted.

Ofsted (2004a) *Promoting and Evaluating Pupils' Spiritual, Moral, Social and Cultural Development*. Available online: http://www.ofsted.gov.uk/Ofsted-home/Publications-and-research (accessed 23 October 2010).

Ofsted (2004b) *Subject Conference Report: Religious Education*, London: Ofsted.

Ofsted (2007) *Making Sense of Religion: A Report on Religious Education in Schools and the Impact of Locally Agreed Syllabuses*, London: Office for Standards in Education.

Ofsted (2008) *Recent Research on Gender and Educational Performance*, London: Ofsted.

Ofsted (2010) *Transforming Religious Education: Religious Education in Schools 2006–09*, Manchester: Ofsted.

Olson, D. R. and Bruner, J. S. (1996) 'Folk psychology and folk pedagogy', in D. R. Olson and N. Torrance (eds) *The Handbook of Education and Human Development: New Models of Learning, Teaching and Schooling*, Oxford: Blackwell.

ONS (Office of National Statistics) (1971) *Annual Abstract of National Statistics*, London: Office of National Statistics.

ONS (Office of National Statistics) (2006) *Focus on Religion.* Available online: http://www.statistics.gov.uk/focuson/religion/ (accessed 27 July 27 2010).

Organisation for Security and Co-operation in Europe (2007) *The Toledo Guiding Principles on Teaching about Religions and Beliefs in Public Schools,* Warsaw: Office for Democratic Institutions and Human Rights. Available online: http://www.osce.org/item/28314.html (accessed 10 July 2010).

Osler, A. and Starkey, H. (2005) 'Education for democratic citizenship: a review of research, policy and practice 1995–2005', *BERA Academic Review.* Available online: http://www.bera.ac.uk/pdfs/OslerStarkeyBERAReview2005.pdf (accessed 19 October 2006).

Østberg, S. (2003) 'Cultural diversity and common citizenship: reflections on ethnicity, religion, nationhood and citizenship among Pakistani young people in Europe', in R. Jackson (ed.) *International Perspectives on Citizenship, Education and Religious Diversity,* London: RoutledgeFalmer.

Ota, C. (1997) 'Learning to juggle – the experience of Muslim and Sikh children coping with different value systems', *The International Journal of Beliefs and Values,* 18: 227–234.

Ota, C., Erricker, C. and Erricker, J. (1997) 'The secrets of the playground', *Pastoral Care in Education,* 15, 4: 19–24.

Ouseley, H. (2001) *Community Pride, not Prejudice (Report of the Bradford District Race Review Team),* Bradford: Bradford Vision.

Palinscar, A. and Brown, A. (2008) 'Reciprocal teaching of comprehension fostering and comprehension monitoring activities', *Cognition and Instruction,* 1: 117–175.

Panjwani, F. (2005) 'Agreed syllabi and un-agreed voices: religious education and missed opportunities for social cohesion', *British Journal of Educational Studies,* 53: 375–393.

Papert, S. (1982) *Mindstorms: Children, Computers and Powerful Ideas,* New York: Basic Books.

Parekh, B. (2000) *Rethinking Multiculturalism: Cultural Diversity and Political Theory,* Basingstoke: Macmillan Press/Palgrave.

Parker-Jenkins, M., Hartas, D. and Irving, B. A. (2005) *In Good Faith: Schools, Religion and Public Funding,* Aldershot: Ashgate.

Passey, D. and Rogers, C. with Machell, J. and McHugh, G. (2004) *The Motivational Effect of ICT on Students,* England: DfES/University of Lancaster.

Paterson, L. (2003) *Scottish Education in the Twentieth Century,* Edinburgh: Edinburgh University Press.

Peatling, J. H. (1974) 'Cognitive development in pupils in grades four through twelve: the incidence of concrete and abstract religious thinking', *Character Potential,* 7: 52–61.

Peatling, J. H. (1977) 'On beyond Goldman: religious thinking and the 1970s', *Learning for Living,* 16: 99–108.

Petrovich, O. (1989) *An Examination of Piaget's Theory of Childhood Artificialism.* Unpublished D.Phil thesis, University of Oxford.

Phillips, V. and Bond, C. (2004) 'Undergraduates' experiences of critical thinking', *Higher Education Research and Development,* 23: 277–294.

Pickard, W. (2008) 'The history of Scottish education, 1980 to the present day', in T. G. K. Bryce and W. Humes (eds) *Scottish Education (3rd edn) beyond Devolution,* Edinburgh: Edinburgh University Press.

Pike, M. (2006) 'From beliefs to skills: the secularization of literacy and the moral education of citizens', *Journal of Beliefs and Values,* 27: 281–289.

Pike, M. A. (2007) 'The state and citizenship education in England: a curriculum for subjects or citizens?' *Journal of Curriculum Studies,* 39: 471–489.

Pike, M. A. (2008) 'Faith in citizenship? On teaching children to believe in liberal democracy', *British Journal of Religious Education,* 30: 113–122.

Pike, M. A. (2009) 'Religious freedom and rendering to Caesar: reading democratic and faith-based values in curriculum, pedagogy and policy', *Oxford Review of Education*, 35: 133–146.

Poole, J. (2010) 'The orientation theory of dyslexia: uniting current schisms through an ecological perspective', *Educational Review*, 92: 215–229.

Poole, M. W. (1995) *Beliefs and Values in Science Education*, Buckingham: Open University Press.

Poole, M. W. (2007) *User's Guide to Science and Belief*, Oxford: Lion Hudson.

Preston, C. (2004) *Learning to use ICT in Classrooms: teachers' and trainers' perspectives: An Evaluation of the English NOF ICT Teacher Training Programme 1999–2003*, London: MirandaNet and the Teacher Training Agency.

Priestley, J. (1996) *Spirituality in the Curriculum*, Frinton on Sea: The Hockerill Foundation.

Priestley, J. (2001) *The Spiritual Dimension of the Curriculum – What are Ofsted inspectors Looking For and How Can We Help Them Find It?* unpublished lecture to Hounslow SACRE.

Priestley, J. (2006) 'Agreed syllabuses: their history and development in England and Wales, 1944–2004', in M. de Souza, G. Durka, K. Engebretson and R. Jackson (eds) *International Handbook of the Religious, Moral and Spiritual Dimensions in Education (Part 2)*, Dordrecht, The Netherlands: Springer Publishing.

Priestley, J. and Copley, T. (1991) *Forms of Assessment in Religious Education: The FARE project*, Exeter: University of Exeter.

Pring, R. (2001) 'Education as a moral practice', *Journal of Moral Education*, 30: 101–112.

Pring, R. (2004) 'The skills revolution', *Oxford Review of Education*, 30: 105–116.

Qualifications and Curriculum Authority (1994) *Model Syllabuses for Religious Education*, London: QCA.

Qualifications and Curriculum Authority (1997) *The Promotion of Pupils' Spiritual, Moral, Social and Cultural Development*, London: QCA.

Qualifications and Curriculum Authority (1998) *Education for Citizenship and the Teaching of Democracy in Schools*, London : QCA.

Qualifications and Curriculum Authority (1999) *Citizenship: The National Curriculum for England*, London: HMSO.

Qualifications and Curriculum Authority (2001) *Citizenship through Religious Education at Key Stage 3*, London: QCA.

Qualifications and Curriculum Authority (2004) *Religious Education: Non-Statutory National Framework*, London: QCA.

Qualifications and Curriculum Authority (2007a) *GCSE Subject Criteria for Religious Studies*, London: QCA.

Qualifications and Curriculum Authority (2007b) *Religious Education: Programme of Study (Non-statutory) for Key Stage 3 and Attainment Targets*, London: QCA.

Qualifications and Curriculum Authority (2007c) *Religious Education: Programme of Study (Non-statutory) for Key Stage 4 and Years 12 and 13*, London: QCA.

Qualifications and Curriculum Authority (2009) *A Framework of Personal, Learning and Thinking Skills*, London: QCA.

Qualifications, Curriculum and Development Authority (2008) *The Secondary Curriculum*, London: QCDA.

Qualifications, Curriculum and Development Authority (2010a) *Assessing Pupil Progress in the Foundation Subjects: Standards Files for RE*, London: QCDA.

Qualifications, Curriculum and Development Authority (2010b) *Community Cohesion in Action*, London, QCDA.

Raine, A. (1999) *Using ICT in the Teaching of Primary Religious Education*, Oxford: Farmington Institute.

Ramsey, I. T. (1964) *Models and Mystery*, Oxford: Oxford University Press.

Rawls, J. (1993) *Political Liberalism*, New York: Columbia University Press.

Religious Education Council (REC) (2005) *The Campaign against Terrorism: A National Strategy for Religious Education* with *Salutary Afterword: The London Bombers and their Schools*, letter to Lord Adonis, 29 July.

Religious Education Council of Northern Ireland (1978) *Design for Religious Education*, Belfast: Christian Journals Limited.

Revell, L. (2010) *Christian and Atheist Student RE Teachers' Attitudes to Objectivity and Professionalism*, report on research project, in Religious Education Council, June Newsletter.

Revell, L. and Walters, R. (2010) *Christian Student RE Teachers, Objectivity and Professionalism*, Canterbury: Canterbury Christ Church University.

Richardson, N. (2007) 'Sharing religious education: a brief introduction to the possibility of an inclusive approach to R.E. in Northern Ireland', Belfast: Stranmillis University College: Belfast (unpublished paper).

Richardson, N. (2008a) 'Faith schooling: implication for teacher educators. A perspective from Northern Ireland', *Journal of Beliefs and Values*, 29: 1–10.

Richardson, N. (2008b) 'An introduction to religious education: the development of religious education in Northern Ireland', Belfast: Stranmillis University College (unpublished paper).

Richmond, R. C. (1972) 'Maturity of religious judgements and differences of religious attitudes between ages of 13 and 16 years', *Educational Review*, 24: 225–236.

Robbins, M. (2000) 'Leaving before adolescence: profiling the child no longer in the church', in L. J. Francis, and Y. J. Katz (eds) *Joining and Leaving Religion: Research Perspectives*, Leominster: Gracewing.

Robbins, M. (2005) 'Attitude to smoking among female adolescents: is religion a significant but neglected factor?' in L. J. Francis, J. Astley and M. Robbins (eds) *Religion, Education and Adolescence: International Empirical Perspectives*, Cardiff: University of Wales Press.

Robbins, M. and Francis, L. J. (1996) 'Are religious people happier? A study among undergraduates', in L. J. Francis, W. K. Kay and W. S. Campbell (eds) *Research in Religious Education*, Leominster: Gracewing.

Robbins, M. and Francis, L. J. (2010) 'The Teenage Religion and Values Survey in England and Wales: an overview', *British Journal of Religious Education*, 32: 307–320.

Robinson, J. (1999) *Methods of Teaching Religious Education using ICT*, Oxford: Farmington Institute.

Robinson, J. A. T. (1963) *Honest to God*, London: SCM.

Rose Review/Department for Children, Schools and Families (2009) Independent Review of the Primary Curriculum: Final Report, Nottingham, DCSF.

RPA (Review of Public Administration) (2007) *Policy Paper 21: Sectoral Support Post-RPA*, Bangor: Department of Education Northern Ireland. Available online: http://www.deni.gov.uk (accessed 8 July 2008).

Rudge, J. (2000) 'The Westhill Project: religious education as maturing pupils' patterns of belief and behaviour', in M. Grimmitt (ed.) *Pedagogies of Religious Education*, Great Wakering, Essex: McCrimmons.

Rudge, L. (2001) 'Task setting in religious education at Key Stage 2: a response to Barbara Wintersgill', *Resource*, 23, 2: 4–8.

Runnymede Trust (1997) *Islamophobia: A Challenge for us All*, London: Runnymede Trust.

Russell, B. (1972) *Religion and Science*, Oxford: Oxford University Press.

Sacks, J. (1995) *Faith in the Future*, London: Darton, Longman & Todd.

Sacks, J. (2002) *The Dignity of Difference: How to Avoid the Clash of Civilisations*, London: Continuum.

Sacred Congregation of the Clergy (1971) *General Catechetical Directory*. Available online: http://www.vatican.va/roman_curia/congregations/cclergy/documents/rc_con_cclergy_doc_11041971_gcat_en.html (accessed 16 August 2010).

Sahin, A. and Francis, L. J. (2002) 'Assessing attitude toward Islam among Muslim adolescents: the psychometric properties of the Sahin-Francis scale', *Muslim Education Quarterly*, 19, 4: 35–47.

Sampson, P. J. (2000) *6 Modern Myths about Christianity and Western Civilization*, Downers Grove, IL: InterVarsity Press.

Sardar, Z. (2004) *Desperately Seeking Paradise*, London: Granta Books.

Schihalejev, O. (2010) *From Indifference to Dialogue: Estonian Young People, the School and Religious Diversity*, Münster: Waxmann.

Schools Curriculum and Assessment Authority (1994a) *Glossary of Terms in RE*, London: SCAA.

School Curriculum and Assessment Authority (1994b) *Model Syllabuses for Religious Education*, London: SCAA.

School Curriculum and Assessment Authority (1995) *Spiritual and Moral Development*, SCAA Discussion Papers No. 3, London: SCAA.

School Curriculum and Assessment Authority (1996) *Education for Adult Life: The Spiritual and Moral Development of Young People: A Summary Report*, SCAA Discussion Papers No. 6, London: SCAA.

Schools Council (1971) *Working Paper 36: Religious Education in Secondary Schools*, London: Evans/Methuen.

Schreiner, P. (2007) 'Religious education in the European context', in E. Kuyk, R. Jensen, D. Lankshear, E. L. Manna and P. Schreiner (eds) *Religious Education in Europe*, Oslo: IKO.

Scottish Catholic Education Service (SCES) (n.d.) *This is Our Faith*. Available online: http://www.sces.uk.com/this-is-our-faith-2.html (accessed 10 February 2011).

Scottish Central Committee on RE (1978) *Bulletin 1: A Curricular Approach to Religious Education*, Edinburgh; HMSO.

Scottish Central Committee on RE (1981) *Bulletin 2: Curricular Guidelines on RE*, Glasgow: Consultative Committee on the Curriculum.

Scottish Education Department (1972) *Moral and Religious Education in Scottish Schools* (the Millar Report), Edinburgh: HMSO.

Scottish Executive (2005) *Circular 1/2005. Provision of Religious Observance in Scottish Schools*. Available online: http://www.scotland.gov.uk/Resource/Doc/37428/0023554.pdf (accessed 30 March 2011).

Scottish Government (n.d.) *About the Scottish Government*. Available online: http://www.scotland.gov.uk/ (accessed 16 August 2010).

Scottish Government (n.d.) *Curriculum for Excellence Religious and Moral Education Principles and Practice*. Available online: http://www.ltscotland.org.uk/learningteachingandassessment/curriculumareas/rme/nondenominational/principlesandpractice/index.asp (accessed 16 August 2010).

Scottish Government (n.d.) *Curriculum for Excellence Religious Education in Roman Catholic Schools Principles and Practice*. Available online: http://www.ltscotland.org.uk/learningteachingandassessment/curriculumareas/rme/rerc/principlesandpractice/index.asp (accessed 16 August 2010).

Scottish Government (2004a) *A Curriculum for Excellence The Curriculum Review Group*. Available online: http://www.scotland.gov.uk/Resource/Doc/25954/0023749.pdf (accessed 30 March 2011).

Scottish Government (2004b) *The Report of the Religious Observance Review Group*, Edinburgh. Available online: http://www.scotland.gov.uk/Publications/2004/05/19351/37058 (accessed 23 October 2010).

Scottish Government (2009) *School Estate Statistics 2009*. Available online: http://www.scotland.gov.uk/Publications/2009/10/08104324/3 (accessed 16 August 2010).

Scottish Office Education Department (1991) *Circular 6/91*. Available online: http://www.edlaw.org.uk/wp-content/uploads/pdfs/guidance/religion.pdf (accessed 16 August 2010).

Scottish Office Education Department (SOED) (1992) *Religious and Moral Education 5–14*, Edinburgh: SOED.

Scottish Office Education Department/Catholic Education Commission (1994) *5–14 Religious Education (Roman Catholic Schools)*, Edinburgh: SOED.

Sefa Dei, G. (2008) 'Schooling as community: race, schooling, and the education of African youth', *Journal of Black Studies*, 38: 346–366.

Shaw, D. W. D. (1978) *The Dissuaders, Three Explanations of Religion*, London: SCM.

Short, G. (2003) 'Faith schools and social cohesion: opening up the debate', *British Journal of Religious Education*, 25: 129–141.

Shropshire Religious Education Artefacts Project (1992) *Sikh Artefacts*, Shropshire Education Curriculum Resources Unit.

Simon, B. (1981) 'Why no pedagogy in England?' in B. Simon and W. Taylor (eds) *Education in the Eighties*, London: Batsford.

Skeie, G. (2007) 'Religion and education in Norway', in R. Jackson, S. Miedema, W. Weisse and J.-P. Willaime (eds) (2007) *Religion and Education in Europe: Developments, Contexts and Debates*, Münster: Waxmann.

Slee, N. (1986) 'Goldman yet again: an overview and critique of his contribution to research', *British Journal of Religious Education*, 8: 84–93.

Smalley, S. (2005) 'Teaching about Islam and learning about Muslims: Islamophobia', *Resource*, 27, 2: 4–7.

Smart, N. (1973) *The Phenomenon of Religion*, London: Macmillan.

Smith, A. (2003) *Accelerated Learning: A User's Guide*, Edinburgh: Network Educational Press.

Smith, A. (2007) *Growing up in Multifaith Britain*, Cardiff: University of Wales Press.

Smith, D. (1999) *Making Sense of Spiritual Development*, Nottingham: The Stapleford Centre.

Smith, D. L. (1998) 'That burning bush again: the psychometric assessment of stages in religious thinking', *Journal of Beliefs and Values*, 19: 71–82.

Smith, D. L. and Kay, W. K. (2000) 'Religious terms and attitudes in the classroom, (Part 2)', *British Journal of Religious Education*, 22: 181–191.

Smith, F. (1931) *A History of English Elementary Education 1760–1902*, London: University of London Press.

Spencer, N. (2006) *Doing God: A Future for Faith in the Public Square*, London: Theos.

Spender, D. (1982) *Invisible Women*, London: Writers and Readers.

Stenhouse, L. (1975) *An Introduction to Curriculum Research and Development*, Oxford: Heinemann.

Stern, J. (2006) *Teaching Religious Education*, London: Continuum.

Stern, J. (2010) 'Research as pedagogy: building learning communities and religious understanding in RE', *British Journal of Religious Education*, 32: 133–146.

Sullivan, A. (2001) 'Cultural capital and educational attainment', *Sociology*, 35: 892–912.

Tacey, D. (2001) 'Youth spirituality as a response to cultural crisis', in J. Erricker, C. Ota and C. Erricker (eds) *Spiritual Education – Cultural, Religious and Social Differences*, Brighton: Sussex Academic Press.

Tacey, D. (2004) *The Spirituality Revolution –The Emergence of Contemporary Spirituality*, Hove: Brunner-Routledge.

Talbot, M. and Tate, N. (1997) 'Shared values in a pluralist society?', in R. Smith and P. Standish (eds) *Teaching Right and Wrong: Moral Education in the Balance*, Stoke-on-Trent: Trentham.

Taylor, M. (2005) 'Two-thirds oppose state-aided faith schools', *Guardian*, 23 August.

Teacher Development Agency (2011) *Skills Test*. Available online: http://www.tda.gov. uk/training-provider/itt/qts-standards-itt-requirements/skills-tests.aspx (accessed 31 January 2011).

Teare, B. (1997) *Effective Provision for Able and Talented Children*, Edinburgh: Network Educational Press.

Tearfund (2009) *Church is Where the Heart is*. Available online: http://www.tearfund. org/News/Press+release+archive/January+2009/Church+is+where+the+heart+is. htm (accessed 28 January 2011).

ter Avest, I, Jozsa, D-P., Knauth, T., Roson, J. and Skeie, G. (eds) (2009) *Dialogue and Conflict on Religion: Studies of Classroom Interaction in European Countries*, Münster: Waxmann.

Teece, G. (2001) *Pocket Guides to the Primary Curriculum: Religious Education*, Leamington Spa: Scholastic Press.

Teece, G. (2010) 'Is it learning about and from religions, religion or religious education? And is it any wonder some teachers don't get it?' *British Journal of Religious Education* 32: 93–104.

Temple, W. (1942) *Christianity and the Social Order*, Harmondsworth: Penguin.

The Fourth R: the Durham Report on Religious Education (1970) London: SPCK.

Thatcher, A. (1991) 'A critique of inwardness in religious education', *British Journal of Religious Education*, 14: 22–27.

Thiessen, E. (1993) *Teaching for Commitment: Liberal Education, Indoctrination and Christian Nurture*, Leominster: Gracewing.

Thiessen, E. (2001) *In Defence of Religious Schools and Colleges*, Montreal: McGill Queen's University Press.

Thiselton, A. (2009) *Hermeneutics: An Introduction*, Grand Rapids, MI: Eerdmans.

Thompson, E. P. (2002) *The Making of the English Working Class*, London: Penguin. First published in 1963 by Victor Gollancz.

Thompson, P. (2004) *Whatever Happened to Religious Education?* Cambridge: LutterworthPress.

Thompson, P. (2007) 'Religious education from Spens to Swann', in M. Felderhof, P. Thompson and D. Torevell (eds) *Inspiring Faith in Schools: Studies in Religious Education*, Aldershot: Ashgate.

Toynbee, P. (2001) 'Keep God out of class', *Guardian*, 9 November.

Transferor Representatives' Council (2007) *Response to Consultation on Policy Paper 21 – Sectoral Support Post-RPA*. Available online: http://www.ireland.anglican.org (accessed 8 July 2008).

Tulasiewicz, W. and To, C-Y. (eds) (1993) *World Religions and Educational Practice*, London: Cassell.

Underkuffler, L. S. (2001) 'Public funding for religious schools: difficulties and dangers in a pluralistic society', *Oxford Review of Education*, 27: 577–592.

United Nations (UN) (1948) *Universal Declaration of Human Rights*, General Assembly of the UN, New York.

UNESCO (1996) *Learning: The Treasure Within* (the Delors Report), The Report to UNESCO of the International Commission on Education for the Twenty-first Century, Paris: UNESCO.

Valk, P., Bertram-Troost, G., Friederici, M. and Béraud, C. (2009) *Teenagers' Perspectives on the Role of Religion in Their Lives, Schools, and Societies: A European Quantitative Study*, Münster: Waxmann.

van der Want, A., Bakker, C., ter Avest, I. and Everington, J. (2009) *Teachers Responding to Religious Diversity in Europe: Researching Biography and Pedagogy*, Münster: Waxmann.

van Geest, F. (2004) 'Deepening and broadening Christian citizenship: going beyond the basics without succumbing to liberal or communitarian ideals', *Christian Scholars Review*, 34: 91–118.

Van Till, H. J. (1996) 'Basil, Augustine, and the doctrine of creation's functional integrity', *Science and Christian Belief*, 8: 21–38.

Vertovec, S. (2006) *The Emergence of Super-diversity in Britain*, Oxford: Centre on Migration, Policy and Society.

Von der Lippe, M. (2011a) 'Young people's talk about religion and diversity: a qualitative study of Norwegian students aged 13-15', British Journal of Religious Education, 33: 127–142.

Von der Lippe, M. (2011b) 'Youth, religion and diversity: a qualitative study of young people's talk about religion in a secular and plural society – a Norwegian case', unpublished PhD Thesis, University of Stavanger.

Vygotsky, L. (1987 [1934]) 'Thinking and speech', in R. Rieber and A. Carton (eds) *The Collected Works of L. S. Vygotsky, Volume 1, Problems of General Psychology*, New York and London: Plenum Press.

Walford, G. (2000) *Policy, Politics and Education: Sponsored Grant-maintained Schools and Religious Diversity*, Aldershot: Ashgate.

Walford, G. (2008) 'Faith-based schools in England after ten years of Tony Blair', *Oxford Review of Education*, 34: 689–699.

Walker, D. (2008) *How Many Penguins Does It Take To Sink An Iceberg. The Challenges and Opportunities of Web 2.0 In Education*, Oxford: Farmington Institute.

Walker, T. (2006) *Creationism debate moves to Britain* (18 May). Available online: http://www.independent.co.uk/news/education/education-news/creationism-debate-moves-to-britain-478576.html (accessed 21 June 2010).

Walshe, K. and Copley, T. (2001) 'The Jesus of Agreed Syllabuses in Keys Stage 1 and the Jesus of Theology and Religious Studies', *British Journal of Religious Education*, 24: 32–40.

Warburg, M. and Hojsgaard, M. (2007) *Religion and Cyberspace*, London: Routledge.

Watson, B. (2000) 'Privileging secularism: meeting the challenge for religious education', *Muslim Education Quarterly*, 17.2: 4–14.

Watson, B. (2004) *Truth and Scripture: Challenging Underlying Assumptions*, Castle-upon-Alun: Aureus.

Watson, B. (2009) 'What is education? The inhibiting effect of three agendas in schooling', *Journal of Beliefs and Values*, 30: 133–144.

Watson, B. and Thompson, P. (2007) *The Effective Teaching of Religious Education*, London: Pearson Longman.

Watson, J. (2007) 'Spiritual development: constructing an inclusive and progressive approach', *Journal of Beliefs and Values*, 28: 125–136.

Weaver-Hightower, M. (2003) 'The "boy turn" in research on gender in education', *Review of Educational Research*, 73: 471–498.

Wedell, K. (2010) 'Evaluating the impact of the Hampshire agreed syllabus: "Living Difference" on teaching and learning in religious education', *British Journal of Religious Education*, 32: 147–161.

Weller, P. (2008) *Religious Diversity in the UK*, London: Continuum.

Wenger, E. (1999) *Communities of Practice, Learning Meaning and Identity*, New York: Cambridge University Press.

West-Burnham, J. and Huws-Jones, V. (2007) *Spiritual and Moral Development in Schools*, London: Continuum.

Westhill College (1989) *Attainment in RE*, Birmingham: Westhill College.

Westhill College (1991) *Assessing, Recording and Reporting RE: A Handbook for Teachers*, Birmingham: Westhill College.

White, J. (1997) 'Three proposals and a rejection', in R. Smith and P. Standish (eds) *Teaching Right and Wrong – Moral education in the Balance*, Stoke-on-Trent: Trentham.

White, J. (2004) 'Should religious education be a compulsory school subject?', *British Journal of Religious Education*, 26: 152–164.

White, R. S. (2007) *The Age of the Earth*, Faraday Paper No 8, Cambridge: The Faraday Institute for Science and Religion.

Whitehouse, E. (1972) 'Children's reactions to the Zacchaeus story', *Learning for Living*, 11: 19–24.

Whittall, A. (2009) 'Developing principles and strategies for teaching gifted students of religious education', in J. Ipgrave, R Jackson and K. O'Grady (eds) *Religious Education Research through a Community of Practice: Action Research and the Interpretive Approach*, Munster: Waxmann.

Whyte, J. (2003) *Bad Thoughts: A Guide to Clear Thinking*, London: Corvo.

Wilby, P. (2010) 'Social class still matters more than top of the class', *Questa*, 1: 54–58.

Williams, K. (2005) *Faith and the Nation: Religion Culture and Schooling in Ireland*, Dublin: Dominican Publications.

Williams, R. (2000) *Lost Icons*, Edinburgh: T and T Clark.

Wilson, A. N. (1991) *Against Religion*, London: Chatto and Windus.

Wingate, A. (2005) *Celebrating Difference, Staying Faithful*, London: Darton, Longman and Todd .

Wintersgill, B. (2000) 'Task-setting in religious education: a comparison with history and English', *Resource*, 22: 10–14.

Wittenberg, J. (2002) *A Faith-based School for Many Faiths*, London: Multi-faith Secondary School Trust.

Wolterstorff, N., Joldersma, C. W. and Stronks, G. (1994) *Educating for Shalom: Essays on Christian Higher Education*, Grand Rapids, MI: Eerdmans.

Wood, C. (2009) *The RE Teacher's Handbook*, London: Continuum

Woodward, R. (2006) *Adding a Global Dimension to the Teaching of RE*, Nottingham: Stapleford Centre.

Wright, A. (1993) *Religious Education in the Secondary School: Prospects for Religious Literacy*, London: David Fulton.

Wright, A. (1996) 'Language and experience in the hermeneutics of religious understanding', *British Journal of Religious Education*, 18: 166–180.

Wright, A (1997) 'Hermeneutics and religious understanding. Part one: the hermeneutics of modern religious education', *Journal of Beliefs and Values*, 18: 203–216.

Wright, A. (1998) 'Hermeneutics and religious understanding. Part two: Towards a critical theory for religious education', *Journal of Beliefs and Values*, 19: 59–70.

Wright, A. (1999) *Discerning the Spirit: Teaching Spirituality in the Religious Education Classroom*, Abingdon: Culham College Institute.

Wright, A. (2000a) *Spirituality and Education*, London: RoutledgeFalmer.

Wright, A. (2000b) 'The Spiritual Education Project: cultivating spiritual and religious literacy through a critical pedagogy of religious education', in M. Grimmitt (ed.) *Pedagogies of Religious Education*, Great Wakering, Essex: McCrimmon.

Wright, A. (2003) 'Freedom, equality, fraternity? Towards a liberal defence of faith community schools', *British Journal of Religious Education*, 25: 142–152.

Wright, A. (2004) *Religion, Education and Post Modernity*, London: RoutledgeFalmer.

Wright, A. (2007) *Critical Religious Education, Multiculturalism and the Pursuit of Truth*, Cardiff: University of Wales Press.

Wright, D. and Cox, E. (1967a) 'Religious belief and co-education in a sample of sixth form boys and girls', *British Journal of Social and Clinical Psychology*, 6: 23–31.

Wright, D. and Cox, E. (1967b) 'A study of the relationship between moral judgement and religious belief in a sample of English adolescents', *Journal of Social Psychology*, 72: 135–144.

Wright, N. T. (1996) *Jesus and the Victory of God*, London: SPCK.

Younger, M. and Warrington, M. (1996) 'Differential achievement of girls and boys at GCSE: some observations from the perspective of one school', *British Journal of Sociology of Education*, 17: 299–313.

Ziebertz, H-G. (2005) 'Models of inter-religious learning: an empirical study in Germany', in L. J. Francis, M. Robbins and J. Astley (eds) *Religion, Education and Adolescence: International Empirical Perspectives*, Cardiff: University of Wales Press.

Ziebertz, H-G. and Kay, W. K. (eds) (2005) *Youth in Europe 1: An International Empirical Study about Life Perspectives*, Münster: Lit Verlag.

Ziebertz, H-G. and Kay, W. K. (eds) (2006) *Youth in Europe 2: An International Empirical Study about Religiosity*, Münster: Lit Verlag.

Ziebertz, H-G., Kay, W. K. and Riegel, U. (eds) (2009) *Youth in Europe 3: An International Empirical Study of the Significance of Religion for Life Orientation*, Münster: Lit Verlag.

Index

Also from Routledge

Learning to Teach Religious Education in the Secondary School:
A Companion to School Experience, 2nd edition
Edited by L. Philip Barnes et al
Paperback ISBN 978-0-415-42046-4

The leading text for student teachers of Religious Education, the aim of this textbook is to enable student teachers to learn to teach RE in a way that pupils will find interesting, enjoyable and purposeful.

Learning to Teach in the Secondary School:
A Companion to School Experience, 5th edition
Edited by Susan Capel, Marilyn Leask and Tony Turner
Paperback ISBN 978-0-415-47872-4

'I found this book a great help in preparing effective lessons and developing classroom management skills. It gave me confidence and support in my placement schools. When I started looking for a job, the section on professional development proved really useful with clear and practical tips and I still use the book as a reference today.' – *Fabienne Collombon, French Teacher, Dulwich, London*

This best-selling core textbook – now in its 5th edition – is a sound and practical introduction to the knowledge and skills needed to qualify as a teacher.

Readings for Learning to Teach in the Secondary School:
A Companion to M Level Study
Edited by Susan Capel, Marilyn Leask and Tony Turner
Paperback ISBN 978-0-415-55210-3
Hardback ISBN 978-0-415-55209-7

'This timely publication provides a readily accessible source of the most stimulating and relevant published research in the field of education. Readings include those which directly influence day-to-day practice, consider educational policy, and explore new areas of interest, such as neuroscience.' – *Sheila King, Director of the Secondary PGCE, Institute of Education, University of London, UK*